Ngũgĩ wa Thiong'o

Studies in
African Literature

EAEP Nairobi
HEINEMANN Portsmouth (NH)
JAMES CURREY Oxford

Ngũgĩ wa Thiong'o

An Exploration of His Writings

Second Edition

DAVID COOK
Formerly Professor of English, University of Ilorin,
and Professor of Literature, Makerere University, Kampala

&

MICHAEL OKENIMKPE
Professor of Education (English), Department of Adult Education,
University of Lagos

James Currey
OXFORD

EAEP
NAIROBI

Heinemann
PORTSMOUTH (NH)

James Currey Ltd
73 Botley Road
Oxford OX2 OBS

Heinemann
A division of Reed Elsevier Inc
361 Hanover Street
Portsmouth, New Hampshire 03801-3912

East African Educational Publishers
PO Box 45314
Nairobi

British Library Cataloguing in Publication Data
Cook, David
Ngugi wa Thiong'o : an exploration of his writings. - 2nd ed. - (Studies in African
literature)
1.Ngugi wa Thiong'o, 1938- - Criticism and interpretation
I.Title II.Okenimkpe, Michael
823

ISBN 0–85255–539–3 (James Currey Paper)

**Library of Congress Cataloging-in-Publication Data
available on request**

ISBN 0–435–07430–X (Heinemann Paper)
ISBN 0–435–07432–6 (Heinemann Cloth)

Typeset in 10pt solid Monotype Garamond by
Nicholas Hardyman, Oxford
and printed in Britain by
Villiers Publications Ltd,
London N3

Contents

PART I Introduction

PART II The Novels

PART III Short Stories, Plays & Non-Fiction

PART IV Conclusion

Acknowledgements

We would like to thank the University of Lagos for supporting Michael Okenimkpe during a visit to Kenya to carry out supplementary research relevant to the initial edition of this book; and also the University of Ilorin for sending David Cook on study leave to East Africa and England for the same purpose. We are also happy to acknowledge the helpfulness of the Department of Literature and the University Library in Makerere University in following up early texts in *Penpoint*.

We are grateful to Dr Arthur Ravenscroft, Professor Arnold Kettle and Professor Andrew Gurr for guiding us on certain biographical data. Mr Henry Chakava and Mr Laban Erapu of Heinemann Educational Books, Nairobi gave us very good advice; while they and Mr Aig Higo of Heinemann Educational Books, Ibadan, Nigeria, provided crucial encouragement and inspiration.

Mrs Philomena Okenimkpe allowed herself to be a captive audience for the authors' vigorous debates and nurtured their minds and bodies at moments of stress and elation during the preparation of the original manuscript. Mr John Butler has been indefatigable in helping to correct errors, omissions and stylistic lapses, as well as playing a key role in the thankless chores of proof-reading and laboriously finalising the index both in 1982–3 and again in 1997.

Several of those who helped us with typing early on became personally involved as promoters of the project: in this respect we were initially particularly indebted to Mrs Marie Luwaji and Mr David Adesuyi. Mr James Currey has been guide and friend throughout, and Miss Lynn Taylor, also of James Currey Publishers, has been ever helpful in the latest stages.

D.C.
M.O.

Preface

The writing and the present updating of this book has realised long-standing aspirations for its authors. We have each had the privilege of knowing Ngũgĩ personally and being associated with him at different times and in different phases of his life. In preparing the original version of the book, and now working on this enlarged edition, we have had the advantage of standing at a distance and observing his achievements objectively. Like many of his readers, we continue to be impressed by Ngũgĩ's spectacular growth as a writer and as a social thinker. We hope the book in its original form and in its latest extended version fairly represents our respect for our author as a person, and our assessment of the considerable stature of his works.

It is understandable that publishers feel many reservations about promoting a collaboration between writers: this may involve many pitfalls and delays. Nevertheless, we are now gratified that we have, as envisaged throughout our partnership, completed and revised a work which is significantly different (and probably much better) than either of us could have achieved alone. We have both worked on every chapter, and indeed on every paragraph, during the entire evolution of this study. We have thrashed out successive points about which we originally differed; and we have at every stage reached not just a tentative compromise, but a carefully considered joint vision to which we are both committed. It is neither our wish nor our intention that self-evident traces should remain to indicate which of us first drafted any particular chapter. We jointly accept full responsibility for the entire book in its final form.

D.C.
M.O.

PART I

Introduction

Career

Ngũgĩ wa Thiong'o was born in 1938 in Kamiriithu Village, near Limuru in Kiambu District of Kenya, 12 miles north-east of Nairobi. He himself has disclaimed any precise knowledge of the date — 'I'm sure of the year but not of the month and day' — but two different critics[1] both specify 5 January.

Like the majority of Gikuyu in 'the White Highlands', as this fertile area was often called, Ngũgĩ's father, Thiong'o wa Nducu, was an *ahoi* — a dispossessed peasant farmer forced to become a squatter on the estate of a well-to-do landowner. Most such landowners were British, but Thiong'o wa Nducu farmed on the property of one of the few propertied Africans. The British Imperial Land Act of 1915 had transferred official ownership of all land to the British Crown, giving the Governor authority for its disposal, a power widely exploited, especially in the Highlands, so that most Gikuyu were left without any legal rights over the soil of their homeland. Ngũgĩ's mother was one of four wives, and Ngũgĩ was one of about 28 children in the family.

At about the age of nine he went to the mission-run Kamaandura School in Limuru for two years, and then to a school of the Karing'a, the Independent Schools Movement, in a village called Maanguu.[2] Schools organized by this movement were run entirely by the communal effort of Kenyan Africans, like that of which Waiyaki is headmaster in *The River Between*.

Ngũgĩ received his secondary education from 1954 to 1958 at Alliance High School situated at Kikuyu, 8 miles north-west of Nairobi. Founded in 1926, this was Kenya's first full-fledged secondary school for African students and was run under the auspices of an alliance of all Protestant denominations in Kenya. Ngũgĩ studied there during the time of Carey Francis, the second and perhaps most notable of the school's principals, of whom Anderson writes that 'although strict and often very narrow in his views, [he] brought to his teaching qualities of perseverance, integrity and empathy that touched the hearts of the nation at a crucial time of its development.'[3] Later Ngũgĩ's view of Carey Francis remained equivocal:

3

while he had fallen a little under his spell and rightly admired his effectiveness as a headmaster, he also repudiated many aspects of his Spartan missionary stance and uncompromising western bias.

At Alliance High School Ngũgĩ developed a complex religious awareness, reflected in the integral use of biblical references and Christian mythology in the novels. Quotations from Kihika's much-thumbed Bible are structurally significant in *A Grain of Wheat*, as even the title itself reminds us. In replying to Micere Mugo's question as to what the Bible meant to him, Ngũgĩ said:

> The Gikuyu society is somewhat lacking in mythological background and the Bible conveniently provides one with a relevant framework. For instance, the idea of destiny with regard to the Israelites and their struggle against slavery. The Gikuyu people have had similar experiences. Biblical mythology is also widely known and has the advantage of being easily understood by most audiences.[4]

Alliance High School figures repeatedly in Ngũgĩ's works as Siriana Secondary School, and no doubt Ngũgĩ's later attitude to Carey Francis colours the portrait of at least one of Siriana's fictional headmasters.

Ngũgĩ's childhood and adolescent experiences are woven into his fiction. He was not a writer to expend all his first-hand material in a first novel: he draws on his background judiciously in a number of works. In particular his family situation in an extended African household provides a framework, transmuted into fiction, for *Weep Not, Child* (1964). The parallels between fact and fiction are numerous. Like Nducu, Ngũgĩ's father, Ngotho is an *ahoi* on the estate of an African landowner. Boro, Njoroge's brother, goes into the forest to join the Mau Mau forces as did Ngũgĩ's real-life brother, Wallace Mwangi, between 1954 and 1956. Ngũgĩ's parents, besides others of his relatives, were put into detention, as were members of Ngotho's family and major characters in *A Grain of Wheat*. A striking parallel from the latter novel is found in the fact that in 1954 or 1955 a stepbrother of Ngũgĩ's, of the same name and condition as the deaf and dumb Gitogo who is shot dead by government forces in *A Grain of Wheat*, died in identical circumstances.

Up to the point at which he drops out, Njoroge follows a school career in *Weep Not, Child* closely parallel to Ngũgĩ's own. Micere Mugo confirms the similarities between Siriana School and Alliance High School, and claims that the portrait of the Reverend Livingstone in chapter 10 of *Weep Not, Child* bears a close resemblance to Carey Francis.[5] Ngũgĩ himself recalls that Kamiriithu, the village where he was born was forcibly moved to its new site as New Kamiriithu just as Rung'ei becomes New Rung'ei. Moreover the relationship between Mahua Village and Kipanga Town in *Weep Not, Child* is the same as the actual relationship between Kamiriithu and Limuru at that time.

By the time he comes to write *Petals of Blood* (1977), Ngũgĩ employs the actual name of his father, Nducu, for one of his characters, and of his school, Kamaandura. But this is only an extension of his already established practice of deploying in his novels the names of those near and dear to him — as of his mother, Wanjiku, and his wife, Nyambura — as well as of familiar places. Asked by fellow students in Leeds University whether his writings were autobiographical, he replied: 'Every writer's books are autobiographical, that is, you write about your experience, your immediate experience.'[6]

It may be asked how it is that Ngũgĩ, who was to become a leading exponent of Mau Mau as a heroic struggle for independence, should not have been personally involved in any episode in the campaign. He was 14 in 1952 at the start of the Emergency; open hostilities had considerably subsided by 1954, but intensive clandestine activities persisted up to 1956. Waruhiu Itote ('General China') in his book, *Mau Mau General,*[7] records that Mungai Thiga, at the age of 16, was a leading member of the company of forest fighters who sacked Naivasha Police Station on 26 March 1953. As an outstanding scholar, the young Ngũgĩ would certainly have been encouraged by Gikuyu of all shades of conviction to continue with his studies: the universal passion for education among his people is faithfully represented in *Weep Not, Child.* But schoolboys often served vital roles in obtaining and transporting arms and ammunition since their passes allowed them to travel with minimal constraint. However, Ngũgĩ's age and role made him at most a marginal candidate for even a minor militant role in the struggle.

The opportunity for a lad like himself to become an activist would have been a matter of chance in terms of contacts and being in an opportune place at an apt time. There is evidence by inference in *Weep Not, Child,* which we shall discuss later, that Ngũgĩ had some sense of guilt and failure as a non-combatant, but there is no evidence that he had any specific opportunities for participation in the active struggle. He himself records that the crisis did not cause any total disruption of the routine of life in Gikuyu country. The populace was in the main both ignorant and confused about what was happening, thanks to the colonial government's propaganda campaign and high-powered social pressurization. Ngũgĩ himself actually expresses in his writings his own process of re-appraisal and re-evaluation through which he reached the conviction that Mau Mau had been not only a heroic but also a very effective movement in the struggle for Gikuyu, Kenyan and African liberation, and at the same time presented a model in the continuing fight for social justice in the framework of the continuing class conflict.

The successful conclusion of Ngũgĩ's school career led him on to Makerere University College in Kampala, Uganda, the only institution at the time conferring degrees in East Africa. Here he was engaged in many activities. He continued to be an outstanding student, who gained a good Upper Second degree in Honours English at the end of his four years there in 1963. He could certainly have gained First Class Honours, an opportunity which he in no sense frittered away but deliberately sacrificed because he believed that varied and vigorous participation in literary and creative activities was part of his obligation as an undergraduate, a conviction which bore much fruit.

It was during his Makerere days, in 1961, that Ngũgĩ's marriage partnership with Nyambura began. Their eldest son, Thiong'o, was born on 19 September 1961 and his brother Kimunya on 22 July 1963. Then followed a daughter, Mukoma (28 February 1971). Wanjiku arrived on 31 March 1972; whereas Ngũgĩ was to learn of the birth of her sister, Njooki, on 3 May 1978, while he was in detention. He writes in the third section of Chapter Six of *Detained* about his wife, the birth of Njooki who, 'born again as Wamuingi, belonged to the people', and of his agonized refusal to allow himself to be chained while an innocent political detainee as the price of receiving a visit from his family in prison.

During this period Ngũgĩ worked hard on the novel which was to become *The River Between,* taking into consideration suggestions from his prospective publishers and from other sources. Between drafting and recasting this work, he wrote *Weep Not, Child,* which thus became his first published novel, completing its progression through the press after he had graduated. He wrote a full-length play, *The Black Hermit,* and was deeply involved in its production for Uganda Independence in 1962. And he wrote short plays for Makerere's regular literary competitions, two of which appeared much later in *This Time Tomorrow and Other Plays.*

He became editor of the student journal of creative writing, *Penpoint,* and through his very perceptive interpretation of this role was, for a period, a key figure in monitoring Makerere's important contribution to the development of East African literature. A number of his short stories appeared in *Penpoint* both before and during his editorship, four of which, newly carpentered, figured in the edited collection of writings from *Penpoint, Origin East Africa,* in 1965. These and others from this period were at length included in the collected short stories in 1975 under the title *Secret Lives.* Altogether he was a very live wire in the Makerere generator, and was himself remarkably productive as a writer, considering that he was also on the way to graduating very well: Upper Seconds were then a rarity for those working in English as a second language.

During this period also he contributed to a column in the *Daily Nation* (a newspaper published in Nairobi) a total of 44 lively articles on various burning issues under the caption 'As I See It'. These were thoughtful and provocative pieces of journalism, which now chronicle for us the early stages in the formulation of his ethical and political viewpoint.

At Makerere he was subjected to a conventional British syllabus in British literature, which would already have looked a little outmoded in the United Kingdom. No one had yet seriously considered the possibility of including African literature in the English curriculum. But what the college offered it offered well, in a coherent administrative pattern. The literature Ngũgĩ studied inevitably had a great impact on him — notably the novels of Lawrence and Conrad, about whose undoubted and very positive influence on Ngũgĩ's writing too much may already have been said. Caught up in a well-established pattern of studies, Ngũgĩ did not perhaps really begin to survey and ask pertinent questions about the syllabus as a whole, in particular about what it ignored, until he had left Makerere and could survey his undergraduate experience as a whole.

Before he went on to Leeds University, Ngũgĩ followed up his vacation work and part-time writing for the *Nation* group of newspapers in Nairobi by taking up the position of junior reporter with the newspaper from March to September 1964. While he learnt much from this experience, he also realized that full-time journalism was stultifying for a developing author like himself, and he did not later follow up this early opening.

Leeds opened up new perspectives. He made friends with radical fellow students, some of whom he met at discussions on literature in Arnold Kettle's house. He now moved in a society where all questions were open and which encouraged him to rethink many issues — political, social, literary and academic. 'I think I was confused at Makerere,' he wrote later. 'I had more questions than answers and by the time I left I was disillusioned about many things. Leeds systematised my thinking.'[8] He moved around England and Scotland, and visited the continent. All this time his main preoccupation was with the writing of *A Grain of Wheat*. He wrestled with its structure. He took his time, and worked and reworked the material.

He was required in Leeds University to register first for the Diploma in English Studies. Arthur Ravenscroft, who was administering this programme and conducting and teaching the course on the Use of English, found Ngũgĩ's creative use of the language brilliant and at the end of one term recommended that he should move straight to the two-year MA course by research. He opted to work in the field of Caribbean Literature, and Professor Douglas Grant was appointed as his supervisor. In due time Ngũgĩ submitted a draft of his thesis, which was also seen by John Hearne, who was Visiting Fellow in Commonwealth Literature at Leeds at this time. Suggestions were made for a fairly radical revision of the draft. In the event Ngũgĩ did not undertake this revision, and concentrated on the more important challenge of *A Grain of Wheat*. Among various reasons for his lack of interest in concluding his MA may well have been a growing scepticism about the value of postgraduate awards.

But Ngũgĩ did find time to attend important literary conferences in Damascus, the United States and Moscow, where again he had the opportunity of meeting many new people and further extending his horizons. The last mentioned connection was to have a sequel: the dateline 1970–5 for *Petals of Blood* is placed in Yalta, where he completed the novel in a chalet near the Black Sea on a special grant, as well as in Evanston and Limuru.

Returning from Leeds in July 1967, Ngũgĩ took up a Special Lectureship in English in Nairobi University. His view of changes which were needed in the whole structure and syllabus of the department was now clearly formulated during this period of first-hand experience. In March 1969, after only some 20 months, Ngũgĩ resigned this post because of his strong reactions during a confrontation between the university, especially the student body, and the government. Reporting this event, a Nairobi newspaper claimed that he had 'clinched his case as a man of social conviction [by resigning] his lectureship at Nairobi University, alleging that the academic staff were hypocritical to the principle and practice of academic freedom'.[9] He has given his own reasons for resigning as

> . . . the failure of the college administration and a large section of the staff to make a clear and public stand on the issues that led to the crisis at the University College, the mishandling of the crisis by the same administration, and the consequent suspension, itself a form of victimisation, of five students.[10]

On leaving Nairobi he returned to Makerere for a year as Fellow in Creative Writing. Here he played a vigorous role in the active Writers Group, and organized a successful writers' workshop as the climax of his Fellowship. He busied himself in putting together the collected edition of his short stories and saw the publication of his short plays in a volume named after the longest of them, *This Time Tomorrow.*

During this period the Makerere English Department was in the second stage of reorganizing its syllabus from a traditional British structure to one based primarily on African Literature (including in particular Oral Literature) and, secondly, on World Literature (with special attention to Caribbean and Black African writing) — a process which Ngũgĩ had sparked off in Nairobi. He arrived in Makerere in time to play a constructive role in discussions of ways and means of implementing this scheme, which was eventually approved and put into practice under the new title of Department of Literature just as he was completing his one year's Fellowship.

At the end of the Fellowship, he went, again for one year, to North-western University, Evanston, Illinois, to teach African Literature. His earlier visit to America in 1966 as a guest of honour at the International PEN Conference had elicited a most sour comment on American society:

> Well, I was impressed by the actual material progress. But in the streets of New York, one of the richest cities in the world, I found beggars crawling in the streets and people who had nowhere to sleep. I couldn't believe it. This progress soon sickens you when you go to a place like Harlem and see how run-down they really are — in fact, worse than I somehow expected. In Chicago I found some of the worst slums that surely exist anywhere in the world. These slums stand side by side with some of the wealthiest areas in the world. Some friends of mine who took me round these slums — they were white — would never come to the same area after 6 p.m. because they were afraid of being murdered. So it did not surprise me that there were riots in this area a few days after I left. The Negro in America has been exploited for over 300 years and yet people still try and explain racialism as a psychological phenomenon. It is surely the economic aspect of racialism which is of prime importance. The Negro community in America is part of the exploited working class. The colour of the skin is a convenient excuse for using state economic and political machinery to continue this kind of ruthless exploitation.[11]

However, about his one-year tenure at Northwestern he has remained reticent, beyond good-humouredly blocking further inquiry by saying, as if finally, 'I taught African literature.'[12]

In 1972 his collection of occasional writings, *Homecoming: Essays on African and Caribbean Literature, Culture and Politics,* was published. It takes up and follows through the growth of his ideas from where his contributions to the *Daily Nation* column had left them in 1963.

In August 1971 he returned to the Nairobi English Department, where eventually as Chairman of the Department he again took up and master-minded the demand to reorientate the focus of literary studies at the university. Not all the proposals were accepted: the new title of 'The Department of Literature', authorized in 1970, was not further changed, but the restructuring of the old, outmoded and irrelevant pattern of studies was carried further along the lines he had been advocating. Defending the proposed changes, Ngũgĩ and two of his colleagues argued before the Board of Studies of the Arts Faculty in the following terms:

> Here then, is our main question: If there is need for a 'study of the historic

continuity of a single culture' [as the then alien Chairman of the department had claimed], why can't this be African? Why can't African literature be at the centre so that we can view other cultures in relationship to it?

This is not mere rhetoric: already African writing, with the sister connections in the Caribbean and the Afro-American literatures, has played an important role in the African renaissance, and will become even more and more important with time and pressure of events. Just because for reasons of political expediency we have kept English as our official language, there is no need to substitute a study of English culture for our own. We reject the primacy of English literature and culture.

The aim, in short, should be to orientate ourselves towards placing Kenya, East Africa, and then Africa in the centre. All other things are to be considered in their relevance to our situation, and their contribution towards understanding ourselves.

We therefore suggest:

A.   That the English Department be abolished;

B.   That a Department of African Literature and Languages be set up in its place.

The primary duty of any literature department is to illuminate the spirit animating a people, to show how it meets new challenges, and to investigate possible areas of development and involvement.

In suggesting this name, we are not rejecting other cultural streams, especially the western stream. We are only clearly mapping out the directions and perspectives the study of culture and literature will inevitably take in an African university.[13]

In a discussion with one of the present writers in more recent years Ngũgĩ remarked that now that they had got their priorities right in the University of Nairobi by putting African writing in the forefront of attention, they were in fact studying more non-African writing than before — though by definition more relevantly selected.

In 1977 his fourth novel, *Petals of Blood*, was released. This key work, not only in Ngũgĩ's development but also in the development of radical African literature, was launched in Nairobi by a minister of Kenyatta's government. It appeared close on the heels of a dynamically popular play which presented the cause of Mau Mau as the inspiring starting point of the continuing struggle for social justice. *The Trial of Dedan Kimathi* was published earlier in 1977 following a whirlwind production which allowed the Kenya National Theatre for a brief moment to live up to its name.

Later in the same year Ngũgĩ collaborated with Ngũgĩ Mirii in writing a play in Gikuyu, *Ngaahika Ndeenda*, and in November became deeply involved in the staging of the play at Kamiriithu Community Educational and Cultural Centre in his home town, Limuru — at first with official permission. After the first performances, however, the district commissioner of Kiambu revoked the licence he had given for the performance of this 'massive 3 hour long play',[14] in which 'the audience is invariably led to the conclusion that man's position in society is a variable of how much money and power he has'.[15] It tells of the underhand manoeuvres by which the wealthy Kioi achieves possession of the 1½ acres of land belonging to 'the down-trodden poor labourer Kiguunda' for the purpose of building an insecticide factory on it in partnership with foreigners. In the eyes of a local journalist, the play

> attempted to interpret some aspects of modern Kenyan life to the average villagers in terms which the government authorities on the scene thought too provocative. The play was said by the DC to be an attempt to stir up animosity between various sections of the community on the basis of their respective roles during Kenya's bloody Mau Mau rebellion.[16]

Banning the play was not the end of the matter:

> On 31 December, in the early hours of the morning, two police vehicles arrived at Ngũgĩ's home near Limuru. Nearly a dozen uniformed policemen came out of the vehicles and entered Ngũgĩ's home. According to his wife, Nyambura, the policemen went to Ngũgĩ's study and after an hour or so in which they were engaged in conversation with the author, they came out carrying bundles of books . . . As they were leaving the house, the police told Ngũgĩ they wanted him to accompany them to the local police station. The police told Nyambura that they were taking her husband away . . . for questioning, that there was nothing serious and that her husband would be back home the following day or even earlier.[17]

In the event he was not to return for nearly twelve months.[18]

We can take up the story in Ngũgĩ's own words in an interview given on 12 December 1978, following his release in the generally conciliatory atmosphere of the early months of President Arap Moi's new regime:

> When I was arrested, I was taken to Kamiti Maximum Security Prison, in Kiambu, where I was kept behind stone walls for a whole year . . . I was not tried in an open court of law. I have never, even now, been told any specific reasons for my detention . . . I had no access to radio or newspapers. I was for a period confined to a cell for 21 hours a day under the full glare of an electric bulb. This is mental torture . . . I had no privacy whatever. I was also told that I had to be chained as a condition for my seeing my family or for medical treatment . . . So though I personally had no direct experience of physical beating in detention, I was always under extreme mental and psychological torture.[19]

Yet characteristically he was open to positive experience even here; the interview goes on:

> I was lucky in that I was put where there were 19 other detainees. And I was very impressed by the way in which these detainees had been able to withstand prison pressures for the last three, four, ten years. The detainees also struck me, on the whole, as people who were extremely patriotic, people who loved Kenya and people who had been put in because they had spoken out about the poverty of the masses, or rather people who had spoken for the rights of the poor. So, I should say, I was very impressed with them, and I shall never forget my one year of interaction with them in prison. I learnt a lot.

During Ngũgĩ's imprisonment, appeals, protest meetings in various parts of the world (notably in London) and delegations to Nairobi, including one from Nigeria led by Wole Soyinka, produced little effect before the change of government.

Ngũgĩ himself made the English translation of *Ngaahika Ndeenda* which he has published under the title *I Will Marry When I Want*. In the appropriate chapter we draw attention to the importance Ngũgĩ has placed in this play on the role of land-ownership in the relationship between rich and poor, in the determination of social status, and in the ruthless acquisitiveness shown by the wealthy in edging peasants and workers out of the few parcels of land left to them. In this collaborated play Ngũgĩ has at length turned to writing in a Kenyan language, primarily so as to make readier contact with the common man, to whose cause he has dedicated so much of his energy and talent. At the same time he has been relieved of the embarrassment of denouncing colonialism and its ethnocentric assault on African cultures while himself writing exclusively in English.

Three months after his release from detention, in March 1979 there was another flurry in the Kenyan press when it was feared that a minor (or trumped up) charge might be made an excuse for confining him again. He and Ngũgĩ Mirii, having been arrested for drinking after authorized hours, were charged with behaving in Tigoni Police Station 'in a disorderly manner by shouting and banging the counter . . . They were also alleged to have banged cell doors, abused policemen on duty and demanded the release of all suspects locked up in the station.'[20] The scene is not hard to conjure up. However, the matter blew over and there was no further imprisonment.

Ngũgĩ's first novel in Gikuyu, *Caithani Mutharaba-ini*, [21] was published in 1980 and his own English translation of it under the title *Devil on the Cross* and of *Ngaahika Ndeenda* as *I Will Marry When I Want* in 1982;[22] meanwhile in 1981 two further works of non-fiction appeared — *Writers in Politics*, and his record of his experiences and thoughts while in Kamiti Maximum Security Prison, *Detained: A Writer's Prison Diary*.[23] As we record more fully in Chapter 7, Ngũgĩ engaged himself during his monotonous and enervating months in detention in writing *Devil on the Cross* in Gikuyu. His schedule for completing it and translating it into Kiswahili and English is also outlined in the same chapter.

Ngũgĩ was not reinstated in Nairobi University. In the prison diary he sets out in detail his correspondence and negotiations with various university officers in an effort to regain his post. Asserting that his detention had been an 'Act of State', the university terminated Ngũgĩ's appointment soon after his detention was announced, and paid him six months' salary in lieu of notice. He learnt of this from his wife who was only vaguely informed by word of mouth. Not till after his release did he receive his terminal benefits. The university claimed that his reinstatement was beyond its powers and suggested he re-apply for a post (at no guaranteed level). Ngũgĩ steadily affirmed that since he had not resigned, and no charge had ever been brought against him in connection with his detention, reinstatement was his right. However, he did re-apply but was rebuffed. Ngũgĩ quotes a report in the *Kenyan Weekly News* of 11 July 1980:

Last week when speaking to a church group in his home town in Kabarnet, the President startled many Kenyans when he said ex-detainees who were detained after Kenya received her political independence, would be the last to be considered for available jobs . . . since they had been 'undermining' the government of the late President Jomo Kenyatta. 'Was President Kenyatta's government a colonial one to deserve such agitators?' he asked. Is my government a colonial one? (232)

In June 1982, while in London for the launching of *Devil on the Cross*, 'on hearing of his impending arrest in Nairobi' he determined to remain in exile.[24] When he published an English translation of his second novel in Gikuyu, *Matigari*, in 1989, three years after it had appeared in its original language in Nairobi, Ngũgĩ comments dryly that his protagonist and the novel itself had 'joined their author in exile'.[25] The fictional Matigari had already been hunted in the real world by the Kenyan police.

He has added to his earlier arguments four works of non-fiction: *Barrel of a Pen: Resistance to Oppression in Neo-colonial Kenya* (1983), *Decolonising the Mind: the Politics of Language in African Writing* (1986), *Moving the Centre: The Struggle for Cultural Freedoms* (1993) and an enlarged and significantly revised edition of *Writers in Politics* (1997).

Ngũgĩ has travelled widely since 1982, attending conferences and seminars, and giving lectures, particularly in Africa, the USA, Germany and Sweden. In the autumn of 1991 he was The Five College Visiting Distinguished Professor at Amherst, Massachusetts, on detachment from his much longer period from 1989 till 1992 as Visiting Professor of English and Comparative Literature in Yale University. In 1992 he made a further move within the USA, becoming Professor of Comparative Literature and Performance Studies in New York State University, a role which he still fills as we write in a Named Chair as The Erich Remarque Professor.

In 1986 on scanty evidence he was accused in the Kenya Parliament of leading a clandestine opposition political group — Mwakenya, and was also implicated in that group's predecessor, the 12 December Movement.[26] In October 1987 he was unquestionably made chairman in London of Umoja, an organization linking a cross-section of Kenyan anti-government bodies.

Between 1982 and 1984 Ngũgĩ widened his scope by publishing three children's books in Gikuyu based on the character Njamba Nene (two being also published in English translations), hoping to inform Kenyan youth through fiction of the socio-political realities of their lives, and by studying film-making as a new medium in which to reach a wider popular audience. In an interview with Jane Wilkinson in 1989, he confirmed his new stance on language when she pressed him on his statement that *Decolonising the Mind* was his 'farewell' to the use of English:

> Yes, it's still my position. It just means I shall be using Gikuyu mainly, like some people operate in English, in French, in Chinese. [27]

In 1994 Ngũgĩ was made Honorary Doctor of Human Studies by Albright College.

His publications from 1979 onwards demonstrate that, far from being cowed, intimidated or silenced by his prison ordeal, Ngũgĩ has gained a new determination and mental resilience from that experience, strengthening his will to continue the battle for social justice. Individually these volumes add new dimensions to his writing, and together they document a transition in his campaign towards rousing his countrymen to act in practical ways against exploitation and inequality.

His appointment as professor in New York State University also marks a new phase in his career. Since his experiences to date appear to have cast him in a heroic mould reminiscent of certain of his fictional characters, he will be sure to keep the ear of his considerable following in Kenya, in Africa and widely in the world at large.

Notes

1. Eddah Gachukia, *Notes on Ngugi wa Thiong'o's 'The River Between'* (Heinemann, Nairobi, 1975, 1; Micere Githae-Mugo, *Visions of Africa in the Fiction of Achebe, Margaret Lawrence, Elspeth Huxley and Ngugi wa Thiong'o* (Kenya Literature Bureau, Nairobi, 1978), 21. Micere Mugo uses the spelling 'Kamirithu' whereas Ngũgĩ uses 'Kamiritho' *(Petals of Blood)* or 'Kamiriithu' *(Detained: A Writer's Prison Diary).*
2. Ngũgĩ wa Thiong'o, *Detained: A Writer's Prison Diary* (Heinemann Educational Books, London, 1981), 73.
3. John Anderson, *The Struggle for the School* (Longman, London, 1970), 27.
4. Micere Githae-Mugo, op. cit., 24.
5. Ibid., 23–4.
6. Interview by Allan Marcuson, Mike Gonzalez and Dave Williams, *Leeds University Union News,* 18 November 1966, 6; reprinted in *Cultural Events in Africa,* 31 (June 1967), p. ii of the Supplement.
7. Waruhiu Itote (General China), *'Mau Mau' General* (East African Publishing House, Nairobi, 1967), 82.
8. Micere Githae-Mugo, op. cit., 25.
9. Philip Ochieng, 'Ngugi, the Writer, Extends "Exile"', *Sunday Nation,* no. 538 (Nairobi, 12 July 1970), 14.
10. 'Ngugi Quits at College: Mishandling of Crisis', *Sunday Nation,* no. 469 (Nairobi, 16 March 1969), 15.
11. Interview by Allan Marcuson *et al.,* op. cit., pp. iii–iv of the Supplement.
12. Ngũgĩ has been unwilling to grant interviews on personal aspects of his life, saying that facts of one's private life are an armour against inimical forces, and to reveal them is to expose oneself to grave dangers. He retorts to such requests, 'There is nothing to tell beyond what is already in print,' which may suggest modesty rather than an urge towards secrecy as the motive for his reticence.
13. 'Appendix: On the Abolition of the English Department', *Homecoming* (Heinemann Educational Books, London, 1972), 146.
14. Karugu Gitau, a review of *Ngaahika Ndeenda, The Weekly Review,* 151 (Nairobi, 9 January 1978), 13.
15. Ibid.
16. 'Ngugi wa Thiong'o: Writer in Trouble', *The Weekly Review,* 151 (Nairobi, 9 January 1978), 5.
17. Ibid.
18. In *Detained,* Ngũgĩ writes:
    I am told . . . that some time in December 1977, two gentlemen very highly placed in the government flew to Mombasa and demanded an urgent audience with Jomo Kenyatta. They each held a copy of *Petals of Blood* in one hand, and in the other, a copy of *Ngaahika Ndeenda.* The audience granted, they then proceeded to read him, out of context of course, passages and lines and words allegedly subversive as evidence of highly suspicious intentions. The only way to thwart those intentions — whatever they were — was to detain him who

harboured such dangerous intentions, they pleaded. Some others had sought outright and permanent silencing, in the manner of J. M. Kariuki, but on second thoughts, this was quashed for 'national stability'. And so to detention I was sent! (xvi)

19. Interview with Margaretta wa Gacheru, 'Ngugi wa Thiong'o Still Bitter over His Detention', *The Weekly Review*, 203 (Nairobi, 5 January 1979), 30.
20. Andy Akporugo, 'Famous Kenyan Author in Court', *Daily Times* (Lagos, 12 March 1979), 9.
21. Heinemann Educational Books, Nairobi, 1980.
22. Heinemann Educational Books, London, 1982.
23. Heinemann Educational Books, London, 1981.
24. Carol Sicherman, *Ngugi wa Thiong'o: The Making of a Rebel* (Hans Zell, London, 1990), 14.
25. *Matigari*, viii.
26. Carol Sicherman, ibid., 16.
27. Jane Wilkinson (ed.), *Talking with African Writers* (James Currey, London; Heinemann Educational Books, Portsmouth, NH, 1992), 133.

Points of Departure

Ngũgĩ's activities over the years indicate a steady development in his thinking about social issues. Now, in the 1990's, he is clearly committed to the reform of society, particularly African society, along radical leftist or socialist lines, though he shows no dogmatic conformity to any specific political doctrine. We can identify three phases in the growth of this philosophy of life.

First, during an early period up to the end of his first degree studies at Makerere in 1963, he evinces an essentially moralist-humanist outlook on human affairs, characterized by a confident hope in a better future, and an innocent, youthful trust in people's good intentions and goodwill in the process of bringing about that future. This period of varied interests, not yet fully digested or integrated, includes his brief excursion into journalism.

Secondly, there is an intermediate phase, embracing Leeds and his earlier teaching career, a period of maturing vision in which his attention is focusing upon such large ideas and events as Mau Mau, capitalism, socialism and nationalism. In this period most of the essays collected in *Homecoming* were written and what might be called his theory of history was formulated.

The most recent period is marked by a corrosive disillusionment with the character of social forces in independent Africa, particularly Kenya, and a bitter revulsion against the emerging African elite and middle class.

Our penultimate chapter explores more fully the history and scope of Ngũgĩ's ideas. At this point we shall concentrate on the early formative phase of his thinking which is most expressly embodied in the newspaper articles he contributed in 1962 and 1963 to a column in the Nairobi *Daily Nation* under the general title 'As I See It'.

The concerns to which Ngũgĩ gave his attention in the early period were numerous: he responded to most issues of topical public interest. However, viewed in a historical perspective, his articles record the beginnings of a coherent body of reformist thought which in later years veered considerably further to the left. They reflect the conciliatory humanist–moralist orientation which dominated Ngũgĩ's mood at this time: their common theme was to urge justice and fair play in human affairs.

The first aim of the struggle in colonized Africa was political independence. However, Ngũgĩ saw this as only the first step towards total liberation — spiritual and mental — of the African. Such complete freedom presupposes self-supporting economies which ensure decent living standards for ordinary citizens, genuine and incorruptible democracies which depend for their survival and growth on the mental maturity of the people and the nurturing of a true nationalist spirit. Consequently Ngũgĩ foresaw independence developing in three stages which he defined in 1963 in his last newspaper column.

The first of these stages is political independence: an African country becomes free of foreign political authority and power passes from whites to blacks. The immediate benefits go to members of the educated elite who rise to positions of responsibility, influence and affluence as a result of the nationalization and Africanization of public services and of the private sector. The second stage is that of economic independence which aims at improving the financial condition of the uneducated and underprivileged masses whose only stake in political freedom lies in the improvement of their material wellbeing — the only possible measure of their 'sense of dignity and self-respect'. The third stage is psychological independence. At this stage the people should have attained such a level of wellbeing — material and spiritual — and such a level of mental maturity and confidence that they no longer feel the need to assert their independence, their personality or their culture aggressively. They also outgrow the urge to avenge the injustices which they have suffered at the hands of alien races. The ultimate outcome is that the African 'be free from fear and destructive anxiety, physically free to journey towards the heights he can reach, and ready to affirm the worth of life, in spite of its tribulations.'[1]

Thus in this early period, Ngũgĩ saw freedom from colonial hegemony as merely a prelude to the realization by the African of his full human potential. In his fiction and non-fictional writings opposition to colonialism is depicted not merely as a historical phenomenon, but as a process of growth. In a nutshell, Ngũgĩ wrote to urge the African to lift himself above colonialism and its continuing constraints on his mind and thought, and above all such other limitations and circumstances which could hamper his aspiration towards true equality of status with all other peoples.

In spoken pronouncements, and in writings in newspapers and magazines, Ngũgĩ's commitment to the ideal of African emancipation was borne out by the recurrence of certain motifs which included: a relentless siege on colonialism and capitalism; a commitment to the economic wellbeing of the African masses; a distrust of the ruling and materially affluent African elite; a campaign against tribalism in African social relationships; a persistent proclamation of all the basic freedoms of man and a profession of a leaning towards the ideas of Frantz Fanon and Karl Marx.

Colonialism was the chief handicap; so Ngũgĩ attacked colonialism with the utmost virulence and persistence. Perhaps his most moving repudiation of colonialism at this time was a passionate outcry in an early contribution to his newspaper column:

We Africans who have been under colonial rule for many years believe that colonialism, whatever its advantages, is basically immoral. For anyone of whatever country to be content with alien rule, however sweet, is to be less than human.[2]

In this early period, Ngũgĩ thus admitted that there had been some benefit from colonialism, but he went beyond the rejection of colonialism as military conquest, political control and suppression to reject also its subtler manifestations. One of the most pernicious of these is mental indoctrination, a process of conditioning, subduing or conquering the mind and, therefore, of altering the personality, of which colonial education was guilty: 'The worst colonialism was a colonialism of the mind, a colonialism that undermined one's dignity and confidence.'[3] In another astringent pronouncement, he condemned colonial education as totally harmful:

> In the past [the educational] system was designed to fit people into a colonial regime. It produced a whole group of people with a colonial mentality whose two facets were an inferiority complex that was ready to be apologetic of a people's past when not outright ashamed of it, and an extreme dependency — a feeling that only the white man can do things for us.[4]

Ngũgĩ believed that colonial indoctrination had penetrated the entire sense and psyche of the African and that in the years following independence the African would consequently exhibit negative traits of behaviour in many situations. One such situation would relate to racial discrimination. In one of his articles, Ngũgĩ asked whether Kenya Africans should after independence revenge themselves on other races for having been made victims of racial discrimination for over a century. Exhibiting his humanist–moralist instinct at perhaps its most magnanimous, he warned that such 'reverse discrimination' would show Africans as still subject to the tentacles of colonialism.

The challenge of independence is to live for the freedom of the human spirit — the freedom of every man and woman of whatever race. Colonialism, he claimed, failed because it was built on contradictions: 'For it was these very nations whose culture was built on Christianity and on the concept of rights and freedom of the individual, that denied the same things to the Africans.'[5]

He proclaimed African nationalism as a 'liberating force', and condemned retaliatory racial discrimination as 'a black mark'[6] on it. He insisted that to accord equality to all races was not an act for which the African or Kenyan should be lauded: it was merely a matter of proving their humanity, of participating in a struggle to promote and preserve a universal human ideal:

> But perhaps it is unfair to call this an African challenge. The challenge to uphold right, to sow the seeds of truth and light, is the challenge to build for a wider humanity, a humanity that goes beyond the confines of our race and territory.[7]

Commenting on a suggestion by Semei Nyanzi, one-time Economics Lecturer at Makerere University and member of the East African Legislative Assembly, that education in Uganda should be placed on a scientific basis by abolishing both character training — physical and spiritual — and missionary control, Ngũgĩ once again advocated universal values, professing a characteristic humanist–moralist sensibility. He reiterated all his reservations about missionary education, but went on to stress the importance to man of spiritual values:

> There is something wrong in an education system that brings up a child to value and know about Europe when he does not know even the very simple facts about his own country. Not that there is anything wrong in studying and knowing things related to other countries. But education as well as many other things should be related to life and the immediate requirements of the people. Education should begin at home.
>
> The history of Africa is always taught as an extension of Europe, and the African child, for a long time, thinks that he has no past; his past and history beginning with the colonizing missions of the imperial powers.
>
> A civilizing mission, no doubt, but at what spiritual cost to the colonized people and their mentality . . . I still think that a society which bases its life on materialism without a corresponding search for lasting values is doomed to failure and destruction . . .[8]

He sounded a similar warning elsewhere, insisting that education must cater not only for society but also for the individual, for only thus could a man develop his full capabilities and rejuvenate his society, creating an interplay between man and environment which would enable the society to 'grow with full intellectual and moral vigour'.[9]

Ngũgĩ identified the tendency in the African to attribute all the problems of Africa to imperialism as a manifestation of colonial mentality. Two dangers were inherent in this tendency:

> [It] can be a form of self-delusion: for often it leads people away from the real issues involved in a problem and clouds their thoughts . . . Besides, this attitude portrays Africans as idiots without minds of their own, as culpably innocent, immature, unintelligent.[10]

Africans are also subject to the failings and weaknesses common to humanity:

> It is time we recognized that a conflict like the ones between Algeria and Morocco, Somalia and Kenya (and so many others ever since then) can be due to the fact that Moroccans are Moroccans, Algerians, Algerians; all human beings capable of varying and conflicting interests.[11]

In his humanist–moralist mood, pursuing his ideal of universal values, Ngũgĩ was provoked into making his famous pronouncement against what he called 'Africaphobia':

> I am now tired of the talk about African culture; I am tired of the talk about African socialism. Why must I always try to discover something inherently African in every system of thought, ranging from democracy to culture — as if none of these things could be really useful to me unless they were prefaced by the word 'African'?[12]

He deplored the common practice in independent Africa of avowing a policy of neutrality in international relations. For, first, it was 'a hollow concept': African nations pretended neutrality as a cover for subservient subordination to one or other of the world powers. Secondly, were neutrality practicable, it would be 'a cowardly form of escapism', encouraging indifference as to 'right and wrong . . . truth and falsehood'.[13] Only a bold stand on issues that plagued the world could do honour to Africa and project her dignity and integrity.

Ngũgĩ praised the conduct of affairs in the 1962 Kampala Conference of African writers for the reason that, although the participants had disagreed violently on certain issues, yet

> the whole conference was almost quiet on such things as colonialism, imperialism and other -isms. In this it differed from the 1956 and 1959 World Congresses of Negro Writers where political discussions clouded the atmosphere.[14]

He noted that the stance at the conference, far from signifying that the African writer was indifferent to the problems confronting his continent, rather reflected his maturing intellectual vision, and his ability to induce the right atmosphere for creative work in which he could '. . . sit down and observe and, at times, "poke sophisticated irony" at the foibles and vagaries of a fully realized society'.[15]

The purist artistic sentiments examined so far represent a major facet of Ngũgĩ's outlook in the early period. There was also a more radical side to that outlook which forms the groundwork of his later more emphatically leftist position: ten years after he had written the rather restrained utterances above, the following much more severe denunciation of European exploitation of Africa had become characteristic:

> Literature does not grow or develop in a vacuum; it is given impetus, shape, direction and even area of concern by social, political and economic forces in a particular society. The relationship between creative literature and these other forces cannot be ignored, especially in Africa, where modern literature has grown against the gory background of European imperialism and its changing manifestations: slavery, colonialism and neo-colonialism. Our culture over the last hundred years has developed against the same stunting, dwarfing background.
>
> There is no area of our lives which has not been affected by the social, political and expansionist needs of European capitalism: from that of the reluctant African, driven by whips and gunpowder to work on the cotton plantations of America, the rubber plantations in the Congo, the gold and diamond mines in southern Africa, to that of the modern African worker spending his meagre hard-earned income on imported cars and other goods (razor blades and Coca Cola even), to bolster the same Western industries that got off the ground on the backs of his peasant ancestors and on the plunder of a continent.[16]

This radical approach is foreshadowed early on in the views which Ngũgĩ expressed about such large issues as pan-Africanism, the regeneration of African cultures, capitalism, the need for integrity among the new ruling elite, the welfare of the masses, tribalism and the basic freedoms of man.

Pan-Africanism received a great deal of his attention, such as, for instance, when he urged the consolidation of the three states of East Africa into a federation as 'a test case for a United States of Africa',[17] or when he counselled the teaching of English and French in schools all over Africa,[18] and when he decried the then current secessionist tendencies of the Baganda of Uganda. In a spirited pronouncement, he declared pan-Africanism to be essential to the survival of black Africa:

> The consolidation of [an African country's] independence will be helped or accelerated by a progressive union with the other African States, leading finally to a United States of Africa. This ; . . is not a dream.
>
> The African countries have no choice. They must either unite, or singly, sink into obscurity or insignificance in the world scene. Pan-African unity as a strategic position for the battle for world peace should transcend personality and national sovereignty.[19]

Ngũgĩ was of course aware that the ideal of pan-African solidarity did not have universal appeal for all African states, to some of which it was hardly more than a slogan. It was out of this concern that he queried whether the 1963 Afro-Asian solidarity Conference which met in Moshi, Tanzania, was tackling serious issues or merely coining resonant slogans.[20] Enumerating such urgent problems as the Sino-Indian conflict, the Kashmir dispute, the collapse of the Mali Federation and of the Guinea/Ghana Union, the *coup d'état* in the then Togoland and the Kenya/Somali border clashes, he warned that meaningful objectives of Afro-Asian solidarity lay only in seeking solutions to such dilemmas. Nevertheless, he cried, 'Still, I would like to talk about Africa! Africa! Africa!',[21] giving explicit expression to his more radical temperament which was evolving alongside his predominant outlook of moral rectitude.

Another focus of his radical instinct at this time was his exhortation to Africans to rescue and regenerate their indigenous culture which was all but annihilated by the colonial onslaught. He has consistently castigated Christian missions which, apart from their alien role in education, had actively helped to suppress African cultures. To him imported religious organizations were a great fraud, for, as a powerful arm of colonialism, the European churches operated with a single-minded determination to discredit and undermine African culture and to drive it underground. In his most sustained early attack on the Christian missions, he declared:

> Christianity, whose basic doctrine is the equality of man, was an integral part of the colonialism which in Kenya was built on the inequality of man, and subsequent subjugation of one race to another.
>
> But even more than this contradiction, the coming of the missionaries set in train a process of social change at times involving rapid disintegration of the tribal set-up and framework to which people could cling . . .[22]

He repeated this accusation in much the same phrasing many years later, and claimed that the missionaries, having destroyed the indigenous culture of the people whom they had ostensibly come to save, imposed on them 'European civilisation . . . [a] European scale of values and [European] customs', rejecting traditional modes of behaviour as evil: 'Thus . . . was created (in Kenya) a people without spiritual roots which could anchor them to the soil. Education could not be a substitute.'[23] He charged further that while 'in Kenya the European settler robbed the people of their land, the missionaries robbed them of their soul'. That was why the people saw the missionary and the settler as one. He attributed to a reaction against negative tendencies in missionary religion the emergence in Kenya of the Independent Schools Movement and the religious characteristics of the Mau Mau revolt. The object of the new religious inclinations was

> . . . to create a form of worship and an education more in tune and harmony with the people's hopes, incorporating the best in our traditional approach to God . . . They wanted a place to feel at home.[24]

He knew that not all Kenyans were Christian, but he believed that no Kenyan had escaped the influence of Christianity, for that influence had been all-pervasive.

To recover from the cultural degeneration caused by colonialism and the Christian missionary religion, Africans must not only directly confront these forces, but must also energetically exert themselves in creative endeavours, so that the dignity of their cultural past would be vindicated, and their capability for cultural growth demonstrated. It was out of this instinct that Ngũgĩ became in this period involved in varied cultural activities: he expressed enthusiastic support for East African writing, hailed the work of the East African Literature Bureau, commended African art, and urged the replacement of English with Swahili as a national language in East Africa. He once declared: 'I do not think for a moment that we can ever be a nation of any importance unless we have a language of our own through which our national aspirations and spiritual growth can be expressed.'[25] Perhaps his most moving early expression of his devotion to the cultural regeneration of Africa was his commendation of Jomo Kenyatta's book, *Facing Mount Kenya,* for identifying the cultural roots of the African.[26] He characterized Kenyatta as one of those people who recognized that dignity for the African 'could only come out of a people's revaluation of their past, their song, dance and ritual — in fact all those things that are concerned with the spiritual development of man'. This was why, according to Ngũgĩ, Kenyatta wrote the book in 1938, 'a time the African way of life was seen as all savagery, devoid of any lasting values'. Hence the book, in Ngũgĩ's judgement, 'was an impassioned plea for a search into the historical roots that connect a people to their institutions, for only through such an awareness could our people be given that dignity that the world denied them'. In enthusiastic agreement, he quoted the conclusion to the book:

> It is all those aspects of life together that make up a social culture. But it is the culture which he inherits that gives a man his human dignity as well as his material prosperity. It teaches him his mental and moral values and makes him feel it worth his while to work and fight for liberty.

Regarding creative writing and other artistic activities in Africa, he insisted on universal standards of excellence. He demanded that the budding African writer must be subjected to the same rigours of judgement as his European and Asian counterparts. Sympathizing with the restrictive conditions under which South African writers under apartheid worked, he warned writers in independent Africa against imposing upon themselves similar disabling constraints, which could only impair artistic genius and vigour. This is why he has never shown much enthusiasm for the concept of negritude, or for its chief African exponent, Leopold Senghor, whom he once accused of being 'only committed to the colour of [his] skin', as one of those people 'who used to be so vocal and yet now that they are in power do not want to change anything'.[27]

Having, as it were, settled his score with the colonialist and the missionary, Ngũgĩ turned his attention, in an even more radical and partisan vein, to his fellow Africans. His foremost concern here was with the welfare of the masses.

Perceiving African society as consisting of two strata, the socially privileged, politically powerful and materially affluent elite, and the disadvantaged and deprived generality (groups which Ngũgĩ was later to designate 'the emergent bourgeoisie and the masses'[28]), he saw the former as predator and the latter as victim in all their relationships. He contended that the educated elite of Africa had to recognize two important challenges: first a strong influence on, and a heavy responsibility towards, the masses, and secondly the need to prevent 'a possible rift in society . . . a horizontal cleavage dividing the upper crust of Africans from those below, the few educated from the many uneducated'.[29] In a query addressed specifically to the elite of Kenya just before Kenya's independence, he asserted that the first test of the elite's ability to meet the challenge would be the kind of Public Service which would be set up after independence:

> Africanisation is now being carried on rapidly, and the question appears: is the Kenya African going to build a Civil Service imbued with integrity and honesty or one tainted with corruption and bribery?[30]

He bemoaned the emergence in early independent Kenya of the social scourge of bribery which was becoming so powerful an instrument of material gain that the poor who could not afford bribes were doomed to perpetual penury. He acknowledged that gift-giving was a feature of African peasant life, but decried bribery as 'a perversion of generosity, a gift corrupted', which inflicted on the individual the worst of all spiritual injuries, the enslavement of the mind. In defence of the rights of the masses, he once strongly rebuked the Asian community of Kampala for exploiting the masses through the private school system, calling the schools, 'a shame on the country'[31]

For Ngũgĩ, the economic upliftment of the poor was of primary importance. One scheme which he advocated for accomplishing this goal was the modernization of agriculture. He urged whichever of the two Kenyan pre-independence political groups succeeded the colonial administration to see to it that farming became an economically viable enterprise. Such a party must 'come out with a bold long-term agricultural policy designed to lay a sound basis for farming', for 'Kenya rests on the back of the farmer'.[32] Warning that 'soon there will be no imperialist scapegoat to blame for all our troubles',[33] he commended the spirit of hard work and self-help with which people had returned from detention, and urged the government to provide them with appropriate employment on which to expend their energy and enthusiasm so as to ensure their prosperity for the future. In a similar vein, he urged a resolute attack on the problem of street beggars.

Perhaps even more than with the economic welfare of the masses, Ngũgĩ was concerned with their mental development. He considered youth —

who constitute the bulk of the masses — to be 'the spearhead of progress . . . who are going to bear the burden of democracy after independence'.[34] To be able to bear this burden, they must be given an education which 'inculcates in them the basic qualities needed for healthy leadership — honesty, truthfulness, sympathy and courage'. Comparing the provision for the farmer of capital and equipment, or of education, Ngũgĩ rated the provision of education as more important, for it is only the enlightened farmer who can make prudent and profitable use of loaned capital. It was in view of this need for education that he lamented that the university colleges of East Africa of those days were merely 'Oases in the midst of poverty',[35] from which the poor masses could hardly expect to receive any help.

Ngũgĩ was already in this early period demonstrating significant interest in the fundamental freedoms of man. In a *Sunday Nation* article in 1962, he urged that freedom of expression should be instituted as an inalienable end-product of education, and that truth should be enshrined 'as the greatest striving and mark of a good press'.[36]

He saw two major threats to the freedom of political thought and expression: tribalism and the dictatorial tendencies of African governments. He once warned: 'The immediate obstacle to the creation of a Kenya nation is now not so much racialism as tribalism.'[37] He urged the integration in Kenya (as well as in other African states) of the various tribal groups as a necessity for the creation of a national culture. He disapproved of tribal unions and associations in towns and higher educational institutions, the clandestine activities of such pressure groups as the 'Land Freedom Army' in Kenya, racial segregation in schools and, particularly, tribe-based political parties.[38] In this cause he took the Kenya African Democratic Party to task. He accused the party of 'perpetrating a dictatorship of the mind' (while, ostensibly, it had been formed to prevent political dictatorship in Kenya) by trying to protect the tribal groups within which it was influential (the Masai and the Kalenjin) from what it considered to be dangerous influences from the Kikuyu. He warned the party that: 'Tribal dictatorship over the individual is hardly more desirable than a countrywide dictatorship by one leader.'[39] He pointed out that there were 'some people surely who would like the right and freedom to hear the opposite point of view'. Furthermore:

> Far from wanting to shield the other man from what is a wrong opinion or policy, according to us, we should expose him fully to it. It is the only way that he can develop into a man of integrity and intellectual and emotional maturity.[40]

He acclaimed the political awakening which made it possible for the Masai and Kalenjin to act together to seek solutions to the political problems of Kenya, but regretted that the Kenya of those days should be seen in terms of KANU and KADU areas. Upholding sport as an activity which nurtures a national spirit, he once exploded into this great delight over a Kenyan athlete's success at a world sports event: 'He was a Kenyan. I too was a Kenyan. I knew that his victory was mine. And I was glad to share it.'[41] In an early article, 'Kenya: The Two Rifts',[42] in which he volubly lamented the conflicts which Kenya had had to live through — racial, economic and, later, tribal — he declared:

In Kenya then, there is really no concept of a nation. One is always a Kikuyu, a Luo, a Nandi, an Asian or a European. I think this diminishes our strength and creative power. To live on the level of race or tribe is to be less than whole. In order to live, a chick has to break the shell shutting it out from the light. Man too must break the shell and be free. Political freedom from foreign rule, essential as it is, is not *the* freedom. One freedom is essential. This is the freedom for man to develop into his full potential. He cannot do this as long as he is enslaved by certain shackles. Two of these are racism and tribalism. To look from the tribe to a wider concept of human association is to be progressive. When this begins to happen, a Kenya nation will be born. It will be an association, not of different tribal entities, but of individuals, free to journey to those heights of which they are capable. Nationalism, by breaking some tribal shells, will be a help. But nationalism should not in turn become another shackle. Nor should it be the end. The end should be man ultimately freed from fear, suspicion and parochial attitudes: free to develop and realize his full creative potential.

Ngũgĩ's concern for the economic wellbeing of the masses had begun at this time to develop into a vision of political power for this disadvantaged group. Thus his present socialist temperament in political thought is traceable to this early time. He had begun to entertain the design that the masses should exercise real and effective control of African governments and determine the policies and character of such governments. Hence as early as 1962 he already formulated the idea of 'the people's government': 'The image of the people's government must be felt in all the economic, educational and other social developments that are of immediate urgency to the people.'[43] Similarly, he considered the idea of a 'traditional African concept of community' to be worthy of emulation and adoption in modern African governments:

> The community serves the individual. In it he finds the fullest development of his personality in two-way service to all. Extreme individualism tending towards self-interest is tempered with the concern for the community tending towards selflessness. Wealth, while not communally owned, is yet for all.[44]

Another of Ngũgĩ's developing ideas concerned the role of violence and revolt in the struggle for liberty and social justice. Reacting with contempt to the characteristic cynicism with which Fred Maidanaly in his book, *A State of Emergency: The Full Story of Mau Mau*,[45] had portrayed the Kenyan uprising, he declared:

> Violence in order to change an intolerable, unjust social order is not savagery: it purifies man. Violence to protect and preserve an unjust, oppressive social order is criminal, and diminishes man. To gloat in the latter form of violence, as Ian Henderson does in his *The Hunt for Dedan Kimathi*, is revolting. In Kenya, then, we were confronted with two forms of violence. The British perpetrated violence on the African people for fifty years. In 1952, once the political leaders were arrested and detained, the colonial regime intensified its acts of indiscriminate terrorism, thereby forcing many peasants and workers to take to the forests. For about four years, these people, with little experience of guerrilla warfare, without help from any outside powers, organized themselves and courageously resisted the British military forces . . . The disorganized end of

Mau Mau should not be confused with its heroic beginnings and its four years of spectacular resistance to the enemy forces. Mau Mau violence was anti-injustice; white violence was to thwart the cause of justice . . .[46]

These egalitarian concerns were soon to attract Ngũgĩ to the ideas of the Martiniquan revolutionary and philosopher, Frantz Fanon, and through Fanon to the Marxist tenets of his social theory. These developments were subsequently to steer Ngũgĩ's thinking away from its earlier idealistic humanist-moralist approach to its later militancy.

Meanwhile multitudinous implications of the peasant revolt — for the individual, the home, the village, the tribe and the nation — form the theme of *Weep Not, Child* and several of his short stories, while issues concerning cultural heritage are central in *The River Between* and also in a number of stories. *The Black Hermit* is primarily concerned with the question of establishing an equilibrium, between the individual's responsibilities to self, to those close to him, and to the society at large.

Notes

1. 'As I See It: The Three Levels of Independence', *Sunday Nation* (hereafter *SN)* 189 (27 October 1963), 39.
2. 'As I See It: Respect Will Come When We Are Self-sufficient', *Daily Nation* (hereafter *DN*) 157 (17 March 1963), 29.
3. Ibid.
4. 'As I See It: Mboya is Right -- Education is an Investment', *DN* 162 (21 April 1963), 10.
5. 'As I See It: Let's Get Out of the Dark and Take a Look at the Sun', *DN* 118 (17 June 1962), 39.
6. Ibid.
7. Ibid.
8. 'As I See It: Don't Forget Our Destination', *DN* 152 (10 February 1963), 12.
9. Ibid.
10. 'It's Time We Recognised that the Root of our Troubles May Be In Us', *SN* 191 (10 November 1963), 12.
11. 'Must We Drag Africanness into Everything?', *DN* (2 September 1962), 30.
12. Ibid.; quoted in Roland Hindmarsh, 'Africa: The Inward Exploration', *Transition,* vol. 2, nos 6 and 7 (October 1962), 41.
13. 'As I See It: What Do We Really Mean by Neutralism?', *DN* 127 (19 August 1962), 30.
14. 'As I See It: Here Are the Heralds of a New Awareness', *DN* 120 (1 July 1962), 32; republished as 'A Kenyan at a Conference', *Transition,* vol. 2, no. 5 (July/August 1962), 7.
15. Ibid.
16. *Homecoming* (Heinemann Educational Books, London, 1972), xv-xvi.
17. 'As I See It: What is Happening About Federation?', *DN* 128 (26 August 1962), 30.
18. 'As I See It: Lack of Communication may be Barrier to an African United States', *DN* 184 (22 September 1963), 14.
19. 'As I See It: What Do We Really Mean by Neutralism?', op. cit., 30.

20. 'As I See It: Even Brothers Can Cut Throats', *SN* 153 (17 February 1963), 4.
21. Ibid.
22. 'I Say Kenya's Missions Failed Badly', *SN* 147 (6 January 1963), 5.
23. Ibid.
24. Note the title of the book by F. B. Welbourn and B. A. Ogot, *A Place to Feel at Home: A Study of Two Independent Churches in Western Kenya* (OUP, London, 1966).
25. 'As I See It: Swahili Must Have Its Rightful Place', *DN* 132 (23 September 1962), 12.
26. 'As I See It: Respect Will Come When We Are Self-sufficient', op. cit., 29.
27. See first chapter, Note 6.
28. Interview by Heinz Freidberger, *Cultural Events in Africa* 50 (January 1969), supplement, p. ii.
29. 'Can the Educated African Meet This Challenge?' *SN* 115 (27 May 1962), 31.
30. Ibid.
31. 'The Letter that Made My Heart Sink Inside Me', *SN* 183 (15 September 1963), 15.
32. 'As I See It: The Future and the African Farmer,' *DN* 116 (3 June 1962), 33.
33. Ibid.
34. 'As I See It: Adult Education Must Be Tackled', *DN* 118 (24 June 1962), 43.
35. 'As I See It: The Oasis That Is Makerere', *DN* 158 (24 March 1963), 30.
36. 'The Role of the Press', *SN* 145 (23 December 1963), 6.
37. 'Let's See More School Integration', *SN* 121 (8 July 1962), 25.
38. 'There Must be Freedom to Hear Opposite Views', *SN* 122 (15 July 1962), 11.
39. Ibid.
40. Ibid.
41. 'As I See It: Here is a Spirit Kenya Must Encourage', *DN* 138 (4 November 1962), 22.
42. *Homecoming*, 22-5.
43. 'As I See It: It's Time We Broke Up this Tribal Outlook', *DN* 188 (20 October 1963), 33.
44. 'Can the Educated African Meet this Challenge?' op. cit., 31.
45. Houghton Mifflin, Boston, 1963.
46. 'Mau Mau, Violence and Culture', *Homecoming*, 28–9.

PART II

The Novels

The River Between

Ngũgĩ's first four novels make up a roughly chronological sequence in relation to historical time, and so it may be helpful to begin by identifying the position of *The River Between* within this sequence. It is well known that while *The River Between* was the second novel to be published, it was the first to be drafted.[1] One cannot say for certain whether or not Ngũgĩ envisaged fairly early a series of novels following through some half a century of Gikuyu history, but it seems quite likely. *The River Between* is set at the beginning of this period. The two villages which the novel depicts, Kameno and Makuyu, separated by the River Honia, were in relative social harmony before being affected by alien religion and colonial politics. During the course of the story, missionary Christianity has been so recently introduced that a convert can still be referred to as a 'white man's slave' (5).[2] Tribal customs are intact. Circumcision is still ritually enacted as an expression of manhood and courage: the people take pride in their ancient heroes and the mythical origin of the villages. Physical courage is prized. Knowledge of tribal secrets is treasured and seen as a mark of noble birth. The concept of the ritual purity of the tribe remains alive.

As the novel opens there is no school within walking distance of these ridges, so pupils must become boarders at distant Siriana. Events in *The River Between* are centred on the first school to be set up locally, as a communal enterprise, to offer an alternative when Siriana closes its doors to children who fail to renounce their traditions, particularly circumcision.

As yet Kameno and Makuyu harbour no white men. There are no settlers here. Visits by colonial officials and missionary agents are rare. No land has, therefore, been alienated through the European administrative policy of resettling World War veterans. Only isolated plots have been acquired by missionary agents. Mau Mau lies in the future. This is Ngũgĩ's setting for the clashes between viewpoints and personalities within this society confronted for the first time by the thrust of imported innovations.

The underlying themes which provide fundamental links between the first four novels find their first expression in *The River Between*. The exceptional speed with which change has come to Africa in the twentieth century has brought sharp contrasts between life patterns and assumptions. Ancestral and modern ways of living, traditional religion and Christianity, have clashed violently, while statesmen, reformers and career politicians have differed widely in their prescriptions for containing the resultant conflicts and the emphasis they have placed on various possible antidotes. The crying need is for the unity which would enable society at large to retain its positive traditions and withstand the disintegrating force of power groups and vested interests, whose pressures inevitably deepen rather than alleviate social injustice. Reform must spring from popular movements. There is an innate wisdom in working folk that needs to be fostered and given a sense of direction by far-sighted, selfless leadership. Unless dynamic and humane individuals rally support for more constructive policies, demagogues and fanatics like Kabonyi and Joshua will dictate the directions in which society is to move.

In a rapidly changing society like modern Kenya, it may be hard for older men to keep pace with the inexorable movements of history. Young men and women are needed, in key with the times, who are free from self-interest and immune to the prejudices both of power-magnates and of their own teachers. *The River Between* is no mere attempt to reconstruct the past. It offers stern schooling to younger readers in Africa today who themselves aspire to become responsible leaders, and also to their potential advisers and followers. How can the young distance themselves sufficiently from the personal dilemmas of youth to contribute towards building a balanced, unifying force in their own communities? Even if they are willing to put the interests of the majority before their own, can they hope to co-ordinate the various needs of society without being carried away by individual obsessions or diverted into private dramas? Waiyaki may be seen as a model, but his story serves even more forcefully as a warning. Leadership must not become distanced from the throng. United action presupposes the mustering of a corporate will, not the mass following of a self-ordained saviour.

Linked to these issues is the need in a community like Kenya for effective education so that group attitudes and decisions may be well informed. There is danger in adopting a narrow, authoritarian form of schooling which may condition rather than teach. Real education must embrace the social arts, and will involve above all a sensible training in political concepts, and so be a basis for making real choices. This would be the opposite of indoctrination. *The River Between* poses questions which remain urgently relevant today as to what form of education is desirable in Africa — or elsewhere. It depicts a situation in which a properly unified programme for defending the integrity of indigenous society is dangerously split between rival policies. Education and political activism, instead of being partners, become antagonists. This contention is the pivot of both plot and characterization.

Varying creeds, both religious and political, may preach a valid social morality, and could in theory be reconciled with one another. But Christianity is so encrusted in its missionary form with racist, class-ridden bigotry that it is seen as doing more harm than good in Kenya as an entrenched vested interest, even though its unperverted tenets may be unassailable. The possibility of reconciliation between tradition and the more liberal elements of the incoming creed is a further crux in *The R iver Between,* and the degree to which either education or political militancy is conducive or antagonistic to such a reconciliation. Amid these forces the will of the people is vital. They crave for both change and continuity. They respond dynamically to the rhetoric and the personalities of specific leaders.

These themes lead to a fundamental exploration of how the good of society is to be achieved. Our second chapter introduces, and our last but one chapter expands, the subject of Ngũgĩ's practical recipe for the political emancipation, economic strength and cultural dignity of an African state, and of his demand for a high ethical standard in the conduct of affairs. The novels express the processes by which these ideals are achieved or denied in the lives of individuals and of communities. Ngũgĩ thus tests in his fiction the manhood of his protagonists in the pursuit of certain goals. He asks how far these key figures, unpredictable as they are like all mankind, inevitably subject to psychological imbalance, can cope with the challenges which must accompany high aspirations. Whatever the verdict in each case, all Ngũgĩ's novels pay tribute to the high-mindedness and moral courage that lead men to outface hardships and sacrifices in the pursuit of excellence, above all for the good of society at large.

In all the novels we get to know how characters, as victims of their situations, struggle inadequately against the forces around them: Joshua, Waiyaki, Ngotho, Njoroge, Howlands, Thompson, Mugo, Gikonyo, Munira, Wanja, Abdulla. And also we are invited to pass judgement on those who are in themselves essentially deficient in humanity like Kabonyi, Jacobo, Robson, Karanja, Kimeria, Chui, Nderi wa Riera, Mzigo. In significantly different degrees each group shares some responsibility for the setbacks of society. No character escapes his or her due portion of blame; and there is even a dispensation of poetic justice in the kind of retribution each has to endure.

Ngũgĩ's thinking about the qualities required by a revolutionary personality — the ingredients of mind and temperament needed to equip the individual to help propel a society forward — has had a long period of gestation stretching across the composition of all the novels to date. In *The River Between* he is already scrutinizing his key characters as potential leaders of a new society. Joshua and Kabonyi obviously fail all the tests; but even Waiyaki is found sadly wanting.

The storyline skilfully and truthfully relates the larger issues to the perplexities facing key characters at the centre of the action. The immediate outcome of the social struggles already outlined is determined by the strengths and weaknesses of specific individuals, and the alliances, antagonisms and jealousies among them. Waiyaki's and, to some extent, Nyambura's problems are multiple. Called by his special opportunities to early leadership, Waiyaki is restrained in every course of action by the inevitable inner doubts of a sensitive young man faced prematurely by complex responsibilities. He is asked to solve the problems of society long before he can solve the problems of his own identity. Then, also, the group divisions that separate the ridges hold Waiyaki and Nyambura apart. The strong allegiance of each to parental and group demands pulls against the powerful attraction between them. So the question of individual freedom arises. How far is it right and proper for the private person to assert deep-seated emotional links if these are in conflict with the group demands of a cause or a campaign?

The strong patterning of the novel clarifies its interrelated themes. The image linking the two ridges, together with the river which both unites and divides them and from which the novel takes its title, is fundamental, reappearing time and again as central statement and subtle inference. The metaphor is so firmly imprinted on our awareness from the very first page that we may begin to take it for granted and fail to see how exactly apt it is, and how skilful a use is made of its detailed implications. This is already evident when Chege and Waiyaki reach the sacred grove: from this significant vantage point, 'Kameno and Makuyu were no longer antagonistic. They had merged into one area of beautiful land (19/16).' After his second birth Waiyaki 'came out clean' (15/12) from his dip in Honia River, which later serves as anaesthetic and ritual participant in the circumcision ceremonies. The ridges indeed adopt a symbolic life of their own: Waiyaki sees them 'glaring at one another menacingly' (68/59). And later, as he works himself into a state of enthusiasm at the first parents' meeting, 'He had awakened the sleeping lions. They would now roar, roar to victory' (107/94). The image is developed more minutely in the vivid passage on the rain when Waiyaki becomes quaintly angry with the downpour for collaborating with the white man in carrying off the soil, till he laughs at himself for his absurdity. But the point is made. The insidious network of local forces permitting the alienation of the land is like the myriad tiny runnels eroding the soil into the Honia: 'From the scoops flowed little narrow streams that ran through the grass. They mingled and flowed on to join the main stream, like a small river, like Honia' (75/64). And at the end of the novel the river still flows enigmatically, the repository of so many unresolved possibilities: 'And Honia river went on flowing through the valley of life, throbbing, murmuring an unknown song' (173/150).

Though the extended metaphor of the ridges is in essence perfectly clear, upon closer inquiry there are aspects of this symbolism which are less easy to interpret. This is not necessarily a criticism of the concept but perhaps rather an indication of its ability to express the full complexity of the situation. If Kameno basically represents traditional society and Makuyu the Christian minority, what or who is symbolized by the intervening river? Is Waiyaki to be understood as the Honia — 'redeemer and destroyer', the saviour, the reconciler, and at last unintentionally the divider? Or are all the successive prophets and would-be saviours embodied in the element of life and death?

The imagery of the ridges and the river is not the only factor creating a sense of pattern and unity in *The River Between*. There is the point of reference in the sacred grove and the journey that Chege and the youthful Waiyaki make together there, which is constantly remembered and alluded to throughout the novel. Even more central is the special place beside the Honia where so many of the crucial episodes are enacted. This scene of our first meeting with Muthoni and Nyambura when they discuss circumcision is also the arena where both Waiyaki's and Muthoni's actual circumcisions take place in common with those of all the true members of the ancient tribe. Here also the first love scene occurs, to which

Nyambura harks back whenever she can, and later this is where love is consummated. Here and in the adjoining area the fateful last gathering called by Waiyaki takes its course. Sometimes the links between the various actions which focus on this place are spelt out; at other times we are left to realize them for ourselves through the powerful geographic awareness we are given of the whole district. Again the boyhood fight between Kinuthia and Kamau which is controlled by Waiyaki — who already has a strange power of command in his 'large and rather liquid' eyes (12/10) — is remembered on a number of occasions when the relationship between them is in question.

The prophetic forebodings of Mugo wa Kibiro and of Chege are frequently invoked as further points of reference throughout the narrative. The foretelling of the emergence of a saviour lies behind the rivalry between Kabonyi and Waiyaki who, as far as we know, are the only aspirants privy to this vision. The ritual effect in recalling the words of these seers is reinforced by the ritual enactment of circumcision. Traditional preparations for this rite are emphatically juxtaposed with Christian ceremonies when, twice during the course of the novel, the highpoints of the year in the two religious camps coincide (or are about to coincide) at Christmas. This strain in the novel culminates in a passage at the beginning of the very last chapter which counterpoints with narrative events a kind of traditionalist litany, made up of ritualistic restatements of Mugo's prophecies:

> And he stood at a raised piece of ground and looked at the people; at their expectant faces and eyes. *Salvation shall come from the hills.* And he saw that many people had come and had filled up the initiation ground and the slopes of the hills. Some had climbed up trees. *A man shall rise and save the people in their hour of need* . . . (168/146)

There are naiveties within the fabric of the work. For instance, Waiyaki's vision of a united society adopts something of the tone and language of revivalist rhetoric. It could be argued that this is a deliberate exposure of Waiyaki's own immaturity. However, the way in which the passage is built into the text makes it appear inextricable from the voice of the novel at this point, especially since the central imagery of the river is involved. No deliberate irony is suggested:

> It was the vision of a people who could trust one another, who would sit side by side, singing the song of love which harmonized with music from the birds, and all their hearts would beat to the rhythm of the throbbing river. The children would play there, jumping from rock on to rock, splashing the water which reached fathers and mothers sitting in the shade around, talking, watching. Birds sang as they hovered from tree to tree, while farther out in the forests beasts of the land circled around . . . In the midst of this Nyambura would stand. The children would come to her and she would talk to the elders. The birds too seemed to listen and even the beasts stopped moving and stood still . . . (137/119–20)

Ngũgĩ would remark privately in later years that he found *The River Between* somewhat embarrassing to turn back to. This may in part have been the result of a shift in his own vision which might, for instance, have made the idea of reconciliation with even a purged and Africanized Christianity less congenial to him. On the other hand, most mature writers are likely to find artless passages such as this in their early works which make them wince. Perhaps even more gauche is the glib phrasing of Muthoni's dying words which provide such an important thematic refrain in the book: 'tell Nyambura I see Jesus. And I am a woman, beautiful in the tribe' (61, 117–18, 121/53, 103, 106). Happily such lapses are rare while the marks of a rapidly maturing talent are numerous: not least in the forms of structural patterning which we have been sampling.

In the main, strongly as the author feels his subject, over-simplifications are, as mentioned earlier, uncommon. Complexity is insisted upon, even within the framework of the structural imagery. After all, Kabonyi, the renegade Christian who leads the reinstated tribal council, the Kiama, and conducts the campaign for immediate action, is from Makuyu, the heart of Joshua's territory. This may remind us that Makuyu and Kameno were already rivals for precedence even before the incursion of Christianity.

The novel clearly deplores the rigid, doctrinaire rejection by hardline Christians of all traditional beliefs and values. Joshua's evangelical work is essentially dehumanizing and mechanical. He is subservient to ideas which he makes no claim to have mastered:

> Not that Joshua saw anything intrinsically wrong in having a second bride. In fact he had always been puzzled by the fact that men of the Old Testament who used to walk with God and angels had more than one wife. But the man at the Mission had said this was a sin. And so a sin it had to be. Joshua was not prepared to question what he knew to be God-inspired assertions of the white man. (113/99)

His obsession nourishes personal antagonisms. Waiyaki's progressiveness is a threat to conditions under which conversions to missionary Christianity proliferate: 'What worried Joshua was not just that many people had returned to the cursed things of the tribe like circumcision . . . The rise of Waiyaki as a young, intelligent leader of the tribe was the menace' (113/99). Waiyaki becomes for Joshua the embodiment of Kameno. And so Joshua intensifies rather than relaxes the hostility between the two ridges. In his reaction to Muthoni's death, we see Joshua's blind extremism growing into a perverted denial of natural feeling and of reason alike. At length he disowns his other daughter for her faithfulness to the man she loves. Those who can thus suppress their human nature in the fanatical pursuit of a creed identify themselves and their faith as obstacles to all social progress.

Yet Joshua is no mere caricature. Time and again the sincerity and the twisted integrity with which he pursues his chosen dogma are impressed upon us:

> Whenever Joshua preached there was something fascinating in his voice. It carried a deep sense of conviction, a passionate commitment to the moral truths revealed to him through the Bible. His church was always packed full. (97/84)

Conversely ancestral piety provides no simple, clear-cut solutions. When Waiyaki deliberately visits the sacred grove again on the day before the fateful assembly, his inner uncertainties and confusions find no immediate resolution: 'Waiyaki now thought it was time to go. The sacred grove had not lit the way for him. He did not quite know where he was going or what he really wanted to tell his people. He was still in the dark' (163/142).

Ngūgī's novel presents to us a society divided between Christians and non-Christians. Loyal traditionalists from Kameno do not, it would seem, belong to or even conceive of a non-missionary, African-oriented Christian church in sympathy with Gikuyu traditions. We hear of no counterpart to the African Orthodox Church or the African Independent Pentecostal Church with which the Kikuyu Karing'a Educational Association and the Kikuyu Independent Schools Association were increasingly connected in historical fact. Yet Ngūgī has not so much simplified history in this respect as dramatized its complexities through the activities, beliefs and aspirations of his most significant characters. While the emphasis in *The River Between* is on the self-assertive rejection by inflexible Christians of everything pertaining to traditional religion and the way of life inseparable from it, Christianity is taken seriously. Waiyaki does not match the mission Christians in intolerance — as Kabonyi perhaps at length does. The young idealist is drawn by nature to the non-controversial aspects of their creed: 'After all, he himself loved some Christian teaching. The element of love and sacrifice agreed with his own temperament. The suffering of Christ in the Garden of Gethsemane and His agony on the tree had always moved him' (114/100).

Muthoni puts her dual convictions into practice, but it is Nyambura who attempts to work out the doctrinal basis for such a reconciliation:

A religion of love and forgiveness stood between them. No! It could never be a religion of love. Never, never. The religion of love was in the heart . . . If the faith of Joshua and Livingstone came to separate, why, it was not good. If it came to stand between a father and his daughter so that her death did not move him, then it was inhuman. She wanted the other. (154–5/134)

She finds this 'other' in the Bible itself, in the vision of the leopard lying down with the kid: 'That was her religion. That was what she now wanted for her tribe. It was the faith that would give life and peace to all' (155/135). Waiyaki follows the same winnowing process:

For Waiyaki knew that not all the ways of the white man were bad. Even his religion was not essentially bad. Some good, some truth shone through it. But the religion, the faith, needed washing, cleaning away all the dirt, leaving only the eternal. And that eternal that was the truth had to be reconciled to the traditions of the people. A people's traditions could not be swept away overnight. That way lay disintegration. Such a tribe would have no roots, for a people's roots were in their traditions going back to the past, the very beginning, Gikuyu and Mumbi. (162/141)

This honesty which embraces complexity is a mark of developing maturity. When a novel written in this vein speaks out we are more ready to be convinced. And those readers who have already thought much about the issues which such a work takes up, still find within it new dimensions and insights.

The clear outlines which *The River Between* achieves are thus not the result of naivety but of contact with fundamental issues faced truthfully and directly. This approach leaves the author, like his protagonist, open to doubts which lead at length to re-examination of his premises and to a new understanding. Thus Waiyaki is properly conceived as the central figure of this work. Already Ngũgĩ is concerned not with happy endings nor neat resolutions but with having some impact on his actual society by provoking and stirring his readers. If he is necessarily almost always one step ahead of Waiyaki·in resolving contradictions, it is seldom more than one step, and so instead of looking back at his protagonist with complacent self-assurance the author views him with compassionate fellow-feeling and a sense of direct involvement. To understand Waiyaki better is to understand East Africa and its problems better. The journalese employed by the *Guardian* critic quoted in the 'blurb' on the cover of the novel should not provoke us into dismissing the perceptiveness which leads him to acknowledge that *The River Between* 'sometimes touches the grandeur of tap-root simplicity'.

Such grandeur may in part be attributed to the constant assertion of the integrity and coherence of traditional values:

> These ancient hills and ridges were the heart and soul of the land. They kept the tribes' magic and rituals, pure and intact. Their people rejoiced together, giving one another the blood and warmth of their laughter. Sometimes they fought. But that was amongst themselves. (3/3)

Chege, Waiyaki's father, declares uncompromisingly that Kabonyi, in first going over to Christianity, has 'betrayed the tribe' (24/20).

There is a great awareness of the holiness and mystery of traditional beliefs. In spite of the level-headed realism which is expressed, the sacredness of the sacred grove is never seriously in question. Indeed the tentative scepticism makes the countervailing conviction much harder to dismiss:

> And the sacred grove seemed to be no more than ordinary bush clustering around the fig tree. But there was something strange about the tree. It was still huge and there was a firmness about it that would for ever defy time; that indeed seemed to scorn changing weather. And Waiyaki wondered how many people before him had stood there, where he now was, how many had indeed come to pay homage to this tree, the symbol of a people's faith in a mysterious power ruling the universe and the destinies of men. (161/140)

At the same time, in the very process of demonstrating the perverse intransigence of the Christians and their converts, the religious mystery that their creed embodies is also celebrated: 'Joshua, their leader, was inspired. He now preached with vigour and a strange holiness danced in his eyes' (68/58).

Indeed, Ngũgĩ seems more interested in the two religions as creeds than Achebe is in, say, *Things Fall Apart*. Achebe and Ngũgĩ share an understanding of the manner in which beliefs blend into ways of life and social organization; but Ngũgĩ is also concerned to explore the extra-logical forces on which each faith depends. This in turn helps him to weave all the events and rituals that he portrays into the fabric of his story and his character-ization. The design marked out in the opening pages of the book merges into an account of the mystic Gikuyu tradition embodied in the creation myth, a motif taken up again by Waiyaki in the final movement of the work. The significant figures from the tribe's past — seer, witch and great warrior — stand in the shadows behind the more substantial characters who constantly (so to speak) glance over their shoulders at these spirits, conscious that they are expected to carry on the heritage: 'These, who had the courage to look beyond their present content to a life and land beyond, were the select few sent by Murungu to save a people in their hour of need' (3/3).

Complex reactions to religious awareness are faithfully portrayed, notably in the strange weeping state in which Waiyaki finds himself in the final stages of the second-birth ceremony. The adolescent Waiyaki is filled with awe, both exhilarating and petrifying, when he conceives that he may be inheriting a great ancestral responsibility:

> The knowledge that he had in him the blood of this famous seer, who had been able to see the future, filled him with an acute sense of wonder . . . For the first time, Waiyaki felt really frightened. Unknown terror gripped him. He fought with it . . . Waiyaki felt as if a heavy cloud was pressing down his soul and he felt a strange sensation of suspension in his stomach. (22–3/19–20)

Already touched by the doubts and perplexity which are to characterize his emergence into manhood, he turns for escape to the possibility that Chege is demented, but this thought cannot subdue his awareness of forces beyond him, too great for him to grapple with:

> And then for a time he began to doubt the sanity of his father. Perhaps the whole thing had been an old man's dream. He almost laughed at the serious manner in which his father had taken it all. But there was no mirth in his heart. Instead he felt a heaviness making him a man . . . (25/21)

Waiyaki never seriously thinks of rejecting his spiritual kinship with his father, and as he takes up his own 'mission' (a word used more than once to express his dedication to education, as well as Kabonyi's commitment to immediate political action) Chege's earlier strength of conviction influences him more strongly: 'Maybe the very spirit that was in his father had entered him' (81/70).

Tribal tradition remains dominant in the protagonists' lives. The novel is true to Gikuyu history. Muthoni is consumed with the idea of becoming a *real* woman in the process of circumcision. After his initiation Waiyaki experiences the sensation that his blood is linking him to the earth. Circumcision is comprehended as the ritual and spiritual basis of the tribe's communal awareness:

> Waiyaki had realized many things. Circumcision of women was not important as a physical operation. It was what it did inside a person . . . If the white man's religion made you abandon a custom and then did not give you something else of equal value, you became lost. (163/142)

In Waiyaki the realization is here dramatized which Kenyatta expressed more formally in *Facing Mount Kenya* 25 years before Ngũgĩ was writing, soon after the actual historic events that form the framework of *The River Between*:

The real argument lies not in the defence of the surgical operation or its details, but in the understanding of a very important fact in the tribal psychology of the Gikuyu, namely that this operation is regarded as the very essence of the institution which has enormous educational, social, moral and religious implications ... The overwhelming majority of [the Gikuyu] believe that it is the secret aim of those who attack this centuries-old custom to disintegrate their social order and thereby hasten their Europeanisation. The abolition of *irua* will destroy the tribal symbol which identifies the age-groups, and prevent the Gikuyu from perpetuating that spirit of collectivism and national solidarity which they have been able to maintain from time immemorial.[3]

Waiyaki has acquired his passion for education in Siriana, the missionary citadel, where Chege (like Ezeulu in *Arrow of God*) sends his son to acquire the white man's magic so that he and his people can deploy it for their own ends instead of fighting against it blindly. But in Chapter 13 when we first hear of Marioshoni School, we first hear also of Waiyaki's lack of interest in radical social thinking:

And why should they, who had been educated in Siriana, be so vehement against it? It was just like his father, who had sent him to the Mission to which he had all his life objected. Perhaps life was a contradiction. Waiyaki felt something stir in him as he listened to Kinuthia. Perhaps Kinuthia was speaking for the sleeping hills, for the whole of Gikuyu country. Then he suppressed the feeling and thought of the new drive in education. (75/64)

And so Waiyaki allows his lazy-minded conservatism to override Kinuthia's advice and to pervert his overmastering passion for teaching. From the beginning Waiyaki is shy of involvement with the wider Gikuyu movement. He cannot find scope in his life for this other dimension. If Waiyaki had possessed a more comprehensive imagination he might have seen these two spheres of activity as complementary, indeed as necessary to each other. But for all his fiery idealism, in this he fails, and so he retreats within his more limited conceptions: 'Waiyaki feared they would give him a place in the leadership of this Kiama, which was meant to embrace all the ridges. He did not feel enthusiastic about it. He wanted to concentrate on education' (75–6/65). He is indeed recruited but soon rashly withdraws of his own volition. Later we hear that 'He was thankful that he had left the Kiama' (126/110): 'He did not see any connection between what his education mission and what the Kiama was doing' (115/101). Ngũgĩ expects us to deplore Waiyaki's lack of vision. The Teacher's nerve fails him. He foregoes the opportunity to relate his school and its syllabus to the environment and the social climate in which his pupils live. Instead he runs for the familiar protective cover of Livingstone's doctrine: 'Perhaps the teaching of Livingstone, that education was of value and his boys should not concern themselves with what the government was doing or politics, had found a place in Waiyaki's heart' (76/65).

So the picture is complex. Waiyaki is independent but with a qualified and conditioned independence. We remember that 'In starting self-help in education, Waiyaki had seen it as a kind of mission' (78/67). He genuinely partakes of the life of the villagers in numerous respects: 'Waiyaki was superstitious. He believed the things that the people of the ridges believed'

(83/71), yet in some sort his mission turns out to be an echoing of the voice of the parent school in Siriana. The schools stood as 'symbols of people's thirst for the white man's secret magic and power' (79/68). It is apparent success in this aim that fosters the parents' enthusiastic acknowledgement of the Teacher: 'Their children could speak a foreign language, could actually read and write' (105/92). Deep down Waiyaki had his own qualms — 'Was the education he was trying to spread in the ridges not a contamination?' (83/72) — yet he does not act upon these doubts. On the contrary, he opts out of the Kiama. This partial sidestepping of his destiny leaves him troubled with misgivings which he can never quite identify: 'Yearning. Yearning. Was life all a yearning and no satisfaction? Was one to live, a strange hollowness pursuing one like a malignant beast that would not let one rest?' (85/73). And when his ambivalent longings draw him to visit Joshua's church, 'he again felt that insatiable longing for something beyond·him, something that would contain the whole of himself' (100/87). His sense of emptiness no doubt derives in part from his need for private fulfilment in love and marriage: his chosen path proves a lonely one — 'The hut was cold and everything in it spoke of desolation' (94/82). Yet other factors are certainly involved. Waiyaki is half-aware that his programme for rejuvenating the tribe is lop-sided, incomplete. Filled as he is with a dedicated passion for service, he nevertheless allows himself to become 'obsessed' with schools and dreams of unity while 'in spite of all this Waiyaki was losing that contact with people that can only come through taking part together in a ritual' (128–9/113); 'at times he felt isolated' (80/69).

Before too readily blaming Waiyaki for his blindness and naivety in believing that education in independent schools and a politically independent society were different issues that could be monitored separately, and in failing to see (as Kinuthia so clearly can) how Kabonyi is maliciously fomenting antagonism against him and his work, we should take a sympathetic look at the very difficult situation in which he is placed. This is a situation into which Ngũgĩ, surely through analogous experience of his own, has deep insight.

At the same time as Ngũgĩ was working on the manuscript which was to become *The River Between*, a number of his undergraduate contemporaries were exploring in apprentice plays the relationships between the young educated East African and his elders in the village as epitomized in confrontations on the question of choosing a wife — a theme Ngũgĩ was to touch upon in *The Black Hermit*. But in his early novel Ngũgĩ first addressed himself to the less fashionable but equally fundamental issue of the social responsibility of such an educated young man, and the dilemma he was likely to face if he tried to respond to this responsibility honestly. The village as a rule took great pride and placed great hope in those who first went off to eat the white men's wisdom. The older generation was eager to listen to and learn from the new kind of knowledge that these youthful pioneers were expected to bring back home. Naturally they hoped to receive useful advice in the context of problems they had already identified. No doubt the returning bookman often felt and sometimes expressed his own kind of pride in this prematurely elevated position of supposed wisdom and potential authority. But even if he were relatively humble, and in the innocence of his heart simply poured forth the new kinds of ideas and convictions he had acquired, he was still likely to meet (contrary to everyone's expectations) a frigid, disappointed, increasingly hostile reaction. His seniors assumed that he had mastered new skills to bolster and protect their traditional way of life against the inroads of the foreigner, whereas in the event he often appeared to those who had remained behind to have become a renegade, an iconoclast, who has joined the enemy instead of arming himself and his society against them. Such a situation was in many respects inevitable. There was no way for the older generation to foresee the true impact that access to the world of books would have on their sons. They simply desired new weapons in the form of knowledge. They had not envisaged a transformation of the outlook, values and horizons of the individuals being educated.

Achebe explores the same problem in *No Longer at Ease*. But whereas Obi Okonkwo is a relatively callow individual who has been conditioned by a full training in a metropolitan university and is both self-preoccupied and in many ways insensitive, Waiyaki is a would-be selfless idealist who has neither proceeded so far through the educational process nor become so alienated from his background. Yet, despite very real and well deserved initial successes, the problem of adequate communication with his society ultimately defeats him. He is unwilling to think through the problems that face him and his community in their entirety. He labours devotedly towards limited goals but this piecemeal approach proves to be self-defeating and he is prevented from full and open contact with his people. He insists on his own partial solutions to the complex problems ahead. So, entrenched group solidarity thwarts his liberal determination to break down barriers and antagonisms, a determination spurred on both by social ideals and by private emotions. In this new dispensation the young man is expected to become an active leader in society, but he finds himself condemned for the initiative he shows when his inquiring, only partly trained mind leads him along paths which society does not wish to follow. Yet his stubborn infatuation with his own partial programme of reform shuts from his sight any fuller perspective and precludes a complete give-and-take between himself and those he seeks to serve.

But to say this much is still to overlook a further crux. Waiyaki finds himself in the ambiguous role of leadership, which strains his youthful capability, at the very time in his life when the sensitive and honest mind is most likely to be at war within itself. This is part of the process of discovering oneself, trying to find out who one is (as it is frequently expressed), a process which generates self-doubts, questionings, uncertainty as to where one stands morally and metaphysically. If, then, Waiyaki stumbles when he most needs a clear, undivided sense of direction and purpose, this is not the result of weakness of character but (as with Hamlet) of strength of character. His hesitancy is the consequence of honesty, integrity, a deep-seated reluctance to proceed without resolving one's reservations and self-questionings: 'Waiyaki was a man of strong emotional moods' (76/66); 'Where was his place in all this? He felt a stranger, a stranger to his land' (69/60); 'Where did he stand? Perhaps there was no half-way house between Makuyu and Kameno . . . Just now he did not know his ground. He did not know himself' (99/86).

However, Ngũgĩ's sympathetic insight into Waiyaki's plight does not qualify his unswerving message. His concern for Waiyaki is real enough but this is not the ultimate issue. In Waiyaki's position, only a man who can master his fate and go beyond the impasse that confronts him will be able to achieve his reformatory purposes. This is what the reader is to grasp.

The novelist must understand Waiyaki's quandary exceptionally well. He too is likely to question himself more than most men, especially in his formative years. He too, as a uniquely articulate member of an educated elite, may have little choice but to take a lead in various social spheres. He too, with his heightened sense of responsibility, will wish to respond to the call, and yet he may find that the kind of lead he feels bound to offer is unwelcome and unpopular. Waiyaki is not the man to turn aside from demands made upon him, yet he is so preoccupied in grappling with himself that he cannot adopt a sure and confident stance. For all his real achievements, Waiyaki muffs his opportunities, fails his own ideals and confounds his own cause. Yet in his defence we can say that life and society have demanded too much of him too soon. If Waiyaki had died at the end, his death would have been fatalistic. But he lives on. True, he lives on in failure and defeat. Yet these, we may conjecture, he will survive. In this novel of challenge rather than of despair — a point to which we shall return — it is appropriate to wonder what the protagonist may be able to achieve when the first tumult has passed and he has at length come to terms with himself.

For the moment, however, as a result of these inner confusions, Waiyaki fails in his careful plan to use the first mass meeting of parents to preach reconciliation. He is aware of his failure and reproaches himself with it to the end of the story. The project starts as hardly more than a well-meaning impulse: 'inside him he felt vaguely that it would be good to reconcile all these antagonisms' (81/69). Then he sees the big meeting which he will control as a golden opportunity to crown his achievements: he weighs the risks and refuses to be deterred:

> The gulf between them was widening and Waiyaki wanted to be the instrument of their coming together. A word from him in the coming meeting might be a big start. Now was the time to show his stand . . . Would this not be a risk to his growing popularity? Yet he would try. (104–5/91)

However, in the event he is so carried away by his deeper obsession with the schools that only after the big meeting is enthusiastically concluded does he uneasily recall that he has neglected his plan: 'And with a fleeting feeling of guilt he remembered that he had forgotten to preach reconciliation' (112/98). But was this really a pure oversight, or was it a subconscious ordering of his fundamental priorities? He does not in his heart altogether regret the omission, even as he reproaches himself:

> The moment had come. The moment had passed. Had he remained calm he would have spoken outright for reconciliation.
> 'Another time. Next time,' Waiyaki always told himself when these moments of self-blame came. And in a way he was glad. Education was really his mission. (115/100–1)

From beginning to end the true creative brilliance of *The River Between* as a young man's venture into the art of the novel lies in its authentic dovetailing of the complex public themes with the private drama of individual characters. Waiyaki's excursion into the realm of books has not 'spoilt' him in tribal terms but it has subtly affected his outlook. He has developed a conscious personal inner life which makes it hard for the new man to accept the kind of total communal involvement that both tradition and his 'mission' demand, even though ironically his contact with more formal patterns of thought has heightened his awareness of human rights and the need for social justice: 'His activities were being watched by everyone. His freedom was being curbed. Yet was this not what he wanted? Service! Service! Always standing by the tribe like his father and the ancestors before him' (94/81). He has indeed a burning desire to be useful to his people, and he is in the true sense dedicated to education: 'he would never forsake them. He would serve them to the end' (100/87). Yet the modern craving for personal freedom may distract even the most determined reformer. In insisting on such rights Waiyaki drops his mildness and moderation. He becomes the angry young man who will brook no restraints. He makes no attempt to explain patiently his unfamiliar stance to the elders in the Kiama or the traditionalists in his village. When his private life is infringed, the Teacher ceases to persuade and begins to assert and dictate. Little wonder that the outcome is confrontation rather than accommodation.

This posture is not only a by-product of a certain type of formal education in an unAfrican milieu, but is also shaped by the clash of powerful forces within the rural environment. Waiyaki first contemplates this issue as he visits the fatally sick Muthoni after she has been circumcised in defiance of her fanatical father: 'Waiyaki thought: "Is she paying for the disobedience?" He shrank to think of this. Was everyone to pay with suffering for choosing his way, for being a rebel?' (56–7/49). Both Waiyaki and Nyambura will indeed also pay with suffering for choosing their way: 'After all, was he himself free from fear?' There is a significant patterning in the reactions at different ages by Waiyaki and Nyambura in the face of paternal control. When Chege confronts his son with a mysterious burden of responsibility which appears too great for the boy to bear, Waiyaki wants to protest but is mesmerized by the spell of his father: 'Waiyaki wanted to cry out: "Don't tell me more. I don't want to hear more. No! No! No, Father!" Instead he only whispered, "Ye-es!" ' (23/19). Later Nyambura reverses this position under the same kind of hypnosis when she reluctantly holds Waiyaki at arm's length:

> Why had she said 'No' when she would have been happier saying 'Yes'? She loved him. She wanted him. He was her only saviour. Yet when he came to her she had run away from him. It was difficult for her to rebel against her father. (130/114)

The feuds between Christians and traditionalists, and the growing divergence between the proponents of education and of political action as solutions to Gikuyu problems, criss-cross in creating Waiyaki's inner bewilderment:

> And so the ancient rivalry continued, sometimes under this or that guise. It

was all confusion building up and spreading under the outward calm of the ridges. Where did people like Waiyaki stand? Had he not received the white man's education? And was this not a part of the other faith, the new faith? The Kameno group was strengthened by the breakaway group led by Kabonyi. Waiyaki felt himself standing outside all this. (80/69)

And in the burgeoning drama, Kabonyi is spurred on by jealousy, in particular of Waiyaki's youthful aspirations. Why should this whipper-snapper usurp what he regards as his appointed position as the prophesied saviour? He sees himself as mature in wisdom; he believes that his son Kamau ought to be at least the equal of his contemporary. He, Kabonyi, is already the driving force within the Kiama. Is not he, then, in every way more eligible to lead the community than this boy they call 'Teacher'?

In the first place Kabonyi revives the Kiama ostensibly to restore the purity of the tribe; but his more immediate motive is his corrosive bitterness against Waiyaki's growing eminence in the community, overshadowing his own son. So the Kiama in his hands is an offensive weapon against Waiyaki. Like a number of his counterparts in African literature such as T.M. Aluko's Teacher Royasin and Benjamin Benjamin, Okara's Dr Abadi, Achebe's Nwaka and Chief Nanga, Kabonyi is well-versed in the issues at stake, accomplished in the art of mob rhetoric, utterly lacking in personal integrity, and endowed with a belligerent capacity for sheer vindictiveness. He seizes upon Waiyaki's genuine efforts to unite the ridges as supposed indications of double-dealing and betrayal of trust. In front of the Kiama he takes full advantage of Waiyaki's reluctance to retaliate in underhand combat. Kabonyi is in a position of civil authority and so has a lethal weapon for doing harm. In confrontation with Kabonyi, Waiyaki has been doomed from the start. In this way Ngũgĩ impresses upon us that those capable of undermining the revolutionary process are not numbered among the uneducated masses, but come from within the knowledgeable few. A revolution is threatened far less by mistaken actions than by deliberate sabotage. Kabonyi is an even more virulent and dangerous enemy of social enlightenment and progress than is Joshua.

In vain and too late Kinuthia warns Waiyaki: ' "Kabonyi is angry. I found him saying to everybody that you are too young to be let into the secrets of the tribe" ' (96/83); 'He pleased many. But not everybody. At such moments jealousy and ill-will are bound to work' (105–6/92). The whole complex of circumstances plays into Kabonyi's hands. His challenge to Waiyaki in front of the Kiama at length finds the protagonist ready to assert the rights of his personal love for Nyambura, while angry pride silences him, and so the denouement is upon us: 'Waiyaki rose. He was now really exasperated. What had Nyambura got to do with them? What? Could he not do whatever he wanted with his own life? Or was his life not his own?' He would tell them nothing about Nyambura' (148/128). Nyambura similarly goes through the mill:

> She now wished to rebel. Muthoni had done it. Nyambura had not Muthoni's courage. And so the struggle went on in her heart. At one time she would want to go to seek Waiyaki out and ask him to take her again. She would whisper to him, 'Waiyaki, I love you.' At others she would fight against her feelings for him and she would feel proud that she had stuck to her father. (130–1/114)

43

And like Waiyaki before the Kiama, so she at a Christian meeting in her father's house must suddenly make her decision. Whereas he turns on his heel in silence, she offers her testimony. In warning Joshua, Waiyaki has waited beyond the eleventh hour to champion the cause of reconciliation. So in making this precipitate, unplanned gesture he is disbelieved and dismissed by Joshua before he is finally cast out by his own community at the instigation of Kabonyi. But Nyambura chooses this moment of Waiyaki's commitment and rejection to link herself to him publicly:

> She saw her Waiyaki being humiliated. Her obedience to her father fought with her love for Waiyaki. And at last, when he turned his back, rejected, she stood up. Her voice was clear and almost commanding . . . 'The teacher is not telling a lie.' (155–6/135)

The weaknesses of the novel, like its strengths, are related to the paradoxes inherent in its themes. Some aspects of the social conflict involved were as yet no clearer to the author than to his characters, and this leads to some underdevelopment in areas where a more explicitly committed writer (as Ngũgĩ has now become) might have left fewer gaps. The African novel, in the main, has adopted a briefer and more concentrated form than the traditional European novel, which was one of its progenitors. This economy is powerful in its compactness, in its rejection of over-explicitness and multiplicity, and in its disciplined directness. *A Walk in the Night, The Wedding of Zein, The Voice* are startling examples for which the diminutive and deprecating term 'novelette' is inappropriate. Even *Things Fall Apart* can barely exceed 50,000 words. It is not to underrate this well-established and all-too-little-considered African mode to suggest that its abruptness can sometimes be overdone. *The River Between* is one of a number of novels that might have been strengthened by further judicious development in places. It would have greatly helped our understanding of the situation and the characters, for instance, if we had seen Waiyaki at an early meeting of the Kiama and learnt more of the mood and manner in which he withdrew from that body. Chapter 13 is finely conceived and it provides intriguing variations in style and presentation. The meditation on the falling rain is interwoven with an account of the creation and development of Marioshoni School from its inception to the point where it is already in a state of disrepair, and leads to Waiyaki's first deliberate separation of education from politics. Yet, fine a piece of writing as it is, the passage remains somewhat too terse and abstract. Such an intricate and important sequence could well have sustained more than its six or seven pages. Again, concentrated and exciting as the last climax of the story is made, we are left with scarcely enough time to take in fully its final recasting of the principal themes.

On the other hand the trenchant force of the novel's manner is effectively clinched by the chapter endings: 'He was ready for initiation' (15/12); 'The war was now on' (66/57); 'Waiyaki was his rival to death' (123/108). And the design of the book is pointedly controlled by the way it pivots on the death of Muthoni, as she attempts in action to blend the warring sets of beliefs and ways of life. The ironies are often left implicit; they are never laboured: for instance, that it is Nyambura rather than Muthoni who feels guilty about her thoughts concerning circumcision when we first meet the sisters beside the River Honia. The somewhat staccato dialogue blends into passages which enter the stream of consciousness of one or other of the main characters — notably Waiyaki's or Nyambura's at key points — so that we are intimate with their inner thoughts and feelings, a technique that Achebe did not choose to experiment with in his first, monumental novel. And the constant casting back to certain key experiences and points of reference which has already been discussed — such as the trip to the sacred grove, the boyhood fight, the events beside the river — ensures that the characters' memories are also our memories. This brings us even closer to them since we find ourselves sharing their own vision of the surroundings. The same device is exploited increasingly in the more mature novels.

The themes of *The River Between* are brought to life for us in the experiences of individual characters, and (to look at it the other way round) our awareness of the characters is deepened because they are involved in crucial affairs which affect the whole society. These two complementary facets of the narrative come together in depicting 'the people', those who are not named, but who make up the various components of the community and who live out the story. The majority of the tribe (as opposed to the Christian enclave) 'remained conservative, loyal to the ways of the land' (33/28), as is true of any stalwart agricultural peasantry. They resent innovations imposed on them from without, but unless a natural leader arises they tend to remain passive in the face of encroachments:

> The white man should never have set a foot in Siriana. A Government Post was being built on the ridge next to Makuyu. And it was now clear that people would have to pay taxes.
>
> What could they do? It was now too late to take action . . . (67/58)

But once given the chance, they eagerly follow the lead offered by Waiyaki in annexing the new magic of education: 'The children caught the enthusiasm of their parents. Perhaps they saw they were the hope and the glory of the tribe' (80/68). This response is without prejudice to their inherent support for traditional culture, with circumcision as its focus: 'The cry was up. Gikuyu Karinga. Keep the tribe pure. Tutikwenda Irigu. It was a soul's cry, a soul's wish' (79/68).

If, in terms of the novel, one man could have harnessed both these impulses — the desire for education and the devotion to tradition — the two forces might have coalesced and such a man might have fulfilled Mugo's prophecy. In historical reality, Kikuyu Karing'a and similar movements were in fact to work along these lines, but one may suspect that their Africanized Christianity, while by definition reconciled to tradition, was not adequately 'washed' for Ngũgĩ's — nor, by implication, for Waiyaki's — liking. Perhaps Kinuthia captures something of this desired spirit when he laments his friend's shortsightedness: 'Yet he wondered if Waiyaki knew that people wanted action now, that the new enthusiasm and awareness embraced more than the mere desire for learning' (135/118). The African Orthodox Church, to which Kikuyu Karing'a was linked, and other indigenous sects, may have appeared to the youthful Ngũgĩ, looking back sceptically from his Alliance High School experience, too narrowly doctrinaire to match up to 'the other' of which Nyambura dreams. In the event Waiyaki disastrously leaves the way open for the more demagogic Kabonyi both to lead the Kiama, and to rally popular political sentiment: 'Yes. The Kiama was right. People wanted action now' (164/143).

Yet in his self-assertiveness Kabonyi also misunderstands those whose support he seeks to marshal. The heart of man — at all times, in all places — is drawn by the allurements of newness and everything that it promises. The people want the new age on their own terms, but they want it. And, whatever his misgivings, our author is clearsighted about this:

> Not that Kabonyi knew exactly where he would lead the people. For he too was grappling with forces awakened in the people. How could he understand that the people did not want to move backwards, that the ridges no longer desired their isolation? How could he know that the forces that drove people to yearn for a better day tomorrow, that now gave a new awareness to the people, were like demons, sweeping the whole country, as Mugo had said? . . . (166/144)

And so Waiyaki's failures are real failures, because his lost opportunities were real opportunities. Yet the demands made upon him were excessive. And at the last he has that rarest and most disarming of all human virtues, the readiness to admit his own mistakes. Too late in terms of the narrative, he comes to see what Kinuthia has seen all along:

> New thoughts are coming into my mind. Things I might have done and said. Oh, there are so many things I did not know. I had not seen that the new awareness wanted expression at a political level. Education for an oppressed people is not all. (160/138–9)

The militant Ngũgĩ of *Petals of Blood* is, as we said earlier, already stirring. Waiyaki blames himself for having abandoned his self-elected task of re-unification:

> What if he had made his stand clear at the meeting? That was now a lost opportunity and he had to reckon with the present. Still he wondered if he had not betrayed the tribe; the tribe he had meant to unite; the tribe he had wanted to save; the people he had wanted to educate, giving them all the benefits of the white man's coming. (162/141)

Thus, while at the human level Ngũgĩ extends much sympathy and fellow-feeling to Waiyaki, at the social level he represents his failure starkly as failure pure and simple. Ngũgĩ is giving a stern reminder to himself as well as confronting his readers. This theme is developed in the novels ahead. The cause of society succeeds or fails not as the result of the absence or existence of obstacles — obstacles are always present — but according to whether or not the leaders of society are of a calibre to surmount such obstacles as must be faced. Waiyaki fails, as it were, by a narrow margin, and so there is much to learn from him, from his positive qualities and, even more important, from the factors that nullify his good intentions: his lack of insight and foresight, and his readiness to be carried away by one part of his vision at the expense of the whole.

Waiyaki's self-doubts may be honourable, an aspect of his integrity and his ability to grow, but they inhibit him as a fullfledged mentor of social change. He allows his personal passion for Nyambura to become, instead of an incidental matter from a public standpoint, a major cause of conflict between himself and the Kiama, refusing to plead his case and keep the issue in perspective. Waiyaki's good-will and enthusiasm are great virtues in the ethos of the novel, and so the wastage of such potentiality is the greatest possible disaster for the community as a whole.

Muthoni and Nyambura, in their small ways, much more nearly fulfil Ngũgĩ's ideal. They do not seek martyrdom. They suffer in the pursuit of the fullness of life. Within the small spheres in which they can hope to exercise any influence, they stand up to defend their convictions fearlessly and unequivocally. Nyambura is contrasted with Waiyaki in her undeviating steadfastness in all her beliefs. For her, religion has no meaning without her man. For her, Waiyaki is that man and no social perversities may stand between them. Waiyaki loves Nyambura in return, but his clumsiness exposes her to grave dangers. While Waiyaki fails and fumbles, Nyambura remains undefeated.

As for Muthoni, Waiyaki himself admits her success where he himself is found wanting. She makes serious efforts to reconcile the conflicting ethics and mores of indigenous and adopted religions:

> Muthoni had tried. Hers was a search for salvation for herself. She had the courage to attempt a reconciliation of the many forces that wanted to control her. She had realized her need, the need to have a wholesome and beautiful life that enriched you and made you grow. (163/142)

In so far as either Nyambura or Muthoni falters, they do so because they have leaned on Waiyaki in trust and he has not proved able to maintain even his own course, let alone to reinforce their own.

Late in the day as it is, nevertheless Waiyaki's vision is at last coherent. We are left in no doubt, by his own honest account, of where or why or how he has failed. The implications of this must be plain to Ngũgĩ's readers. Waiyaki now knows that in refusing to seek the political kingdom, he has emasculated his own ideal of education. But he no longer has time even to try and relate his two failures to each other. Was success in both spheres ever possible? Even if his own perspective had been much broader from the start, would he not have been bound to make a choice? Was there ever any way of achieving both political freedom and reconciliation between Kameno and Makuyu? To have come to terms with the Christians not as he (and Nyambura) imagine they might become, but as they actually were in Joshua's meetings, would surely have meant compromising demands for real political emancipation. The predicament involved, as we have seen, is dramatized in Waiyaki's bewilderment.

The novel embodies contradictory possibilities and leaves us to arbitrate between them. The ferment within this society at a crossroads is dynamically communicated: the past is re-created alive and, more importantly, the many issues which still remain relevant are thrust at us for urgent reconsideration. We recall that the first draft of the novel was entitled *The Black Messiah*,[4] and that it brought Waiyaki and Nyambura to their deaths in the last scene. Just as, on the one hand, it is better that we should continue to wrestle with the dilemmas which the work impresses upon us rather than that we should sit back and listen to a set of forced remedies, so, on the other hand, it is well that Ngũgĩ eventually abjured private tragedy in order to leave his challenge to the reader central at the end. The irony remains: the community rejects Waiyaki because of his own personal commitment to the very unity which he forgot to foster publicly, but which he feels impelled to practise privately in order to remain true to his personal passion. And yet the people themselves are stunned, embarrassed, alarmed at what they have done: there is clearly much rethinking ahead for them as well as for ourselves: 'They went away quickly, glad that he was hidden by the darkness. For they did not want to look at the Teacher and they did not want to read their guilt in one another's faces' (175/152).

Specific solutions to the larger problems raised we might have rejected; melodrama we might have rejected; the reality and the urgency of the questions posed we cannot reject. These remain with us long after we have closed the book, and draw us forward to explore the later novels.

Notes

1. In an interview at Makerere University, Ngũgĩ wa Thiong'o explained that *The River Between* was submitted for an East African Literature Bureau creative writing competition on 31 December 1961, but was not released for publication till March 1963. In the intervening period in 1962, *Weep Not, Child* was written and published.
2. The first set of page references to *The River Between* relate to the first edition (Heinemann Educational Books, London, 1965). The second refer to the reset edition of 1975, subsequently reprinted.
3. Jomo Kenyatta, *Facing Mount Kenya: The Tribal Life of the Gikuyu* (Secker & Warburg, London, 1938), 134–5.
4. The phrase 'black messiah' appears several times in the first edition of *The River Between* (pp. 45, 117, 154).

Weep Not, Child

It is reasonable to suppose that *Weep Not, Child* opens, in terms of our real-world calendar, 15 years or so after the final incidents of *The River Between*. Both are, of course, works of fiction and there is no purpose in quibbling over a precise historical ordering of events. Nevertheless each of the stories seeks to re-create meaningfully a recognizable epoch in Gikuyuland and it is therefore hardly surprising that we can relate the principal milestones in the narratives to an actual sequence of happenings. *Weep Not, Child*, then, probably begins towards the end of 1945 and spans some ten years, from the time Njoroge is about to join Kamae Primary School for the first time to the traumatic months after he has become a first-year drop-out from Siriana. By a minor exercise of artistic licence, the general strike, which took place in May 1950, is made to coincide with the announcement of Njoroge's first public success in qualifying to go beyond lower primary school. He spent two of his four years in Kamahou Intermediate School when the news of Jomo Kenyatta's conviction is heard — that was on 8 April 1953. So we may presume that he passes his Kenya African Preliminary Examination (KAPE) at the end of 1954.[1] He has been in secondary school for only two terms when Jacobo is killed and his formal education is brought to a halt — this is when he is 19 or thereabouts. And so the fictional Njoroge was imagined to be two years older than his author. His perception of the Mau Mau campaign may thus very well have been similar to Ngũgĩ's own.

Like *The River Between*, *Weep Not, Child* is intensely concentrated. It epitomizes a crucial and complex phase in Gikuyu, Kenyan and indeed African experience. Resentment against the colonial alienation of land is now at a menacing pitch: it has been estimated that a quarter of the whole Gikuyu population had been forced to leave their family homes by 1948.[2] Restrictions imposed on farming activities in the 'Native Reserves' were crippling. Discrimination was humiliating as well as educationally and economically restrictive. Men returning from the Second World War had seen too much of social intercourse in the world at large ever again to

49

accept tamely the repressive conditions they found in their own country. Demands for political emancipation were in the air. In 1950 the Mau Mau Central Committee was formed.

Weep Not, Child is a novel of challenge. Most immediately it challenges Kenyan youth to identify the powerfully positive elements in their heritage. It challenges a whole age-group to refuse to sit on the fence or retreat from a complex situation into self-pity or despair. It is not Njoroge alone who needs to accept the responsibility of building on the sacrifices and achievements of the Boros, of the Nyokabis and Njeris, and even — for what can be learnt from their sturdy determination to survive — of the Ngothos. Such commitment could enable the new generation to find ways of realigning the drive and direction of society (which is in danger of losing its way) through concerted policies and action.

Ngotho's age-group lacked foresight and determination and so failed to stand out against colonial and elitist appropriation of the land. But in spite of this failure to unite against a takeover by invading interests, they retained a certain staunch integrity, and a traditional social morality — except for traitors like Jacobo. Boro's age-group has united, fought, conquered — and been betrayed. They are angry and frustrated men, but they seek to hand on their will to resist, their readiness to suffer in a communal cause, their insistent demand for social justice. What can our Njoroges make of these invasions, survivals, submissions, battles and betrayals? Will they turn their backs, or (still worse) seek to step into the shoes of the exploiters? Will they wring their hands in despair or will they come together to pursue the struggle for an equitable and just society? In posing these questions, the novel sets Njoroge at the centre of the scene as subject for our concern and, indeed, for our severe criticism. He does not sell out. He does not join, or seek to join, the extortioners. Ngũgĩ searches more subtly into these issues by presenting a protagonist who means well but who is deficient in moral insight, courage and stamina, like so many of us who read the novel. Njoroge finds himself on the sidelines of the struggle. He dithers, loses heart, opts out. His heroic, individualistic daydreams undermine rather than strengthen his resolve as they fail and fade. Yet he has the makings of a constructive member of the community and so can be rescued and set on the road to more active participation. Significantly, he is recalled by those who have worked unassumingly yet determinedly for the welfare of their group all their lives.

Again like *The River Between*, *Weep Not, Child* offers both a subtle portrayal of particular human dilemmas and conflicts, and a dramatic social commentary. Ngũgĩ handles his characters with great compassion and understanding as individuals who are suffering intensely, assailed by contrary forces beyond their control or indeed their comprehension. But in his role as recorder and monitor of society the author has no place for narrow sentiments (let alone sentimentality). If at the private level we are allowed to sympathize with inadequacy, confusion, bewilderment, at the public level whereon we must learn from the past if we are to reshape the future, failure is baldly acknowledged to be failure, and misjudgements and misinterpretations are observed as actually or potentially disastrous. A good deal of careful understanding goes into the characterization of Jacobo and Howlands, but little sympathy is wasted on these essentially self-centred go-getters. On the other hand Ngũgĩ's insight leads the reader to sorrow profoundly over the broken Ngotho. Yet at the same time we acknowledge the calamitous effects of his generation's short-sightedness in imagining that the land crisis caused by colonial exploitation would somehow solve itself in the fullness of time: 'Would these people never go? But had not the old Gikuyu seer said that they would eventually return the way they had come?' (36/32).[3] The younger generation may somewhat brashly underestimate the intricacies of the problem that confronted their forebears, but the fact still stares us in the face from the pages of *Weep Not, Child* that in such a situation inaction is indistinguishable from total capitulation. The prophesied people 'with clothes like butterflies'[4] came unresisted; and the elders waited passively for the arrival of 'a son' whose 'duty shall be to lead and save the people'.[5] Boro exclaims, ' "How can you continue working for a man who has taken your land? How can you go on serving him?" ' (30/27).

Njoroge cannot be said to have failed, since he is a youngster who has not been harnessed for action. Yet he has spent a protected youth in the midst of a social cataclysm dreaming about his future heroic role as a messiah. Then, when the field is left open for him to enter, he is overwhelmed by the scale and complexity of the problems. So at length he is prepared to betray the fight for Gikuyuland and for social justice by his own form of capitulation in suicide.

It is sometimes implied that in perceiving the growing corruption and class privilege in pre-independent and independent Kenya, Ngũgĩ looked back at Mau Mau as a venture which did nothing but expose society's inability, or refusal, to build a juster future. Certainly the insurrection was plagued and splintered by mammoth contradictions. Between 1952 and 1956 Ngũgĩ as a schoolboy must have shared the doubts and bewilderment which the novel so faithfully depicts, and may even have come to question the whole rationale of Mau Mau. But as an undergraduate in 1962 he had disentangled these doubts. His journalism, which we discussed earlier, expresses the optimism with which he now viewed the future of Kenya. The despair and failings which *Weep Not, Child* records, the fear which it voices for the future, are to be seen therefore not only as a truthful expression of the uncertainties and ironies inherent in the situation between 1956 and 1962, but also as a provocative challenge from novelist to reader.

Weep Not, Child emphasizes the pressing need for joint action by the community, as opposed to individual self-assertion. It does this in recalling the heroism and the impact of Mau Mau, and also by depicting the unhappy effects of disunity and lack of social harmony. If Ngotho is the sad reminder of the demoralizing effect of servile compliance with foreign demands, Njoroge embodies an even more negative passivity which repudiates the example offered by Mau Mau in its maintenance of the campaign for corporate rights against all odds. However confused the scene, everything is to be fought for and won. There is no possible justification for despair or retreat. At the end of *Weep Not, Child,* the discredited Njoroge has the chance for a new beginning, which he shares with a considerable proportion of the novel's readership. The egotism of imagining himself singled out to redeem his people by personal inspiration must now be expiated. We conceive of him working in future constructively and unpretentiously within the framework of the society which his mothers have so long helped to sustain.

Ngotho is at the centre of the protest from first to last. The protest is against the colonial situation which has allowed the land to be stolen while in the process a whole way of living and being has been undermined. As Chege tells the youthful Waiyaki in *The River Between*, the Gikuyu believe that Murungu bequeathed the land to them at the beginning of the world: and Ngotho hands down the myth to his children in *Weep Not, Child*. Land has thus from time immemorial been the key factor in the unity, cohesion and strength of the family, linking the living and the dead in an unbroken chain. Ngotho has been robbed of his very heritage:

> And yet he felt the loss of the land even more keenly than Boro, for to him it was a spiritual loss. When a man was severed from the land of his ancestors where would he sacrifice to the Creator? How could he come into contact with the founder of the tribe, Gikuyu and Mumbi? (84/74)

Added to this, the younger generation with their new political organizations have become aware that every branch of mankind exerts an ancestral right over its allotted area of the earth. At the end of Chapter 9 Ngũgĩ leaves Njeri, one of the mother figures, to analyse the confidence trick that the white man has played. The process must indeed be transparent if a village woman can grasp it so clearly, and fundamental, if a young mother can deplore it so passionately:

> 'The white man makes a law or a rule. Through that rule or law or what you may call it, he takes away the land and then imposes many laws on the people concerning that land and many other things, all without people agreeing first as in the old days of the tribe. Now a man rises and opposes that law which made right the taking away of the land. Now that man is taken by the same people who made the laws against which that man was fighting. He is tried under those alien rules. Now tell me who is that man who can win even if the angels of God were his lawyers.' (84–5/75)

We are reminded of the fable of the elephant and the hut in Jomo Kenyatta's *Facing Mount Kenya*.

For Ngotho his white employer is the ever-present perpetrator of the loss he has suffered. In a way their feeling for the land holds Ngotho and Howlands incongruously together:

> Not that Mr Howlands stopped to analyse his feelings towards him. He just loved to see Ngotho working in the farm; the way the old man touched the soil, almost fondling, and the way he tended the young tea plants as if they were his own. (33/29–30)

But it is a love-hate relationship at the best. What superficially unites them, at a deeper level divides them irrevocably. Ngotho is at one with the land, co-operates with it: Howlands triumphs over it, possesses it assertively as a conqueror.

> Ngotho felt responsible for whatever happened to this land. He owed it to the dead, the living and the unborn of his line, to keep guard over this *shamba*. Mr Howlands always felt a certain amount of victory whenever he walked through

it all. He alone was responsible for taming this unoccupied wildness. (35/31)

' "This is my land." Mr Howlands said this as a man would say, This is my woman' (145/129). And it is hatred which dominates their relationship in the end as Howlands pursues his vendetta against Ngotho: 'Mr Howlands always felt that soon he would come to grips with Ngotho. Ngotho was his foe' (111/97).

But Ngũgĩ's protest is at the same time wider and deeper. He is appalled by the human condition which, however inexorably time may catch up with the usurpers, seems for the moment to collaborate with them in crushing the good, gentle, powerless man; in holding apart those who have a deep love for each other; and in tormenting the brave and selfless with a sense of failure. In spite of all his setbacks Ngotho has gently but firmly moulded a united household:

> The feeling of oneness was a thing that most distinguished Ngotho's household from many other polygamous families. Njeri and Nyokabi went to the *shamba* or market together. Sometimes they agreed amongst themselves that while one did that job the other would do this one. This was attributed to Ngotho, the centre of the home. For if you have a stable centre, then the family will hold. (45–6/40)

Yet this of all households is the one that circumstances ruthlessly tear apart.

Ngotho is a characteristic figure in Ngũgĩ's works. His aspirations and dreams are in the long run unfulfilled: 'He had all his life lived under the belief that something big would happen' (44/39). Instead he is progressively undermined and at last paralysed by Boro's anger and contempt. ' "You know how bitter he is with father," ' Kamau reminds Njoroge, ' "because he says that it was through the stupidity of our fathers that the land had been taken" ' (47/41). Thus, like Waiyaki at the end, and Mugo from the very beginning, Ngotho is increasingly weighed down by a sense of guilt. He succumbs to all Boro's recriminations and is bowed under the shame of having failed his own sons: 'He had not wanted to be accused by a son any more because when a man was accused by the eyes of his son who had been to war and had witnessed the death of a brother he felt guilty' (83/74); 'The awareness that he had failed his children had always shadowed him. Even before this calamity befell him, life for him had become meaningless, divorced as he had been from what he valued' (134/119). And the last sour irony is that finally even Njoroge looks on his father as a shadow of his old self: 'Could this be the father he had secretly adored and feared?' (140/123).

At the same time, in the midst of his frustration Ngotho anticipates Mugo as a momentarily heroic anti-hero. His gesture at the strike meeting can be compared to Mugo's leaping into the trench to save the woman being beaten by the homeguard. Ngotho too is a loser. His courageous act of defiance defeats its own purpose. When Njeri and Kori are seized for breaking curfew, Boro blames the helpless old man for taking no action: ' "And *you* again did nothing?" ', and will listen to no explanation: 'Ngotho had nobody to whom he could explain' (92/81). After he has already condemned himself for cowardice, he must crouch in a prolonged agony of self-abasement:

He felt like crying, but the humiliation and pain he felt had a stunning effect. Was he a *man* any longer, he who had watched his wife and son taken away because of breaking the curfew without a word of protest? Was this cowardice? It was cowardice, cowardice of the worst sort. (91/80)

Yet he proves himself to have that most exceptional kind of courage which a meek man can show in spite of possessing no ounce of bravado. This is true at the strike meeting, but even more tellingly later when he goes to the DC and confesses to a crime he believes his son Kamau to have committed, knowing full well that he is walking into the leopard's jaws.

Though the youthful Ngũgĩ is not yet fully equipped to free a moment of tragedy from sentimentality or cliché, yet there is some sense of release for the characters and the reader at the old man's death, when Boro in a flash realizes the whole truth, asks Ngotho for forgiveness, and accepts his blessing. But, as we shall see later, this miniature dramatic resolution is not part of the final movement of the novel. Njoroge has inherited his father's role and still has to endure the climax of his own sense of guilt and self-condemnation. The pattern is recurrent.

In the underlying design, Nganga stands between the alienated Ngotho and the quisling Jacobo. The pattern has gradations. The presence of Nganga reminds us that not all middle-aged Gikuyu are landless, nor are all the luckier, conservative elders ruthless traitors to their people. Kamau deeply resents Nganga's old-fashioned, slow-moving type of apprenticeship and feels he is being exploited. Yet he and his brother have to eat their words when Nganga comes unasked to rescue the homeless family: 'It was then that Njoroge realized that the man's rough exterior and apparent lack of scruple concealed a warm heart. His old hatred of Nganga vanished. Even Kamau could now speak of him with enthusiasm' (69/61). We shall find many more instances of such balance and complexity in this novel.

Boro embodies another major aspect of the design. Ngũgĩ himself (like Njoroge) was too young to have been directly involved in Mau Mau. Much of the tone of *Weep Not, Child* may well derive from his own uncomfortable feeling that, in the seclusion of school and college, he has had an easy ride as a non-combatant. The writing of the novel was perhaps an act of reparation — even of expiation — for his own irrational sense of guilt for having been born too late to participate in the conflict. Ngũgĩ certainly knew the Boros of his home area well and, in talking to them during holidays and vacations, he may well have nursed a self-critical awareness of his own immunity. Significantly, it is Njoroge in the novel who loses faith in education as a cure-all, not Boro, nor indeed any of the older folk.

Boro, a pattern of the Mau Mau hero, has carried the brunt of society's ill-fortunes and has been incurably bruised in mind and spirit in the process: 'All the wrong done to the people was concentrated in the plaintive voice of Boro' (85/75). The bitter ironies of his having fought in the Europeans' war are compounded by the fact that he was apparently present when his most-loved brother was killed in some by-water of that struggle. Boro is pictured as an indomitable fighter for social principles. Yet he has become morose and introverted. His rejection of his father, sincerely motivated as it is, at the same time gives perverse solace to his injured psyche. Boro has become the husk of his old self. He lives negatively, destructively, for revenge. As General China relates of himself in *Mau Mau General*,[6] Boro wishes only to turn the deathly skills he has been taught in the world war against those whom he sees as accountable for the theft of Gikuyu lands — and for his brother's death. 'The ripe hour of his youth had been spent in bloodshed in the big war. This was the only thing he could do efficiently' (116/102). In anatomizing Boro, Ngũgĩ is plumbing the harshest dimensions of the Mau Mau struggle:

'Don't you believe in anything?'
     'No. Nothing. Except revenge.'
     'Return of the lands?'
     'The lost land will come back to us maybe. But I've lost too many of those whom I loved for land to mean much to me . . . What great cause is ours?'
     'Why, Freedom and the return of our lost heritage.'
     'Maybe there's something in that. But for me Freedom is meaningless unless it can bring back a brother I lost. Because it can't do that, the only thing left to me is to fight, to kill and rejoice at any who falls under my sword.' (115–16/102–3)

The novel is concerned with the wider problem of non-communication. Boro is 'withdrawn' (84/75); Ngotho fears his own son and eventually has no one to whom he can explain himself. Whites and blacks are irrevocably apart: '"Europeans cannot be friends with black people. They are so high"' (41/37). Africans and Indians are mutually alien: 'You could never like the Indians because their customs were strange and funny in a bad way' (8/7); and even the gentle and humane Nyokabi is shocked into an unseemly outburst when her child goes to accept the spontaneous gift of a sweet from an Indian counterpart. All forces are at work to separate Njoroge and Mwihaki when they first start getting to know each other as children. On a different level, Njoroge finds himself tongue-tied when he tries to communicate his private dreams:

Whenever he was with Mwihaki, he longed to impart some of these things to her. Yet when he tried to define them in words, he failed. So he kept them all to himself, walking alone in the fields and sometimes finding companionship with the nights. (56/49)

All Gikuyu have in common one great unifying call which ideally extends to all Kenyans, to all Africans: ' "Black people must rise up and fight" ' (85/75). Yet this itself is a cry of reaction against the ironic divisions which hold the people apart:

'All white people stick together. But we black people are very divided. And because they stick together, they've imprisoned Jomo, the only hope we had. Now they'll make us slaves. They took us to their wars and they killed all that was of value to us . . .' (85/75)

The defiant plea of the poor villager is a lost cause before it is spoken:

'Let Africans stick together and charge very low prices. We are all black. If this be not so, then why grudge a poor woman the chance to buy from someone, be he white or red, who charges less money for his things?' (9/8)

Yet it is the economic dominance of the Asians that enables them to undercut small African traders. Social conditions make unity impossible.

There is, then, no easy idealism for the author. He is starkly realistic about the problems he identifies. Ngũgĩ never deliberately addressed himself to a foreign readership: his challenge has always been to his own people. His sad analysis of black disunity plays into the hands of no alien lobby, but is directed towards righting those wrongs within society which mirror the very things its members are fighting against: ' "Blackness is not all that makes a man," Kamau said bitterly. "There are some people, be they black or white, who don't want others to rise above them" ' (24/21). Later the temperate Ngotho keeps his reservations to himself when the forthcoming strike action is being explained to the elders: ' "We black people are brothers." Ngotho knew of one or two who were certainly *not* brothers. But he did not say so' (59/51). The confrontation between generations fans the flames of dissension. Boro condemns unreservedly the passive stance of his father's age-group: 'There was no land on which he could settle, even if he had been able to do so . . . How could these people have let the white man occupy the land without acting?' (30/26–7). The fact that the renegade Jacobo is identified and resisted by Ngotho is taken not as an assurance of unity but of the inevitability of division: ' "It shows that we black people will never be united. There must always be a traitor in our midst" ' (68/60).

Individual discord swells into hatred between factions as the villagers stand helpless between brutalities of the homeguard and reprisals of the forest fighters, a situation in which opportunist marauders find it easy to camouflage themselves. Ngũgĩ chronicles the internecine struggle through the unsophisticated rivalries of schoolboys:

'Jomo is bound to win. Europeans fear him.'

'No. He can't win. My father said so last night.'

'Your father is a homeguard,' another boy retorted. The two boys began a quarrel.

'The homeguards with their white masters. They are as bad as Mau Mau.'

'No. Mau Mau is not bad. The Freedom boys are fighting against white settlers. Is it bad to fight for one's land? Tell me that.'

'But they cut black men's throats.'

'Those killed are the traitors! Black white settlers.' (81–2/72)

The sympathies of the novel lie inevitably with the freedom fighters. The novel exposes the dissension that has existed in order to highlight the imperative need for a new sense of unity among the shattered fragments of the community. For Ngũgĩ is keenly aware that villagers, trapped between two fires, are left with a sense not only of helplessness but of anarchy. The colonized are given no chance to react against their condition coherently. The barber, hub of life in the township, and Nganga, the man with the honest success story, are among six murdered civilians: ' "Who killed them really, the white men?" "Who can tell these days who kills who?" ' (97/86). Divide and rule assumes a new and even more sinister meaning. Howlands, the militant settler, is gratified: 'The blacks were destroying the blacks. They would destroy themselves to the end. What did it matter with him if the blacks in the forest destroyed a whole village? . . . Let them destroy themselves' (110/97). Even Njoroge is repelled when his wild-eyed brother, his hair 'long and unkempt', emerges from the forest: 'Njoroge instinctively shrank from him' (140/124). Writing some years later amid cries of 'Uhuru' and 'Harambee', Ngũgĩ points to the unhealed scars that must be recognized and tended if the prevailing euphoria is to inspire a campaign for unity and justice.

The one figure in this pattern of contradictions for whom we are allowed to feel no real compassion is, as in *A Grain of Wheat*, the man who has sold out long ago to the alien power: 'Jacobo, the richest man in all the land around, had been brought to pacify the people . . . For one single moment Jacobo crystallized into a concrete betrayal of the people' (66/58). Jacobo deliberately frustrates his fellow Africans' attempts to move forward and regain effective control of the land. He surpasses Kabonyi as an evil and destructive figure. His cynicism entails not only ruthless ambition geared to self-aggrandizement, but the shame of betraying his own people to achieve his ends. The first sight of his home 'looked like a European's house' (20/18). This lackey of the white man is in fact held in contempt by the man he so eagerly serves: 'Mr Howlands despised Jacobo because he was a savage. But he would use him' (88/77). Howlands grins like a schoolboy at the prospect of kicking his minion. In return for prostituting himself, Jacobo receives favours which help him to defy retribution for a while and acquire affluence — and through affluence power, power over the lives of others. Only by totally suppressing his conscience can he maintain this position. But at length his time runs out and he is dispatched.

Ngũgĩ does not deny him touches of humanity: 'Jacobo looked tired. He was not the proud farmer of old' (104/92). And Jacobo shows a real flicker of interest in Njoroge's schooling, though as he does so Njoroge glances at the homeguards' red jerseys and remembers the dead barber. Even Mwihaki, the dutiful daughter, is estranged: ' "But now he is uncommunicative. The gun and the pistol he carries make him a stranger to me" ' (106/94). Jacobo is an exceptional figure in the novel, to be grouped — if at all — with Howlands rather than with his countrymen.

Njoroge, on the other hand, is central and in many ways typical, above all as a victim of circumstances rather than an instigator of action. As an adolescent he can — like the women — be politically and publicly inactive without loss of face, except in his own eyes. For different reasons Ngotho, and in essential respects Boro, are also victims who cannot change their physical or psychological environments. Njoroge is thus appropriate as a focal figure for a variety of reasons: on thematic grounds because in muted form he parallels aspects of the experiences of other key characters; and, at a narrative level, since he is well placed to observe what passes in Gikuyuland during this formative decade.

Like Waiyaki, Njoroge is alert and sensitive, over-sensitive indeed: 'he did not like plucking a flower in bloom because it lost colour. He said, "Let's not play with flowers" ' (41/36). Until he is tested under the pressure of intense experience, he is willy-nilly, formalistically Christian, though he puzzles over and wrestles with the contradictions inherent in his faith in emergent Africa. But for the moment, in spite of all he sees, he accepts the idea of an all-powerful, all-good God, and so rather glibly assumes that somehow everything will be for the best. When he discovers that he has passed the secondary entrance examination, 'His first impulse . . . [is] to kneel down and thank God for all' (118/104).

Njoroge lives a large part of his early life, like Waiyaki, in imagining a rosy future in which he will play an important role in the redemption of his society (a destiny which he tries to sidestep when it faces him in starkly realistic terms): 'Njoroge had always been a dreamer, a visionary who consoled himself faced by the difficulties of the moment by a look at a better day to come' (135/120). And, as for Waiyaki, his pole star is education:

> He knew that for him education would be the fulfilment of a wider and more significant vision — a vision that embraced the demand made on him, not only by his father, but also by his mother, his brothers and even the village. He saw himself destined for something big, and this made his heart glow. (44/39)

Learning will equip him for this undefined task ahead, as a saviour of the tribe — a conception which also preoccupied Waiyaki; and in the process the shambles of the guerrilla war will be sublimated:

> Only education could make something out of this wreckage. He became more faithful to his studies. He would one day use all his learning to fight the white man . . . When these moments caught him, he actually saw himself as a possible saviour of the whole God's country. (93/82)

In making knowledge his ideal, he has committed himself to the one goal that unites all the conflicting elements of Gikuyu society:

> Whatever their differences, interest in knowledge and book-learning was the one meeting point between people such as Boro, Jacobo and Ngotho. Somehow the Gikuyu people always saw their deliverance as embodied in education. (119/104–5)

Yet it is interesting that all these characters take it for granted that education must mean exactly the same thing to everyone. Waiyaki in *The River Between* is, indeed, implicitly criticized for his refusal to reconsider the role of education in his changing environment and to reform its content accordingly: he is no Karega. Always Njoroge's personal aspirations, his sense of mission, his desire to serve, his hopes for himself and his people, coalesce in the belief in education: 'Njoroge was still sustained by his love for and belief in education and his own role when the time came' (92/82); 'He saw himself rebuilding the whole country' (104–5/92). But will a rigidly conservative approach to schooling provide an adequate basis for this reconstruction? It is characteristic of the ambivalence of Njoroge's ideas that for a while he sees his utopia revealed in the ordered, peaceful harmony of Siriana Secondary School.

Surrounded as he is by evidence that life as he knows it is violent and uncertain — 'War, diseases, pestilence, insecurity, betrayal, family disintegrations — Njoroge had seen all these' (103/91) — his determined hopefulness about a brighter future begins to sound like a set of empty slogans, better calculated to reassure himself than to convince others. It is Mwihaki who perceives the ironic contradiction in this self-appointed reformer of the nation having no adequate concept of what he means either by 'the people' or by 'the country'. In honest confusion she at length turns and faces him, challenges him to vindicate his complacent generalities:' "You are always talking about tomorrow, tomorrow. You are always talking about *the* country and *the* people. What is tomorrow? And what is *the People* and *the Country* to you?" ' (120/106). Deflated, Njoroge limply begs the question by saying that if life were to continue indefinitely as it is now, then it would be utterly meaningless. He clings to a vague faith that there is meaning, significance:

> 'Don't be angry, Mwihaki. For what can I say now? You and I can only put faith in hope . . . Surely this darkness and terror will not go on for ever. Surely there will be a sunny day, a warm sweet day after all this tribulation, when we can breathe the warmth and purity of God.' (120–1/106)

We are reminded of Nyambura's naive vision of the promised land ahead for the Gikuyu — with the important difference that here it is clear that the novelist is not himself caught up in these over-simplifications. Njoroge is to be rudely jolted into disillusionment before long.

Much the same is true of the conventional idyll of young love which Mwihaki fosters, convincingly since she is a solitary and sensitive girl, ripe for emotional experience: ' "I'm so lonely here," she at last said, with a frank, almost childishly hurt voice. "Everyone avoids me" ' (99/87). She is a totally blameless victim of an all-embracing network of circumstance. When she first innocently suggests a kind of platonic elopement — ' "I could be such a nice sister to you and I could cook you very tasty food and —" ' (108/95) — Njoroge panics, not because he is a realist, but because he is too locked up in his own dreams: 'He saw his vision wrecked by such a plan' (108/95). By the time his vision has faded, and he turns to the idea of elopement with Mwihaki as an escape, she has grown up and matured faster than he has, and can no longer live inside adolescent illusions: ' "Don't you see that what you suggest is too easy a way out? We are no longer children," she said between her sobs' (151/133). And when he persists with the idea that they could run away to Uganda together, she responds with a bleak adult realization of the way things are: ' "But we can't. We can't!" she cried hopelessly' (151/133).

As the novel proceeds we must chillingly watch one character after another fall apart. Ngotho disintegrates completely: ' "It's nothing. Ha, ha, ha! You too have come back — to laugh at me? Would you laugh at your father? No. Ha! I meant only good for you all" ' (140/124). But Boro too has been sapped by the enervating contest in the forest which reaches no clear outcome. He performs his symbolic act of revenge in killing Howlands more as a zombie, a shell of his former self, than as an angry man exacting passionate retribution: 'Boro's voice was flat. No colour of hatred, anger or triumph. No sympathy' (145/128). While Mwihaki's growing pains may not prove to have maimed her irrevocably, yet her arrival at womanhood' is bitter:

> Her former softness seemed to have hardened so that she appeared to have all of a sudden grown into a woman. Mwihaki looked at Njoroge. She saw frustration and despair and bewilderment in his eyes. But she was determined to have no pity. So she just eyed him. (148/131)

Despair hangs poised over the characters. The grey facts of life from which Njoroge flees into the classroom as a child will be all around him at the end:

> The place was always the same; men of all sorts hanging around the tea-shops and slaughter houses, idling away the hours. The drudgery of such a life made him fear a future that held in store such purposeless living and weariness. He clung to books and whatever the school had to offer. (54/48)

The valiant Ngotho falls into fatalistic despair: ' "Jacobo wants to ruin me. He wants to destroy this house. He will do it" ' (91/80). He descends into the state dreaded by Njoroge: 'What did he live for now? His days were full of weariness. He had no longer *the waiting* to sustain him' (83/73). 'Njoroge was sure that if a child hit Ngotho, he would probably submit. He was no longer the man whose ability to keep home together had resounded from ridge to ridge' (92/81). Njoroge, a member of the rising generation, tries to grasp the conflicts and ironies which surround him but the sole result is bewilderment: ' "I thought Mau Mau was on the side of the black people" ' (94/83). What is Boro fighting for? ' "And Freedom?" the lieutenant continued. "An illusion. What Freedom is there for you and me?" ' (116/102).

Before we come to the heart of the matter and ask how Ngũgĩ deduces his positive challenge from this sad, ironic vision, we may well stop to consider some of the methods and techniques he uses in the course of the novel. The style itself, the medium in which Ngũgĩ operates, we shall explore more fully in a separate chapter.

There is nothing in *Weep Not, Child* to compare with the structural symbolism of the ridges and the Honia in *The River Between*, though a similar concept is briefly touched upon early in the novel in defining the confrontation between whites and blacks and the alienation of the land:

> The first two valleys went into the Country of the Black People. The other two divided the land of the Black People from the land of the White People . . . You could tell the land of Black People because it was red, rough and sickly, while the land of the white settlers was green and not lacerated into small strips. (7–8/7)

The factual manner, almost like that of a textbook, here presents the misappropriation of the best land objectively, and then through such expressions as 'the Country of the Black People' and 'the Country of the White People' subtly blends this objective presentation with the terminology of political myth (like, say, *1984*), making us feel that reality verges on the bizarre in this black continent dominated by non-blacks.

An image which recurs in *Weep Not, Child* is the shiny tarmac road. Only one narrow salient of the colonial Kikuyu Reserve traversed this road. This alone would make it easy to identify Kipanga, where Njoroge grows up, with Limuru, Ngũgĩ's home town. The then new tarmac road skirted the town on one side before descending the escarpment of the Rift Valley in hairpin loops. Near the bottom was the chapel built in memory of the Italian prisoners who lost their lives in its construction. The shoe factory in Kipanga finally corroborates this identification, since the Bata works is a key feature of Limuru.[7] The most significant fact about this 'big road' (7/6) is that the villagers cannot conceive where it comes from or where it may lead to: 'And the road which ran across the land and was long and broad had no beginning and no end. At least, few people knew of its origin' (5/5) — an attribute which is mentioned again at the very end of the book as Njoroge steps off the tarmac to reach the place where he has determined to commit suicide: 'He moved from the road that had no beginning and no end' (152–3/135). This most dominant reminder in Kipanga of colonialism and 'progress' is thus disconnected. It is an ironic metaphor for Njoroge's well-defined pathway in life which has led nowhere and points towards an unformulated future at the end of the novel. It is also an apt image for the lack — which Ngũgĩ deplores — of any clear sense of direction in this society at large, just at the time when leaders and militants are most determined about their goals and are attempting to map out the shortest route towards them.

The opening paragraph of chapter 5 elaborates another potentially powerful image, of which however we hear no more. This is the hillock of household rubbish outside Ngotho's home — a by-product of the family's landlessness and lack of further space to distribute their debris — from the top of which Njoroge regularly surveys not only his approaching kindred but also the ample fields of pyrethrum blossoms belonging to Jacobo, the only African in this area permitted to grow this crop.

Part Two of the novel opens with schoolboys relating the mythical exploits of Dedan Kimathi, very much a real-life figure of the Mau Mau struggle, who has already joined the ranks of traditional heroes and prophetic seers, such as the shadowy figure whom 'People thought . . . was the man who had been sent to drive away the white man. But he was killed by wicked people because he said people should stand together' (30/26).

While there is no single spot as central to *Weep Not, Child* as the space beside the Honia River in *The River Between,* there is still a very strong sense of place. The ground where Njoroge and Mwihaki meet at significant intervals, the path along which they linger together, the trading centre, Ngotho's hut, become for the reader familiar and recognized localities.

Ngũgĩ is developing a technique in certain passages which will become a major feature of his style as master novelist in *A Grain of Wheat:* a fluent movement between scenes. This is not a constant feature of *Weep Not, Child,* since the calculated juxtaposition of short episodes can lead at times to a certain disjointedness, but it is well illustrated by the first chapter, which appears relaxed and yet blends much dramatized material into a continuum. The chapter opens with Nyokabi offering Njoroge the chance to go to school and shifts to his communicating this news to Kamau. Then the text picks up the tarmac road and follows it here and there till the road discovers Ngotho on his journey to and from home and the shops to buy meat: this particular event merges into other similar occasions before refocusing on the precise time of day in question. Already we have made intimate acquaintance with Njoroge, with both his parents, and with the environment — from family dwelling to trading centre — where most of the action is to take place. We have been present on a specific day and at a key discussion, and have also become familiar with local life in a more generalized way. Yet we have been aware of no awkward transitions or ragged edges. If this novel is in some respects apprentice work, it is part of the apprenticeship of a notable artist.

The biblical tradition which is also to play a structural role in *A Grain of Wheat* is already complexly handled. Christianity is admired and accepted, and yet is also looked at critically and askance, till eventually it loses authority. Since Njoroge formulates his Christian beliefs in parrot fashion, the reader remains sceptical of their validity. The subtle manner in which traditional and acquired religions are interrelated reminds us of *The River Between:* 'he knew it was the House of God. But some boys shouted while they were in there. This too shocked him. He had been brought up to respect all holy places, like graveyards and the bush around fig trees' (16/ 14). This identification is quite specific:

> a belief in a God of love and mercy, who long ago walked on this earth with Gikuyu and Mumbi, or Adam and Eve. It did not make much difference that he had come to identify Gikuyu with Adam and Mumbi with Eve. To this God, all men and women were united by one strong bond of brotherhood. (55/49)

Jomo became Moses.[8] Njoroge sees himself as David rescuing the Israelites from Goliath. He is overwhelmed by the thought that perhaps he has been 'called': 'he felt a bit awed to imagine that God may have chosen him to be the instrument of His Divine Service' (106/94). It is with mixed feelings that we observe the transformation of the memorably unconventional primary teacher Isaka into a Revivalist, who is allowed to read us a long passage from St Matthew. But it is characteristic of Ngũgĩ's determined refusal ever to over-simplify that we are filled with respect for Isaka in the moment that he faces assassination with calm assured dignity, and the contemptuous sarcasm upon his faith is allowed to backfire against the white officer 'with reddening eyes': ' "Come this way and we'll see what Jesus will do for you" ' (115/101).

The novel is full of such complexities: we have noticed quite a number already. But we have not yet remarked upon Njoroge's readiness to feel sorry for the young Stephen Howlands, his contemporary: 'A wave of pity for this young man who had to do what he did not want to do [that is, leave Kenya] filled Njoroge. At least, he, Njoroge, would rise and fall with his country' (126/111) — and in reporting this incident in a letter to Mwihaki, Njoroge adds, ' "He looked lonely and sad" ' (129/114). More intimately, Ngotho is restrained from reacting against Boro's criticisms because of the sympathy he feels for his son in his tortured frame of mind: 'But Ngotho had always wanted to be gentle with Boro because he knew that the son must have been sorely tried in the war' (83/74). And yet the one point on which he cannot humble himself in front of Boro is the only one which might have redeemed their relationship; though we see that Ngotho was justified by tradition in taking this position: 'But whatever Ngotho had been prepared to do to redeem himself in the eyes of his children, he would not be ordered by a son to take oath . . . That would have violated against his standing as a father' (83–4/74).

It has already been said that the feeling for the land that Howlands and Ngotho share and which brings them uneasily together, really means something so different to each of them that at a deeper level it holds them infallibly apart: 'They went from place to place, a white man and a black man. Now and then they would stop here and there, examine a luxuriant green tea plant, or pull out a weed' (35/31). Yet each sees his own son in future possession of this same land! At the same time, Ngotho is aware of a force in Howlands which he cannot grasp: 'There was something in Howlands, almost a flicker of mystery, that Ngotho could never fathom' (32/29). Ngũgĩ senses the settler's genuinely obsessive passion for the land, however warped and arrogant.

The key to Howlands' ambivalent position is its illogicality. When England, and the white race in general — for which he is ready to die — appear to him to have let him down, he rejects them holus-bolus. He seems to demand that fate should function simply to promote his well-being. In apparently embracing Africa, he does so only in so far as it provides him with a means to economic prosperity, not in social or human terms. He is thus completely deculturalized — cut off from his native roots without letting down any new ones. His presumptuous claim to the land is based on the illusion that he has been the first to turn it to account. It has been presented to him by the colonial government on the supposed grounds that no one else has prior or better claims to it. Armed robbery is rationalized into a natural right. In the hands of history, Howlands is thus an almost pathetically vulnerable victim.

The white man is no more nor less a stereotype than several other sketches in the novel. There are subtle convolutions in his holding off from finally exercising his easy brutal power over Ngotho: 'Mr Howlands could not explain to himself why he always waived plans to bring Ngotho to submissive humiliation' (111/97-8). Why, indeed, is he so lividly angry because Ngotho has confessed to a crime in order to protect Kamau? This is not the first time that their thoughts about the next generation have been sharply at variance:

> He had taken on the guilt to save a son. At this Mr Howlands' hatred of Ngotho had been so great that he had trembled the whole night. He had drunk, itching to get at Ngotho but in the morning realized that he could not do what he had contemplated. (144/128)

Twice, both much earlier (86/76) and at this later hour, we are taken back into Howlands' own boyhood memories and dreams, which are carefully paralled to Njoroge's:

> He did not know what had happened to him since he saw something in the eyes of Ngotho's son. He had remembered himself as a boy, that day so long ago when he had sat outside his parents' home and dreamt of a world that needed him, only to be brought face to face with the harsh reality of life in the First World War. (144/127)

And to Njoroge, of course, we must now at length return. His dreams, his aspirations are at an end; even his willpower is broken: as an assistant in the Indian's store he is little more than an automaton. 'He hated being driven on like this. He had lost the will to fight even in a bargain, and he was tired of this game. Life too seemed like a big lie where people bargained with forces that one could not see' (143/126). So the perennial dreamer is jolted out of his dreams: But all these experiences now came to Njoroge as shocks that showed him a different world from that he had believed himself living in. For these troubles seemed to have no end, to have no cure' (135/120).

He prayed earlier that he would not have to repeat his father's experience. Now in so many respects he has to follow in Ngotho's footsteps.

He finds himself entangled in guilt. He blames himself for having brought disaster on his family by maintaining friendship with Mwihaki. In this fervour of self-accusation his whole life-pattern collapses and he relinquishes all that had previously seemed most secure: 'That day for the first time, he wept with fear and guilt. And he did not pray' (137/121). This is a relentless process: he feels that nothing that has mattered to him can survive the sense of dissolution: ' "I have now lost all — my education, my faith and my family" ' (149/131). In this melting-pot everything seems lost: 'But why did he call on God? God meant little to him now. For Njoroge had now lost faith in all the things he had earlier believed in, like wealth, power, education, religion' (152/134).

His sense of guilt is not wholly without justification. Mwihaki, accepting what she is told without relating it to what she knows, allows herself to feel betrayed. Beneath the surface, which is turbulent enough, lie Njoroge's jagged, confused feelings about Jacobo. He loathes Jacobo as the treacherous enemy of his family, the direct and powerful antagonist to both his father and his elder brother. Yet because of his connection with Mwihaki he feels implicated himself as a near-traitor who, through the misinterpretation of his last visit to the Chief's house, has attracted to his family suspicion for Jacobo's death. And yet most of all he hates the memory of Jacobo since his violent death has cut him off from the girl whom he now realizes he loves — to a point where he cannot even allow himself to think about her:

> Everybody and everything for him had a stamped image of the Chief . . . Only once did he think of Mwihaki. That was the night his mother had tried to tell him something. But he thought of her with guilt. He felt as if it was his connection with her that had somehow brought all this ill-luck. He wanted to shout to his mother across the night, *It's I who have brought all this on to you.* He hated himself without knowing why and then hated the Chief all the more. (136/121)

In his despair, sympathy is intolerable, partly because he is reaching a point at which his feelings are becoming deadened, like Boro's; partly because sympathy brings home to him the fact that he is trapped in a position from which there appears to be no way out.

The last phase can be interpreted as one in which Njoroge draws nearer to, and echoes in his own life, the experiences of his father and his elder brother. It was Ngotho and Boro who first sought release from unbearable confrontations and misunderstandings by asking for forgiveness from each other. Boro overhears his father's melodramatic lament: ' "Boro went away. He found me out — a useless father" ' (140/124) — and he responds:

> 'Forgive me, father — I didn't know — oh, I, thought —' Boro turned his head . . . 'Just forgive me.'
> Ngotho exerted himself and sat up in bed. He lifted his hand with an effort and put it on Boro's head. Boro looked like a child. (140–1/124)

But the novel cannot end here. The youthful Ngũgĩ must lay the equivocal burden on his own generation.

Njoroge's slogans are dead: ' "I have no hope left but for you, for now I know that my tomorrow was an illusion" ' (149/132). And so he brings his bewildered guilt to Mwihaki: ' "I wanted to meet you and say that I am sorry" ' (149/131). It is the whole complex of events that he is taking on his head. When she in turn asks for forgiveness for her lack of faith, he will not flinch from his own position of unqualified self-blame: ' "I am sorry for having thought ill of you," she said. "No, Mwihaki. I must take on the guilt and you have all the cause to hate me" ' (150/132). Sparingly as the lines are drawn, they are etched deep: they interpret the society's dilemma in terms of individual drama, as *The River Between* seeks to do, and as the later novels will succeed in doing even more fully.

Ironically, Njoroge does not know of what he is guilty till he stumbles to the edge of his pit of despair. He is expecting the impossible of Mwihaki in asking her to unravel his problems for him. In response she acknowledges that she returns his love, but places the onus on him: ' "No! No!" she cried, in an agony of despair, interrupting him. "You must save *me*, please Njoroge. I love you" ' (150/133). For all his honesty in other respects — he will not pretend that he *would* have betrayed the plan to assassinate Jacobo to her even if he had known it — he is so preoccupied with self-pity that he cannot react positively to her appeal. It is she who faces up to their true moral obligations: ' "But we have a duty. Our duty to other people is our biggest responsibility" ' (151/134). This is a lesson he is still unprepared to learn. Mwihaki delicately brings back to life Njoroge's dead slogans in order to smooth the harshness of reality: ' "We better wait. You told me that the sun will rise tomorrow. I think you were right" ' (151/133). In this context the cliché ceases to be a mere formula. But Njoroge is not attuned to catching her meaning: 'She sat there, a lone tree defying the darkness, trying to instil new life into him. But he did not want to live' (151/133). At the hour when the woman he loves has told him that she too loves him but pleads frankly for them to wait until the time is right, he is filled with a final sense of loneliness because she will not come to him *now*: 'For the first time he knew that he was in the world all alone without a soul on whom he could lean' (151/134). In this crisis he is aware of his need but not of his responsibilities. He walks the way of Boro, his heart deadened by the endless roll-call of loss: 'Nganga, the barber, Kiarie, and many others . . . The path eventually led him to the big and broad road' (152/135) — the road which comes from nowhere and leads nowhere, except to the spot on one side where Mwihaki told him that she loved him but that he should still wait, and on the other where he is determined to end the waiting in suicide. Like Ngotho too, he is trapped in misunderstanding, despair, nullity, purposelessness. And like his author, Njoroge has played no part in the fight. In this frame of mind, not even uhuru could release him from his sense of inadequacy. So he will finish it all. The last free man of his male line, he will be the first to cut the thread himself.

But the mother who opens the story by setting him on the 'long and broad' road to education is also there to hold him back on the verge of self-annihilation. We prefer to believe that she has tracked him to this place by no mere chance: she has clearly observed his moods and movements more closely than he has ever considered hers. This is the last of the 'shocks' that must wake him from the world of dreams which, though he does not realize it, he still inhabits. Suicide, despair, self-pity are denials and indulgences. He seeks to sidestep his destiny and the many calls upon him by this last grim escapade. But it is not to be. Ngotho and Boro have faced the nightmare: he must now do the same. He is rescued from final failure and must eat the bitterness of real remorse for having run away from his responsibility. In having thus dramatized himself he now sees that he has 'failed' his mother — can he dare to say that he is alone when she is there, suffering so deeply but thinking only of him? He has failed 'the last word of his father', who in death took a great stride towards resolving negation: ' "Fight well. Turn your eyes to Murungu and Ruriri. Peace to you all — Ha! What? Njoroge look . . . look – to – your – moth—" ' (141/ 124). He has failed Boro, who even in despair did what he had to do without flinching or turning away. He has failed the voice of Mwihaki as she at length took up his old refrain, to wait for a new day, the day for which his father and brother have been willing to die.

At the end of the novel Njoroge is, like Waiyaki, left by implication with a new chance. His mission is not to compound by his self-appointed death the disasters that have befallen Ngotho and Boro, but, by living, to exorcize them the hard way. Ngotho, who later takes the bravest deliberate action in the whole story, blames himself for cowardice. So now does his youngest son. As he walks back into life behind his mothers, Njoroge at last sees and faces his true guilt, and can therefore grapple with it: 'Njoroge did not speak to Njeri but felt only guilt, the guilt of a man who has avoided his responsibility for which he had prepared himself since childhood' (154/ 136). The counter-voice within pours scorn on his *supposed* cowardice in turning aside from suicide. But when his truer self replies, 'Yes . . . I am a coward', he refers to the cowardice that was egging him on to self-destruction and which he has now finally renounced. He has found his courage. The public and the private themes have merged.

Ngũgĩ perhaps realized half-instinctively, half-conciously that for all the power he had already achieved over structure, and over the fundamentally African art of understatement, he had not yet fully mastered the word in moments of high individual drama. In Muthoni's and Ngotho's death scenes, the language skirts dangerously upon sentimentality. Here at the end of *Weep Not, Child* he relies on the strengths he could marshal more confidently, and which possibly reflected more truthfully his own current mood. In doing so he leaves this early work stamped at the end with a certain ambivalence which may remind us of the ending of Conrad's *Lord Jim*. We are left to work out the implications and perceive the resolution for ourselves, as in many greater works of art. But all the evidence points clearly in the same direction in reinforcing the guarded optimism of the book's title and epigraph. In keeping with its whole tenor, the work abjures over-simplification to the last, but its final lines are as positive and· as challenging as those of *The River Between*.

Those who point the way are, as so often in Ngũgĩ, the mother figures, Nyokabi and Njeri. They throughout have been positive characters, the centre of the harmonious collaboration in Ngotho's family, involved with other people, concerned and informed about their environment. The rescue and possible rehabilitation of Njoroge as a constructive contributor to social endeavour is their triumph, and this, with all its overtones and undertones, is the concluding event of the book, reversing the negative trends, and thrusting us out hopefully, actively into an unknown future.

Notes

1. From 1950 to 1956, four years in 'primary' school were followed by four years in 'intermediate' school, after which KAPE was a passport to four further years in secondary school. The years 1947–9 were those of phasing over the first eight years from the earlier pattern of three years in 'elementary' school, three years from standard IV in 'primary' school capped by two further years in 'tops' (the old forms 1 and 2). That Njoroge had been two years in Kamahou Intermediate School in April 1953 confirms that he went through the later of the two systems. A useful summary of the various stages in school structuring in Kenya is to be found in J. Stephen Smith, *The History of Alliance High School* (Heinemann, London, 1973), 273–4.
2. Paul Maina, *Six Mau Mau Generals* (Gazelle Books, Nairobi, 1977), 3.
3. The first set of page references to *Weep Not, Child* relate to the first edition (Heinemann Educational Books, London, 1964). The second refer to the reset edition of 1976, subsequently reprinted.
4. *The River Between* (Heinemann Educational Books, London, 1965; reset 1975), 22/19.
5. Ibid., 24/20.
6. Waruhiu Itote (General China), *'Mau Mau' General* (East African Publishing House, Nairobi, 1967), 15, 46.
7. In *Detained* (Heinemann Educational Books, London), published considerably later in 1981, Ngũgĩ confirms this identification: 'I have tried to describe the landscape in *Weep Not, Child* where Kipanga town obviously stands for Limuru, or Rũũngai as the town was popularly known' (73). Continuing the passage, he refers to the valleys mentioned in our previous quotation: 'One of the valleys described in *Weep Not, Child* originates from Kamiriithu' (Ngũgĩ's home village near Limuru).
8. Ngũgĩ reflects sadly in *Detained:*

    > The Kenyatta of the 1930s was talking about the imminent inevitable collapse of the old British Empire, falling to the united blows of its enslaved workers and peasants . . . This was the Kenyatta of 'the burning spear', of whom the Kenyan masses then rightly sang as their coming saviour. This was the Kenyatta reflected in my novel, *Weep Not, Child,* about whom the peasant characters whispered at night. (86)

    In Ngũgĩ's view this was a far cry from the later Kenyatta 'now preaching "forgive and forget" who, as an earlier Bishop Muzorewa, sent the army inherited from colonial times to hunt down the remaining Mau Mau guerrillas, describing them as "these evil men, vagrants" '(88).

A Grain of Wheat

The River Between centres on the struggle to free men's minds from the constraints of colonialism in preparation for the assertion of national integrity and individual human identity. *Weep Not, Child* portrays Kenya during the Mau Mau period stumbling towards group consciousness and group responsibility in spite of vicious counter-currents at a time of great confusion and uncertainty. *A Grain of Wheat* again concerns the Mau Mau campaign, placed in its lengthy historical setting, and the relationship of this movement to independence. It is a novel about heroic corporate effort towards a juster society, and about betrayal. It is a fierce, passionate examination of heroism and treachery. Socially positive behaviour is lauded; all that is essentially anti-social is condemned. At the same time it is an infinitely complex work, exploring the nature and causes of frailty and failure, and expressing a humane concern for social misfits and even delinquents, provided they are in some degree capable of self-examination and readjustment.

Individual betrayals are representative of the vast betrayal of a whole society by its power elite. The leaders of Kenya at the moment of uhuru are drawn from among neither the Mau Mau campaigners nor those who cherish the ideals for which the freedom fighters made their sacrifices. The men at the top are a tribe of operators and manipulators who in their own narrow interests are replacing colonialism with neo-colonialism: 'the situation and the problems are real — sometimes too painfully real for the peasants who fought the British yet who now see all that they fought for being put on one side' (Foreword to *A Grain of Wheat*). 'But now,' complains Gikonyo:

> 'whom do we see riding in long cars and changing them daily as if motor cars were clothes? It is those who did not take part in the movement . . . At political meetings you hear them shout: Uhuru, Uhuru, we fought for. Fought where?' (80/60)[1]

It is significant that most readers recognize the brief chain of events

68

portraying a land-hungry politician cheating a new land-cooperative group as expressing one of the novel's most trenchant themes.

If the plot is so handled as to make readers feel compassion for certain characters before they are identified as guilty — in particular Mugo, Gikonyo, and indeed Mumbi — Ngũgĩ has careful purposes in this. The intention is in no degree to exonerate either vicious social conduct, or failure (any more than in the earlier novels he excuses Waiyaki's inadequacy or Njoroge's self-obsessed apathy). But this work is concerned with more than the relatively simple task of objectively identifying and condemning betrayal — though it does this at some length in portraying and repudiating such incorrigible characters as Robson, Thompson and Karanja. The wider purpose is to implicate us all, in the hope of inducing a true self-searching and reorientation in every reader. We are asked to recognize the characters' guilt, and then to acknowledge that we share it in part whenever we ourselves fail the cause of society, so that we will be moved to try and do better in future. Thus the book becomes not simply a social document but a social force. This is Ngũgĩ's aim. It is this aim that justifies the complex patterning of time sequences and the juxtaposition of different scenes, with the intention of bringing home to us the connection between cause and effect, action and responsibility. With such a purpose in view, Ngũgĩ felt understandably disappointed that barriers of language here restricted his potential audience so drastically.

So at one level the novel judges its characters, and condemns the guilty. At another it is a compound of insight, concern, regret, hope and involvement. Yet ultimately the two planes are interdependent, and it is this dovetailing which accounts for the book's depth and richness.

Occupying primarily the last five days before the ritual enactment of Kenyan independence, *A Grain of Wheat* also revisits the turmoil of the Emergency and sets it against the outcome of the struggle for uhuru, while lamenting that as things have transpired, the ceremony is ' "like warm water in the mouth of a thirsty man" ' (273/208): General R. asserts, ' "I know even now this war is not ended. We get Uhuru today. Tomorrow we shall ask: where is the land? Where is the food? Where are the schools?" ' (250–1/192). It is not long before the novel's public political interests are manifest. Of Waiyaki, the early nationalist, we are told in chapter 2: 'Then nobody noticed it; but looking back we can see that Waiyaki's blood contained within it a seed, a grain, which gave birth to a political party whose main strength thereafter sprang from a bond with the soil' (15/13). Here, then, is the core of the work. Our 'grain of wheat' is the political will of the people planted at this earliest stirring of the demand for social justice. But the grain must die in order to be reborn. Ngũgĩ insists that all of us as members of a community must individually and collectively accept responsibility for its growth and well-being. Only by the general discharge of this responsibility can a society progress: this is the sole foundation on which moral order can be built. Individualistic, messianic leadership is rejected. Even more than Njoroge's adolescent day-dreaming, Mugo's self-delusion is exposed as ludicrous and empty: 'And God called out to him in a thin voice, Moses, Moses. And Mugo cried out, Here am I, Lord' (143/108); 'Surely he must have been spared in order that he might save people like Githua from poverty and misery. He, an only son, was born to save'

(153/118).[2] Kihika, politically untutored as he may be, has worked out a coherent alternative to pinning our faith on an isolated saviour figure:

'In Kenya we want a death which will change things, that is to say, we want a true sacrifice. But first we have to be ready to carry the cross. I die for you, you die for me, we become a sacrifice for one another. So I can say that you . . . are Christ. I am Christ. Everybody who takes the Oath of Unity to change things in Kenya is a Christ.' (110/83)

And so it is with the full force of conviction that Kihika declares, ' "Can't you see that Cain was wrong? I am my brother's keeper" ' (113/85). Disastrously, Karanja rejects his mother's early advice, ' "Don't go against the people. A man who ignores the voice of his own people comes to no good end" ' (256/196). It is no longer possible for the twisted and tormented Mugo to benefit from Gikonyo's admonition: ' "You want to be left alone. Remember this, however: it is not easy for any man in a community to be left alone" ' (29/23). He has so completely surrendered himself to his own isolation that he even 'felt deep gratitude to the whiteman' (226/173) as his only point of human contact in the very act of betraying Kihika. We are to learn that General R.'s ultimate verdict that the agent of Kihika's death has ' "really betrayed the black people every-where on the earth" ' (174/134) applies in fact to Mugo.

Like all other characters in the novel, John Thompson is part of the general scheme of exposing human shortcomings. While Howlands in *Weep Not, Child* is spokesman for settler morality, Thompson is the exponent of the ethics of imperial colonialism. His passionate sincerity in adhering to this creed reminds us that pernicious beliefs can assume complete plausibility for the converted. Thus can self-centred prejudices put on a cloak of fine words and dominate large sections of humanity. For Thompson, colonization is the Christian and philanthropic process of civilizing a people and putting them in contact with the benefits of European inventions: it is the implementation of a great moral idea. After talking in English to two African students at Oxford he asks himself,

Where was the irrationality, inconsistency and superstition so characteristic of the African and Oriental races? They had been replaced by the three principles basic to the Western mind: i.e. the principle of Reason, of Order and of Measure. (62/47)

Subsequently, the process of transforming African and Oriental minds into European minds becomes a subject of research for Thompson. One morning he is elated by a great sense of victory:

'In a flash I was convinced that the growth of the British Empire was the development of a great moral idea . . . to be English was basically an attitude of mind: it was a way of looking at life, at human relationship, at the just ordering of human society. Was it not possible to reorientate people into this way of life by altering their social and cultural environment? (63/48)

And so, as colonial administrator he becomes 'the symbol of whiteman's power, unmovable like a rock, a power that had built the bomb and transformed a country from wild bush and forests into modern cities' (176–7/136). In time, the people he has been labouring to convert to European ways of thinking and living are on the verge of independence. But at the first signs of their acceding to nominal equality with himself, far from rejoicing in such evidence of 'progress', John Thompson withdraws from the colonial service.

Thompson embodies for Ngũgĩ that most odious form of political authority, colonialism, so of all his characters it is on Thompson that he pours most scorn. Thompson is a supreme example of those who refuse to admit the logical links between past action and present outcome. As Africa enters the international arena in its own right, this proponent of reorientation is appalled, not triumphant. His hypocritical visions are exposed as sham, and together with them he is shattered and broken. At the same time, he is cuckolded and despised by a forlorn and unfulfilled wife who has grown tired of playing a secondary role to his hollow ambitions. From the vainglory of his little brief authority, he fades into an inglorious retirement. .

It is Mugo, however, the anti-hero of A *Grain of Wheat,* in whom Ngũgĩ most clearly portrays complete failure to accept social responsibility. His resultant alienation entails grave consequences. Like Robson and Karanja, Mugo must face the outcome of his actions. Mugo irrevocably thwarts the will of his society and so he invokes his own fate. His failing is an obsessive unwillingness to participate in the affairs of his community, a refusal to be involved in his social environment. Mugo has been born and bred an outcast and a loner. Nominally he cries out against this fate: 'He wanted somebody, anybody, who would use the claims of kinship to do him ill or good. Either one or the other as long as he was not left alone, an outsider' (11/9). Yet when he is offered the opportunity of reintegrating with his fellows, he recoils into his shell. As Kihika, at a party meeting in Rung'ei before Kenyatta's return, calls for sacrifice upon hearing 'the call of a nation in turmoil', Mugo sits in silent revolt: 'He could not clap for words that did not touch him. What right had such a boy, probably younger than Mugo, to talk like that?' (19/15). An affinity of isolation draws him to the old woman, mother of the deaf and dumb Gitogo, who, Wambui later asserts, dies of loneliness on uhuru day: 'He wandered through the streets thinking about the old woman and that thrilling bond he felt existed between them' (198/152). But ironically when Kihika, and later Mumbi, turn to him as an ally, in a spirit of comradeship, he is terrified and angry: 'He revelled in this mad desire to humiliate her, to make her grovel in the dust: why did she try to drag him into her life, into everybody's life?' (158/122); ' "I wanted to live my life. I never wanted to be involved in anything. Then he came into my life, here, a night like this, and pulled me into the stream. So I killed him" ' (210/161).

Certainly Mugo is mentally sick, and we are given detailed insight into his childhood as the origin of his neurosis. But this does not exonerate him. A human being who submits to the most destructive elements in his own background is at best pathetic, and at worst criminally weak-willed. And we are left in no doubt about the criminality of Mugo's act of betrayal. One of the major symptoms of Mugo's psychopathic state is his refusal to perceive sequential connections between events in general, and specifically between his own actions and their repercussions — the logic inherent in the grain of wheat, in the cycle of nature. Not until Mumbi and circumstance have 'cracked open his dulled inside' does he attempt to piece cause and effect together:

> Previously he liked to see events in his life as isolated. Things had been fated to happen at different moments. One had no choice in anything as surely as one had no choice on one's birth. He did not, then, tire his mind by trying to connect what went before with what followed after. (195/149)

In Mugo Ngũgĩ dramatizes the sad folly and futility of a life of uncommitedness:

> He had always found it difficult to make decisions. Recoiling as if by instinct from setting in motion a course of action whose consequences he could not determine before the start, he allowed himself to drift into things or be pushed into them by an uncanny demon; he rode on the wave of circumstance and lay against the crest, fearing but fascinated by fate. (29/23)

This deliberate opting out has had a conscious basis in pragmatic self-interest:

> . . . all his life he had avoided conflicts: at home, or at school, he rarely joined the company of other boys for fear of being involved in brawls that might ruin his chances of a better future. His argument went like this: if you don't traffic with evil, then evil ought not to touch you; if you leave people alone, then they ought to leave you alone . . . (221/169)

A man who allows himself to drift into things might well accept the consequences of his unplanned actions. But Mugo cannot perceive cause and effect and so lives in a bewildered, debilitating state of tension for all but the very last stage of his life.

Mugo thinks himself immune. For two years he successfully avoids involvement in Mau Mau, and eludes his fate. He gloats over this achievement:

> Had he not already escaped, unscathed, the early operations of the Emergency? Kenya had been in a state of Emergency since 1952. Some people had been taken to detention camps; others had run away to the forest: but this was a drama in a world not his own. (212–13/163)

But suddenly, in a manner which makes evasion impossible, he is drawn into the centre of action. After years of avoiding decisions, he must now choose between supporting the people's cause or betraying it. At first he thinks he can still stand aloof. He cannot see that even in this attempt he is now blatantly siding with the powers of oppression, and is thus involved without realizing it. It is now only one step further to treachery:

> Why should Kihika drag me into a struggle and problems I have not created? Why? He is not satisfied with butchering men and women and children. He must call on me to bathe in the blood . . . have I stolen anything from anybody? No! Have I ever shat inside a neighbour's courtyard? No. Have I killed anybody? No. How then can Kihika to whom I have done no harm do this to me? (220–1/168–9)

In this crisis Mugo must first gain insight into the human condition: man cannot escape from his environment. Confidence in his invulnerability wavers:

'If I don't serve Kihika, he'll kill me . . . If I work for him, the government will catch me. The whiteman has long arms. And they'll hang me' (221/169).

Mugo's attempt to break out of this circle draws him in fact to the centre of the conflict he has evaded. For the betrayal of Kihika attracts to Mugo's village an exceptional concentration of colonialist forces. Mugo is not sadistic, as are Robson and Karanja. His retreat from responsibility stems from a psychopathic fear of action; so he withdraws from decision-making which alone, he wrongly believes, can involve him in action. He is horrified by fighting and blood. So when he later finds himself in the trench, he reacts irrationally and futilely (albeit courageously) against the brutality of the very forces to whom he has betrayed Kihika and his people. We are tangentially reminded of Ngotho at the strike-meeting. Having secretly surrendered the leader to the enemy, Mugo strikes out against their ill-usage of one of the least important of their victims, Wambuku. So he himself becomes suspect. But he has neither taken the oath nor is he privy to any Mau Mau plans. In consequence, no extent of violence can elicit information from Mugo. His inability to help the enemy is construed by his fellow-sufferers as heroism and hence the tragic denouement of the novel becomes inevitable.

In recognition of what they take to be his heroic sacrifice, the elders of Thabai ask Mugo to lead the uhuru celebrations in the village. Alarmed and confused when he finds himself in the midst of activity, fearful that in fact the truth is already known, he can nevertheless for a moment summon his old messianic dreams and aspire to out-manoeuvre his fate:

> For he walked on the edge of a revelation: Gikonyo and Githua had brought him there. He remembered the words: he shall save the children of the needy. It must be him. It was he, Mugo, spared to save people like Githua, the old woman, and any who had suffered. Why not take the task? Yes. He would speak at the Uhuru celebrations. He would lead the people and bury his past in their gratitude. Nobody need ever know about Kihika. To the few, elect of God, the past was forgiven, was made clean by great deeds that saved many. It was so in the time of Jacob and Esau; it was so in the time of Moses. (146/110)

In Mugo's perverse fantasy, Ngũgĩ thus finally mocks the delusions of grandeur of any would-be individualist leader, such as torment Waiyaki in *The River Between* and dazzle Njoroge in *Weep Not, Child*.

But much intervenes to shake Mugo out of this dream into a new reality about himself and his guilt. He at last musters vestiges of a sense of responsibility in time to rescue a few remnants from the wreckage of his frustrated, and eventually corrupt, existence. Both Gikonyo and Mumbi have, ironically, been moved to unburden themselves of their much lesser loads of guilt to him, and each finds a contradictory solace in so doing — especially Mumbi: ' "I have never talked these things to anybody," she said . . . "You make me feel able to talk and look at these things" ' (157/121); ' ". . . I might tell you it already makes me feel better to have opened my heart to you" ' (170/131). Notwithstanding this, Mugo's familiar inner self is still unable to respond: 'Leave me alone, he wanted to tell her' (157/121).

These experiences send Mugo's private thoughts on an altogether new tack. Mumbi reminds him of the villagers' suffering during the digging of the trench. Her account startles him. Was this one of the end-products of his handing Kihika over to the government forces? 'It is not me, it would have happened . . . the murder of women and men in the trench . . . even if . . . even if . . . He was moaning' (199/152). Having thus cracked open his dulled inside, Mumbi's story 'released imprisoned thoughts and feelings' (195/149). He is drawn into the sequence of confessions and tells Mumbi the truth. Ngũgĩ has endowed Kihika's sister with the powerful, almost hypnotic influence over men that he grants to all his most significant women characters. Where her brother failed, she succeeds in drawing Mugo out of his sterile shell, out of the human void he has so long inhabited. The most important single influence impelling Mugo to public confession is his earlier private revelation of his crime to Mumbi. He must live up to all that his new vision of her stands for: 'Why should I not let Karanja bear the blame? He dismissed the temptation and stood up. How else could he ever look Mumbi in the face?' (267/203–4). This new standard of conduct asserts itself, even though, after the unaccustomed warmth of their contact, he believes she has drawn back from him in revulsion:

> Mugo was able to see what he translated as scorn and horror on her face . . . He lay on the bed, aware that he had just lost something. Many times, the scorn on Mumbi's face flashed through the dark, and a shuddering he could not control thrilled into him. Why was it important to him now, tonight, what Mumbi thought of him? She had been so near. He could see her face and feel her warm breath. She had sat there, and talked to him and given him a glimpse of a new earth. She had trusted him, and confided in him. This simple trust had forced him to tell her the truth. She had recoiled from him. He had lost her trust, for ever. To her now, so he reasoned, saw and felt, he was vile and dirty. (266/203)

His fresh concept of life as characterized by Mumbi stirs him to seek deliverance from spiritual death: he will atone for the past, which he has defiled, by admitting his crime at the Rung'ei uhuru meeting. Mugo's resolve falters when he is faced with the crowd and General R.'s over-pitched speech. But he pulls himself together, walks forward — somewhat beside himself — and admits his guilt.

This structural climax of the plot, when so many discoveries and mysteries are made plain and are brought to a new resolution, is an anti-climax for all those present at Rung'ei:

> 'Something went wrong . . . Everybody gone. And a minute before, the field was covered with so many people, like in the days of Harry, you know, at the procession. Then in the twitching of an eyelid, all gone. The field was so empty. Only four (or were we five?) left.' (273/208)

Mugo must die. General R., Lieutenant Koinandu and Mwaura must carry through their mission. The drama must be played out and retribution must be exacted.

The tragic inevitability of Mugo's death is counterpointed against other themes in the complex conclusion which is crowded with implications. This complexity is epitomized by a brief dialogue when Mumbi visits Warui and Wambui after the uhuru meeting and its logical outcome:

'Perhaps I could have saved him . . .' Mumbi lamented . . .

'There was nothing to save,' Wambui said slowly. 'Hear me? Nobody could have saved him . . . because . . . there was nothing to save.'

'But you did not see his face, Wambui, you did not see him,' Mumbi said in a heated voice . . . (274/209)

The two levels of the novel are thus juxtaposed and they interact to create its intricate and gripping conclusion.

It is true that nobody could have saved Mugo from retribution. He himself acknowledges his own accountability just as, ironically, he has glimpsed, through Mumbi, the truly dynamic attraction of living: 'so he was responsible for whatever he had done in the past, for whatever he would do in the future . . . he did not want to die, he wanted to live. Mumbi had made him aware of a loss which was also a possibility' (267/204). But it is too late. After a crime such as Mugo's, there can be no reprieve. As General R. tells him, 'without anger or apparent bitterness': ' "Your deeds alone will condemn you . . . You — No one will ever escape from his own actions" ' (270/206). In the event, he makes no attempt to escape. Death is now no more than a confirmation, and an end, of the perpetual torment of his life which was first wished upon him by circumstance and was then perpetuated by his own total rejection of commitment. But for all the depth of Mugo's perfidy, he is not a Karanja. He is a lost soul who sincerely confesses his guilt, regrets it, and accepts the necessary punishment: ' "I am ready," Mugo said, and stood up' (270/206). Ngũgĩ, like Dostoyevsky in his depiction of Raskolnikov in *Crime and Punishment,* takes us inside the mind of a criminal, and elicits from us not only unqualified condemnation of his act, but also pity for this twisted being, especially as he yearns to untwist himself. In this Ngũgĩ maintains a purpose. Our closeness to Mugo, our real concern for him, must surely inspire in each of us an urgent desire to eschew social treachery of any degree whatsoever and to be positively involved in our community and its aspirations before it is too late. If Mugo leads us to contemplate the terrible possibilities within ourselves, then the novel will have effected change in us and will be an active ingredient in the struggle which Ngũgĩ espouses.[3]

As ever in Ngũgĩ's fiction, it is the women who take us to the heart of the matter and point the way forward. The very women who carry the brunt of the suffering impress us most by the selfless way in which they look upon events. It is Kihika's mother, Wanjiku, who, after witnessing Mugo's confession, tells Mumbi, ' "It was his face, not the memory of my son that caused my tears" ' (252/193). Mumbi, Kihika's sister, who has throughout been passionately devoted to her brother, and who has felt Mugo's fevered fingers on her throat, turns her back on retribution. When she believes Karanja is the culprit, she thinks, 'Karanja would be killed for his part in Kihika's death. Should this be done in the name of her brother? Surely enough blood had already been shed: Why add more guilt to the land?' (206/158). And so she sends Karanja a message to warn him not to attend the meeting. When she knows the identity of the real betrayer, still 'she did not want anybody to die or come to harm because of her brother' (237/181). So, again, she goes to Mugo's hut to persuade him to save himself, and later blames herself for failing to trace him at that crucial moment.

Even Wambui has her reservations about the judgement after the event: 'Wambui was lost in a solid consciousness of a terrible anti-climax to her activities in the fight for freedom. "Perhaps we should not have tried him," she muttered.' (275–6/210).

None the less, Mugo has to die. Ngũgĩ suggests no alternative. His death, however, belongs to the past. Necessary as it is, it is now largely irrelevant. Mugo's death is an inevitable event within the structure of the novel, but the real priority is to examine what the past has led to in the present so that new strategies can be developed to minister to the future.

If the celebration of uhuru in Rung'ei has turned out to be an unwitting praise-ceremony for a traitor, so is Kenyan uhuru itself a giant betrayal of the people who fought for it by those manipulating it: 'why should these men be elected only to enrich themselves' (200/153). Mugo, the archenemy in the past struggle, at least opens his heart and repents, and his crime can be ritually cleansed from the earth by his sacrificial death. What of the whole tribe of politicians represented by the MP who cheats and double-crosses Gikonyo's land-cooperative? Any repentance? Any retribution? It is towards their overthrow that the novel now tentatively looks. This uhuru is indeed 'like warm water in the mouth of a thirsty man' (273/208). The drizzle which symbolically hangs over the whole uhuru celebrations and their aftermath may well 'go on for many days' (271/207).

The novel in general, and the key women in particular, seem to ask, what can be *learnt* from Mugo's properly concluded tragedy that may, instead of stultifying, contribute to the future? After all, if others do not merit death, at least they have their own guilt and inadequacies. We need not speak here of Robson, Thompson or Karanja: they are written off as irredeemable. But what of the characters on whom the future must rest? General R. in his youth had to leave his home village after attempting to kill his own father, and as he begins to speak on uhuru day his eyes are blurred by the visual memory of the excessive brutality with which the Rev. Jackson Kigondu had been assassinated. Lt Koinandu is still distressed by the way revolutionary energies were misdirected into the savage raping of Dr Lynd. Mumbi is unfaithful to her husband at the very moment that she learns he will be returning to her. Gikonyo is haunted by the steps which led him to forswear his faith and forsake his comrades in the prison camp. How are such transgressions to be resolved so that the real achievements of the past can be translated into a continued and effective struggle in the future? If *A Grain of Wheat* is less clear-cut than *Petals of Blood* in its response to these questions, it certainly does propose answers, and to these we must return at the end of our discussion.

The parallels between *A Grain of Wheat* and Conrad's *Under Western Eyes* have often been noticed, and have no doubt sometimes been exaggerated.[4] In Conrad's novel, the revolutionary Haldin assassinates the reactionary Mr de P., and then seeks refuge with Razumov, who betrays him to the authorities. Similarly Kihika shoots Robson, turns to Mugo as an ally, and is betrayed. In each case the sister of the executed revolutionary has an impelling influence on her brother's betrayer. Mugo shares Razumov's social uncommittedness and individualism. Both have been alienated as children and are isolated as adults. At length each has a deep sense of guilt for his self-protective act of handing over a revolutionary activist to his enemies, and confesses to the sister. In employing a somewhat similar structure, Ngũgĩ is inevitably influenced by Conrad's liberal humanism and thus probes deeply into the psyche of the tormented individualist, and like Conrad uses his character to reveal paradoxes in human actions and relationships. But the situation and hence the emphasis are fundamentally different. Conrad is unable to believe that Haldin's arbitrary act of heroism is an effective way of combating a regime (much as Karega repudiates the extermination of the three power-magnates in *Petals of Blood*). In the context of *A Grain of Wheat*, on the other hand, handing over Kihika to the British is seen as an act of criminal treachery against Mugo's whole society, not simply the selfish annihilation of a brave fanatic by the man he trusted and wrongly thought to be of like mind. While the parallels between the two works are critically suggestive and of great interest, there is a danger in pushing the comparison too far.

The love-story between Gikonyo and Mumbi, its breakdown, and eventual revival are structurally and thematically fundamental. The liaison starts as an idyll when Gikonyo's shyness in front of this girl about whom he feels so deeply is broken down by the passionate sincerity with which she offers herself to him. In this work only the relationship between Kihika and Njeri shares a similar integrity. Wambuku fails Kihika. Wounded pride spurs Karanja's persistent infatuation with Mumbi. Margery Thompson's brief and furtive infidelity to a husband who cannot fulfil her needs at any level is pathetic. In contrast the bond between Gikonyo and Mumbi is at once prototypical and yet subtly personalized:

> 'It was like being born again ... I felt whole, renewed ... I had made love to many a woman, but I never felt like that before ... Before, I was nothing. Now, I was a man ... Every day I found a new Mumbi. Together we plunged into the forest. And I was not afraid of the darkness ...' (114/86)

And so the drying up of this deep affection suggests a drought at the very spring of social intercourse.

In prison Gikonyo builds up the image of Mumbi in his mind into the acme of human goodness and love. His longing for her is so all-consuming that he betrays his oath of loyalty to the cause of freedom in order to return to her. But he returns to find her defiled.[5] She for her part has so desperately longed for him to come back to her that she reacts with a kind of hysteria to Karanja's news that the long process of Gikonyo's release has begun, and she gives herself to the ever-importunate bringer of the tidings. It is unfortunate that this is one of the very few episodes in the novel which Ngũgĩ fails to bring to life in any intimate or subtle detail, and so we are left, at least in part, sharing Gikonyo's consternation.

Both are guilty, for both have broken their oaths: one of loyalty to their people, the other the marital vow. Gikonyo is disconsolately shattered because, in his private obsession with his image of perfection, he refuses to take account of the psychological and emotional buffeting which Mumbi has endured. Mumbi has been left unprotected for six years in the midst of a desperate crisis, lonely and hungry. In expecting to find her unchanged, Gikonyo is superimposing his own wishful imaginings upon the realities of the situation. In fact each of the two maintains a bafflingly arrogant posture before the other. Though the sympathies of the novel are with

Mumbi, she makes little concession to Gikonyo's understandable chagrin at her adultery — with Karanja of all men, personal rival and traitor to the society, just at the time her husband is known to be returning — an adulterous union which has borne issue. The woman in Ngũgĩ's story 'The Return' has reason to believe that her husband is dead in somewhat similar circumstances, and so is not as culpable as Mumbi. Nevertheless, whether or not the evidence for such an evaluation is sketched in sufficiently clearly, Mumbi is certainly elevated by the text. Like Muthoni, Nyambura, Nyokabi and Njeri before her, she takes on a certain matriarchal quality, embodying all the good and natural attributes of an African community at its best. It is Gikonyo who is primarily blamed for the failure to heal the breach in the marriage: and certainly he is the more wilful and intransigent. His own mother, Wangari, sides unequivocally with Mumbi:

> 'See how you have broken your home. You have driven a good woman to misery for nothing. Let us now see what profit it will bring you, to go on poisoning your mind with these things when you should have accepted and sought how best to build your life. But you, like a foolish child, have never wanted to know what happened. Or what woman Mumbi really is.' (200/153)

The ironies of concealed guilt, loneliness and a sense of the aridity of living provide strange interconnections between the characters. In the people's misunderstanding of their false hero, in their frenzied admiration and worship of him (in short, in their warped grasp of reality), Ngũgĩ invokes the extremes of irony: 'Independence Day without him would be stale' (204/156). 'The man who had suffered so much had further revealed his greatness in modesty. By refusing to lead, Mugo had become a legendary hero' (200/153). Gikonyo is in a false position different only in degree from Mugo's: 'he was elected the chairman of the local branch of the Party, a tribute, so people said, to his man's spirit which no detention camp could break' (22/18). And he broods over his dreadful secret much as Mugo does: 'Could he, Gikonyo, gather such courage to tell people about the steps on the pavement?' (278/211). His overstatement of the case brings out the links: 'What difference was there between him and Karanja or Mugo or those who had openly betrayed people and worked with the whiteman to save themselves?' (278/212). He forces himself into an isolation comparable to Mugo's: 'One lived alone, and like Gatu, went into the grave alone' (135/102). And Karanja, the renegade, is well placed to understand the pain of such separateness: ' "a time will come when you too will know that every man in the world is alone, and fights alone, to live" ' (165–6/128).

The barrenness of life for those who cut themselves off from others is related to such loneliness. Mugo at the opening finds it hard to distinguish between detention and his own warped version of freedom: 'How time drags, everything repeats itself . . . the day ahead would be just like yesterday and the day before' (4/3). With a nice symmetry, these ideas are re-echoed (more than once) in Mugo's thoughts at the end of the novel: 'Life was only a constant repetition of what happened yesterday and the day before' (269/205). As existence becomes blank for Gikonyo when he learns of Mumbi's falsity, living for him too appears flat and featureless: 'Life had no colour. It was one endless blank sheet, so flat. There were no valleys, no mountains, no streams, no trees — nothing' (132/100). The empty fatuity of a life outside the community is thematic. And in revealing that Githua's claim to have lost his leg fighting for the people in the Emergency is false, General R. universalizes the tendency to create little illusions to cover up the constant bare patches in existence, a minor version of the larger falsifications which Gikonyo and Mugo play out: ' "It makes his life more interesting to himself. He invents a meaning for his life . . . Don't we all do that? And to die fighting for freedom sounds more heroic than to die by accident" ' (172/133).

Such patterning and juxtaposing is fundamental to the form and structure of this novel. An ironic motif is reiterated in the two races. In the first, Karanja seeks to triumph in self-display as he outdistances his rival, who meanwhile has been diverted by Mumbi, the prize, into their first woodland love-scene. In the second Karanja determines to blot out his past defeat, but again in winning the race he loses the reward, for it is the injured Gikonyo who monopolizes Mumbi's attention. This incident will be the beginning of their gradual rediscovery of each other. After the humiliation of the first loss, when his fellows take to the forest Karanja (or so he tells Mumbi) remains behind — and becomes the whiteman's lackey — simply so that he will not again lose touch with the woman who obsesses him. But as the ruthless chief under his colonialist masters, Karanja finally marks himself out as enemy of the people and of all that Mumbi cares for.

The whole story of Mugo as it unfolds in the novel is framed within two occasions when village elders call at his hut, the first time to invite him to speak at the uhuru meeting, the last time as a consequence of what he said when he spoke there.

Ngũgĩ epitomizes the complexity of all actions and reactions by showing us different perspectives at different points in the narrative on the same scene. We watch the exultant villagers dancing round Mugo's hut in joyous celebration on the eve of uhuru; and later we are beside the guilt-ridden Mugo as he grovels inside the hut listening to the celebrants. We hear both Thompson's and Mugo's versions of the moment when the white man spits in the informer's face; and we are offered two variant dramatizations of the raping of Dr Lynd.

Past and present (and by implication the future) are interlinked by incidents that occur in the same place running together in a character's mind. As Mugo walks down the crumbling trench just before uhuru, he recalls the scene there of his abortive and hopeless attempt to save the pregnant Wambuku from the homeguards' whips. As layers of narrative move from present to the past and back to the present, we are familiar with certain features of the scenes that recur, and so the memories of the characters become also our memories, bringing us strangely close to them at most intimate levels and involving us intensely in the life of Thabai Ridge. While the present action of the novel covers five days leading up to uhuru and nine days thereafter, events dating back across seventy years are presented to us. Kihika is introduced through a speech which he made several years previously. Much of the life-story of each major character is intermittently related as various incidents become relevant.

We may in this process identify layers of 'pastness'. For instance, Mugo goes over in his mind aspects of Gikonyo's visit immediately after he has departed, which leads him to recall a day in 1955 which he has come to regard as 'the climax of his life' (143/108), which itself reminds him of an event in his childhood. Particularly suggestive is the recurrent image of Mugo stopping outside the old woman's hut, hesitantly compassionate, characteristically unwilling to commit himself. When Ngũgĩ first introduces this motif it runs in tiers into the past. As Mugo walks by her hut in the present of the Sunday before uhuru, we hear the story of her deaf son being shot in the Emergency; then of Mugo's agitation on seeing the woman on his return to the village, and again of his visit to her with provisions. The sight of her sleeping place reminds him of his own terrifying childhood (of which we are soon to hear more) till we move once again to the end of the first visit, and so back to the present when he falters in his determination to enter.

The time-shifts thus produce many effects, and reveal many connections to us that might not otherwise be obvious. And in so doing they assert the interrelatedness of all time as a single continuum, wherein the future will grow integrally from the present, as the present has done from the past, without any disconnectedness. This is one of Ngũgĩ's preoccupations in *A Grain of Wheat* as he develops a new attitude towards history, leading to his conviction of the inevitability of the success of social revolution as time unfolds.

The reiteration of images and symbols reinforces this sense of design. The railway represents the ruthless advance of colonialism: 'The iron snake spoken of by Mugo wa Kibiro was quickly wriggling towards Nairobi for a thorough exploitation of the hinterland' (15/12). Trains are omnipresent. A train claims the life of Dr Van Dyke as its annual sacrifice from Githima settlement. Our last glimpse of Karanja is as the train, emblem of the whiteman to whose skirts he has clung, leaves him alone and forlorn as it steams away in the darkness. Karanja, as a secondary traitor, is spared the supreme penalty of death. But he has abandoned all communal standards and so is not eligible to embrace the peace and renewed hope which his fellows have won by extreme sacrifice. So he banishes himself from Thabai, and as he goes is left standing abandoned by the iron snake: 'The earth where he stood trembled. When the train disappeared, the silence around him deepened; the night seemed to have grown darker' (262/200).

But unlike the restlessly moving, disruptive train, the railway station serves a dynamic, unifying purpose by attracting villagers of the neighbourhood to weekly gatherings on Sunday at which social issues and the future in general are discussed. The iron road is being deployed by the people as a point of reference in their own affairs. It is being absorbed into the communal framework, free of the menace of those who first brought it and made it a burden instead of an amenity. Ngũgĩ is far from rejecting modernity for Africa — indeed he demands it: but on Africa's own terms, and for its own internal purposes and benefit.

We have already noticed in passing the imagery of weather. The whole countryside is enveloped in drizzling rain throughout the uhuru period, the least productive of all climatic conditions, unwished-for by farmers, antagonistic to all social activity, dull, overcast, vaguely threatening.

Similar images, mostly on a smaller scale, are common. They are precise as physical description, without any explicit metaphorical reference; yet by implication they take on further significance. The well-known opening lines of the novel offer a clear example. Mugo slowly awakens on his bed at home to be aware of a malignant drop of blackened rainwater gathering above his head: 'Sooty locks hung from the fern and grass thatch and all pointed at his heart' (3). Every little object in the village environment seems to be accusing the hidden traitor as the novel opens.

There are numerous special effects supporting a narrative style which deliberately breaks the consecutive order of events. An incantatory rhythm is sustained in Mumbi's account of her life during the Emergency by the interjection of a fateful refrain: ' "Two more women died" ' ; ' "Two men died" ' ; ' "All together, twenty-one men and women died" ' (165–6/127–8), each refrain being isolated in a short paragraph. A kaleidoscope effect of cinematic sequences is produced as each participant in the long-distance uhuru race casts his mind introspectively over his past life. Ngũgĩ creates his own kind of stream-of-consciousness in many other introspective passages: intricate association, idea and memories are interlaced among the events that characters call to mind. Dreams and visions intensify states of mind. A narrator who is a member of the Thabai community, but is different from the voice of the author, is heard from time to time, just as his counterpart will figure continually in *Petals of Blood*: 'Most of us from Thabai first saw him at the New Rung'ei Market . . .' (202/155); 'In our village and despite the drizzling rain, men and women and children, it seemed, had emptied themselves into the streets' (231/177). This produces yet another level of intimacy, now with the community at large.

The Christian religion has been a constant subject and source of material throughout Ngũgĩ's writing career, especially as portrayed in biblical idiom and images. Indeed the treatment of Christianity can be seen as a marker of his ideological development. In *The River Between* there is a basic acceptance of Christian morality but a demand that Christianity should be 'washed' of European bigotry and insolence. Njoroge in *Weep Not, Child* shifts from conviction to scepticism and finally to rejection of his original faith. In *Petals of Blood* the Christian religion will be seen as a mask for a powerful and biased form of power politics, itself a vested interest whose missionaries and evangelists prey upon society. The attitudes in *A Grain of Wheat* are multiple and as a whole form an intermediate stage between the early novels and *Petals of Blood*. Mugo, and at some moments Kihika, seem to interpret Christianity as endorsing a messianic role for themselves; and popular opinion identifies Jomo Kenyatta closely with Moses,[6] much as Mugo sees himself in the same role. This individualistic obsession is to be deplored here as much as in Njoroge of *Weep Not, Child*. But Kihika selects a new emphasis in his favourite biblical quotations, and modifies it to relate to a communal revolutionary situation, as in the passage proposing a multiplicity of Christs which we have already quoted. Christianity is seen at one time as a rote creed used to bludgeon children into conformity, as when the youthful Kihika challenges his Sunday school teacher on the biblical authority for opposing female circumcision. The incident closes with a Dickensian passage of savage half-comic irony:

However, after discussing Sunday's incident with the church elders, he had decided to give the boy a chance to save his soul. The teacher had therefore decided to whip the boy ten times on his naked buttocks in front of the whole assembly — this for the sake of the boy's own soul and of all the others present. After the beating, Kihika would have to say thank you to the teacher and also recant his words of last Sunday. (100–1/76)

But the epigraphs to sections of the novel, being passages underlined in Kihika's Bible, are presented seriously, seldom with any hint of irony. Kihika compares Gandhi to Christ and suggests that he succeeded by using similar methods. But he goes on to make a radical revision of the messianic message in declaring that Christ 'failed because his death did not change anything' (110/83).

On the one hand, the Rev. Jackson Kigondu collaborates with the colonial administration and denounces Mau Mau from every available pulpit, so that it is found necessary to liquidate him. On the other, the Rung'ei uhuru celebrations are opened by the Rev. Morris Kingori, who before the Emergency had been a preacher in the Kikuyu Greek Orthodox Church. His brand of religion is that in which 'Protest alternated with submission, meekness with anguish, warning with promise' (247/189). But perhaps the most positive application of the Bible in *A Grain of Wheat* lies in its invocation as a universal mythology to which all mankind has access. We recall, for instance, Mumbi's narration of the course of the Emergency in Thabai during her attempt to explain to Mugo how she came to submit to Karanja. As she cries, ' "Do you know that we all thought the end of the world had come?" ' (163/126) — which is set for heightened effect as a paragraph on its own — she rouses a profound sense of pathos because her simple question endows the calamity of the Kenyan Emergency with all the horrors associated with the biblical deluge and the prophecy of destruction by fire. In the same account, she recalls some of the songs which the villagers sang to sustain their spirits as they worked at their enforced tasks. By reference to the universalized mythology of the Old Testament, the scale of their labours and of their sufferings is conveyed more powerfully:

> The children of Israel
> When they were in Misri
> Were made to do work
> Harder than that done by cows and donkeys. (164/126)

However, the final message of *A Grain of Wheat* is not of unmitigated suffering and frustration, but of challenge and hope. The epigraph to the whole book from Corinthians — 'that which thou sowest is not quickened, except it die . . .' — is reinforced by the quotation from St John which prefaces the last part of the novel: 'Except a corn of wheat fall into the ground and die, it abideth alone: but if it die, it bringeth forth much fruit' (229/175). The death of Kihika and the agony of Mau Mau have not been sterile, though the true rebirth is still awaited. In the first instance, perhaps, the biblical quotation following that from St John *is* ironic. The 'new earth' of uhuru is a vast confidence trick played by the power elite upon the peasants and workers of Kenya. But this is only in the short view. Ngũgĩ looks beyond without irony to the real uhuru when the revolution will become a reality. The paramount needs in bringing this about are solidarity and the strength that grows out of solidarity. Kihika is aware of this as a strategist in the Mau Mau campaign, and (irony upon irony) propounds his finds to Mugo of all men during the fateful visit to him which leads to the great betrayal:

> 'We want a strong organization. The whiteman knows this and fears. Why else has he made our people move into these villages? He wants to shut us from the people, our only strength. But he will not succeed. We must keep the road between us and the people clear of obstacles.' (218/167)

That he is speaking this to the man who will soon prove to be the greatest single obstacle to Kihika's cause, strengthens rather than weakens the force of the statement.

Ngũgĩ embraces the whole history of the movement for freedom from the early days of the pioneer Waiyaki, through the saga of Harry Thuku, to the Mau Mau forest fighters. This reminds us that, as well as looking far back, he is also looking far forward — beyond the false dawn of the mock uhuru which is warm water to the thirsty — to a truer liberation beyond. So Kihika's most telling words, trumpeted forth by his author, speak not only for the time of the Mau Mau struggle, but also for 1967 when the novel was published, for our own time now, and again far beyond. This is virtually the same voice as that of Dedan Kimathi in *The Trial* and of Karega in *Petals of Blood,* who sound out clearly the message which was tentatively expounded by Boro in *Weep Not, Child.* It is characteristic of *A Grain of Wheat* that Kihika, unlike Karega, strengthens his battle-call by employing an Old Testament myth once more:

> They say we are weak. They say we cannot win against the bomb. If we are weak, we cannot win. I despise the weak. Let them be trampled to death. I spit on the weakness of our fathers. Their memory gives me no pride. And even today, tomorrow, the weak and those with feeble hearts shall be wiped from the earth. The strong shall rule. Our fathers had no reason to be weak. The weak need not remain weak. Why? Because a people united in faith are stronger than the bomb. They shall not tremble or run away before the sword. Then instead the enemy shall flee. These are not words of a mad man. Not words, not even miracles could make Pharaoh let the children of Israel go. But at midnight, the Lord smote all the first-born in the land of Egypt, from the first-born of Pharaoh that sat on the throne unto the first-born of the captive that was in dungeon. And all the first-born of the cattle. And the following day, he let them go. That is our aim. (217/166)

This is the final burden of *A Grain of Wheat.* Everyone who can be mustered is needed: the reader is to feel this for himself or herself. Even the repentant perpetrator of the most unspeakable crime (unlike the unrepentant Karanja) can contribute: though not in life since he has put himself beyond the pale. But Mugo's remorse (inspired by his first whole-hearted response ever — to Mumbi), which leads him to speak out the truth and denounce his own treachery, can in death fire others to a new self-examination. This may help to liberate their wills so that they can look beyond the false independence now being offered and fight on for something better. New weapons, new strategies will be needed for the new battle, but unity remains the key to victory.

It is not Gikonyo and Mumbi alone who are significantly affected by Mugo's climactic speech. All are touched by it. Even the stubborn quisling, Karanja, knows that Mugo has saved him (for whatever his life may be worth): ' "He seems to be a courageous man . . . Yees. He is a man of courage . . . He even saved my life: for what?" ' (258–9/197). As soon as he has confessed, 'Mugo felt light. A load of many years was lifted from his shoulders. He was free, sure, confident' (267/204). The transformation is complete, even if it lasts 'Only for a minute', since he must almost at once face retribution in death. But it is now a very different sort of death from the one, perhaps years later, in which he might have taken his evil secret to the grave with him. The people in general are shocked, partly no doubt because they have been shown what they now regard as their own blindness in allowing themselves to be deceived for so long: by Mugo, but also by their new MP and his like. This disillusionment, the sense of anti-climax which permeates society for the greater part of the last section of the novel, is an essential preamble to any true reawakening.

We watch this reawakening begin in Gikonyo. Mugo's testament is an essential agent in his change of heart. It all begins with self-examination. Every one of us needs to be cleansed through such a process: ' "Which of us does not carry a weight in the heart?" ' (203/155). It is Gikonyo who crystallizes this realization and speaks Mugo's true epitaph. We are surrounded by those who cling to honours which they would not be vouchsafed if the whole truth about them were generally known. Gikonyo himself is dogged by those footsteps:

'He was a brave man, inside . . . He stood before much honour, praises were heaped on him. He would have become a Chief. Tell me another person who would have exposed his soul for all the eyes to peck at . . . Remember that few people in that meeting are fit to lift a stone against that man. Not unless I – we –– too – in turn open our hearts naked for the world to look at.' (265/202)

Gikonyo now, in consideration of his own shortcomings, forgives Mumbi. Mumbi, perceiving in a flash that a true change of heart cannot be expressed on the spur of the moment, pauses before finally bending the slightly stiff-necked stance she has still retained, but we now feel completely certain that a sincere reconciliation is imminent between them.

So all are stirred by Mugo's final action, and the novel can end on the contemplation of the sanctity of life and of life-renewing processes. This shift of tone is dependent on Ngũgĩ's conviction that the success of the struggle for a juster society is part of an inevitable historical progression, and is thus as certain in due time as the natural cycle of death, regeneration and rebirth in the grain of wheat. It is true that the preparations for uhuru have come to nothing because a heinous misdeed in the past has come to light. The penultimate chapter is suffused with an air of despondency. Warui, Wambui and Mumbi are weighed down by an awareness of the inexplicable paradoxes in life. Warui harps on the death of the old woman: ' "Why on that day, I keep on asking myself . . . But why on that day?" ' He continues, ' "And that day . . . that day! First Gikonyo breaks his arm . . ." ' (272-3/208). Mumbi's first words are, ' "It's cold." ' The day of independence, so long fought for, has been far from auspicious.

But relief from this general sense of doom comes with the renewed recognition that the individual is caught up as a small, though significant, part of the whole machinery of life and time. Whatever happens life will, and must, go on. Our only responsibility is to try and ensure that it continues, cumulatively day by day, month by month, in a manner more conducive to the happiness of all members of society than it proceeded in in the past. Mumbi, who has been more shocked and shaken than anyone else by Mugo's end, now puts this nucleus of events into a wider perspective: ' "Perhaps we should not worry too much about the meeting . . . or . . . about Mugo. We have got to live" ' (275/210). And the old folk join in and build up the dialogue between the three of them into a miniature chorus in celebration of the natural cycle of living positively in a community:

Warui:	'Yes, we have the village to build.'
Wambui:	'And the market tomorrow, and the fields to dig and cultivate ready for the next season.'
Mumbi:	'And children to look after.' (275/210)

This hope for a new beginning is epitomized in the final chapter in the reconciliation of Gikonyo and Mumbi. Their reconciliation is itself symbolized by the carved stool which will be Gikonyo's peace-offering to Mumbi. And in the stool, their reunion becomes an image for the unified strength of the whole society. The carving is to be an example of true traditional African craftsmanship. The gift had first been determined as a stool in response to a passing remark by Wangari: ' "These days there are no wood-carvers left . . . so you only get chairs and seats joined together with nails" ' (126/95). It is to be a craftsman's artefact inspired by a deep creative urge: 'he had wanted to give her a gift, a creation of his own hands' (126/95). It would be moulded with all the artist's passion for his medium: 'he became more and more excited and his hands itched to touch wood and a chisel' (279/212). As Gikonyo lies in hospital, the images — first of Kerinyaga, the mountain which is the source of spiritual values for the people and of their ancient, communal concepts of the good life, and secondly of the irrigation canals which he helped to dig as a prisoner 'converting the dry plains into rice-growing fields' (277/211) — merge into his renewed impulse to fashion this special stool. Its design grows and develops in his mind, but its basic form is clear from the start. Three figures are to support the bowl of the stool representing the family. The man and woman will be depicted 'with hard lines on the face' (279/212), figuring the peasants' tough existence. He will bear, with bent shoulders, the main weight of their world. Their hands will be joined, and their other hands will meet on the head of the child. At first the bead design on the bole is to represent the irrigating 'river and a canal'. A jembe (the villager's hoe) or a spade is to lie beside the canal symbolizing purposeful cooperative effort. This design is at length tentatively transformed into the even more significant image of 'A field needing clearance and cultivation' (279/212) — as Kenya still does after this trial uhuru. As an alternative or an addition to the jembe, there may now be a bean-flower, a fertility symbol in all its natural beauty. And, with the marriage pact about to be resealed, the female figure is finally metamorphosed into that of a pregnant woman. Communal and private love and effort are fused in the coming generation.

Notes

1. The first set of page references to *A Grain of Wheat* are to the first paperback edition (Heinemann Educational Books, London, 1968). The second refer to the reset edition of 1975, subsequently reprinted.
2. See also *A Grain of Wheat* pp. 214/164 and 223/171.
3. Ngũgĩ states in *Detained* (Heinemann Educational Books, London, 1981): 'In the novel *A Grain of Wheat*, I tried, through Mugo who carried the burden of mistaken revolutionary heroism, to hint at the possibilities of the new Kenyatta' (90). He admits to having been utterly mistaken in his notions about Kenyatta at this time: 'But that was in 1965–6 and nothing was clear then about the extent to which Kenyatta had negated his past, nor the sheer magnitude of the suffering it would cause to our society today' (90). The implication is that it would have required at least a symbolic death of Kenyatta and the values he epitomized as a condition for creating a new just Kenya.
4. See in particular: Ebele Obumselu, '*A Grain of Wheat:* James Ngũgĩ's Debt to Conrad', *The Benin Review* no. 1, June 1974, 80–91.
5. In *Detained*, Ngũgĩ comments on the origins of the theme of 'return' in his writings:

   I came back [from the Alliance High School, Kikuyu] after the first term and confidently walked back to my old village. My home was now only a pile of dry mud-stones, bits of grass, charcoal and ashes. Nothing remained, not even crops, except for a lone pear tree . . . I stood there bewildered. Not only my home, but the old village with its culture, its memories and its warmth had been razed to the ground . . . Many critics have noted the dominance of the theme of return in my novels, plays and short stories, particularly in *A Grain of Wheat*. But none has known the origins of the emotion behind the theme. It is deeply rooted in my return to Kamiriithu in 1955. The return of Mau Mau political detainees was to come later. (73–4)

6. See *A Grain of Wheat*, pp. 248/189–90.

Petals of Blood

Petals of Blood is the first of Ngũgĩ's novels which is fairly and squarely about independent Kenya. It is an exposé of the nature of capitalism, of the insensitivity, callousness and insatiable ambition of those who control vested interests in order to gain power and wealth, impoverishing the unprivileged, imposing misery and suffering upon the majority. In order to anatomize this monster, capitalism, Ngũgĩ dramatizes the destructive and demoralizing effects of the whole social system which it creates. The setting is not incidental background but is of the very essence of the novel's subject. The arena juxtaposes the conflicting interests within contemporary African society: the city and the village. These are presented as opposite extremes at the beginning of the novel's time-scheme. We are to watch the tentacles of the city reach out and lay hold of its rural neighbour as the novel progresses. Ngũgĩ particularizes the characteristic features of each community as they play out their respective roles of victim and destroyer.

The city is the seat of opulence with its tall buildings; its houses set in idyllic gardens; its bright lights and smooth, wide avenues; and, in particular, its places of entertainment catering for every perverse taste and sensual whim. It is the hotels, bars, restaurants and other places of resort that breed the hapless community of barmaids, prostitutes and down-and-outs who are sacrificed to this materialistic culture. Exploited and trampled upon, this multitude populates the shanty locations of drooping mud-and-wattle shacks, with unplanned mud-tracks for roads, where the barest necessities of the wealthy suburbs would be undreamed-of luxuries. These drudges service the capitalist citadel but are an irksome threat to their privileged countrymen, undermining their complacency and asserting ominous reminders of the squalor on which affluence rests. The picturesque estates of the elite are occupied by Chui, Mzigo, Kimeria, Nderi wa Riera, Ezekiel Waweru, the Reverend Jerrod and their fellows, who are seen as malignant and vicious, hypocritical and exploitative public officers: school administrators, legislators, church dignitaries — Christians. While basking in their good life, they seek to bolster up a social order which protects their selfish comforts and relegates the multitude to perpetual poverty. The city also harbours rich and corrupt expatriates — one of whom we see luring Wanja to his exotic house to 'perform' with his dog. The occasional champion of the poor within the privileged circle — Pinto, the lawyer J. M. (who shadows Josiah Mwangi Kariuki in real life), are hounded at every opportunity by their less scrupulous peers.

In contrast to the city, Ngũgĩ elevates the countryside, represented in the novel by the outpost village of Ilmorog. Early on we learn something of its distant past:

> Ilmorog, the scene of the unfolding of this drama, had not always been a small cluster of mud huts lived in only by old men and women and children with occasional visits from wandering herdsmen. It had had its days of glory: thriving villages with a huge population of sturdy peasants who had tamed nature's forests and, breaking the soil between their fingers, had brought forth every type of crop to nourish the sons and daughters of men. How they toiled together, clearing the wilderness, cultivating, planting: how they all fervently prayed for rain and deliverance in times of drought and pestilence! And at harvest-time they would gather in groups, according to ages, and dance from village to village, spilling into Ilmorog plains, hymning praises to their founders. (120)[1]

Ngũgĩ endows Ilmorog with an ideal setting and tradition: '[its] ridge, as it drops into the plains along which Ilmorog river flows, must form one of the greatest natural beauties in the world' (67). The tiny stream had once in all probability been a large river. Ngũgĩ suggests that oral traditions, 'recent archaeological and linguistic researches' and even colonialist records might be able to teach us much more about ancient Ilmorog:

> [Its] plains are themselves part of that Great Rift that formed a natural highway joining Kenya to the land of the Sphinx and to the legendary waters of the River Jordan in Palestine. For centuries, and even up to this day, the God of Africa and the Gods of other lands have wrestled for the mastery of man's soul and for the control of the results of man's holy sweat . . . (68)

Ilmorog had been founded by a herdsman of undaunted courage, Ndemi, who ventured out in search of a higher mode of living. He was followed by 'Nyangendo of the famous gap in her upper teeth and Nyaguthii of the black gums and breasts that were the talk of herdsmen wherever they met' (121), who became his wives. Such is the history of this setting for Ngũgĩ's story of the despoliation of rural peace and dignity by urban greed and degradation. In time Ilmorog is invaded by European settlers and colonists, and exploited by Indian petty traders, till after independence it is no more than a ravished, abandoned ghost of its former self. When the disillusioned and demoralized inhabitants initiate action to redeem the lost glory of their homeland, they trigger off a confrontation with city financiers which forms the centrepiece of Ngũgĩ's novel, until the old Ilmorog is buried for ever beneath a promoter's paradise.

The urban elite — Kimeria, Chui, Nderi wa Riera and the like, and the village stalwarts — Nyakinyua, Muturi, Njuguna, Ruoro, offer a total contrast in values which is central to *Petals of Blood*. Intermediate between these extremes are the principal protagonists of the novel who partake in varying degrees of both worlds. Through them the confrontation is set actively before us. Characteristically, Ngũgĩ creates for Godfrey Munira, Wanja, Abdulla and Karega rounded life histories which give the story depth and authenticity but, more than this, also express one of the principal themes of the book: a realization that this modern African community is a tangle of disoriented, isolated lives which, when they interrelate at all, more often than not do so to the mutual disadvantage of the individuals concerned.

Hawkins Kimeria is perhaps the most repulsive of the urban group. He has fully imbibed the cynical city dictum as it is later propounded by Wanja: ' "You eat somebody or you are eaten. You sit on somebody or somebody sits on you" ' (291). He is without conscience, and so utterly inhuman: he pursues self-interest unquestioningly, almost like an automaton. During the Emergency he got rich transporting the dead bodies of Mau Mau victims killed by the British. His financial success endears him to Wanja's father and thereby he finds the opportunity to ravish the young girl, so that she is barred from school and is thrown into a degrading and precarious life of prostitution as a bar-girl. At a later encounter he delights in subjecting Wanja to intense humiliation by forcing her to bed to the knowledge of her imprisoned companions, after, ironically, they have approached him for help for a sick child. At length, Kimeria plays a key role in the invasion of the countryside by the city which destroys old Ilmorog in the process of dispossessing and making destitute its inhabitants. For Kimeria, money is alpha and omega; with a sickening matter-of-factness, he coolly deploys its power in the ruthless pursuit of his interests.

Chui mirrors Kimeria in the unstinting pursuit of wealth, power and status. Since he misdirects what are undoubtedly exceptional gifts and talents, he might have cut an even more sinister figure than Kimeria had not Ngũgĩ suggested, perhaps unintentionally, that he is in part corrupted by external, and therefore extenuating, circumstances. At school he is a luminary in every field: classwork, sport and dress, setting the pace for others. So he finds himself the leader of a student strike agitating for better school conditions. Through the prefect system, the colonial education policy sows in him the seeds of self-conceit which were later to fester into his morbid contempt for his people's culture, and his off-hand repression of their interests. Expelled from school after the strike, he drifts off — significantly — to South Africa, and then to America and elsewhere, and in the process he is conditioned and brainwashed.

So when, after another student protest, this time against alienating syllabuses, he becomes the acclaimed new headmaster of his alma mater, in fact he outdoes his ousted predecessor, Cambridge Fraudsham, in pursuing the prefect system and promoting foreign values. Later, not surprisingly, he too participates in the final demise of old Ilmorog.

Nderi wa Riera is Ngũgĩ's prototype of the new politician, conforming to the egocentric assumptions of the power group without questioning its ethics or seeking to reform the system. Characteristically, he grabs political office for personal ends and then remembers his electorate only when an election is approaching or when as a hardened demagogue he must needs quieten the rumblings of discontented voters. He is willing to cheapen his society's culture and prostitute its womanhood. Such a man will go through the motions of public concern or of Christian piety as at the turn of a switch. His hypocritical posturing and hollow rhetoric are a facade for clandestine deals and comfortable rackets. Ngũgĩ pictures such men as a social plague.

In contrast, the rural group is materially poor but rich in values. They uphold human dignity and integrity. Their guiding spirit is Nyakinyua, Wanja's grandmother, Ngũgĩ's archetype elder — like Chege in *The River Between* — the repository of legends, lore and secrets of the tribe, preserver of bygone ideals. Her impassioned tributes to her dead husband's courage and love of honour fill the young with respect for their ancestors and the desire to emulate them in the present. In a crucial scene she re-creates the ancient mystique of alcoholic drink which can relax the nerves, open the senses and release latent mental powers if properly handled. Today drink is used to drug the mind against despondency engendered by our crude and brutal life. On her deathbed Nyakinyua asserts that drink of old was not 'this concoction you and Abdulla are cheating people with' (324).

'. . . they would drink it only when work was finished, and especially after the ceremony of circumcision or marriage or itwika, and after a harvest. It was when they were drinking Theng'eta that poets and singers composed their words for a season of Gichandi, and the seer voiced his prophecy.' (204)

'Theng'eta. It is a dream. It is a wish. It gives you sight, and for those favoured by God it can make them cross the river of time and talk with their ancestors. It has given seers their tongues; poets and Gichandi players their words; and it has made barren women mothers of many children. Only you must take it with faith and purity in your hearts.' (210)

Among the villagers we meet Mwathi wa Mugo, the occult priest, most extraordinary of men, who is portrayed by Ngũgĩ with a rare double-edged irony, ambivalence and scepticism which call into question the validity of fundamental metaphysical beliefs of the Ilmorog villagers, perhaps of Africa at large. He is seen as the mentor of the clan. Youth may not enter his shrine, and even among the elders no one claims certainty about who he really is or what he is really like. Eventually, the Trans-Africa Highway nudges its way to Mwathi wa Mugo's sacred compound with bulldozer and pickaxe as it cleaves Ilmorog irrevocably into two and forces it into the modern age. The villagers watch with bated breath as the gang approaches Mwathi's domain:

We said: it cannot be. But they still moved toward it. We said: they will be destroyed by Mwathi's fire. Just you wait, lust you wait. But the machine uprooted the hedge and then it hit the first hut and it fell and we were all hush-hush, waiting for it to be blown up. Even when the Americans landed on the moon . . . we were not as scared as when Mwathi's place was razed to the ground. The two huts were pulled down. But where was Mwathi? There was no Mwathi. He must have vanished, we said, and we waited for his vengeance. Maybe he was never there, we said, and the elder who might have helped, Muturi, had become suddenly deaf and dumb at the sacrilege. (265–6)

Modern science may see Mwathi as a fraud; at several points in the novel Ngũgĩ allows his reforming characters to decry the preservation or worship of the past for its own sake. But Mwathi wa Mugo as an idea (if not a scientific reality) has served the vital purpose of providing inner meaning and coherence for a community. Does not the destruction of that meaning usher in the disintegration of Ilmorog?

The group that straddles town and country includes Godfrey Munira who, though himself strangely inactive most of the time, is nevertheless a centrifugal cause of action. In his catalystic inaction he is reminiscent of Mugo in *A Grain of Wheat* Dusk is his element:

> Munira relished twilight as a prelude to that awesome shadow. He looked forward to the unwilled immersion into darkness. He would then be part of everything: the plants, animals, people, huts, without consciously choosing the links. To choose involved effort, decision, preference of one possibility, and this could be painful. He had chosen not to choose, a freedom he daily celebrated walking between his house, Abdulla's place and of course Wanja's hut. (71)

Munira is son to Ezekiel Waweru, the pious operator who uses everything — but above all his Christianity — to advance his material interests. At Siriana Munira is willy-nilly part of Chui's strike and is expelled, which is the beginning of a shiftless life. Munira stands out in an aggressively successful family as a mere beggarly primary school teacher:

> it pained [Munira] that he still depended on his father for a place in which to set a home. He had always thought of striking out on his own but he had remained circling around his father's property without at the same time being fully part of it. This was unlike his more successful brothers. (13)

Ngũgĩ mocks these determinedly well-to-do kindred among whom acquisitiveness has replaced conscience: Munira's opting out is a protest which he stands by quite deliberately. His participation in the school strike closes the door to affluence. Lucklessly, he chooses the pagan Wanjiru for his wife 'maybe as a prompting from the heart against what his father stood for' (91) and because 'Her voice, her dancing, her total involvement had attracted him' (203), only to find her embracing his parents' empty religion: 'She could never get it out of her mind that she had married into a renowned Christian house, and she tried to be the ideal daughter-in-law' (91). So Munira's dream of fulfilment in love 'had vanished on the marriage bed' (203): 'Munira could have forgiven her everything but those silent prayers before and after making love. But he had never lifted a finger to fight against the process' (91).

Like Ngotho, like Mugo, Munira is a born loser. He runs towards exile as a release. In an odd mixture of assertion and self-negation, he abandons his wife and family and their aggressive vitality, and goes to famine-ridden Ilmorog to try and bring education to an unwilling and even hostile people. And he ends up performing the most important single act in the whole novel in challenge and scorn of a repugnant social set-up which has steadily squeezed the life out of him — and many others.

Wanja is both the instinctively wise perennial innocent, and the temptress, in spite of herself. It is she who will link together the straying, alienated characters of the story, and will animate both energies and desires. Her physical appeal fits her for the role of barmaid and prostitute, yet she remains insulated from degradation by an acute and shrewd intelligence, an endless zest for life, and unfailing human sympathy. Her childhood leaves only painful memories of feuds between her parents and the shame of a schoolgirl pregnancy induced by a debauched and callous older man. Fleeing from home, she gets rid of her infant and throws herself into prostitution, a career in which her talent for human relationships produces flashes of joy amid much suffering and squalor. Her adaptable and buoyant nature saves her: she survives not only to repay those who have abused her, as an instrument of retribution, but also to attain fulfilment in at last being granted a. longed-for child which this time we know she will cherish and nurture.

Frustrated though he becomes, Abdulla, the half-caste, is also essentially active. We meet him as an inconsequential storekeeper in Ilmorog, but Ngũgĩ presents him as a gallant figure who links in his private history the heroic past of the Mau Mau uprising against imperialism, and the inglorious present which he nevertheless leads us to feel is, just beneath the surface, alive with positive human potentials. His lame leg is testimony to a betrayed generation of honourable men who forsook the comforts of home and braved the hardships of the forest in order to rescue their homeland from shameful oppression. He stirs his companions in the great journey to new courage and new sense of purpose by recalling the earlier campaign in which he figured:

> He had indeed endured thirst and hunger, briars and thorns in scaly flesh in the service of that vision which first opened out to him the day he had taken both the oath of unity and later the Batuni oath.
>
> He was then a worker at a shoe-factory near his home, where strike after strike for higher wages and better housing had always been broken by helmeted policemen. He had asked himself several times: how was it that a boss who never once lifted a load, who never once dirtied his hands in the smelly water and air in the tannery or in any other part of the complex, could still live in a big house and own a car and employ a driver and more than four people only to cut grass in the compound?
>
> How he had trembled as the vision opened out, embracing new thoughts, new desires, new possibilities! To redeem the land: to fight so that the industries like the shoe-factory which had swallowed his sweat could belong to the people: so that his children could one day have enough to eat and to wear under adequate shelter from rain: so that they would say in pride, my father died that I might live: this had transformed him from a slave before a boss into a man. That was the day of his true circumcision into a man. (136)

Born of an African mother and an Indian father — who at least sent him to school and started a savings account for him — he is agitated by his 'divided self'. He abandons school for the streets to be with. other children of his age and condition. His period of working in the shoe-factory geared him for combat in the Mau Mau rebellion. His unpremeditated flight to the forest is movingly related. He and Nding'uri (who turns out to be Karega's brother) go by prearrangement to collect bullets for the fighters, but are betrayed by Kimeria. Abdulla escapes to the forest but Nding'uri is hanged. He joins the troop led by Ole Masai, a charismatic leader who arouses a nationalist fervour in him. Abdulla is shot in the leg during the raid in which Ole Masai is killed when his gun jams. Abdulla's lame stump becomes a significant symbol in the novel.

After detention he naively hopes that his past patriotism will be rewarded: but the scales have turned against people of his kind. He is thrust aside as unemployable while Kimeria bustles in as the successful entrepreneur. Ngũgĩ insists on the irony:

'The clerks were saying after he had gone inside: Uhuru has really come. Before independence no African was allowed to touch the company's goods except as a labourer. Now Mr Kimeria handles millions!' (255)

Thus, like Munira, Abdulla has recourse to self-exile: ' "I wanted to go deep deep into the country where I would have no reminder of so bitter a betrayal" ' (255). But after a few years in old Ilmorog the brash new destructive society catches up with Abdulla there. He loses even his humble shop and bar, and finds himself living in a hovel and selling oranges by the roadside to landlords and road-hogs. Abdulla has a special importance in the novel as a link between specific experiences in the past and the present. There is special significance in his eventual brief union with Wanja and (we are left to assume) his fathering of her child. But his future remains a question mark at best at the end of the novel.

The fourth full-length portrait is that of Karega. He is Ngũgĩ's prototype of the oppressed poor who learn to resist their oppression and envisage the reconstruction of society. He enjoys neither good education nor a decent stable income, yet he optimistically and courageously fights for the righting of social wrongs. As he moves around Kenya, hounded from job to job for rousing his fellow workers into being aware of their rights, he becomes the representative worker, now on a plantation, now as a Mombasa docker, now selling skins at the roadside, now in a new-town factory. He is the authentic revolutionary figure, making fertile the dormant soil, one who points the way to the possibility of a better future.

His mother, Miriamu, is a peasant farmer on the land of Munira's father. She has fled from the cruel conditions of peasant tenancy under which her husband worked. Following in Munira's footsteps, Karega goes to Siriana, leads a strike, and is expelled. He becomes an itinerant worker, taking on whatever employment is to hand wherever he arrives. He too comes to Ilmorog, and is later drawn back there a second time as he quests for some meaning in his life. Munira takes him on as a schoolteacher, but in time he becomes the successful rival for Wanja's affection and then reveals his own involvement with the tragic death in the past of Munira's sister, and so his first stay in Ilmorog is terminated. He continues his rovings; for a while on the coast he is one of those who 'loaded and unloaded the ships . . . handled all that wealth . . . with our naked bodies sweating in the steamy sun' (288). When he returns to the new Ilmorog, divided like Nairobi between poor and well-to-do quarters, it is to lead the workers in the Theng'eta Breweries in a confrontation with their exploiting employers. However, as we shall see, it is no part of Ngũgĩ's scheme to have Karega exterminating the handful of individual oppressors whose deaths shape the plot — though at the level of a 'who-done-it?' detective story, we are meant wrongly to suspect him, and at another level to find food for thought when we discover our mistake.

Ngũgĩ fashions Karega's character with care. In his first act of manhood, his love affair with Mukami, we glimpse something of his own distinctive temperament through the attraction that Mukami's strange personality and tragic inclinations exert upon him. He meets her for the first time sitting on the edge of the quarry, 'her legs swinging in the menacing caved hollow' (216). To join her on that spot puts Karega's courage to a severe test. Ngũgĩ describes the eerie setting for their embraces:

> 'In the middle of Manguo lake were two humps which were never covered by water no matter how much it rained, they always seemed to float above the water. Later I learnt that these were sides of a dam built by the young men of Kihiu Mwiri generation at the insistence of Mukoma Wa Njiriri, then a chief, as a condition of his giving them licence for initiation. But . . . legend among us boys had it that they were the humps of two giant shark-like animals that used to dwell in the lake, and the reeds were supposed to be their puberty hair. On one of them we went and sat down.' (218)

Mukami's father discovers the affair. He knows that Karega's brother has been a member of Mau Mau and accuses him of leading the attack in which his right ear was cut off after accusations of collaborating with the white men and preaching against Mau Mau in church. Because of this and because of the poverty of Karega and his mother, Waweru forbids the liaison. Unable to resolve this dilemma, Mukami leaps off the edge of the quarry and kills herself. Such is the girl who could satisfy Karega's own tempestuous and rebellious nature. His later love is Wanja, even more of an enigma.

When Munira asks him what the protest he led at Siriana was really about, he replies,

> 'I don't really know . . . when the lawyer spoke, I seemed to get it . . . an inkling . . . but it eludes the mind . . . an idea . . . I mean, we were men . . . a communal struggle . . . after all, we were the school, weren't we? We imagined new horizons . . . new beginnings . . . a school run on the basis of our sweat . . . our collective brains, our ambitions, our fears, our hopes . . . the right to define ourselves . . . a new image of self . . . all this and more . . . but it was not clear . . . only that the phrase African populism seemed to sum it all!' (173–4)

Karega mobilizes Ilmorog's collective will for the great march to the city, the protest against starvation: he harnesses the immemorial power the tribe has always invoked in times of affliction. Karega helps draw from Nyakinyua and from Abdulla the wisdom of old and the new patriotism to combat the challenge of new injustice. He reveres the lawyer for his insight into the wrongs of the new social order. But the lawyer aspires to dissuade the architects of this unjust society from pursuing their courses, whereas Karega is convinced that the only way forward is to destroy the corrupt elite. Karega is thus the natural leader of the people in the struggle against their oppressors.

These principal portraits are fundamental to the pattern of power — either for maintaining the *status quo* or for change — and of impotence which the novel presents. We must watch characteristic figures from city and village, and from among those who link these two worlds, interacting and clashing to bring to life Ngũgĩ's picture of capitalist society in Africa, and the possibility of transforming it by determined joint action. Thus the links provided between these key intermediary figures not only tighten the plot, but imply a network as strong as or stronger than that of the vested interests. Njogu, the old man of Ilmorog, is maternal grandfather of Ole Masai, Abdulla's Mau Mau chieftain in the forest. It was Ole Masai's Indian father who built the shop which Abdulla later revives. Nding'uri was both Karega's brother and Abdulla's confederate and was betrayed by Kimeria who also first debauched Wanja. Karega and his mother worked and lived on the land of Munira's father. Karega had first been the lover of Munira's sister and the helpless cause of her suicide, then becomes Munira's pupil, and at length his colleague. Both had been pupil leaders of strikes at Siriana. There can be little doubt that Ngũgĩ sees significance in this interweaving of past, present and future as an expression of historic coherence and inevitability. Many of these links emerge from a murky past as surprises to characters and readers alike. It is true that the reader may sometimes feel more bewildered than enlightened in the process; and we do not always see why these mysteries are revealed to us in a covert and even contorted manner, which greatly adds — perhaps in some instances unnecessarily — to the difficulty of the book. But they do enrich the texture of the story at many levels.

Out of these complex elements Ngũgĩ constructs his drama of belligerent capitalism. As a prelude to the city's lethal embrace of the village, the disparities between them widen. While city buildings grow grander, roads more imposing, gardens more lush, the controlling elite and middle class more opulent, Ilmorog dwindles into a drought-convulsed wasteland:

> But the Ilmorog they now came to was one of sun, dust, and sand. Wanja and Karega were especially struck by the change in the face of Ilmorog countryside.
> 'So green in the past,' she said. 'So green and hopeful . . . and now this.'
> (107)

> Cows and goats and sheep were skeletons . . . by mid-May . . . two cows died; vultures and hawks circled high in the sky and then swooped in hordes, later leaving behind them white bones scattered on stunted and dry elephant grass.
> (110)

From this setting, the plot of the novel emerges. Led by Karega, the four key characters rouse Ilmorog from lethargy and despair, invoking the collective will, the spirit of solidarity and a common destiny by which the tribe sustained itself in past ages. So the village undertakes the great journey to the town to seek deliverance from natural disaster and human neglect. Ironically the journey is the ultimate cause of the annihilation of old Ilmorog: for the new Ilmorog which rises in its place is the complete negation of everything the old village had stood for, a transformation for which the petitioners had not bargained.

Ngũgĩ exerts all his literary skills to emphasize the wickedness and inhumanity of capitalism and its effects. Hearts are hardened; emotions are coarsened; minds are enslaved; the psyche is depraved. Life becomes meaningless, a thing to be endured rather than enjoyed. The negation operates at two levels. As individuals, the poor are trodden down and the rich are brutalized (even the nominally religious). As a society, upright old Ilmorog dies and new Ilmorog rises in moral ignominy.

The degenerate characters we have already surveyed embody the vices of capitalism. Kimeria, Chui, Nderi wa Riera, Mzigo, Rev. Jerrod Brown, Waweru have all risen by standing on the backs of the poor whom they have used and discarded at will. When this unholy alliance combines to swallow old Ilmorog, they need exert little effort in replacing it with their own dehumanized settlement. They set up first a police post to keep the underdogs in check; then a church to tame them; and a government office to colonize them. Village-folk have no choice but to pawn their ancestral lands and homes for bank loans which, predictably, they cannot pay, and so by a purely nominal process of law, property passes into the hands of the city promoters and financiers. In the name of town-planning, small shopkeepers are evicted: Abdulla must now sell oranges to the floating population. Even though Wanja in a futile gesture of resistance briefly redeems Nyankinyua's property, she cannot save the old woman nor for very long her own building. Bulldozers move in. Money-spinning concerns, typified by Theng'eta Breweries and Enterprises Limited, which have prostituted the theng'eta tradition, mushroom everywhere. A tourist centre epitomizes the social decadence: here a depraved European can pick up an African girl for whatsoever he will, while tribal culture is made into a casual peepshow. Farmers of long standing perforce become day-labourers, no longer living in family dwellings but in the shanty-town which inevitably neighbours every urban centre in Africa:

> Within a year or so of the New Ilmorog shopping centre being completed, wheatfields and ranches had sprung up all around the plains: the herdsmen had died or had been driven further afield into the drier parts, but a few had become workers on the wheatfields and ranches on the earth upon which they once roamed freely. The new owners, master-servants of bank power, money and cunning, came over at weekends . . . The peasants of Ilmorog had also changed. Some had somehow survived the onslaught. They could employ one or two hands on their small farms. Most of the others had joined the army of workers . . .
>
> There were several Ilmorogs. One was the residential area of the farm managers, County Council officials, public service officers, the managers of Barclays, Standard and African Economic Banks, and other servants of state and money power. This was called Cape Town. The other — called New Jerusalem — was a shanty town of migrant and floating workers, the unemployed, the prostitutes and small traders in tin and scrap metal. Between the New Jerusalem and Cape Town, not far from where Mwathi had once lived guarding the secrets of iron works and native medicine, was All Saints Church, now led by Rev. Jerrod Brown. Also somewhere between the two areas was Wanja's Sunshine Lodge, almost as famous as the church . . .
>
> The breweries were owned by an Anglo-American international combine but of course with African directors and even shareholders. Three of the four leading local personalities were Mzigo, Chui and Kimeria.
>
> Long live New Ilmorog! Long live Partnership in Trade and Progress! (280–1)

Ngũgĩ also makes outright denunciations of capitalist practice through his leading characters: for instance when Karega declares that all humanity is made up of prostitutes. He is provoked into this when Munira, jealous and frustrated, calls Wanja a prostitute:

> 'But we do not have to heap insults on others. We are all prostitutes, for in a world of grab and take, in a world built on a structure of inequality and injustice, in a world where some can eat while others can only toil, some can send their children to schools and others cannot, in a world where a prince, a monarch, a businessman can sit on billions . . . taken from the world's poor, in such a world, we are all prostituted.' (240)

Earlier the lawyer, advocate of the poor, tells a thinly veiled parable about the decadence into which independent Kenya has fallen. This is perhaps Ngũgĩ's most sustained attack on the excesses of the middle class. Tracing the baleful worship of 'the molten god' to colonialists who introduced a cash economy, he laments that far from this malady being arrested when black people took control, matters turned out to be even worse:

> 'So we go on building the monster and it grows and waits for more, and now we are all slaves to it. At its shrine we kneel and pray and hope. Now we see the outcome . . . dwellers in Blue Hills, those who have taken on themselves the priesthood of the ministry to the blind god . . . a thousand acres of land . . . a million acres in the two hands of a priest, while the congregation moans for an acre! and they are told: it is only a collection from your sweat . . . let us be honest slaves to the monster-god, let us give him our souls . . . and the ten per cent that goes with it . . . for his priests must eat too . . . and we shall take it to his vassal, the bank . . . meanwhile let's all pray and the god may notice our honesty and fervour, and we shall get a few crumbs. Meanwhile, the god grows big and fat and shines even brighter and whets the appetites of his priests, for the monster has, through the priesthood, decreed only one ethical code: Greed and accumulation.' (163)

While in America Karega has seen the true worship of Mammon, but on returning home, .

> 'as in a flash of lightning I saw that we were serving the same monster-god as they were in America . . . I saw the same signs, the same symptoms, and even the sickness . . . and I was so frightened . . . I was so frightened . . . I cried to myself: how many Kimathis must die, how many motherless children must weep, how long shall our people continue to sweat so that a few, a given few, might keep a thousand dollars in the bank of the one monster-god that for four hundred years had ravished a continent? And now I saw in the clear light of day the role that the Fraudshams of the colonial world played to create all of us black zombies dancing pornography in Blue Hills while our people are dying of hunger, while our people cannot afford decent shelter and decent schools for their children. And we are happy, we are happy that we are called stable and civilised and intelligent!' (166)

An equally direct denunciation of capitalist exploitation occurs in the passage after Karega has resolved to read history books to trace the basis of the master-servant relationship between rich and poor.

In condemning the Kamwene Cultural Organization — a covert organization for controlling the peasantry — Karega casts his rejection of middle-class values in the form of a question: ' " . . . how could a whole community be taken in by a few greedy stomachs — greedy because they had eaten more than their fair share of that which was bought by the blood of the people?" ' (112).

Ngũgĩ's imagery is part of the framework of exposure of all that is repugnant to him in contemporary Kenyan — and indeed African — society. Virtually every episode, almost every paragraph, reproaches one group or another for some transgression against society. We may distinguish between narrative ironies and thematic ironies.

The narrative ironies are embedded in nominally narrative passages which at the same time imply destructive traits in a person, an action, an institution, or the entire social system. Such innuendoes permeate the whole text. The police investigation, upon which the whole plot hangs, nominally underwrites the process of law and order, but implicitly sympathizes with the assassination which expresses public indignation at the repression of legitimate aspirations. The personal confessions of the protagonists, especially of Munira and Wanja, involve much self-examination and self-recrimination, but to the reader express more tellingly an indictment of the conditions in which these individuals find themselves trying to operate. It is Kimeria, Chui, Nderi wa Riera, Mzigo, Waweru, the Reverend Jerrod, patrons and administrators of the social system, who are separately and collectively responsible for wrecking the lives of their fellow citizens, rendering Munira an outsider, depriving Wanja of the basic joys of motherhood, shattering any prospects for the crippled Abdulla, encumbering Karega with a life of indeterminate wandering. Three of them (to come full cycle) write the scenario for their own assassination. When Mukami leaps to her death from the quarry-edge, it is her father whom we pillory and the pious frauds with which he surrounds his whole environment. The razing of old Ilmorog indicts a whole society and all the key characters who serve its purposes.

The account of the great trek to the city is crowded with such ironies. Remorselessly, one after the other, Ngũgĩ has the opulent residents of Blue Hills abandon these destitute pilgrims and the desperately sick child among their number to their fate. These pages epitomize man's inhumanity. First 'hakuna kazi', the familiar denial: no work. Then the well-to-do black Christian priest who leaves the starving to feed only on 'the food of the spirit, the bread and fish of Jesus'. Next, to the house of Chui, old friend, nominal reformer, big man in the administration, where the lady-guests, 'red-lipped with huge Afro-wigs', who are engaged in singing bawdy versions of traditional Gikuyu songs with their dark-suited gentlemen friends, faint at the sight of hungry villagers and have them pursued with gunshots. Finally at the house of Kimeria, by now a familiar figure, the elders are imprisoned, and Wanja is forced to submit once again to the will of the dominating bully. From all that we learn throughout the novel we recognize these reactions as no isolated incidents but as prototypical behaviour of the privileged when face to face with the drudges of society.

We attend the false ritual of the forced oathtaking ceremony at the 'tea-party', to which the populace is herded in the hope that traditional awe will inhibit them from any action against their lords and masters. This is linked to Munira 's visit to his father's estate, a complex of mocking irony to expose Waweru's pretensions for what they really are. Though Munira finds his father at prayer, and, 'weak at the knees', kneels with him, for a moment proud 'of a father so serene, so sure and secure in both wealth and faith' (93), yet, true to form, Munira's scepticism leads Waweru to curse him before he leaves. He washes his hands both of his son, and the daughter whom he had driven to her death: ' "You will come to a bad end: just like your sister" ' (94). He honours the KCO secret cult, and despises his schoolteacher son as a failure.

As a final example of narrative irony, we might recall that the novel's anonymous voice reports how 'progress' comes to Ilmorog, and how the local member of the legislative assembly comes to rationalize all the people's ills, and subdue their murmurings. The passage ends: 'Long live Nderi wa Riera. We gave him our votes: we waited for flowers to bloom' (268).

It might be objected that what we have called narrative irony is simply a form of character presentation and plot development — revealing the protagonists in action — which is common to the whole art of fiction. What is being emphasized here is the constant ironic level just beneath the surface that underlies so much of Ngũgĩ's narration and characterization. We have been familiar with this in the earlier novels, for instance in the insistence with which we learn of the different doctrines of Waiyaki and Kabonyi in order to expose the shortsighted limitations of the one and the demagogic speciousness of the other in actual practice.

Ngũgĩ by now treats with unceasing irony the Christian religion as practised in Kenya. At school Ngũgĩ absorbed a strong feeling for Christianity, though no doubt he was like Njoroge in constantly associating it with traditional religion. The early works draw a sharp division between the practitioners of Christianity, like Jacobo and Livingstone, and the Christian principles and concepts so acceptable to Muthoni and Waiyaki once these concepts are 'washed' and interrelated with tribal piety. Indeed in *Petals of Blood* no single direct word of criticism is expressed against Christianity, or even against Rev. Jerrod or Waweru — the two representative Christian characters; but these two are among the most hateful characters in the novel. The episode just referred to of Munira's meeting with his father is characteristic of Ngũgĩ's ironic treatment of this theme. The inherent anomalies in evangelism are epitomized in Lillian, the prostitute-turned-hot-gospeller, and in the transformation of Munira, the conscientious teacher, into her fervent convert: they embody the irrational force by which Chui, Mzigo and Kimeria are wiped out. Ngũgĩ accepts the often-observed linkage between missionary Christianity, colonialism and capitalism; but whereas he openly damns the latter two, he is satisfied with an ironic demolition of the exponents of Christianity, an attitude so constant as to become the second theme of the novel. On the first page we are caught up in a biblical aura since Munira 'had just returned from a night's vigil on the mountain' and the Bible is mentioned four times. When asked why he is carrying his Bible to the police station, Munira replies, ' "We must always be ready to plant the seed in these last days before His second coming. All the signs — strife, killing, wars, blood — are prophesied here" ' (2). Munira is serious: the biblical quotations are correct; every reverent capital letter is in place. It is the tone and context alone that remind us of Ngũgĩ's antagonism to (at best) the irrelevance and (at worst) the hypocrisy of alienated Christians.

The other important aspect of Ngũgĩ's bitter satire against social injustice which we are now to consider is his symbolism and consistent imagery. We have observed Ilmorog and Nairobi as settings representative of the countryside and the city. The contrast between old and new Ilmorog embodies the collapse of social morality. In the city human values have long been eroded. The novel seeks to stir up righteous indignation in the reader against the course Kenyan society is pursuing. It is the injection of the degraded standards of the city into Ilmorog which marks its falling apart in human terms. Rampant materialism, the commercialization of alcohol, the high priority given to tourist demands, the abjectness of the shanty town and the central role of Wanja's brothel characterize this new paradise for vested interests, culminating in the emergence of a class system, divided between the privileged and the unprivileged.

The new trans-Africa road splits old Ilmorog apart as, by implication, it splits Africa, letting in the alien predators who transform the land according to their own preconceived image. The road is seen to evoke fear and consternation. It is first associated with the aeroplane which appears as a shadow over Ilmorog, throws Munira's school into chaos, frightens the donkey (a foreshadowing of its fate), and alarms the whole village: 'What did it want?' (33). Premonition and fear deepen when strange men 'in khaki clothes' tow a clangorous chain across the fields and plant red sticks. The people argue that their telescope 'could see from where they were to the end of the world' (34). Munira ruminates:

An International Highway through Ilmorog. I suddenly wanted to laugh at the preposterous idea. Why, I asked myself, had they not built smaller serviceable roads before thinking of international highways? (48)

The aeroplane returns carrying more surveyors and engineers and on one trip manoeuvres alarmingly over Ilmorog before crashlanding, narrowly missing Karega, Wanja and Abdulla, and killing the donkey. Sightseeing at the scene of the crash proves popular for the surrounding inhabitants and so Wanja and Abdulla set up their bar and restaurant to serve the crowds: thus the plane is connected in several ways with the turning point in Ilmorog's history. Karega leaves Ilmorog soon after the accident, and when he returns five years later it is unrecognizable.

On this issue the voice of the novel also speaks out directly without equivocation:

And so the road was built, not to give content and reality to the vision of a continent, but to show our readiness and faith in the practical recommendations of a realist from abroad. The master, wily architect of a myriad divisions, jealous God against the unity of a continent, now clapped his hands and nodded his head and willingly loaned out the money to pay for imported expertise and equipment. And so, abstracted from the vision of oneness, of a collective struggle of the African peoples, the road brought only the unity of earth's surface: every corner of the continent was now within easy reach of international capitalist robbery and exploitation. (262)

The people of Ilmorog watch from the roadside cars 'whining and horning their way across the seven cities of Central Africa in an oil-company sponsored race' (262–3), disturbed by the ravages of the new order: 'before the road . . . did we live in the New Jerusalem?' Frontal attack may be displaced by subtle irony: 'little boys and girls prance about the banks, trying to spell out LONRHO, SHELL, ESSO, TOTAL, AGIP beside the word DANGER on the sidebelly of the tankers' (263).

This mysterious tarmac road reminds us of its counterpart in *Weep Not, Child*, with no known beginning or ending: an image of undirected turmoil.[2] The anonymous voice pines for the peace and purposefulness of the old Ilmorog 'before the aeroplane crashed into our lives' (266). When Wanja is asked towards the end of the novel why she clings to the old hut when all else is gone, she replies: ' "I don't want to forget the Old Ilmorog. I never shall forget how we lived before the Trans-Africa Road cleaved Ilmorog into two halves" ' (323). It is the symbols that assert the dominant atmosphere of anxiety reaching into despair across large stretches of the book quite as much as the incidents or the plot.

Not all the symbolism in the novel is successful. An instance of relative failure is to be found in one of Nyakinyua's instalments of her husband's history (224–5). A great light which is spat out by a strange animal seen by Wanja's grandfather during the war seems to embody a kind of prophecy about a future African armed uprising against the European oppressors. But the reader is uncertain of the true significance of this image and so the outcome is confusion rather than revelation.

We may indeed consider some sort of balance sheet regarding what is lost in terms of style and what is gained between *A Grain of Wheat* and *Petals of Blood*. The closeknit texture of the earlier novel, in which the intensity of the imagery and the complexity of the structure constantly relate to the main figures and holds us in tension from beginning to end, slackens in its successor. This greater intensity in *A Grain of Wheat* partly arises from the characterization. We are less gripped by the later group of characters as individuals for all the fullness of the portraits in certain respects. Some readers feel on first reading *Petals of Blood* that in order to stir our consciences and even to reach the ears of stubborn civil authority, Ngũgĩ has relaxed his hold on individual private worlds and psyches. The essentially public nature of the themes, the fact that what in many works would be a background is here the foreground, leads to a certain restriction in literary range and depth.

Ngũgĩ is no longer satisfied to leave his message deeply entwined in the fabric of the story and characterization. He wishes to be more explicit than this, to spell out his major points so that they stand clear from the narrative didactically, unmistakably. In doing so he leaves us to debate whether he has thereby strengthened or weakened his proposals. For instance, he lectures us somewhat sententiously on history and the positive mythology of Kenya's 'great past' (67–8, 120–3). In propounding this theme to his schoolchildren (and to us) Munira makes them sing. 'They sang it, but it seemed too abstract' (109) and we echo this reaction. Questions of national politics, so frequently dramatized throughout, are on occasions also expounded directly by the author, as on page 78. Karega's education in social history deliberately aims at educating us as well (198 ff). And when the pamphlets issued secretly to trades union members are summarized, the novel itself momentarily takes on the manner of a pamphlet (304). Perhaps the most heavy-handed sequence in *Petals of Blood* is that which occupies much of the latter half of Part Two, starting with the disquisition from the Lawyer and continuing into Karega's discursive description of incidents in Siriana, objectively recounted and even including a long and difficult quotation from Shakespeare. No doubt Ngũgĩ had the worthy intention of enlightening average Kenyans. In such passages he may rather deflect their attention from the more dynamic communication of the same themes elsewhere.

Furthermore there are occasions, which surprise us in a novel by Ngũgĩ, when the author attempts to force emotions out of an episode which it will not yield. We may miss the emotional impact which the author seems to have been determined to evoke, and this can be specially true where we are led into mystic intimations about the significance of human life. Nyakinyua's evocation of her dead husband's experiences is again a case in point:

> And your man? somebody asked.
>
> He came back. He came back all right, but not the same man with whom I had earlier coiled together thighs and bodies made smooth by mbariki oil and sweat.
>
> She was again silent. She stirred the Theng'eta pot once then let her hand just touch the stirring stick. She was not with them now, she had, just as when she had told them the story in the plains, descended into a private gloom of memories and uncertainties. She remained thus, hand on the stirring stick, head inclined to one side, eyes on the floor, answering none of the questions on their silent faces. (214)

Ngũgĩ seems to overrate the mystic effect on his readers here. Coiling thighs and bodies, and war experiences, are nothing new to us, and, as stock topics, will raise our feelings only if more sensitively touched upon. The sense that material is being strained too far destroys any artistic effect.

These elements create an unduly mundane atmosphere at times. And this is sometimes heightened by dullness of diction. Words and phrases which are bare of imaginative force sometimes strike us as unlike the Ngũgĩ we have known: this is particularly so in earnest passages of retrospective narrative or historical background. Speaking of the distant past of Ilmorog, the author tells us of villagers who worked hard to bring forth 'every type of crop' (120) to feed the people (part of the passage is quoted on page 88 above). The effect is flat: the writer is doing his duty but the wheels are not catching fire. Such phrases as 'with occasional visits', 'according to ages', 'with a huge population', 'hymning praises to their founders' are desiccated in their context. 'Sturdy peasants', 'days of glory', 'the sons and daughters of men', 'fervently' (and so on) are hackneyed.

However, gains in style are to be set against these losses. Let us first consider some details. One skill that has developed further since *A Grain of Wheat* is the use of dialogue for a retrospective account so as to create the illusion that the event is taking place here and now — a crucial technique in a work which constantly alludes to past time. When Karega returns to Ilmorog, he and Munira meet Wanja at the brothel; the parting appears to be a final separation. Two years later Wanja sends to ask Karega to meet her at her old hut (306). But nothing is detailed about this meeting till Munira, Abdulla and Karega are interrogated; so we are in a state of impatient expectancy. But although the moment is now so specifically in the past, when Wanja re-creates it in her evidence in the actual words of the conversation, it is the 'now' of the meeting of which we are aware rather than of Wanja speaking to the police.

On the other hand when it suits his purpose Ngũgĩ will neatly condense a time sequence. For instance on page 294 we hear Karega proclaiming his faith in 'another world, a new earth'. On the next page, without any jarring break in continuity, Munira is quoting this episode and developing our knowledge of it in his police statement. Taking this constant process a step further, the author actually fuses in the narration two quite separate times so that, far from there being an awkwardly abrupt transition, the instant juxtaposition helps us share the characters' identification of two different experiences: as when Abdulla tells the story of the raid in which Ole Masai was killed and he himself lamed to the band of Ilmorog folk as they trek to the city:

> There was pandemonium everywhere . . . people were shouting . . . catch . . . catch . . . and for a second Abdulla had the illusion of a double vision.
>
> For indeed, around him, the children were shouting catch, catch, meat, meat . . . then he too saw what they had seen. The procession had surprised a herd of antelopes which were now leap-leaping across the plains. (138)

The complex skills in manoeuvring time patterns so apparent in *A Grain of Wheat* have grown still more sophisticated.

The anonymous voice in *Petals of Blood* is not altogether unfamiliar either, though its use is more frequent and more significant. It is neither the voice of any of the main characters nor of the omniscient author, who is a different presence in the novel. This technique must be distinguished from the quite long stretches in which Ngũgĩ delays before revealing to us the name of the narrator. This extra presence is never named, but identifies itself as a member of the community by the use of the first person 'we'. The effect is at once of an individual and also of the collective voice of the whole Ilmorog fellowship. Munira 'became one of us', it tells us very early in the text (10). This presence is selectively deployed to convey a group sensitivity to certain intimate events taking place in the village: 'we were soon intrigued, fascinated, moved by the entwinement and flowering of youthful love and life and we whispered: see the wonder-gift of God' (242–3). Africa is 'our continent' (262). The communal perspective adds an important dimension to the story, relating private relationships to group responses. Movements of the many-faceted story are separated by this means, and bridges are provided for reflecting on happenings in the past and conjecturing on those to come. The rhythm of time-shifts is often thus harmonized and the complex structure more clearly articulated.

The reiteration of issues till they grow into recurrent motifs also imposes pattern on the otherwise potentially fragmented presentation. The motifs become part of the novel's symbolism. This is true of the strikes and expulsions at Siriana. Again, the male protagonists constantly question what can have transpired after Wanja's schoolgirl pregnancy, till the long-awaited truth at last emerges, its significance emphasized. A striking instance is the reappearance of the 'petals of blood' with their strange potency until they are metamorphosed into the devouring tongues of fire which at length destroy three leading social parasites.

The structural deployment of songs, as well as dreams, helps to remind us of the relationship in time of composition between *Petals of Blood* and *The Trial of Dedan Kimathi.*

The structuring and patterning of *Petals of Blood* also progress from the striking achievements of *A Grain of Wheat.* The subtle arrangement of time sequences, the deliberate overlappings, juxtapositions and repetitions assert symmetry of form, which expresses the overall significance of each segment in relation to the whole. The division into four parts helps to emphasize the more straightforward progression which underlies the movements to and fro. Part One pictures old Ilmorog up to the great drought and proposals for the journey to the city. Part Two comprises that journey and its immediate outcome. An interim period of relative peace occupies Part Three. Rain and good harvests return, and relief begins to arrive following the journey, so that there is a final rekindling of the earlier life of Ilmorog, and in this environment the romance between Karega and Wanja springs to life, eventually however leading to the rift with Munira and setting Karega off once more on his wanderings. In Part Four the forces that have been gathering join to annihilate old Ilmorog and to allow the financiers to create the new Ilmorog to suit themselves. But three of the key exploiters who have created this situation are wiped out and a tentative vision of hope for a different future is fostered even though the prospect for the years immediately ahead is extremely bleak.

The superstructure of the novel rests on four pillars: the depiction of the present (with the four principals at the police station); time past (in gradations of remoteness and immediacy); the two unnamed narrators (the omniscient narrator and the anonymous voice); and the cyclic patterning with its reiterations creating running motifs, and its distinctive rhythm.

The character with whom we spend most time in the present of the novel is Munira. Indeed his statement to the police, which recollects the variegated history of Ilmorog over the previous twelve years, conveys the bulk of the story to us. His physical presence and living voice bring the reader back time and again to the period of police investigation. He is the compass who directs us through other passages of the text. His personality is thus related to the structure, texture, atmosphere and tempo of the novel from beginning to end.

We listen to voices of other protagonists, including Nyakinyua. And Munira's account is further interspersed with more impersonal accounts of far history. We begin and end with people living, breathing and talking *now*, as in *A Grain of Wheat*, and from here we take long strides into the past to unravel the mystery that confronts us at the beginning. But the climax of the novel is dependent on our full knowledge at the last of the tangled events that have led up to the present. The complex time-scheme coalesces into a denouement. All four of the principal protagonists assist in monitoring this scheme, but pivotal among them is the enigmatic figure of Munira.

The contradictions inherent in Munira's personality are thus central to the themes as well as the story of *Petals of Blood* and so we must consider him now in this context. He rejects the norms and comforts of his family's conformist bourgeois existence. At school he is an active rebel against 'the system'. He virtually disowns his psychopathic wife. At length he deliberately makes his way to the harsh terrain of Ilmorog to set up a school for the underprivileged. In such a summary he sounds like a very positive character. Yet as a reformer he is a strangely muted figure. He makes a mark but only a faint one compared to Karega. Under the strain of jealousy and anger his principles fail him and he has Karega dismissed. And faced by the dissolution of his little world as New Ilmorog replaces the old, he too falls apart, drifts helplessly, and at last becomes a psychopathic disciple of an eccentric Christian sect. Yet it is he who ends by annihilating at one savage stroke three influential exploiters of society against whose operations Karega has been steadily mobilizing all the forces at his command.

The contradictions are rooted in Munira's character. He is not a decisive man: his most important and radical decisions are made hesitatingly. In this he reminds us of Mugo in *A Grain of Wheat*. Each stumbles along, unsure of himself, unable to print his personality decisively on the projects he undertakes, wavering in his beliefs and his goals. We have already quoted the passage in which Munira identifies himself with the twilight. But, like Mugo, he too blames himself for his lack of dynamism:

> Yet he felt guilty about being propelled by a whirlwind he had neither willed nor could now control. This consciousness of guilt, of having done a wrong, had always shadowed him in life.
>
> Munira was a refugee from a home where certain things were never mentioned. His own family life was built and he supposed now broken on the altar of Presbyterian Christian propriety and good manners. (71)

This trait in his character determines his first contact with Wanja — ironically, since this will lead to his confusion and decline. His diffidence blurs his awareness of Wanja's triumphant womanhood, and his indecision holds him back from committing himself to her. He seems to wait for her to take the initiative. And so she is caught up with the forceful and intense Karega. We watch with pain and some irritation Munira's self-induced loss of the person he really needs. This loss releases a sinister strain in him. He abuses Wanja as a prostitute and has Karega packed off. Pining in the bars of new Ilmorog, he eventually despairs and rebounds upon Lillian, a bar-girl and dubious earlier acquaintance, who is herself close to a demented state of religious fanaticism. He becomes a determined evangelical witness. Ngũgĩ pictures Kimeria, Chui and Mzigo as fit prey for the irrational forces now bottled up within Munira. Truly revolutionary impulses are aimed at more permanently significant targets, as we shall shortly see. Ngũgĩ's choice of Munira as a pivot of the novel emphasizes its thematic complexity and the challenge with which it faces the reader. There are no easy solutions to social ills. Something more coherent and determined is needed than Munira's well-intentioned but undirected idealism. Those who are going to change society will need to know themselves and their purposes more clearly than this. But in the spin-off of tangential events a Munira may almost at random strike an unco-ordinated but telling blow against oppression.

Wanja too has her contradictions. She is an intelligent and highly sensitive prostitute. She possesses that positive forcefulness which characterizes the women whom Ngũgĩ presents for our admiration. As a girl thrown upon the sexual market by cynical exploitation, she is a victim of the collusion of social forces. But she is both humane and socially aware, and discovers her true self when she adopts a key role in the great march to the city. She is an unconquerable victim who will not be cowed by this insensate environment. She has all the positiveness that Munira lacks.

In following her career, we are able to enter the grey but lurid world of bars, brothels, sexual commerce and degradation which the novel deplores. In this world she plays constantly shifting roles so that we see into it from all sides. But Wanja retains her human dignity and integrity, her ability to love, to be loved, and to care intensely about others. She has no guilty conscience about the life she has been subjected to; guilt is thrown back in the teeth of those who are responsible for such conditions — to some degree all of us. If we strike moral attitudes we shall not come to understand Wanja. The most enigmatic aspect of her life is her exultant assertion of prostitution as a weapon for revenge in the new Ilmorog. She now has other options, but she prefers to set up her perfected brothel in Sunshine Lodge and to outface all those who have belittled and degraded her and her sisterhood. Her final rejection of all this allows her a future, beyond the end of the novel, to fulfil her essentially untrammelled womanhood. She goes through symbolic chastisement by fire and emerges fit to bear a child of love, and to be reunited with her mother. Yet here too there is a contradiction which underlines the evolving theme as does Munira's case. Her redemption and restoration are at the same time an opting out of what is perhaps her more important role (as the novel sees these things), that of social motivator. Her personal salvation is just as equivocal in its implications as Munira's inner spasms.

As we have said, Abdulla links a heroic past with a present in which he and his like are trampled down by a society indifferent to their sacrifices and to their needs. He is a good man, and he suffers from first to last because of his goodness. Finally we are left to assume that he has been chosen to father Wanja's much-longed-for baby. His courage and achievements are unsung but crucial. Yet he remains socially helpless. The responsibility for mobilizing the social energy and insight needed to counter the evils from which Abdulla suffers can be exercised only by those with Karega's deliberate self-training and self-discipline.

Wanja sidesteps her public destiny; Abdulla is powerless to fulfil his vision; Munira stumbles into an episode of unconsidered public involvement. It is Karega, for all his fragility, who takes on the role of spokesman and proponent of revolutionary change. Like Wanja and Abdulla, he is one of the commonality, a victim; like Munira — but more consistently — he follows his vision; like Abdulla — though more fortunate and more suitably endowed — he translates his convictions into coherent action. The Lawyer is the intellectual, the deeply involved theorist. It is Karega's versatile experience, his indefatigable searching for enduring truths, his resilient endurance, his largeness of mind, his courage and his optimism that identify him as Ngũgĩ's prototype for setting about the reforms that the novel shows to be so desperately needed. At the end of *Petals of Blood* he is behind barbed-wire:[3] there is no easy optimism, no naive simplification. But the work ends in hope rather than despair. It is this realization that we are finally to explore.

But before this last critical task, we must, in analysing a novel which handles time with such complexity, re-examine Ngũgĩ's attitude towards the past, and then we shall be in a position to look with him towards the future. His concept of the role played by the past in man's dealings in the present, which develops from his earliest days of authorship, is both a doctrine and a way of perceiving experience. We are concerned on the largest scale with the past of Africa, of a race; and also on a smaller scale with the past of a community and its individual members as a basis for assessing present-day society and its members. However, whereas in previous writings Ngũgĩ has seen in the African past a standard of moral excellence, of social justice and communal pride, of political sovereignty against which the present must be measured, in *Petals of Blood* he now calls that past in question. Late in the work Karega defines the conditions upon which the past is to be accepted:

'You used to argue that the past was important for today . . .'

'True . . . but only as a living lesson to the present. I mean we must not preserve our past as a museum: rather, we must study it critically, without illusions, and see what lessons we can draw from it in today's battlefield of the future and the present. But to worship it — no. Maybe I used to do it: but I don't want to continue worshipping in the temples of a past without tarmac roads, without electric cookers, a world dominated by slavery to nature.' (323)

Here Karega repudiates his faith in what he earlier called the idea 'Of a past. A great past. A past when Ilmorog, or all Africa, controlled its own earth' (125). He is no longer ready to assert that ' "To understand the present . . . you must understand the past. To know where you are, you must know where you came from" ' (127–8). It is highly significant that the final break between Karega and Wanja follows her account of the heroic death of her grandfather, as she heard it at Nyakinyua's deathbed, to which Karega replies: ' "That is the kind of lesson we can learn from our past . . . as a guide to action . . . but also learn from your grandfather's tendency to act alone —" ' (325–6). Here is a re-enactment of the futile, singlehanded action of Ngotho in *Weep Not, Child;* just as the relationship between Munira and Waweru recalls the relationship between Nyambura and Joshua. We are invited to reassess the characters from Ngũgĩ's early fiction — Ngotho, Njoroge, Joshua, Waiyaki, Mugo and so forth — and to reproach their falterings. Extenuating circumstances are not to mask relative failures in social effectiveness.

This radical rejection of the African past was anticipated when Karega, in ransacking the books sent to him by the lawyer for a vision of the future rooted in a critical awareness of the past, finds only a futile tour conducted by history professors who 'took him to pre-colonial times and made him wander purposelessly from Egypt, or Ethiopia, or Sudan' (199).

For a community or an individual, Ngũgĩ looks to the past to provide a meaningful continuum with the present and the future. As offspring of the past, the present and the future will be influenced by the good and the bad they have inherited. The past stores up rewards or retribution: nemesis. One must accept responsibility for the impact of one's past actions on the present. There is a certain historical inevitability in men's modes of life, and in their progressive action. Karega embodies this idea on the morning after his union with Wanja in ruminating that it has been possible for him to meet and inherit her because 'what has gone before has a logic and a rhythm inevitably leading him to that moment of candour in the flesh' (234).

Ngũgĩ harps frequently on the past as being imminent in the present, stirring the conscience or conjuring up forebodings. A distressed Wanja cries to Karega: ' "Sometimes there is no greatness in the past. Sometimes one would like to hide the past even from oneself . . . My past is full of evil. Today, now, when I look back, I only see the wasted years . . ." ' (128). The elaborate presentation of the principal characters serves to relate their past to their present. One person may earn a reward, another chastisement. One may be fit to help create, to move forward into a more just future, while others peter out into insignificance.

Beyond the pillorying of human wickedness and the tragedy of human debasement, the novel asserts a great hope that the mass of humanity will in time prevail over the malignity of the privileged few. This hope is envinced in a variety of ways in the novel: in the implicit message of the plot; in direct statements; in the exaltation of incidents in which individuals or groups overcome forces which are bearing down upon them and humiliating them; in affirmative symbols and images; and above all in the personal qualities of the protagonists and the ideals which they embody and uphold. Clearly for Ngũgĩ small successes by lowly members of society in their perpetual conflict with those who seek to overmaster them are of immense significance. He builds such incidents carefully into the text and celebrates them. There is no reason to doubt that he has been influenced by the socialist doctrine of the historical inevitability of the ultimate triumph of those who have traditionally been oppressed, and through it expresses an optimistic faith in a future egalitarian social order.

The outcome of the main storyline marks an early stage in the cleaning up of society. Three leading individuals who have thrived on the misery of the poor are destroyed in a symbolic fire oblation, which also burns away the centrepiece of degenerate new Ilmorog, the elegant brothel. Wanja herself is chastened for being its proprietress as a condition for her to set out upon a new dispensation. It is by careful manoeuvring of the action that a four-pronged attack is launched simultaneously on these adversaries of society: Wanja and Abdulla operate separately against Kimeria; while Karega by careful planning through the trade union, and Munira in his distracted religious state operate against the whole trio. The persistence of this attack reflects the hatred engendered by its targets. It is a crowning irony at one level that Karega, the main exponent of mass revolt, is anticipated by Munira in high action against the vested interests. But Ngũgĩ is no author to work to a simple, pat design. Chance and fate operate in a real-life situation very often before careful plans are fulfilled. Nemesis, in overtaking Kimeria, Chui and Mzigo, is as ready to employ a fevered hand as a deliberate one. There may well here be a conviction that there is an inbuilt balancing factor in human affairs which will fitfully propel them towards the overall good of man. If these wily operators can survive a strike, they cannot evade the verdict of time.

Indeed we witness a series of successes which hearten those who are struggling forward. Rarely are they allowed in the novel to descend into group despair or complacency. The journey to the city, whatever its intermediate disasters, is a triumph for the will of the group over the malevolence of man and nature. So, again with certain qualifications, are the strikes at Siriana, and even more the greater one at Ilmorog: a demonstration of the will of the majority to fight for a better life. The Lawyer says:

'Then came that strike in Siriana and, reading between the lines, I thought I saw a new youth emerging, a youth freed from the direct shame and humiliation of the past and hence not so spiritually wounded as those who had gone before. So different from our time; so different shall I say, from those who had seen their strong fathers and elder brothers fold a kofia behind them in the presence of a white boy. I said to myself: here is our hope . . . in the new children, who have nothing to prove to the white man . . . who do not find it necessary to prove that they can eat with knife and fork; that they can speak English through the nose; that they can serve the monster as efficiently as the white ministers; and therefore can see the collective humiliation clearly and hence are ready to strike out for the true kingdom of the black god within us all . . . the total energy, the spirit of the people, the collective we, working for us . . . sisi kwa sisi.' (167)

Such direct avowals abound; cumulatively they form the most distinct motif of the book. After his consummation with Wanja, Karega ponders on Africa's history of tribulation, but at length dwells exultantly on a long line of brave African leaders: Koitalel, Waiyaki, Nat Turner, Cinque, Kimathi, Cabral, Nkrumah, Nasser, Mondhlane, Mathenge (236–7). For Wanja in deep despair, Karega pictures a new, better horizon: ' "we must create another world, a new earth" ' (294). Karega pays tribute to the lawyer after his death as an embodiment of courage and selflessness characteristic of the protectors of the black race. He recalls how the lawyer would say, ' "So I can speak fearlessly for the poor and for land and property reforms — put a ceiling on what a person can accumulate . . . one man, one kiosk . . ." ' (301). Symbolically, the Lawyer's house is decorated with Third World images:

Che Guevara with his Christlike locks of hair and saintly eyes; of Dedan Kimathi, sitting calmly and arrogantly defiant; and a painting by Mugalula of a beggar in a street. At one corner was a wood sculpture of a freedom fighter by Wanjau. (161)

To Karega the Lawyer was:

Such a fine stock . . . with all his faults, he represented the finest and most courageous in a line of courageous and selfless individuals from among the propertied men and women of Kenya; from some of the feudal mbari lords at the turn of the century who, despite bribes of beads and calico and the lure of white-protected power, would not side with the hordes of colonial invaders but died fighting with the people, to others in the thirties and fifties who, despite education and property, refused to betray the people for a few favours from the British. (301)

The Lawyer's death makes Karega wonder how society can be altered to prevent the cream of the community from meeting untimely death at the hands of those who wield power for their own personal ends. In advocating mass action to defeat oppression, he declares Africa's past to be irrelevant to present needs: 'China was saved, not by singers and poets telling of great past cultures, but by the creative struggle of the workers for a better day today' (301). Karega bluntly states the goals of socialist revolution:

'I have told you, I know nothing about the arson . . .1 had nothing to do with it. I don't believe in the elimination of individuals. There are many Kimerias and Chuis in the country. They are the products of a system . . . It's the system that needs to be changed . . . and only the workers of Kenya and the peasants can do that.' (308)

When warned by Wanja that the KCO plan to kill him and destroy his organization, Karega declares:

'They are bound to fail . . . we, the workers, the poor peasants, ordinary people, the masses are now too awake to be deceived about tribal loyalties, regional assemblies, glorious pasts . . . when we are starving and we are jobless, or else living on miserable pay. Do you think we shall let foreign companies, banks, insurances . . . and the local rich with their Theng'eta companies, the new black landlords with their massive land-holdings and numerous houses — do you think people will let a combination of these two classes and their spokesmen in parliament, at universities, in schools, in churches and with all their armies and police to guard their interests — do you think that we shall let these owners of stolen property continue lording it over us for ever? No . . . it is too late . . . we shall no longer let others reap where they never planted, harvest where they never cultivated, take to their banks from where they never sweated . . . There are a million Karegas for every ten Kimerias. They can kill the lawyer or ten such lawyers. But the poor, the dispossessed, the working millions and the poor peasants are their own lawyers. With guns and swords and organisation, they can and will change the conditions of their oppression. They'll seize the wealth which rightly belongs to them . . . The workers and the peasant farmers of Kenya are awake.' (326–7)

The prophecy of social upheaval at the end of Achebe's *A Man of the People* is thematic throughout the whole structure of *Petals of Blood*. It makes the deaths of Kimeria, Chui, Mzigo almost irrelevant; they are merely apt prey for irrational forces of destruction. Wryly the three become even more ignominious in death than in life.

The romance between Karega and Wanja is a celebration of the happiness of the common people when fortune smiles on them. Joseph's success at school is a new birth for the underdog which gives a lasting joy and sense of fulfilment to Abdulla, and also to Wanja. The circumcision ceremony underlines communal continuity. The ceremonial Theng'eta drinking which follows also hymns the successful harvest and leads to the mystic tradition having a great impact through this moment of truth on all the protagonists' lives. There are also symbols affirmative of the positiveness, courage and strength of the poor when they are united. Ilmorog is, at its most expansive, an image of peace and harmony. Its heroic past is conjured up by Nyakinyua. It is the spirit of this Ilmorog that inspires all four main protagonists. Munira early in the novel recognizes the tenacious grip of Ilmorog on his sense:

Whatever it was it had driven him to Ilmorog, to me, to Abdulla, to Wanja, to this riddle: truth and beauty — what illusions! We are all searchers for a tiny place in God's corner to shelter us for a time from treacherous winds and rains and drought. (46)

Reflecting on the quiet dignity with which Abdulla bears his suffering, Wanja says to Karega, ' "perhaps we all carry maimed souls and we are all looking for a cure" ' (73). When Munira recaptures Wanja and Karega, so to speak, in a bar far from Ilmorog, he triumphantly hails them back, 'all going to seek a home in Ilmorog' (106). And even new Ilmorog, for all its corruption — perhaps because of it — is the workshop in which are soldered the progressive forces that are to hoist the land into a new era of social justice.

These various expressions, both rhetorical and literary, of the determination of the common people to persevere in their pursuit of a more upright society culminate in the carefully placed final scene, the exchange over the barbed-wire prison fence between Karega and the young woman, Akinyi. At this apparently unpropitious moment, Karega, the militant reformer, is in prison. And yet the talk and the thought is all of hope and of the future. Karega's efforts are not sterile but fruitful:

'The other workers . . . with a message. They are with you . . . and they are . . . *we* are planning another strike and a march through Ilmorog . . . The Movement of Ilmorog workers . . . not just the union of workers at the breweries. All workers in Ilmorog and the unemployed will join us. And the small farmers . . . and even some small traders . . .' (343)

This is not an isolated incident; it is part of a network of activity. Another important member of the elite has been assassinated, this time it seems not by a random fanatical stroke but as part of a concerted operation:

'According to Ruma Monga it's more than that. They left a note. They called themselves Wakombozi — or the society of one world liberation . . . and they say it's Stanley Mathenge returned from Ethiopia to complete the war he and Kimathi started . . . There are rumours about a return to the forests and the mountains . . .' (344)

These fervently inspired rumours are important not as fact but for the way the popular imagination is working. And so the novel can end, like *A Grain of Wheat,* on a determinedly confident note of hope for the future. Akinyi, speaking for all the oppressed poor of society, pledges support and solidarity, and again intense concern for the individual in a group context: ' "You'll come back," she suddenly said, looking up at him boldly' (344).

We shall in our last chapter discuss the controversial subject of the appropriateness and effectiveness of deploying literature as a tool in a social campaign. But for the moment we can dwell on the fact that the end of *Petals of Blood* affirms Ngũgĩ's bold and powerful attempt to combine the intimacy of the traditional novel with a public rhetorical manner in a new and perhaps itself artistically revolutionary amalgam in order to analyse social injustice and the human dilemmas it creates, and to mark out the practicable path to social change.

Notes

1. Page references refer to both the original edition of *Petals of Blood* (Heinemann Educational Books, London, 1977), and to subsequent reprints.
2. In *Detained* (Heinemann Educational Books, London, 1981) Ngũgĩ explains the name of his home village, Kamiriithu: 'The name is a diminutive form of Miriithu, meaning a flat place on which rests a pool of water defiant to drought' (72). He adds in a footnote: 'A trans-Africa highway has now been built through Kamiriithu and has for ever drained the defiant pool' (72).
3. Ngũgĩ remarks in *Detained,*

> Many critics have pointed out the parallels between my own arrest and detention and similar but fictional events in the opening and closing chapters of my novel *Petals of Blood*. It opens with the arrest of a progressive worker — he is deceived into believing that he is wanted at the police station for a few questions — and it closes with his eventual detention on suspicion of being a communist at heart. (128)

Devil on the Cross

Devil on the Cross was first drafted in Kamiti Maximum Security Prison on toilet paper. Ngũgĩ set himself the exacting task of completing the manuscript in Gikuyu by 25 December 1978, just under a year after he had been detained without trial. On Friday 22 September when the draft had reached an advanced stage, it was confiscated in a prison search, all but two chapters hidden in a prison Bible. 'The next three weeks,' Ngũgĩ records

> were the worst of my stay in Kamiti. It was as if I had been drained of all blood. Nevertheless I made a new resolution: no matter what happened I would start all over again. I would reconstruct the novel in between the printed lines of a Chekhov, or a Gorky, or a Mann, or of the Bible (I would even ask the chaplain for three or four bibles of different sizes as evidence of a new-found devotion!), or of any book in my possession. It would not be the same novel, but I would not accept defeat.[1]

However, no reconstruction of this nature was in the event needed since, incredibly, the senior superintendent in charge of Kamiti returned the pile of hand-written papers three weeks later with terse words of reprieve: ' "I see nothing wrong with it . . . You write in very difficult Gikuyu!" '[2] Ngũgĩ tells us that by his day of release, 12 December 1978, he was 'on the last chapter'.[3]

The imprisoned author had dared to cast his mind forward over what might be a terrifyingly long incarceration, and had tried to stiffen his resistance to the psychological assault of detention by making courageous long-term plans: a year to write his novel in Gikuyu, a second to translate it into Kiswahili and another to make an English version.[4] With different but complex pressures upon him following his release, he maintained this programme. The original Gikuyu version was actually published in Nairobi in early 1980. Ngũgĩ handed over the manuscript of his own English translation to the publishers in London in January 1981.

The prison diary also tells us much of the author's conscious planning of the novel in principle, of the mood that pervaded him while he was writing it, and of the actual occasion which determined its precise design. The revolutionary determination to write a challenging novel in an indigenous Kenyan language, which would immediately reach the commonality of his people, is inherent in Ngũgĩ's initial conception:

Free thoughts on toilet-paper! I had deliberately given myself a difficult task. I had resolved to use a language which did not have a modern novel, a challenge to myself, and a way of affirming my faith in the possibilities of the languages of all the different Kenyan nationalities, languages whose development as vehicles for the Kenyan people's anti-imperialist struggles had been actively suppressed by the British colonial regime . . . and by the neo-colonial regime of Kenyatta and his comprador KANU cohorts. I had also resolved not to make any concessions to the language. I would not avoid any subject — science, technology, philosophy, religion, music, political economy — provided it logically arose out of the development of theme, character, plot, story, and world view. Further I would use any and everything I had ever learnt about the craft of fiction — allegory, parable, satire, narrative, description, reminiscence, flashback, interior monologue, stream of consciousness, dialogue, drama — provided it came naturally in the development of character, theme and story. But content — not language and technique — would determine the eventual form of the novel. And the content? The Kenyan people's struggles against the neo-colonial form and stage of imperialism![5]

Ngũgĩ's reconstruction of his riposte to the prison chaplain during their first meeting tells us much of his inner frame of mind at this time:

'Hold it!' I cried out. 'Who needs your prayers, your Bibles, your leaves of holiness — all manufactured and packaged in America? Why do you always preach humility and acceptance of sins to the victims of oppression? Why is it that you never preach to the oppressor? Go. Take your Bibles, your prayers, your leaves of holiness to them that have chained us in this dungeon. Have you read *Ngaahika Ndeenda*? Did you ever go to see the play? What was wrong with it? Tell me! What was wrong with Kamiriithu peasants and workers wanting to change their lives through their own collective efforts instead of always being made passive recipients of Harambee charity meant to buy peace and sleep for uneasy heads? Tell me truthfully: what drove you people to suppress the collective effort of a whole village? What has your borrowed Christianity to say to oppression and exploitation of ordinary people?'[6]

The choice that faces Wariinga and Gatuiria in the novel Ngũgĩ posed to himself in prison as he reviewed Kenya's history of revolutionary patriots, of renegades, of neo-colonial sell-outs:

Yes, No. Ndio, La. Two of the tiniest words in any language. But yes or no, one had to choose between them. To say 'Yes' or 'No' to unfairness, to injustice, to wrong-doing, to oppression, to treacherous betrayal, to the culture of fear, to the aesthetic of submissive acquiescence, one was choosing a particular world and a particular future . . . But writing aside, I knew, in my heart of hearts, that my sanity depended on my being able to continually say 'No' to any and every manifestation of oppressive injustice and to any and every infringement of my human and democratic rights, a 'No' that included detention itself. I would seize any and every occasion to denounce detention without trial. Yes or No . . . two great words in their own way but the greatest of them was No when spoken in sound or silence or action against oppression.[7]

Ngũgĩ grappled with his theme in an attempt to find an appropriate form in which to express it. This was at length suggested to him by a news item found in part on a scrap of newspaper accidentally thrown into a rubbish-bin by a warder, and then wheedled in greater detail from prison guards:

'Magendo [black-marketeering] in ivory, gem-stones, game-skins, coffee, maize, rice, sugar, *unga,* tea has been a way of life among the ruling circles in Kenya . . . Why then pick on these two law-breakers? Or were they only two sacrificial lambs to propitiate an angry populace and buy time for a rotting, falling-apart system? Capitalism itself is a system of unabashed theft and robbery. Thus theft, robbery, corruption can never be wrong under capitalism because they are inherent in it. Well, they are the structure. Without a systematic robbery of peasants and workers, a robbery protected and sanctified by laws, law courts, parliament, religion, armed forces, police, prisons, education, there is no capitalism. It is worse, the robbery, when a country is under the higher capitalism of foreigners which is imperialism . . . Two M.P.s put in the cooler for small offences while the fat cats continue unabated.'
And suddenly I discover the hitherto elusive theme of my prison novel. I grow literary wings. I am ready to fly. All because of a piece of newspaper little larger than a square inch retrieved from a rubbish-bin.[8]

Devil on the Cross is, on the one hand, both thematically and stylistically a logical development from Ngũgĩ's earlier fiction. His socio-political stand is now confident: it crystallizes the viewpoints towards which he was finding his way in the first three novels and which he embodied in a somewhat more complex and enigmatic manner in *Petals of Blood*. On the other hand, *Devil on the Cross* is a startling new departure, a work which no faithful reader of Ngũgĩ up to the time of his imprisonment without trial could reasonably have predicted.

In some respects the new-found certainty as to where he stands enables Ngũgĩ to simplify his writing and present his ideas in bolder strokes. This helps him to fulfil his intense desire to reach a less exclusive readership — a desire epitomized by the fact that at long last he has composed a novel initially in his own first language, with the intention of translating it first into the national lingua franca — Kiswahili — and then as third priority into an international language — English. This sequence expresses Ngũgĩ's determination to speak to the masses of the Kenyan nation, awaken them to a serious appraisal of their predicament, and propel them into combined action to right the situation. Ngũgĩ still values literary art as a purposeful instrument, but there has been a shift in emphasis away from subtle suggestion and implication, to new kinds of structural control — of which he has long been a master. In a later chapter we shall note the clearly patterned ritual performances in *I Will Marry When I Want*. The bold shifts between juxtaposed movements in *Devil on the Cross* have a stylized purpose analagous with ritual. Throughout, the purposes behind literary creation exercise a new level of control.

The characters are now in the main less wayward, more predictable than formerly, and so the characterization is less complex. The chronological sequence is less involved. When we move back in time, it is to catch up on the past life of one of the characters in the familiar form of a flashback or 'reminiscence' rather than in the metaphysical counterpointing and paralleling of different periods of time adopted in both *A Grain of Wheat* and *Petals of Blood*. Yet it would be naive to suggest that this is a simpler composition than its predecessors. Ngũgĩ has here brought off one of the most difficult technical ventures that any fictional writer can embark upon: the fusion of at least two distinct modes of writing.

Ngũgĩ's deep-seated irony, which we have noted all along, now blossoms into a full-scale set-piece of ironic satire. It recalls Swift's exposure in *Gulliver's Travels* of the social injustices and calculated corruptions in his own society. The savageness of the attack brings *A Modest Proposal* to mind. As sustained ironic fiction it also provokes comparison with Fielding's *The Life of Mr Jonathan Wild the Great*. The epic competition for precedence among the rogues more specifically recalls Pope's *Dunciad*. When inevitably one sees a connection with *Animal Farm*, one returns to the realization of parallels much nearer home in the African fable tradition. In referring to the intermingling in *Devil on the Cross* of 'at least two' literary modes, we had in mind these further relationships with oral tradition — not only with the fable itself in the use of song and satire, but also with public debate.

The reader imbued with traditional literary critical assumptions is at once challenged in 'placing' this book according to familiar criteria. Can time-honoured critical canons be applied here? What in particular makes this work dissimilar in the main from others already cited is the impertinent proclamation by many of the leading characters of their own criminality, combined with the enormity of the universal embezzlement which they proudly insist on having engineered. In most previous ironic indictments, either a third person or an omnipotent author is describing the deeds of others, or the characters operate on the ironic presumption that their activities or proposals are lawful and benign. In *Devil on the Cross,* on the other hand, the reader is asked to believe in a satiric world in which loud-mouthed villains assert their own villainy, a villainy which is exultantly sabotaging the well-being of a whole nation. This now allows their impoverished and down-trodden victims to jeer for once at their tormentors, and even pity them for the moral self-destruction which they so eagerly embrace.

Thus Ngũgĩ is breaking away from many literary norms. He does so for more than one purpose. Clearly his use of Gikuyu has released previously untapped aspects of his creative talent which may very well have been stirred by the ways the language has been traditionally deployed. The self-denunciation we have been discussing springs from a language which is used with great directness: the self-abandon with which characters express themselves persuasively represents their inner nature. The currency of obscene reference is moulded into an exposure of the depth of their depravity and worthlessness — for instance in the constant reference to the defiling of the mother figure. The use of proverbs is only one way in which advantage is taken of indigenous turns of phrase.

Devil on the Cross has closer analogies with certain African works than with its distant European forebears. Gabriel Okara's *The Voice* and Camara

Laye's *The Radiance of the King* also combine out-and-out ironic satire of the exploiters with a realistic, more life-like story of some of their victims. To dovetail these two modes is a literary *tour-de-force*.

This integration of two styles in *Devil on the Cross* has demanded that the heroic figures in the more realistic parts of the story shall be much closer to stereotypes than the protagonists of Ngũgĩ's earlier novels. This tendency has been encouraged by the author's wish to present clearcut contrasts between social classes, each of which is typified by certain characters in the novel. The integration of modes requires some relative simplifications within the parts. But this will not obscure from us the sophistication implicit in such a marriage of techniques. Ngũgĩ's determination to communicate more generally has led him not towards technical crudity but to a new and more appropriate kind of technical brilliance. The initial evidence suggests that Ngũgĩ has succeeded in his democratic aim. *Caitaani Mutharaba-ini* (the novel's original Gikuyu title) went into a second printing within weeks of its first appearance in Nairobi bookshops by sheer force of popular demand.

The blending of formalized realism and extreme ironic satire is more than a technical triumph. It expresses something of the temper and frustration of contemporary radical thinkers in the Third World as typified by Kenya. The scene in the Cave mirrors the brazen confidence now being expressed by comprador capitalist society in parts of Africa. So sure of themselves are the moneyed elite that they feel little need to conceal their real methods or motives. While the competition to crown Kenya's leading extortioner is satirically exaggerated, the assertive cocksure tone that emanates from the body of the meeting will be menacingly familiar to many readers. This unqualified satire gives the victims of neo-colonialism a rare opportunity of seeing their tormentors reduced to comic caricatures by being made to boast in public of their conscienceless excesses. For once the depth of horror and alarm that this situation evokes is adequately expressed. Those who feel themselves paralysed by the triumphant confidence trick being practised upon them can for a breathing space relax their muscles in defiant revolt. They can, as they read the novel, feel a sense of community with others who are seething like themselves. And they can feel a new upsurge of hope in the possibility of joint action.

The competition forms the centrepiece of this unusual novel, occupying, together with ancillary happenings, about half its pages. It is hard to maintain such a lengthy static scene without either monotony or the sacrifice of relevance and intensity. But Ngũgĩ handles his project with verve and skill. He has made use of almost all the techniques he lists in the passage quoted above from the prison diary.

The book opens at a crux in the realistic story as society crowds in on Wariinga, the city typist. Then it shifts to the journey in a mini-bus taxi (or 'matatu') from Nairobi to Ilmorog during which the driver and five passengers discuss the social issues which form the central themes of the work, relating them to their own experiences in life, and differing in their reactions and moral assumptions. These long realistic passages, involving already both dramatic narrative and debate, are punctuated by flashes of satirical absurdity as the various invitation cards to the Devil's Feast in Ilmorog are scrutinized. These amaze and bewilder the characters themselves, but from the start Ngũgĩ succeeds in containing these extravagances within a single credible fictional world.

In handling the shifts of mode which characterize this novel, a writer needs deftness and courage. Ngũgĩ's bold transitions eliminate dull repetitions and mechanical explanations of how we get from one point to the next. After we have been informed of the intentions of the travellers in the matatu to attend the bizarre gathering in Ilmorog, the scene in the mini-bus simply melts into the voice of the meeting's Master of Ceremonies — though at first we do not know who is speaking — as he propounds for the first time what will become a linking motif.

This motif is the capitalist interpretation of the parable of the talents. Those who receive and multiply the ten and five talents respectively are seen as the comprador managers and middlemen conducting business on the spot for their distant, alien master, who returns only to reap where he has not sown and to praise his intermediaries, who will obviously receive their 'cut'. The small man with his one talent, who correctly analyses the cunning materialism of his foreign overlord, refuses to play along, and buries his tiny capital in the ground to keep it intact and return it, is denounced as a lazy and treacherous good-for-nothing and dismissed. This is a keynote address which launches the public rivalry in local exploitation, monitored by giant foreign vested interests — the multinationals. We at once recognize, for all the unexpected content, the familiar bland tones of international intercourse:

> 'And now, before I sit down, I shall call upon the leader of the foreign delegation from the International Organization of Thieves and Robbers (IOTR), whose headquarters are in New York, USA, to talk to you. I think you all know that we have already applied to become *full members* of IOTR. The visit of this delegation, plus the gifts and the crown they have brought us, marks the beginning of an even more fruitful period of co-operation.' (87)[9]

Satiric methods are very varied. They range from visual symbolism in the dress of the seven representatives of neo-colonial powers, each wearing suits made out of the paper money of their respective homelands, to the frank divulgence by the contestants of the methods and motives with which they manipulate the Kenyan economy. These boastful confessions analyse the actual processes by which money-magnates milk the national resources, above all the blood and sweat of the workers and peasants. Specific areas of extortion are singled out. Big-bellied Gitutu wa Gataanguru, trailing his despoiled sugar-girls, battens on the land. Expropriation of the land is the key to the whole colonial and neo-colonial outrage in Kenya and so this topic naturally takes pride of place. Gitutu proudly relates how he has taken over vast estates from white settlers, sub-divided them into derisory plots and sold them at exorbitant prices to citizens. A woman might occasionally be bribed — as the Rich Old Man offers to bribe Wariinga in the last throes of the drama — with absentee ownership of a ranch or plantation which should be the heritage of ranks of honest workers. Gitutu does not mince matters:

> 'The land wasn't mine, and the money with which I'd paid for it wasn't mine, and I hadn't added anything to the land — where did I get the 200,000 shillings?

From the pockets of the people. Yes, because the land really belonged to the people, and the money with which I bought it came from the people!' (106)

Ngũgĩ does not now wish simply to repeat time and again the pattern established with Gitutu for each of the areas of Kenyan life he wishes to satirize. Before Gitutu we have seen the chicken-thief, Ndaaya wa Kahuria, chased off the stage for confusing his own petty thieving with great feats of exploitation achieved by the rich and the powerful. Now following Gitutu, the lanky adulterer Kihaahu wa Gatheeca is allowed to expound three key areas in which social welfare is transformed into big business: education, local government and housing. In education he has discovered that fraudulent schools with illusory standards cannot attract wealthy parents if their false prospectuses are based on an indigenous syllabus. Only the glittering façade of a fully westernized programme can trick the status-seekers.

It is by rigging the local elections and bribing his way into office against equally ruthless opposition that Gitutu reaches the rich goal of chairmanship of the local housing committee. Now he can pocket the fabulous percentages offered by foreign speculators in exchange for building contracts, and then corruptly allocate the jerry-built maisonettes that result to line his pockets even more richly. The community endures debased local administration while publicly subsidized housing is hawked on the black market.

Among these savagely comic rhetorical self-exposures, Ngũgĩ injects more active, though still highly relevant, conflicts among the thieves. While rules for the competition are being agreed upon, a ludicrous but pointed confrontation flares up between the pot-bellied and the cadaverous extortioners about which group truly embodies dedicated racketeering. At length the meeting is led to accept examples of gross self-indulgence and lean, obsessive relentlessness as twin aspects of unscrupulous commercialism. Again after Kihaahu's uninterrupted testimony there is a storm of protest about the way he has been battening on his own class, on the grounds that the elite should hang together and exploit only the unmoneyed, whether as adulterers, as false educators, as business tycoons or merely as hurlers of abuse. The angry exchanges mount to the verge of a gun duel before the session is hastily disbanded for lunch.

Of the three speakers after lunch, the second, Nditika wa Nguunji, adds one more area of exploitation to those already enumerated — *magendo,* a generic term from Swahili for the whole practice of smuggling, black marketeering, of cornering goods and forcing up prices of essential commodities. This vogue in East Africa sparked off the concept of *Devil on the Cross* through the scrap of newsprint that infiltrated Kamiti Maximum Security Prison.

Before Nditika, Mwireri wa Mukirai, whom we first met overnight in the matatu, creates an eddy in the general current by demanding that exploitation be made exclusively indigenous, cut free from foreigners who take the richest pickings. In the process he reveals how multinationals force local enterprise out of the market by underselling — whether in cooking oil, skin lighteners or contraceptives. Seen as a militant nationalist, Mwireri is later murdered for questioning the neo-colonial basis of exploitation. Ironies are interlocking.[10]

There is yet another dimension to the satiric scenario. Each speaker outlines, as his claim to the crown of social crime, a brand new scheme for exploitation. In these proposals Ngũgĩ outbids Swift in horrific burlesque. As in all great satire, these ludicrous extremes enable us to contemplate, grasp and oppose a level of human viciousness which might otherwise be safe from survey because of the repugnance an audience or readership would feel. Such grotesque mockery is in a relatively low key when Kihaahu describes the plastic puppets of white children he deploys to supplement decrepit white headmistresses in enticing parents to send their children to his schools. It is in the contestants' new proposals that the satire reaches its most hysterical pitch. Gitutu looks forward to the day when, instead of tiny plots of land being sold to citizens, they will queue up to buy mere pots or trays of soil in which to grow food for subsistence, and the very air will be sold to workers by the bottleful.[11] Kihaahu forecasts a time when it will no longer be fixed houses that will be peddled to the workforce, but tiny portable tents or 'birds'-nests' that they can pitch nightly like nomads to shelter their heads while their bodies remain at the mercy of the elements. Nditika (following Ngũgĩ's reading about Barnard's visit to Kenya in prison)[12] suggests a final stage of *magendo* in cornering the market in human organs for transplants so that the elite will purchase physical immortality and leave death to the workers. The scheme outlined by Kimeenderi wa Kinyuanjii (and whispered to Wariinga by The Voice) is the last item from the Devil's Feast and caps all that has gone before. In sadistic triumph Kimeenderi outlines his plan to herd all workers into barbed-wire compounds where their blood and sweat will be pumped, squeezed and dripped from them daily and sent out packaged or by pipeline to the home market or for export, while the donors are kept quiescent by means of conditioned religion, education and pseudo-culture. The forces of law and repression will be kept in reserve in the background. The Voice insists that the Christian mass has already pointed the way to Kimeenderi's ideal by urging the regular imbibing of Christ's flesh and blood, a last twist of the knife which may have many readers crying out in protest together with Wariinga herself. The novel challenges everyone.

It might seem hard to follow on from this series of climaxes but Ngũgĩ knows just where he is going. Next comes the weightily ironic passage in which Wangari leads the police to arrest the congregation of thieves only to find that the law is on very good terms with these powerful robbers and that it is she herself who is arrested and imprisoned. The angry march of the workers in which Muturi is involved is another story. It is characteristic of Ngũgĩ's faith in the masses that the marchers achieve at least a short-term victory in their routing of the whole assembly. This rout is symbolic of a full and final victory which lies in the future (towards which Karega was already gazing at the end of *Petals of Blood*). This confidence is embodied in the speeches of exhortation by the workers' leaders for which Ngũgĩ finds due place after the enemy has been put to flight.

It is a deliberate part of the interlocking structure that essential sections of the individual stories of Wariinga and Gatuiria are inset during the lunch-break midway in the festival of misrule.

Biting satire and ribald comedy are inherent in most oral literatures. A stranger at a village gathering which has been convulsed by the words of a singer or narrator may be at a loss to interpret what is happening not because friends are reluctant to explain but because bilinguists in the audience may find it hard to explicate the complex references and local allusions which are derived from daily life within the community and its current controversies. The immediate popularity of *Devil on the Cross* is related to this tradition. Every reader will provide exact features and names for the broad prototypes portrayed in the thieves' gallery, just as listeners to a fable, or to *Drapier's Letters*, or readers of *Animal Farm* have always been aware of who is being exposed to their laughter, derision and profound criticism.

Devil on the Cross's relationship with oral and ritual tradition is embedded as much in its form and techniques as in its content. In his two recent collaborations in drama, Ngũgĩ has learnt to integrate song, dance and formal patterns of celebration and mourning into his writing. The meeting in the Cave is cast in the form of a public discussion, guided by its own rules and procedure. In concept it recalls more closely a meeting of elders than it does a modern platform debate. The novel's narrative is in fact initiated by a traditional village musician and story-teller, though his being almost completely forgotten about except for a side-glance at the beginning of Chapter 10 is a structural weakness. The use of song, on the other hand, is fully integrated into the texture and manner of the work; it emanates in the first instance from the presence of the Prophet of Justice, as the story-teller significantly designates himself in the opening paragraphs.

The use of song develops in an interesting way in the text. After the singer fades into the background, song first infiltrates the prose during Wariinga's trance following her second attempted suicide. Then Muturi consciously describes himself as talking in song when he regrets the perversion of traditional morality:

'They have been taught new songs, new hymns that celebrate the acquisition of money. That's why today Nairobi teaches:

> Crookedness to the upright,
> Meanness to the kind,
> Hatred to the loving,
> Evil to the good . . .' (15–16)

Wariinga also employs song consciously in her semi-autobiographical narrative:

'For today Kareendi has decided that she does not know the difference between:

> To straighten and to bend,
> To swallow and to spit out,
> To ascend and to descend,
> To go and to return.' (25)

And she introduces words from church services which, together with quotations from hymns, will remain throughout in frequent counterpoint with the wisdom of more traditional song-forms.

In their discussion in the matatu Muturi and Wangari introduce excerpts from Nyakinyua dancers and Mau Mau fighters and this sets Mwaura off into highly relevant snatches:

> I shall knock-a-knock the Devil.
> I shall knock-a-knock the Devil.
> I shall tell him: Leave me alone
> I do not belong to demons! (46)

Now Muturi and Wangari actually burst out into song together without any preamble or preparation: so songs have become a medium in their own right without any need for explanation or justification, no longer just in snatches but here in sixteen lines of duet:

> Famine has increased in our land,
> But it has been given other names,
> So that the people should not discover
> Where all the food has been hidden . . . (50)

The singers have become a kind of Brechtian chorus allowing us to stand back and contemplate the issues, as satire will also do in its different way. From now on the prose narrative is freely interlarded with quotations from pop-songs, freedom fighters' songs and hymns. They also become a means of expressing original thoughts, sometimes in quite stylized patterns:

> They walked slowly and silently towards the main road. Then they began to talk. It was not really a conversation. It was more a kind of incantation, as if they were both taking part in a verse-chanting competition, citing verses remembered in dreams.

> Gatuiria: Hail, our land!
> Hail, Mount Kenya!
> Hail, our land,
> Never without water or food or green fields!

> Wariinga: Hail, the splendour of this land!
> Hail, the land ringed round with deep lakes . . . (128)

Another feature taken over from tradition is the frequent use of proverbs. Proverbs are sometimes used in specifically traditional patterns of discussion and debate so that they form an essential part of the argument as when they operate in clusters to reinforce and develop a point. Gitutu asserts his sexual potency with his three women in spite of his obesity thus: ' "As the dancer prepares himself for the arena, it's he who knows how he is going to dance. The elephant is able to carry his tusks, however huge. And again, whoever is able to resist money today is beyond human help" ' (100) — blending proverbs into modern thematic commentary. Wariinga vindicates her choice of a student lover in preference to Boss Kihara in like manner: ' "The yam that one has dug up for oneself has no mouldy patches. The sugar cane that one has picked out has no unripe edges. Those whom one loves do not squint" ' (22–3).

A technique we recognize from *Petals of Blood* is the binding of the plot by miniature coincidences and mysteries interlinking the characters. It turns out that Muturi was the watchman who intervened to prevent Wariinga's first attempted suicide. It is Boss Kihara who tries to seduce Wariinga, against whom Muturi leads a strike, and who hijacks the land allocated to the mechanics' communal workshop. The Rich Old Man turns out to be Gatuiria's father. Hell's Angels act as thugs to eject Wariinga; they are bandsmen at the Devil's Feast; Mwaura is agitated because Muturi accidentally stumbles across his connection with this gang. Whereas Mwaura's fears — 'What's Muturi doing here? . . . Who is Muturi? Who is Wangari?' (126) — create temporary suspense without in the end proving to be of any significance; the Rich Old Man's identity is a pivot of the plot.

As we have previously noticed, Ngũgĩ adopted Biblical imagery and references from early in his career not simply as part of an inbred schoolboy consciousness, but because they formed the most complex mythology generally known to his own and other East African societies. As he comes increasingly to deplore Christianity as a means of conditioning people into an acceptance of colonial and neo-colonial exploitation, biblical allusions are employed with an increasingly ironic edge in *A Grain of Wheat* and *Petals of Blood*. Now in *Devil on the Cross* religious references are primarily critical and satirical. Mwireri earnestly assures his fellow passengers, ' "The majority of those who will be attending the feast believe in God. I, for instance, go to PCEA church at Thogoto, the *Church of the Torch,* every Sunday" ' (76). The Hell's Angels lead the assemblage in the Cave in singing 'as if they were in church:

> Good news has come
> To our country!
> Good news has come
> About our Saviour!' (90)

Christianity is at once a facade for the unscrupulous and a narcotic for those who are suffering

'if you prevented people from breathing, what would prevent them from taking up clubs and swords and guns? Isn't that tantamount to showing how much you despise the masses? Better meanness that is covert: better a system of theft that is disguised by lies. Or why do you think that our imperialist friends brought us the Bible? Do you think that they were being foolish when they urged workers and peasants to close their eyes in prayer and told them that earthly things were vain? Why do you think I go to all the church fund-raising Harambee meetings?' (123)

We have already observed that the ironic re-interpretation of the parable of the talents forms a linking motif in the novel; and that The Voice insists that the Mass prefigures, in its consumption of flesh and blood, Kimeenderi's monstrous scheme to extract the workers' blood and sweat and export them by pipeline. The very title of the novel refers to the ironic inversion of the story of the Crucifixion. It is now the Devil, ruthless genius of the cash nexus, who in a vision is crucified by workers and peasants, and is then taken from the cross and nurtured towards resurrection by the rich and the powerful (immaculately dressed) who live by Satan's creed and prosper as he prospers.

Ngũgĩ invokes biblical mythology to make the abstract concepts of good and evil, so often referred to as warring opposites, concrete and substantial. For all the constant references to God and the Devil throughout, it is evident that they are introduced as a means to an end. They provide 'a way of putting it'. Gatuiria, the young thinker and committed artist, deliberately tries to determine whether or not the Devil exists, as a prerequisite of his coming of age morally and artistically. And it is Gatuiria who at length realizes that the whole paraphernalia of heaven and hell, Christ and Satan, is a vast and deeply significant metaphor which enables human beings to think and feel and act in the light of abstract principles of rightness and goodness. Pressed by Wariinga — ' "So you didn't find a single Devil, not even among the foreigners, for instance?" ' — he responds, ' "What I am saying is that it doesn't really matter if the Devil actually exists or if he's merely a certain image of the world" ' (132).

The symbolism of the partial reversal of the Crucifixion myth must be seen in this light. The issues are complex. If this symbolic substitution were taken for a complete inversion, the message of the novel might be misunderstood. Clearly Ngũgĩ rejects Christian dogma relating to the Deity and to the Trinity. This is essentially a non-religious humanist response to religious orthodoxy (wherever possible paralleling Islam to Christianity). Wariinga plays the part of Christ in her temptation by the Devil, explicitly in her cry of ' "Get thee behind me, Satan" ' (194). She takes over Christ's role as a man and eliminates any suggestion of godhead in doing so. But she thereby identifies herself (without arrogance since this is a visionary sequence) with Christ's moral position. As he has done since *The River Between* and *Weep Not, Child*, Ngũgĩ finds common ground between socialist, humanist ethics and Christian ethics (however misrepresented the latter may be by Christians themselves and their churches).

In her mythical role, Wariinga totally rejects the materialistic worldly-wisdom of Satan's proposals as adamantly as does Christ in the New Testament. It is the wealthy and the socially complacent who minister to the Devil as they lift him from the cross. As has been said, Ngũgĩ sees the vast congregation of 'Holy Joes' in the pseudo-Christian world, notably in Africa, as using their religion as a cynical frontage to conceal their self-seeking opportunism. Like almost every member of the gathering in the Cave, the Rich Old Man is a pillar of his sect. When Wariinga inquires whether he intends to go through a form of marriage with her as his second wife, he reminds her, ' "I am a man of the Church. I just want you to be mine. I'll find my own ways of coming to visit you" ' (253)

We must not imagine that Ngũgĩ is trying to invert morality in placing Satan on the cross in Christ's place. He is not saying that Satan is his Christ, but rather that, whatever they may pretend, it is the Devil whom the capitalist power magnates and their entourage really worship. The message is plain enough to anyone who thinks clearly about the book. But it must be admitted that the potential ambiguities are increased by the fact that it is Satan as The Voice in Wariinga's vision who spells out most clearly in the novel the revolutionary alternative to the present class hierarchy:

> You ask what has been stolen from Muturi. Aren't his sweat and blood worth anything? Where did they teach you the wealth of nations comes from? From the clouds? From the hands of the rich? (186)

> Kimeenderi will show them only two worlds, that of the eater and that of the eaten. So the workers will never learn of the existence of a third world, the

world of the revolutionary overthrow of the system of eating and being eaten. They will always assume that the two worlds of the eater and the eaten are eternal. (188)

It is Satan who in the same discourse exposes the precise methods of the power elite, and their cynical exploitation of religion, as well as some of the anomalies in Christian dogma. It may well be confusing to hear these arguments from the figure who also epitomizes the ideals of the capitalist regime. It is true that this 'spirit' eventually uses these revelations to try and ensnare Wariinga into submission to worldly wisdom. But Wariinga has her work cut out to convince herself later that this was the father of lies speaking and not a prophetic spokesman for the humanist ideal:

> She recalled her recent dream. Had it really been a dream or a revelation? Wariinga put the same question again: Had the voice been real or had it been an illusion?
> No. It had been the voice of Satan, the voice of temptation. For although The Voice had painted a true picture of what was going on in the country, and it had made pertinent observations about neo-colonial Kenya, the way that The Voice had shown her as the escape route from the prison of neo-colonial life was misleading and would have cost Wariinga her life. It had tempted her to walk along a broad highway carpeted with the flowers of self-seeking individualism. It had tempted her to sell her body for money again! (212-13)

Certainly Ngũgĩ avoids glib over-simplifications, as ever; and exposes wiles that can pervert the honest intellect with half-truths. But there must be some danger that the complexity of the half-inverted myth may obscure a clear understanding of the significance of the central narrative and of the ironic satire.

Set against this, however, is not only the unmistakable force of the satiric vision but also the clear statement of the need for revolution that emerges, and the positive conviction that impresses revolutionary ideals upon us. Revolution itself becomes an alternative religion, taking over the very vocabulary of the old religion. Muturi tells Wariinga, ' "Maybe I'm a priest who has not yet been ordained . . . But I belong to an order that has been called to serve by the poverty of the people of Kenya" ' (27). Mau Mau has passed on its tradition of communal self-help: ' "If we don't help each other, we'll become like the beasts. That's why in the days of Mau Mau we took the oath, swearing: 'I'll never eat alone . . . Work is life" ' (38). Their alliance is sanctified: "The Holy Trinity of the worker, the peasant, the patriot" (230). Like Karega, Muturi has suffered for his efforts in going about to raise the consciousness of the workers and rally them to stand up for their rights:

> 'But the profits of the employers increase at the same rate as the increase in prices — in fact, sometimes the rate of profit is higher than the price increases. So when the price of things goes up, the employers benefit, but the lot of the workers gets worse.' (72)

Balanced against the satiric savagery of the witches' high noon in the Cave, we have the direct, representative account of the reality of ordinary people's everyday experience. Law and the police are there to bolster the system, not to assert universal justice. But in the triumphant march of this holy trinity, which sets the power group by the heels, we glimpse a prophetic picture in miniature of a future which Ngũgĩ now clearly and passionately believes in. The pattern of exploitation so boastfully expounded in the thieves' conference is set out in plain language to the marchers' rally:

'. . . we who are gathered here now belong to one clan: the clan of workers — I think all of us saw the incredible spectacle of those who have bellies that never bear children come to scorn us. Those bellies are not swollen by disease. They have been fattened by the fruit of our sweat and our blood. Those bellies are barren, and their owners are barren. What about us, the workers? We build houses; others occupy them; and we, the builders, are left out in the rain. We make clothes; others take them, and dress well; and we the tailors go naked. We grow food; others eat it; and we, the farmers, sleep with our stomachs growling through the night. Look here. We build good schools; other people's children find places in them, and ours go looking for food in rubbish heaps and in dustbins. Today we are taking a stand. Today, here, we refuse to go on being the pot that cooks but never tastes the food.' (208)

The protests expressed in earlier novels are caught up again in this later work. When we learn that Boss Kihara has moved in to purchase the land already promised to the mechanics' community to build a permanent workshop, we are carried back to the MP doublecrossing Gikonyo's co-operative and snatching the plantation he had promised to help them acquire in *A Grain of Wheat;* and also to the trickery by which Kiguunda's land is wrenched from him in *I Will Marry When I Want.* Wangari is ruined by a treacherous public loan just as Nyakinyua in *Petals of Blood.* When Wariinga asks, ' "How can you tell what you love unless you know what you hate?" ' (132), it is as if Wanja is speaking. In their different ways Karega and Gatuiria find history equally arid as a means of illuminating the present:

'I wanted the setting for the music to be a certain village before the advent of British imperialism in Kenya. I thought I would start by telling of the origins of the village . . . But after a few lines I felt the flames die, and the ashes of the work were left without even the tiniest spark.' (66–7)

When Nditika wa Nguunji speciously claims to have been involved in the battle for liberation — ' "We all fought for freedom in different ways, for different sides" ' (177) — it is like a reincarnation of the Politician who appears in Dedan Kimathi's third 'trial'.

Muturi is lightly sketched in as a character. He is a figurehead of the indefatigable few who never despair: ' "Despair is the one sin that cannot be forgiven . . . the sin for which we would never be forgiven by the nation and generations to come" ' (27). He is a figurehead of the force which is tirelessly working towards the 'revolutionary overthrow of the system of eating and being eaten' (188): ' "I'm a delegate from a secret workers' organization in Nairobi. But don't ask any more questions. Wherever I am, I am working for that organization. Look after yourself — and remember, you're not alone" ' (212).

Of course there are renegades among all classes, those who seek only to climb into the place left vacant by those who have scrambled on to the rung of the ladder above them. Mwaura, the matatu driver, is among these opportunists who do not recognize right or wrong, good or evil — the perpetual choice — but only self-interest. Even at his least menacing, Mwaura recalls the voices of the think-nothing people in Gabriel Okara's *The Voice*:

> 'Even today there's no song that I wouldn't sing. I say this world is round. If it leans that way, I lean that way with it. If it stumbles, I stumble with it. If it bends, I bend with it . . . If it is silent, I am silent too. The first law of the hyena states: Don't be choosy, eat what is available.' (47)

The two most developed characters in the book are both dramatically and thematically in the most ambivalent position. They are prototypes of the white-collar workers and the young intellectuals, represented by a secretary-typist and a student. They find themselves with no natural, inevitable class base or class loyalty, and so they have to choose between good and evil, between one moral and social stance, and another:

> 'For each man is part of the forces that have been recruited for creating, building, making our humanity grow and blossom in order to nurture our human nature and create our own Heaven, thus taking on the nature of God — these are the forces of the clan of producers; or he is part of the forces of destruction, of dismantling, of harassing and oppressing the builders and the creators, the forces that seek to suppress our humanity, turning us into beasts in order that we should create our own Hell, thus taking on the nature of Satan — these are the forces of the clan of parasites.' (53)

Men must make the choice both as a community and as individuals. Indeed, each human being is seen as an arena for opposing forces of good and evil, much as in medieval morality plays: hence the ever-present patrons of the two forces: God and Satan. As Muturi puts it:

> 'Heaven and Hell? . . . Both exist, and there is a difference between them, just as there is a difference between good and evil, a good heart and an evil heart. Listen. Our lives are a battlefield on which is fought a continuous war between the forces that are pledged to confirm our humanity and those determined to dismantle it.' (53)

In this battle, Wariinga commits herself to 'the forces of . . . making our humanity grow'. Gatuiria stands trembling on the brink. He makes an active attempt over many years to break away from that group that perhaps makes Ngũgĩ angrier than any other, the 'petty-bourgeois intellectuals at the university who hide ethnic chauvinism and their mortal terror of progressive class politics behind masks of abstract super-nationalism, and bury their own inaction behind mugs of beer and empty intellectualism about conditions being not yet ripe for action'.[13] In his sincere attempt to reject these life-lies, Gatuiria offers a model for the deeply alienated youth of today. In his final failure he acts as a terrible warning to the bold student radical who backslides into becoming one of these petty-bourgeois intellectuals at the very time when faced with the chance of real action and commitment.

In responding to Wariinga we are not confronted with the complexities and contradictions which characterize earlier protagonists in Ngũgĩ's novels. It is true that in the first novels the principal women are admired unequivocally. Not till he created Wanja did Ngũgĩ present us with a woman as ambiguous as virtually all his leading men, though Mumbi in her adultery with Karanja plays her part in the cross-currents which eddy through *A Grain of Wheat*. Wariinga changes radically in the course of the story but in each phase of her being she is a fairly straightforward personality. The brilliant and single-minded secondary student with a flair for maths is undermined by her uncle's pandering and degenerates rapidly into the self-indulgent teenage mistress of the Rich Old Man. Rejected when, with naive confidence, she makes known her pregnancy, she becomes the desperate, abandoned good-time girl and resolutely attempts suicide. Rescued by Muturi and the understanding sympathy of her parents, she qualifies in a commercial college and becomes the city girl who cannot get a job without sacrificing her integrity. Temporarily she breaks lucky with an elderly employer and adopts the role of a wage-earning typist who follows the fashions as well as she can and settles down with a student boyfriend (who tags her along for the sake of the supplementary financial support she offers towards his studies). Then she again suffers elderly male assault on her virtue from her boss, who has merely bided his time to recruit her as his sugar-girl. But this time she is the shocked innocent who will not succumb, and so she is sacked and thus loses her mercenary boyfriend. Melodramatically, she is victim same day of a rapacious landlord and his thugs, and so she finds herself in the street, where, in fact, we first meet her as she is again rescued from suicide.

Her experiences in rubbing shoulders with Wangari, Muturi, and Gatuiria at the thieves' carnival, and as observer of the march of peasants and workers against their oppressors, change her once again. After they have heard the speeches delivered to the marchers by their leaders (including Muturi) both Gatuiria and Wariinga feel challenged. Theirs is one of the two major challenges offered by the novel. The first is to the exploited peasants and workers to reject exploitation and join together in protest and revolt. The other is to Mr and Miss Looking-both-ways, those in the no-man's-land of the struggle, neither labourers nor members of the elite. In giving his gun into Wariinga's safe-keeping, Muturi proves prophetic in trusting her before Gatuiria: ' "Those educated people are often not sure whose side they are on. They sway from this side to that like water on a leaf" ' (211).

Wariinga determinedly chooses her side and transforms her way of life:

> This Wariinga is not the one who used to think that there was nothing she could do except type for others; the one who used to burn her body with *Ambi* and *Snowfire* to change the colour of her skin to please the eyes of others, to satisfy their lust for white skins; the one who used to think that there was only one way of avoiding the pitfalls of life: suicide. (216)

So in her new city context she takes on the heritage of Muthoni and Nyambura, of Nyokabi and Njeri, of Mumbi, of Nyakinyua, of the Woman in *The Trial of Dedan Kimathi*, and — closer to hand — of Wangari. She becomes the spearhead of Ngũgĩ's long battle for women's rights against 'Those who like to belittle the minds, intelligence and abilities of our women' (218); 'the skill that thrilled her most was her ability to take apart and re-assemble internal combustion engines' (219). Ngũgĩ gives Wariinga the opportunity to remind us that the under-estimation of women is indigenous: ' "Even you, the Kenyan men, think that there is no job a woman can do other than cooking your food and massaging your bodies" ' (245).

The process of metamorphosis from typist to a potentially ideal young woman revolutionary is stereotyped and could well seem trite, but Ngũgĩ breathes something of his own convictions into his semi-ritualistic process. The morning scene of Wariinga dressing in her mechanic's rig, grabbing her constant companion — the phase-tester — and striding off to her workplace is perhaps a somewhat self-conscious set-piece. But the scenes in which she wins the respect of her initially sceptical male fellow students at the polytechnic, gets herself employed in the garage by showing a male technician his job, puts an over-amorous male customer in his place with her newly acquired karate skills, and shakes down into a camaraderie with her fellow workers are lively, individualized and convincing for all their didactic brevity.

So Wariinga is fitted at last for her symbolic task, characteristic of Ngũgĩ's thinking throughout his fiction: 'to speak like a people's judge about to deliver his judgment' (253); then to shoot the Rich Old Man as a representative of all the licentious, arrogantly selfish and utterly materialistic hypocrites who dominate the society so fiercely indicted by the novel. In this act she is deliberate, competent, fearless: 'Wariinga heroine of toil'.[14]

The ending is powerful and dramatic. We are shocked and romantically disappointed. The extreme stylization adopted for large parts of the novel, and also the controlled switch from outright ironic satire to formalized realism throughout the development of the love story, will probably have led even the most wary and seasoned reader into anticipating a conventional happy ending. No doubt we expect the sound of wedding bells to be interwoven with the final exposure of the snobbish, reactionary moneyed classes epitomized by Gatuiria's father. The final climax shatters many illusions and unnerves us, leaving us disturbed and disoriented at the last. Of course, it is meant to do so. It is no part of Ngũgĩ's plan to soothe us into complacency as if we were at the dawning of a new age in society already. The brutal facts of neo-colonialist reality confront our lulled senses. The massed forces of the comprador elite smash the idyll.

Wariinga may have grown into an idealized figure of revolutionary womanhood. She has trained as an auto-engineer the hard way. She has gone to evening classes in karate and can defend herself against personal assaults. She is a worker among workers while remaining a very feminine woman in love. But her individual triumph has not altered society. She and those like her are still in the grips of the Rich Old Man and his kind. It is spelt out explicitly to us lest we forget that a destructive social system destroys. It destroys with blandishments, and with sugared lust, backed up ruthlessly by well-armed and legalized forces of self-protection.

The most complex figure is Gatuiria. At the moment of test he fails. The educated young man, the poor little rich boy, has renounced his heritage, has crossed the floor and joined the forces of enlightenment in the struggle between different class interests. He has rejected his father's values and the easy wealth that would go with them. He has forged his own values as a struggling yet dedicated artist. Ngũgĩ presents the scenario of Gatuiria's patriotic oratorio in full as a blueprint for all revolutionary arts. 'For two years Gatuiria concentrated exclusively on his work, and he would literally lock himself into his study whenever the Muse visited him' (224-5). He has come to love Wariinga and all that she stands for as a militant radical thinker. But like Waiyaki, he fails: though within the style of this novel there is less scope for subtle analysis of his failure. Instead of confidently telling Wariinga all that he knows of his family and home and what she can expect at the fateful reception (at least as far as he himself then knows the facts), he dithers and prevaricates and thereby sets the scene for tragedy. And after the event he is helplessly divided in his loyalties. His corrupt father is dead. His beleaguered fiancée is at total risk. But at this moment he does not comprehend his place as being at her side. His priorities are still twisted. In throwing out this challenge to half-committed intellectuals, Ngũgĩ has contrived to recruit the reader's sympathies entirely on Wariinga's side. He makes us feel without doubt that, terrible as the pressures on him are, Gatuiria's place should be with Wariinga, not with his dead father who has done everything calculated to destroy them both as moral beings; nor even with the shadowy figure of his mother who is part and parcel of his father's world. The Rich Old Man has failed to destroy Wariinga. What of his son?

Wariinga's use of the gun at this moment is highly significant. The Rich Old Man boasts of the powers of the rich to circumvent laws and get whatever they want, however great the odds against them, whatever the injuries done to others. We recall that at all other times of confrontation in the past, Wariinga has lost out. As a teenage sugar-girl of the Rich Old Man she was his expendable sex toy in the degenerate power game of the hunter and the hunted. She was the chosen prey of Boss Kihara as much as she was of her ruthless landlord. But now the roles are reversed. With the aid of the gun she will impose an inexorable moral code. It is no accident that the gun has been given into her custody by Muturi, one of the leaders of the workers. Today Wariinga salvages her honour by righteously condemning her elitist persecutor to death. Tomorrow the persecution of a whole society is to be set to rights by armed insurrection.

The melodramatic finale is as symbolic as the great satiric competition between the capitalist thieves. This is a metaphor for the vital role that Ngũgĩ ultimately sees for the gun in the conflict between classes. In this clash of values, Wariinga, the new ideal of womanhood — unlike Gatuiria — is attuned to act. She does so unhesitatingly as an instrument of Nemesis. She guns down the Rich Old Man as retribution for the social evil he epitomizes. Wariinga and the Rich Old Man are stereotypes in a stylized enactment. So there are none of the moral or human complexities which surround the dramas of Waiyaki, Njoroge, Mugo. The issue is stark, clearcut, readily comprehended by a wide-ranging readership. The Rich Old Man is the enemy and he is struck down without regrets, without reservations.

This is a localized, anticipatory day of revolutionary wrath for one of the gang of exploiters and his henchmen. But only one. Wariinga's solitary act dooms her. Avenging justice is as yet an isolated voice. Wariinga has no choice but to act alone. One day the oppressed sections of society will act in concert. Hence the underlying hopefulness of this carefully contrived conclusion. Wariinga marches out of the novel to meet her fate immune for the moment, by virtue of her innocence and her purity of purpose, from the furies around her. She has the future on her side.

Notes

1. Ngũgĩ wa Thiong'o, *Detained: A Writer's Prison Diary* (Heinemann Educational Books, London, 1981), 164.
2. Ibid., 165.
3. Ibid., 11.
4. Ibid., 98.
5. Ibid., 8.
6. Ibid., 24–5.
7. Ibid., 97, 98–9.
8. Ibid., 135–6.
9. Page references are to *Devil on the Cross* (Heinemann Educational Books, London, 1982).
10. In terms of the three ideological orientations described by Ngũgĩ in *Detained*, it is easy to identify Mwireri wa Mukiral with the middle level:

    KANU was a mass movement containing within it different class strata and tendencies: peasant, proletarian, and petty-bourgeois. Leadership was in the hands of the petty-bourgeoisie, itself split into three sections representing three tendencies: there was the upper petty-bourgeoisie that saw the future in terms of comparadorial alliance with imperialism; there was the middle petty-bourgeoisie which saw the future in terms of national capitalism; and there was the lower petty-bourgeoisie which saw the future in terms of some kind of socialism. The upper petty-bourgeoisie can be branded as comprador; the middle and lower petty-bourgeoisie can be branded as nationalistic. The internal struggle for the ideological dominance and leadership of KANU from 1961 to 1966 was mainly between the faction representing comprador bourgeois interests, and the faction representing national patriotic interests. (52)

11. We quote from this section in our final chapter below. It is interesting to compare this whole passage with a sequence in Robert Tressell's *The Ragged Trousered Philanthropists* (new edition by Panther Books, 1967; page 152):

    The only reason they have not monopolized the daylight and the air is that it is not possible to do it. If it were possible to construct huge gasometers and to draw together and compress within them the whole of the atmosphere, it would have been done long ago, and we should have been compelled to work for them in order to get money to buy air to breathe. And if that seemingly impossible thing were accomplished tomorrow, you would see thousands of people dying for want of air — or of the money to buy it — even as now thousands are dying for want of other necessaries of life. You would see people going about gasping for breath, and telling each other that the likes of them could not expect to have air to breathe unless they had the money to pay for it.

12. *Detained*, 138.
13. Ibid., xxi.
14. Ibid., 3.

Matigari

As we said in the last chapter, sympathetic readers of Ngũgĩ's earlier novels up to *Petals of Blood* cannot have seen what would come next. *Devil on the Cross* may have been predictable in its socio-political thrust, but certainly not in its style (or styles) nor its literary mode. During Ngũgĩ's next long pause after *Devil*, enthusiasts may now have wondered whether the well had dried up. And they must have been at a loss to conceive what could possibly follow *Devil on the Cross*. After all, it seemed to have taken an innovative mode of writing to its extreme.

The last short paragraph of 'A Note to the English Edition of *Matigari*' reads:

> Matigari, the fictional hero, and the novel, his only habitation, have been effectively banned in Kenya. With the publication of this English edition, they have joined their author in exile.

But neither Ngũgĩ nor Matigari have been passive exiles. When the police stopped hunting for Matigari in the flesh, identified him as a fictional character — and banned him, the first edition of the Gikuyu version of *Matigari* had already sold out. This amazed the publishers who had never dared to hope that a novel in Gikuyu would become a best-seller. So it was the balance of the second printing that was seized in Kenyan bookshops. And — as the police had already discovered — his reputation in the real world had been as dynamic as it is in the world of the novel.

Ngũgĩ is not of the creative calibre simply to repeat himself. So while much that he had learnt in writing *Devil on the Cross* has been ploughed into writing *Matigari*, this too is unique in its manner. *Devil on the Cross* is a *tour-de-force* which successfully combines two styles — a bizarrely, powerfully extreme form of satire, and a direct socio-political social tale. *Matigari* is stylistically more self-consistent in its manner. It adopts a mode which can be seen as intermediate between the two complementary styles of *Devil on the Cross*. It is certainly an unrelenting satire on contemporary society and its destructive power patterns. But, on the one hand, it only occasionally edges into the extremities of the 'Thieves' Feast' in *Devil on the Cross*. On the other hand, while the satire is comparatively close to actuality, it never shifts to the straight story-telling manner of the Wariinga plot. In asserting his ownership of the house claimed by Settler Williams Junior, and in demanding the right of farmers and factory workers to earn the true value of their sweat (instead of the pittance paid by capitalists), Matigari is an African Everyman — symbolic rather than realistic. But the alienation and exploitation that he describes are directly experienced by his countrymen, rather than being inflated as the plans by the Devil's thieves to commercialize (for instance) the breath and blood and sweat of their victims are deliberately and grotesquely inflated in building up an outrageous satirical case. Exaggerations in *Matigari* are mostly symbolic rather than satirical, as for instance the first view of 'the house':

> and indeed, there on top of the hill overlooking the whole country stood a huge house which seemed to stretch out for miles, as if, like the plantation itself, it had no beginning and no end. (42)

For the most part the methods employed by the two novels are comparable but significantly different in degree.

Devil on the Cross borrows from the fable tradition in many ways. But *Matigari* is modelled much more closely on the essential pattern of fables and parables. The thematic repetitions on which *Matigari* is structured are the stock-in-trade of fables and fairy stories.

The fundamental themes of the two works are similar as is also the challenge to the people to resist being battened down by neo-colonialist and capitalist ruthlessness. *Devil on the Cross* ends with Wariinga firing a pistol to very good effect. *Matigari* opens with an AK47 rifle and a cross-section of weapons being buried as a gesture of peace: but it ends with this miniature arsenal being resurrected. The weapons are dug up and worn by a youthful representative of a new militant generation. When Matigari buries these tools of the guerilla's trade, he determinedly puts on his belt of peace. In the course of the novel, however, he despairs of words alone ever leading to the establishment of truth and justice. Sadly he concludes, 'One had to have the right words; but these had to be strengthened by the force of arms' (131). And he lays aside his belt of peace. At the last it is he who first ignites the flames of the symbolic conflagration. And it is he who leads Muriuki to the hiding place of those very arms which he sought to lay down on first emerging from the fight in the forest. Matigari follows the same path to reluctantly renewed militancy as his author.

Few, if any, of the basic themes in this work are entirely new to Ngũgĩ. So it may be helpful to recall some significant antecedents in the earlier works before determining *Matigari*'s claim to uniqueness in its emphases, focus and mode.

The fig-tree, mugumo, under which Matigari symbolically buries his weapons, has many echoes — in the title of a short story in *Secret Lives* and in the climactic confrontation at the end of 'The Village Priest'. In *The River Between* it is the central feature of the sacred place where Waiyaki is initiated by his father into his heroic role in the society and where he returns in perplexity in a lead-up to the final crisis. Reference to the building of the railway harks back to *A Grain of Wheat* which counterbalances the destructiveness and the positive social role of the metal 'snake' while in *Matigari* the brutal treatment of the construction workers alone is pinpointed.

The statement in the third paragraph of the opening page, 'Well, there was no night so long that it did not end with dawn,' carries us back to the symbolic time pattern in *The Trial of Dedan Kimathi*. Just as rain and dry weather are symbolically significant in *A Grain of Wheat*, so the indeterminate weather, which is emphatically highlighted in *Matigari*, echoes the blank responses which our protagonist faces in his futile tour of the countryside:

> It would have been better if it had clearly rained or clearly shone. Better any of that than this uncertain weather. Yes, better if it were hot or cold, rather than lukewarm like this. (89)

As in his quest for truth and justice he vainly interrogates those going about their business, he encounters simply their fear, despair or resignation manifesting itself as a lukewarm show of indifference or resentment: moods which we shall consider together later as a major theme. The only alternative is the threatening heat of the first day, ominously foreboding aridity and lifelessness:

> Although by now the sun had moved a great deal westwards, and the shadows had lengthened, it was still oppressively hot all over the country. The grass wilted, and the leaves wore a tired look about them . . . the whole land was gripped in a deathly stillness. No wind blew. No leaves rustled. No clothes fluttered anywhere. (40)

The river — forming the centre-piece of *The River Between* — both opens and closes the present tale. In the Ngũgĩ canon it plays a mysterious role, symbolizing both the union of its two banks, and their separation. Also, as in many traditions, it alludes to life and baptism, and by virtue of traversing many lands is imbued with a strange knowledge beyond man's understanding. In *Matigari* it contributes to the fable world in which the chief character is shrouded. It marks the boundary between the world of the forest fighters and the every-day world, lending an uncanny, spiritual element to the forest, making it a strange, inaccessible terrain to which only the brave can go: for in it human relations, interests and exploits, the realities of life and the means of survival, are all drastically altered. At the end of the novel the river receives two major characters into its mysterious bosom — into a sort of eternity — leaving their disciples, personified by Muriuki, to continue the fight.

It is the river which recalls the ritual of circumcision, bringing back the memory of this Gikuyu entry rite into manhood and adult exploits, which was a centre-piece in *The River Between*. As morning breaks and Matigari washes his face in the river, its chilliness

> reminded him of the other waters in the past which had been just as cold. He remembered how, then, they had sung throughout the night in the open air.
>
> > If only it were dawn . . .
> > So that I can share the cold waters with the early bird.
>
> The water had numbed their skin, so that none of them felt the pain as the

knife cut into their flesh. Before this moment, they were mere boys, but by the time they unclenched their fists, they were men. Their blood mingled with the soil, and they became patriots, ready for the armed struggle to come.

This song is repeated as Matigari and Guthera run finally towards the river; and as the dogs tear at them 'their blood mingled and it trickled into the soil, on the banks of the river' (173).

Police brutality against strikers and protesters doubles with passages in *Petals of Blood* and *Devil on the Cross*. This is linked to the inevitable theme of colonial and neo-colonial exploitation from *Weep Not, Child* to *I Will Marry When I Want*. The smooth transition from the older to the newer is skilfully crystallized in the patterning of *Matigari*. The protagonist thinks that after Mau Mau the battle is over, but finds colonialism reincarnated in the neo-colonialism of Williams and Boy Junior:

A white man and a black man sat on horseback on one side of the narrow tarmac road next to the gate. Their horses were exactly alike. Both had silky brown bodies. The riders too wore clothes of the same colour. Indeed, the only difference between the two men was their skin colour . . . The way they held their whips and the reins — no difference. And they spoke in the same manner. (43)

Here we recall from Ngũgĩ's earlier works a procession of black henchmen to alien vested interests, reaching frantic climaxes across history in *The Trial* and in the *Devil*'s Feast. Time and again Matigari epitomizes the bitter sequence in simple, unanswerable terms:

You wouldn't believe, would you, that it was John Boy, a black man, the settler's servant, who saved him? (22)

The drive by Matigari and his two followers through the rich Nairobi suburbs recalls the ultimate bitterness of the village vanguard in *Petals of Blood* as 'The Journey' arrives house by house in just such an environment.

The Minister of Truth and Justice specifically emphasizes that one of the primary thrusts of his Excellence Ole Excellence's government is its association with multi-nationals and neo-colonialists, demonstrated by the acceptance of the gifts from Settler Williams and John Boy's company of shares to himself, other government luminaries and to the party. The gift to the party is deployed as a means of blackmailing the workers to accept the proscription of their strike by proposing that since they are members of the party, they are recipients of the gift, and so by definition they cannot backbite their great benefactor!

Stability, declares the Minister, has the very three legs that we saw in operation so clearly in *Petals of Blood*:

Remember that a country's, any country's, welfare and stability are dependent on three kinds of people: the wealthy, like these capitalists; the soldiers, like our security forces (you all saw how swiftly the police commissioner drew his pistol); and thirdly, leaders, that is people like me, or the priest, or the others whom I shall soon introduce to you. The wealthy, the soldier, the leader — that's all we need. (116)

And we are equally familiar, particularly from *The Trial*, with the specious argument that it is the government and the conservatives who are the loyalists, and it is Mau Mau and the socialists who are the traitors:

> What about the children of those who took axes and home-made guns, claiming that they were going to fight against the rule of law? Where are they today? Where is the independence that we fought for? That is what they are still shouting at the bottom of the ladder.
>
> In fact, it is we who abided by the law who prevented the country from being destroyed. If you look at the situation dispassionately, without the kind of *distortion* you find with some of those *fiction* writers, you can see it is those who obeyed the colonial law who brought about independence. (103)

> We are all freedom fighters. (83)

It is the teacher, condemned by 'instant justice' to detention without trial, who caps Dedan Kimathi's trenchant rhetoric in replying to the Judge's assertion that there is only one law, one justice:

> Two laws. Two justices. One law and one justice protects the man of property, the man of wealth, the foreign exploiter. Another law, another justice, silences the poor, the hungry, our people. (*The Trial*, 25–6)

The teacher proclaims, 'I also know now that there are two truths. One truth belongs to the oppressor; the other belongs to the oppressed!' (121)

The scorn and opprobrium poured on radical teachers who discuss Marx and Lenin with their students calls to mind the Lawyer in *Petals*. The radio announces an event which mirrors the actuality that Ngũgĩ knew:

> This is the Voice of Truth . . . Two university lecturers appeared in court yesterday charged with possessing books on Karl Marx and V. Lenin published in China. All books about the liberation of peasants and workers, particularly those published in China, have been banned since Independence. (70)

Ngũgĩ's long-standing attacks on Christian hypocrisy (notably in *Petals*, and in *The Trial* in the person of the cleric who colludes with politicians and business-men in one of the prison visitations to Kimathi) reach now satiric virulence in the priest in *Matigari* who trembles in terror at rumours of Christ's second coming; falls on his knees on learning of Matigari's seemingly miraculous escape; and then finally reads to the Minister's meeting the New Testament passage against false prophets.

The under-rating and exploitation of women, notably by traditional African society, are exposed in all Ngũgĩ's novels. He always gives key roles to women. In *Matigari* Guthera re-enacts the roles of Wanja and Wariinga: both are defiled and ravished women who in the course of their stories achieve emancipation and spiritual purification through self-sacrificing revolutionary heroism. We first meet Guthera as a young woman of great beauty and sex-appeal who in this cruel world of throttling self-interest has not the remotest chance of maintaining her virtue. But she again displays that innate sense of true human dignity that no buffeting can destroy. Even the corrupt neo-colonialist African discriminates against women. Guthera muses on the chagrin of the Minister's wife and her inamorato, stranded in the bush, when at length they will reach home:

> What problems we women have to go through wherever we are! When that

woman goes home, her husband will beat her, demanding to know what she was doing in the wilderness with a man. When her lover goes home, he will beat his wife for demanding to know what he was doing in the wilderness with a woman. (151)

For all her earlier persecution by the police, and the reasons she has for hating the Minister's wife, Guthera actually finds it in her heart to pity her in this ironic pattern of injustice The wizened old woman who alerts Matigari to the fundamental fact that 'Too much fear breeds misery in the land' (87) reincarnates Wanja's grandmother in *Petals of Blood*.

While these familiar issues are re-blended and given a new look, the crux of *Matigari* gathers many earlier threads with special force. One motif is often embedded in Matigari's retelling of this life-story, which is really the life-story of colonial Africa up to the present:

Matigari was the one who produced everything. But it was Settler Williams who collected the profits. Imagine: the tiller dying of starvation, the builder sleeping on the veranda; the tailor walking about without clothes and the driver having to go for miles on foot. (38)

This plaint, if indeed it is ever simply a complaint, grows into a set of demands, and forms the core of a socialist policy:

This world is indeed upside-down, and it must be set to rights again. The builder wants a place in which to lay his head. The tiller wants his harvest. The worker wants the produce of his labour. We have refused to be the cooking pot that just cooks and never tastes the food. Or do you want our women to continue trading their bodies for a few coins? Our children too, do you want them to continue scavenging in the dustbins for left-overs, like vultures? (138)

Matigari's litany forms a refrain as he virtually sings it to the assembly which is transformed almost into a protest meeting. In this rallying cry the builder, the tailor, the tiller, the worker is each given his own 'verse':

The tiller tends crops in the field.
The one who reaps-where-he-never-sowed yawns for having eaten too much.
The tiller yawns for not having eaten at all. (113)

Each image resounds across the whole Ngũgĩ canon.

Meanwhile, the poor and deprived co-operate in a caring, sharing culture of mutual self-help as one of *Devil on the Cross*'s refrains resurfaces:

Great love I saw there,
Among the women and the children.
We shared even the single bean
That fell upon the ground (6)

— a theme echoed when Matigari distributes his scraps of food among his prison companions (55–6). And Mariuki, like the Boy in *The Trial* embodies the renewal of the struggle in the coming generation, a handing-on.

Anti-colonial protests against the alienation of the land, a central thread in the campaign for independence and then against neo-colonialism, is mainly subsumed in the new novel in Matigari's demand for the return of 'his' house:

Do you see this house? Do you see these tea plantations and this road? Who do you think built them all? And, mark you, I did not begin yesterday . . . Do you think that this house has a story different from the story of these hands? Hands are the makers of human history. (45)

Matigari now said in a raised voice as if addressing a huge crowd, 'Yes, come all, and let us light a fire in the house together! Let us share the food together, and sing joyfully together!' (51)

'. . . according to them, I don't have the title-deed to my house. But tell me — what title-deed is greater than our sweat and blood?' (59)

The 'land' is represented by the vast plantations 'extending far into the horizon' (41) that now 'belong to one person' (41).

In the fight for social justice, Matigari divides people into two camps, whose followers can easily be distinguished in all Ngugi's novels. One camp is of those who play safe, fearfully accepting things as they are: 'A prudent person keeps his mouth shut' (63). The once radical teacher in his intermediate phase explains:

This country has changed from what it was yesterday, or what it was when we fought for it. We have no part to play in it any more. I'm thinking of going to another country where there aren't as many problems as here. (91)

Matigari responds, 'There are two worlds . . . of those who accept things as they are, and . . . that of those who want to change things.' The old woman in the wilderness goes to the root of the problem: 'There is too much fear in this country . . . Too much fear breeds misery in the land.' (87). People exchanging rumours about Matigari discuss fear:

Good God! Who would ever have thought that fear would one day disappear from our land? That a day would come when people would no longer walk with their heads bent in fear? . . . Yes, let's hope for that day. (76–7)

But, as in all the novels, there are those who rise above fear. Once under arrest the university teacher and the student defiantly recover their courage. It is the student who launches one of the songs which begin the rounds of the country as the people surge out of the meeting:

> Even if you detain us,
> Victory belongs to the people.
> Victory belongs to the people! (121)

and the crowd steps up the message by changing 'detain' to 'kill' (127). Guthera follows in the steps of Wariinga as she thinks her way through to a revolutionary stance: 'One can die only once, and it is better to die in pursuit of what is right' (139). Ngaruro affirms that patriots remained in the forest 'to keep the fire of freedom burning' (20). Matigari does all he can to foster renascent patriotism. He assures his disciples, 'Truth never dies' (64, 86). Like Karega, he will not let hope flag. Nor will the voice of the novel:

The true seeker of truth never loses hope. The true seeker of real justice never tires. A farmer does not stop planting seeds just because of the failure of one crop. (84)

Likewise, the novel itself supports Matigari in concluding that the right words alone are, sadly, not enough: 'In the pursuit of truth and justice one had to be armed with armed words' (131).

As we have noticed already, there are certain distinct stylistic affinities between *Matigari* and *Devil on the Cross*. These analogies also involve comparable themes and subject matter to some extent. *Matigari* comes closest to the extended passages of extravagant, flamboyant satire in *Devil* during the meeting conducted by the Minister of Truth and Justice, its longest scene by far. The very title of the ministry is outrageously ironic since it cloaks its true role of disseminating specious government propaganda, in particular through the radio channel carefully misnamed The Voice of Truth in the vein of Orwell's *1984*. The extreme satiric manner adopted in *Devil* is apt only for depicting wickedness, whether in vested interests or in government. Symbolic exaggeration of the attitudes and activities of Matigari and his friends is fabulous rather than ironic.

'Parrotology' in all its branches matches the mutual flattery and self-adulation of the thieves in their feast. It mirrors the self-interested sycophancy of toadies such as Ngũgĩ watched at work in Kenya inside and outside the university. Like the mockery in *Devil on the Cross* it satisfies the indignant but normally impotent reader by cutting down to size those who in real life are impervious to contempt. The legal system is parodied in the form of Instant Justice (bolstered by loans from the UK and the EEC). This draws on bitter past experiences and interrogations of Mau Mau suspects. The sinister hooded figure (reminiscent of the Ku Klux Klan), the quisling employed by the British to identify suspects, is now elevated to the role of virtual judge as The Hooded Truth.

When the MP speaks we might well imagine that we have been transported to an annexe of the Feast of Thieves:

No more children for the poor! Let us give that responsibility to the wealthy! . . . Pregnancies are the result of evil and wild desires. I shall ask the government to ban dreams and desires of that kind . . . Fucking among the poor should be stopped by presidential decree! (119–20)

After Matigari and Ngaruro escape from the mental home where they have been imprisoned, the Voice of Truth announces: 'The Minister of Truth and Justice has authorised the police to shoot down all madmen . . . Shoot at sight!' (134) — except white beatniks.

The most crushing of *Matigari*'s ironies are devastatingly original. The Minister's wife who calculatingly conducts her illicit affairs in the deep bush 'even once said that all barmaids and all prostitutes should be locked up in prison because they are the ones who were causing a lot of homes to break up' (150). The Voice of Truth seeks to allay rumours of Christ's return and other miracles with supreme heretical arrogance: 'Those are false Christs and false Gabriels. There is no way that Jesus could return without first going to pay a courtesy call on His Excellency Ole Excellency' (84).

It may here be recalled that during the confrontation with Matigari,

Settler Williams Junior spurs on John Boy Junior to turn the scene into a theatrical spectacle:

> Amuse him a little, eh? A piece of comic theatre, eh? I will be the audience and you two the actors. (44)

The post-imperialists mock the very African frustrations which they themselves have engendered.

There is one scene where grim reality edges over into grotesque extremes akin to some of the effects in *Devil on the Cross*, again with theatrical overtones. While the destitute children stone Matigari whom they fear as an intruder into their derelict sanctuary, passing cars draw up, not so that their occupants can help to stop the fray and rescue the bleeding elderly victim, but so that they can enjoy the violence as audience to a free peepshow:

> When the children saw him leaving, they jeered and threw more stones with renewed vigour . . . Cars carrying European, Asian and African occupants drove by. Some stopped by the roadside to give the passengers a chance to enjoy the scene of children pelting an old man with stones. Some of them stayed inside the cars and watched the drama through the windows. Others sat on the boots or leaned against their cars, sipping their Cokes or puffing their cigarettes. They were not the only observers. Shopkeepers and their customers crowded the doorways or stood in little groups outside . . . What curse has befallen us . . . that children and their parents should be fighting while our enemies watch with glee? (17)

Rich as *Matigari*'s inheritance from its predecessors is, of special interest must be its own unique contribution to the canon. We have already sketched in *Matigari*'s fable-like symbolic quality linked with the depiction of the actuality of the lives of the wretched of the earth in such a society; and the satiric vein we have already discussed in some detail. The heart of the fable is Matigari's mission to reclaim 'his house', which is really a socialist claim on behalf of African workers for a share in the good life that their 'sweat and blood' have produced.

In seeking to re-motivate his people's claim to their inheritance and birthright, Matigari must come to terms with three facts. First, that re-incarnated colonial usurpation is perpetuating possession of the country's wealth through multi-national commercial monopolies. These successfully gear the repressive power of an outwardy indigenous government so as to hold workers down in slave-labour conditions. Second, this is possible because an indigenous elite, rich in political and economic power — backed up by pervasive social influence — has uncompromisingly adopted the lethal culture of the former settlers. Third, in consequence, the people at large have become so drawn into despair and resignation as to be brainwashed and terrified into abandoning any sense of dignity, pride or human worth: the fight has been knocked out of them.

Late on, Matigari realizes in consequence that it is too early to relinquish his tools of war: a vision that he hands on to Muriuki. Reluctantly, he has no choice but to seek to revive the people's fighting spirit. This is Ngũgĩ's only work apart from *The Trial of Dedan Kimathi* in which a fighter is the key protagonist. In *A Grain of Wheat* Kihika is in the background as a revered hero of a campaign that has been concluded. Now Matigari, who has been a fellow fighter with Kimathi, like him re-activates his co-workers' battle-cry, even more specifically in the present. In no other work of Ngũgĩ's is the claim to national wealth made more unequivocally at a national level, involving the whole country and every stratum of society. Speaking for Kenya, Ngũgĩ now speaks for every African, every third-world nation in which a morally barren group has turned the whole social system upside-down and sentenced the vast majority of citizens to the strangle-hold of penury.

Matigari's quest is interwoven with his own symbolic life story, which is characteristically reiterated a number of times. This is the life story of a colonized African Everyman. It looks back to a purely traditional past. It is centred first on the colonial period, with its alienation of the land and its exploitation of the work-force; followed by the extended struggle for independence (in Kenya primarily the Mau Mau period). And it is now brought up to date in the period of neo-colonialism during which the new quisling elite collaborate in the continued alienation of land and property from their 'rightful owners' — the mass of the people. Settler Williams, Senior and Junior, represent the active colonialist beneficiaries; while John Boy, Senior and Junior, are the sycophantic betrayers contriving to grab all that is left over. The moment when Matigari, as a type figure, revolts against servitude and decides to join the fighters for freedom in the forest, is the moment when John Boy Senior prevents Matigari from shooting Settler Williams (as Wariinga shoots the Old Man in *Devil on the Cross*).

Meshed with these themes is the demand, already discussed, that the tiller, the tailor, the builder, and the industrial worker shall have fair shares of the food/clothes/houses/cash that they generate with their labour; and the angry denial that a pseudo-legal 'contract' gives capitalists the right to abrogate the proper heritage of the masses. Matigari, then, stands proxy for his innumerable down-trodden countrymen: 'I first lost my home; then my children were scattered all over the country' (15). When he first sees Muriuki's fellow orphans

> his heart beat wildly. Let me hurry and tell them that I'm back. Let me tell them that the years of roaming and wandering are over. We shall all go home together. (10)

We have already quoted the passage when Matigari and his friends first see 'the house':

> overlooking the whole country stood a huge house which seemed to stretch out for miles, as if, like the plantation itself, it had no beginning and no end. (42)

And when Matigari addresses Williams and Boy about the house he says

> in a raised voice as if addressing a huge crowd. 'Yes, come all, and let us light a fire in the house together! Let us share the food together, and sing joyfully together!' (51)

Even within the world of the novel, Matigari is not alone in seeking 'To keep the fire of freedom burning' (20) — these are Ngaruro's words. Once they have mustered their spirits, both the radical teacher and the student speak out fearlessly even as they are sentenced in the court of para-law. And it is Ngaruro, the union leader, who argues the most directly socialist case to be presented in the novel in response to the Minister's attempt to force the workers to abandon their strike (109–10). It is a highly representative audience that is assembled for that meeting and they greet Ngaruro's declaration with prolonged applause and ululation; while they respond to the Minister's eulogy of Williams' company for presenting shares to the party with stony silence, prompting the Minister to make a fool of himself by upbraiding them: 'Why are you not applauding ?' (108). Similarly so after he triumphantly announces the end of the strike: 'Who is that booing?' (109).

So the living myth of Matigari develops and spreads far and wide. His first disciples (an apt word as we shall see) — Guthera, Muriuki and Ngaruro — are soon joined by a growing band: the orphans living in the derelict cars (now penitent for their earlier aggression), his fellow-prisoners in the gaol, and then ordinary folk everywhere in market-places, shopping-centres, eating places, crossroads, farmlands. Their minds are stirred with a new hope and dawning courage:

> The patriots . . . are back, and the workers agree with Matigari's call (60) . . . Those who went have come back! . . . to claim the products of our labour (72) . . . imperialists and their overseers should pack their bags, because the owners of the country are back (74) . . . The dogs and the policeman just dropped their tails between their legs and took off (77) . . . Give the stolen wealth back to the owners! Serves the imperialists and their servants right! They have really milked us dry. (78)

Matigari's rallying words have spread like wild-fire (as the police in the real world found when they started tracking Matigari down in earnest!)

But Matigari himself switches his campaign from these stirring calls to action, to more abstract and generalized questions. Repeatedly he asks, 'Where can one find truth and justice in this society?' The people do not recognize this metaphysical seeker for ideals as the very Matigari whom they have been discussing so excitedly:

> What on earth is he talking about? (73) What is he asking now? Let me be off. Me too. And me. I'll go now. (77) Who is this asking such difficult questions? (79)

The psychology of these unassuming citizens can easily be understood. The man in the street may well react positively to the right kind of rallying talk that strikes chords in his heart. But he is likely to turn away from philosophical discussion, which he regards as going over his head. What is less easy to understand is Matagari's strategy in this period of his mission — and Ngũgĩ's. Is Matigari being criticized by his author for misreading those he would rally in expecting too much of them? Ngũgĩ must indeed have been familiar with sincere socialist intellectuals who are publicly anti-productive when they delve into abstract theory. Or are the citizens being criticized for submitting to temporary frustrations, refusing to think about the permanent principles that lie behind their now flagging protests — for playing safe by sticking to the facts, and failing to consider the inspiring ideas that those facts should raise if problems are to be unswervingly addressed — however long it may take to resolve them?

In a still wider perspective, this whole section of the novel relates to Matigari's third problem. People have become wearied by unavailing resistance; even more, they are terrified by active and violent persecution which deliberately aims to drive them into a state of abject silence, an acceptance of impotence. We hear Everyman fearfully retreating into despairing resignation, which then becomes stubborn indifference — spiritual death. As one observer of the police assault upon Guthera puts it:

'The girl was screaming with fright. But people just stood as if their very backbones were made of fear. Or as if their veins and arteries had fear flowing in them instead of blood.' (76)

Even Matigari's former allies — the lecturer and student who were in prison with him — are for a while intimidated into simply protecting their own interests in a highly precarious society. Indeed much of the final public frenzy could be characterized as fundamentalism capitulating into fatalistic hopes for a miracle to rescue the masses without their having to lift a finger.

By implication Matigari is exploring the thesis that no people can be saved until each individual has saved himself; that only those who have freed themselves from terror can know the true value of freedom and be willing to strive towards it. So his roaming the country incognito is not merely justified on a plot level in that an escapee from jail needs to conceal his identity. It is also significant thematically from the standpoint that only choices freely made are uncoloured by moral and social pressures: given Matigari's superhuman reputation, responses to any appeal from him in his public persona would now be conditioned by mob hysteria.

But things have come to such a pass that only dynamic leadership, such as Matigari offers, can electrify the workers to fight again for their rights. So at the Minster's meeting Matigari once more unambiguously offers that leadership. Consequently the very people who appeared to be maimed and dehumanized by fear, now speak up to incite their fellows to challenge the ill-gotten wealth of the rich and sweep away the false social structures they have built; thus demonstrating that it was only the creative insight of good leadership that had been lacking to inspire them. Ngũgĩ has long been amongst those deploring individualistic messiahs and favouring group leadership. But careful consideration of his former writings confirms that he had never denied that group leadership itself needs an infrastructure: just as no democratic committee can function effectively without a good chairman. Matigari throughout accepts his role as a social catalyst, an inspiration to focus a people's joint will. Without such a focus citizens show themselves to be rudderless, swayed only by fear breeding helpless inertia.

Matigari's efforts to re-awaken the people to active and effective protest are counter-balanced by the actuality of their suffering and the intensity of the fear inhibiting them, which are clearly spelt out in the novel. The facts are reiterated in general terms by those whose will-power he has begun to re-kindle:

things will not remain the way they are today. For how can the present conditions continue when foreigner . . . can always get places to pitch their tents? Tents in which to hide their military gadgets? Tents in which to store the wealth stolen from us? And when their black overseers are busy taming the entire population with honeyed tongues or silencing them with police boots! (79)

One of the positive aspects of *Matigari* lies in the new edge of sharpness with which people express their disgust with the government and all its instruments.

The actualities of the society are tellingly personalized in individual stories such as that of Muriuki's mother, harassed by a rapacious landlord for the rent of her tiny hut which at length burns down and kills her. Or the devout Guthera who agonizes over the choices involved in saving her patriot father's life by prostituting herself to the police superintendent; and then continuing to rescue her younger brothers and sisters from starvation by means of this, the only trade open to her.

The prison sequence exposes the squalid conditions in the gaol, where the prisoners, while inhumanly overcrowded, are degraded by piss, shit and vomit. In particular the peasant farmer, the vagrant, the teacher and the student are arrested altogether arbitrarily. Each seizes the chance to tell the circumstances of their being apprehended by the law, and we are thus acquainted with a cross-section of unjust 'justice'.

Cruelty itself becomes a theme, powered as it is by the panicky consciences of the despots in their greed for money, power and status. While its manifestations in police sadism and excesses are evident, its root cause is the tyranny of the government itself, exercised through vicious laws, witch-hunting, threats veiled by bribes, and personified in 'Hooded Truth and Justice'.

While the plight of the oppressed is pictured realistically, the despots and their practices are stripped naked by savage satire. Oppression is conducted systematically by the false leadership and their stooges. At the meeting the Minister openly boasts to the deprived populace of his ostentatious opulence, including a seven-storey house and three swimming pools. At this meeting a parody of justice is vaunted in the form of Instant Justice presided over by The Hooded Truth as a demonstration of 'Christian democracy'; while ruthless neo-colonial business is applauded as 'capitalism with a socialist face' (108). It is clear that the rule of law here means whatever the government decrees in its own interests. The Minister blandly claims to the audience that the party that is oppressing them is *their* party.

Such a regime has inverted the whole moral order:

> In our land today lies are decreed to be the truth, and the truth is decreed to be a lie. Theft and corruption have become the order of the day. That is what people pride themselves on. (137–8)

> The robber calls the robbed *robber*. The murderer calls the murdered *murderer*, and the wicked calls the righteous *evil*. The one uprooting evil is accused of planting evil. The seeker of truth and justice ends up in prisons and detention camps. (150)

But amidst all this, Ngũgĩ does not sentimentalize the oppressed. He sees that all too often the one on the bottom rung of the ladder puts his foot on the head of the one grovelling at ground level. The tractor driver, his two accomplices and the two policemen gang up to charge the destitute children for entrance into the rubbish tip:

> He now understood what was going on. Each child had to pay a fee to enter. A ticket to enable them to fight it out with dogs, vultures, rats, all sorts of scavengers and vermin, for pieces of string, patches of cloth, odd bits of leather, shoe soles, rubber bands, threads, rotten tomatoes, sugarcane chaff, banana peels, bone . . . anything. (11)

And even among the orphans themselves, the bigger bully steals from the weaker child:

> The bigger boy knocked down the smaller one, sat on top of him and held him by the throat, strangling him. The smaller boy kicked about wildly but all the time clinging to the bundle of shoelaces. (12)

It is now time to look at Matigari himself as a character. One thread will link this study. Matigari is a symbolic figure from a modern fable. As such, he might not be expected to have an individual fictional personality at all. The striking thing is that Ngũgĩ does breathe such a personality into his creation. As with *Pilgrim's Progress* and *Animal Farm* so with *Matigari*, it is their authors' skill in creating characters out of symbols that infuses human interest and emotional involvement into what might otherwise be dry, text-book morality. In fact it is not an easy critical task to analyse just how Ngũgĩ has succeeded in this with Matigari. As we go along we shall try to accumulate pieces of contributory evidence.

The initial image of a freedom fighter from the forest carefully burying (not destroying) his weapons under a symbolically beneficent tree is captivating. He does indeed seemingly embody pathos. His boots are patched, his hair is grey, (5) his face is creased with age, (17) he is tired. (5) But in fact he never invites pity nor does he ever see himself as pitiable. There is thus a certain unassuming valiantness about this elderly figure. But is he elderly? There are chameleon attributes in this mythical character. He has extraordinary powers of recuperation, and properly inspired becomes radiant. After 'he felt his bladder and bowels nearly give way as the excruciating pain shot through his body' (18) at the end of the stoning, the help he gets from Ngaruro and Muriuki visibly uplift him:

> he sprang abruptly to his feet as though he had recovered such youthful strength as to overcome all the pain. He picked up his things, his eyes shining brightly as if he could see far into the future. (19)

And he seems able to communicate this inspiration to others:

> Ngaruro wa Kiriro sprung up as if new strength and confidence had been instilled in him by his brief contact with Matigari. (24)

As fearlessly he confronts the policemen who are savagely harassing Guthera,

> The courage of truth had once again transformed him. It seemed to have wiped age off his face, making him look extremely youthful. (31)

His wrinkles disappear as he first gazes at 'his' house:

His eyes shone brightly. All the creases on his face had gone, and youth had once again returned to him. (43)

And the same is reported by the man at the crossroads retelling Matigari's rescue of Guthera: 'the grey of his hair and the wrinkles on his face seemed to disappear' (76). Muriuki wonders at his resilience in their walk across the plantations:

Muriuki felt tired and ached all over. When he looked at Matigari, he could not help wondering: What sort of man is this ? I haven't seen him eat or drink anything, and he does not look in the least tired. (41)

The group weariness perhaps symbolizes the efforts over generations in tending and fighting for this land; just as Matigari communicates the will to throw off such deep exhaustion in the fight for human rights. These transformations are described in a way that makes them seem convincing, so we too marvel at Matigari as a human being. We too never see him eat except perhaps a mouthful when he shares his food among all ten in the prison cell. He orders tea once in an eating house, and asks the old woman in the wilderness for water — that is all.

Matigari's voice has a strangely compelling quality:

Matigari had a quality about him, a kind of authority in his voice and demeanour, which made people listen to him — (51)

even John Boy. The Minister himself cannot resist Matigari's eyes, and the special force that emanates from them:

Matigari stood tall, fearless, full of confidence. It was this quality about him that made people fear him. His glance was piercing, and he made one feel as if he were looking into the very depth of one's soul. (123)

In people's memories these qualities tend to fuse into fabulous imaginings since the people seem to believe anything of him:

Even if you were the one who had a gun, you would have slunk away in a similar fashion. His voice alone was like thunder and his eyes like fire! Smoke was gushing out of his nose, mouth and ears! (77)

The Matigari myth takes on many fabulous features. The petrol-station attendant sums up some of the contradictory reports:

some say that he is as tall as a giant, and that his head touches the sky. Others say that he is as little as a dwarf. Some say that Matigari is a woman, and others maintain that he is a man. Some people think that he is an adult, and others that he or she is a child. Nobody knows what nationality he derives from. (159)

These fabulous extentions broaden Matigari's significance as a symbolic figure. But at the centre of the myth remains a human and humane figure, fearless, confident, soul-searching, with authority.

Something in Matigari's voice made them listen to him attentively. There was a sad note about it, but it also carried hope and courage. (56)

Sadness, hope, courage. He is tenderly, passionately concerned about 'his children' and about all the persecuted: 'His heart beat in rhythm with his thoughts. He wanted to embrace all the children and take them to his home that very moment' (16). And he evokes a corresponding affectionate, self-sacrificing loyalty from those close to him, nourished by gratitude and overpowering admiration. When he suggests parting company with Muriuki and Guthera to preserve them from danger, Muriuki exclaims: 'We are the children of Matigari wa Njiruungi' (139) and they will not hear of leaving his side.

Matigari has a vision 'of himself and his children'

> entering their house together, lighting the fire together and working together for their home, smoke drifting from the roof of their common home . . . They would build their lives anew in the unity of their common sweat . . . A paradise on this earth. (16)

And this is where his constant search for truth and justice culminates: justice for the tiller, the tailor, the builder, the factory worker — and for the children. This is why he will not fearfully seal his lips in the face of oppression.

While Matigari's passionate (near fanatical) dedication to his country and love for its oppressed and impoverished people may be regarded as part of his armour as a fabled hero, it may also be seen as characteristic of certain individuals in the real world. Even more significantly in this respect, he is human enough to have his doubts, his moments of despair, a sense of desolation:

> Where was truth and justice in life ? He felt so lonely. Thoughts of saving himself only and forgetting all the rest crept into him and weakened his resolve. He left behind the paths walked by the people. He went into the wilderness. (86)

He is compelled to fundamental questionings which are never fully resolved:

> If . . .If . . . If . . . If . . . If what? The line that divided truth from lies, good from bad, purity from evil, where was it? What was the difference between right and wrong? Who was the evil one? Was it the one who led another into sin, or the one who actually sinned? Who was the bad one? The one who drove another into bad ways, or the one caught carrying out the evil? (85)

We feel his act of will in refusing to let his determination falter more than momentarily. Thus Ngũgĩ does not let him lapse into a dull and unconvincing moral automaton. Matigari, as the central symbol, is also a man, a character, a troubled thinker.

In most of Ngũgĩ's novels there are biblical references, direct and indirect, and *Matigari* is no exception. While his attitude towards Christianity became more negative from the time of the composition of *Petals of Blood*, the primary thrust against Christianity remained his angry denunciation of hypocritical Christians and the religion's role as a support wing of colonialism, notably in the fight against Mau Mau, and later the support it gives to neo-colonialism. The priest in *Matigari* is an epitome of all that Ngũgĩ has consistently despised and condemned in the international Christian establishment, and in individual hypocritical religious display. Nominal Christians like Settler Williams, John Boy and the Minister and his wife form a chorus on this theme. But Christian humanism has much in common with the morality, personal and socio-political, that Ngũgĩ always espoused. Guthera's father expresses what is close to their author's essential attitude:

> what mattered was God's word and His commandments, and not the differences that any two churches may have had. The real Church of God resided in people's hearts. The rest were mere edifices. (33)

Thus there is no essential contradiction in the parallels that are specifically suggested between Christ and Matigari. During the episode in which Matigari shares his food with the other inmates, the drunk delivers off-the-cuff a para-biblical rendering 'as though he were reading the Bible from the pulpit' with detailed references to the Last Supper and its repercussions in dogma:

> This is my body, which I give to you. Do this unto one another until the Second Coming. He then took the cup, and after blessing it he said: And this cup is a testament of the covenant we entered with one another with our blood. Do this to one another until our kingdom comes, through the will of the people. (57)

The secular modifications are very clear, but the parallel with the original is unmistakable. Immediate references and later reports hint at the escape from prison being effected miraculously by the Angel Gabriel: 'This must be a dream! Or perhaps a miracle' (65). And certain imagined memories picture Matigari holding 'a flaming sword'. Before going to prison Matigari is reported saying, ' "You will see me again after only three days" ' (79). The counterbalancing explanations of how the trick was done perhaps serve the dual roles of calling in question the Bible's own mystique without dispelling the ethereal quality that rubs off on Matigari.

Some of those awaiting trial in the law courts discuss the Matigari rumours, including the idea that he is Christ; and suggest corroboratory evidence in baby Jesus having been carried to Egypt in Africa, and that the longest surviving Christian church is said to be in Ethiopia. In the same discussion, Christ's argument — 'For you were hungry, but they gave you no food . . .' is turned against 'imperialists and their overseers' (81).

Many readers must become increasingly unsure how far Ngugi expects us to go in interpreting this parallel. It is therefore an effective defusing of this mounting but unspoken tension when Matigari is directly questioned on this issue:

> 'Tell us, are you the one whose Second Coming is prophesied ?' asked one of the boys.
> 'Jesus Christ? The Lord who will bring the New Jerusalem here on earth ?' added another. (156)

Matigari's response may well be regarded as the culmination — not of the socio-political issues of the tiller/the tailor/the builder/the worker getting their just dues, nor of Matigari's demand for the restitution of 'his' house — but of major aspects of his ongoing search in general for justice and truth:

> No . . . The God who is prophesied is in you, in me and in the other humans.

He has always been there . . . Imperialism has tried to kill that God within us. But one day that God will return from the dead. (156)

It is almost as if Ngũgĩ's and Matigari's belief system is being presented as a secular arm of Christianity.

Matigari then speaks his credo, which must by definition inter-relate with the more pragmatic socio-political issues which are the practical expression of such moral beliefs:

He will return on the day when His followers will be able to stand up without worrying about tribe, race or colour, and say in one voice: Our labour produced all the wealth in this land. So from today onwards we refuse to sleep out in the cold, to walk about in rags, to go to bed on empty bellies . . . Let the soil return to the tiller, the factory to the worker . . . That God will come back only when you want Him to. (156)

In discussing the conclusion of *Matigari*, we shall have the opportunity to consider more fully the structure of the work, and also to examine critically certain tentative reservations about its execution. For the last part of the novel focuses all such issues.

Matigari is in many respects a symbolic picaresque novel, since its protagonist is always moving on towards only partially defined goals. It adopts the form of a search — a recurrent traditional literary (and oral) pattern. Matigari is, throughout, aiming to find and repossess his home; and in the process is seeking for justice and truth.

True to the widespread journey tradition in the verbal arts, *Matigari* has a tight time sequence which compresses its comprehensive themes into a coherent, easily followed narrative. 'It was only yesterday that the doubts were cleared. Settler Williams fell . . . And so today is my homecoming' (22). 'Today' is here the novel's first day. The scheme occupies three full days and the morning of the fourth. Each of Parts One and Two spans one day, while Part Three covers the third day and the fourth morning. The time scheme is harped upon — we are never allowed to forget it: 'today', 'this morning', 'yesterday', 'tomorrow', 'in three days' time' and so on. This constant awareness of the sequence through the four days of Matigari's visitation gives the tale a compellingly urgent forward thrust, a sense of purpose, progression, of campaigning towards a specific outcome.

In terms of pattern, the penultimate period of, on the one hand, the triumph of Matigari the myth, and simultaneously, on the other hand, the failure of Matigari the man, as he is cold-shouldered in his anonymous tour of enquiry round public places, is deliberately contradictory. It introduces complexity into the basically simple plot. His is not a razzmatazz whistle-stop campaign of mindless cheering and self-congratulation. Building up a solid community of informed and active protest is seen as no easy task. Matigari goes through phases of despair and deep despondency. He is challenged. It is through sheer will-power that he musters an appropriate counter-challenge in the Minister's meeting, when he is again recognized and cheered, and rouses the whole crowd of followers to determined activism. The audience defiantly singing their way out of the hall, and carrying the message of the banned songs across the land, reminds one of the finale of *The Trial of Dedan Kimathi*.

The fever-pitch frenzy of agitation which rocks the whole country as Matigari is expected at 'the house' is also two-edged satirically. The now ludicrously frantic government actually mobilizes its military and police might for a battle — against one man! Conversely, the huge throng of people that has poured into the area either at best yearns naively for a miracle to deliver them from slavery without any effort on their own part; or at the worst merely thirsts for an entertaining spectacle.

From another viewpoint, there is some sense of anti-climax intermixed with the uplift of *Matigari*'s last scenes. The novel is structured as a symbolic quest, as a powerful fable. Yet Matigari falters in carrying through his initial symbolic plans. At the end of the thrilling police chase and its aftermath, we are as disappointed as Matigari that he is unable himself to unearth his symbolic weapons — as he had intended. Nor does he hand them over in person to the younger generation, personified in Muriuki. Furthermore, Matigari does not repossess his representative house intact, nor entertain his fabulously extended family to food there as he promised. The climactic conflagration certainly implies a dramatic clearing of the ground for a new start; but when at last he reaches the house in the midst of a congress of supporters, Matigari does not become the rallying point of a popular, positive crusade as we had hoped — and indeed perhaps expected.

It may be argued that this is a realistic portrayal of the difficulties inherent in such a crusade, just as the end of *Petals of Blood*, and indeed of *Devil on the Cross* each embodies a calculatedly muted sense of triumph to be fulfilled in the future. But clearly, as we have reiterated, *Matigari* is a deliberately simplified symbolic tale; and so the question must surface as to how fitting a symbolic climax, whether similarly muted or not, we find in this work.

Matigari was never going to be an easy work for which to find an adequate ending. Learning perhaps from the underlying who-dun-it plot of *Petals of Blood* (which gives it a skilfully tense structure without obscuring its serious themes), Ngũgĩ resorted in *Matigari* to a different popular pattern. The final climax is approached via a breath-taking car chase (as in many melodramatic action films and novels). The escapee is the hero. Will the misguided police 'get him'? Tension. Suspense. And as all seems lost we reach the surprise shock of his crashing the Mercedes Benz through the front door of the house. All these ingredients of a traditional spine-chilling adventure are now skilfully moulded to serve the turn of a serious work. (Great writers, not least Shakespeare, have always made unpredictable use of popular modes.) Yet when all is said and done, we harbour lingering reservations. Was Ngũgĩ carried away, in finding this ingenious solution to the problem of a gripping ending, into playing down the expected climax for Matigari himself at the serious fable level?

Clearly Ngũgĩ took into account his need to avoid building Matigari up simply into a traditional hero or messiah — a figure which, as we have discussed, he had always found inappropriate for any popular social struggle. And in this he has succeeded. Yet the very last sequence involving Matigari raises questions which are not easily answered. The hints of miracle and apotheosis tend to maintain the shadowy messiah parallel. Matigari (unlike Guthera) seems immune to bullets though surrounded at close quarters by overwhelming armed force. His incredible final crawl to the river in the teeth of innumerable snarling dogs (that have already tasted blood) and 'the whole army of killers' (174) who are doubly motivated to 'get him'; his desperate athletic leap with the wounded Guthera in his arms right into the main current of the stream; are feats worthy of any boyhood hero. His seeming disappearance (and presumably Guthera's) is a clever solution to the tricky problem of extricating him from the plot. But here we are again faced with the symbolic ambivalence of the river into which Matigari plunges. Perhaps his essentially symbolic role made the apparent element of mystic apotheosis acceptable to Ngũgĩ.

However, it seems legitimate to ask whether readers should be left to search for implications in a deliberately simple, straightforward mode. But perhaps they should. Fables themselves often traditionally had, by definition, fabulous elements. One would love to know in some detail how the original Gikuyu audience (whom Ngũgĩ had primarily in mind) grappled with such puzzles It is possible that most Gikuyu simply took them in their stride as part and parcel of the traditional form which Ngũgĩ had entered into with such verve.

'Who was Matigari?' The recurrent question appears twice on the penultimate page, the very last two times his name occurs. To the second and last of these is appended the further question, 'Was he dead, or was he alive?' Here we may do well to remember the challenge that Ngũgĩ has characteristically thrown out to his immediate audience at the end of most, if not all, his novels. On the last page of *Weep Not, Child*, he challenges youthful Kenya not to fall into the escapist trap of suicide or retreat. In *The River Between* the young are again invited to embrace Waiyaki's passionate championing of education while side-stepping his disastrous abandonment of its political corollaries. In *Devil on the Cross* (to curtail the potential list) the choice between following Wariinga or Gatuiria is inescapable. Should we not then presume that at the close of *Matigari* Ngũgĩ's ideal reader would respond to the question 'Was he dead, or was he alive?' with the unhesitating response, 'Alive — in me'.

Indeed, in asking such questions as we have raised, one still surely has no doubt that the central thrust of Ngũgĩ's purposes must have found its mark in intended readerships. Ngũgĩ has brought off the rarely achieved task of creating a socio-political fable of great force and immediate relevance. On the last page, Muriuki — the youngest of Ngũgĩ's key figures apart from The Boy in *The Trial*, the representative of all derelict children and indeed of a whole new generation, and ultimately personifying oppressed Kenyan society at large — joins Karega and Wariinga as each looks forward into the future of their respective novels: not with false optimism — Muriuki cannot but be disarmed before effecting any significant protest in the literal world — but with determined, active, challenging hopefulness. At one level, the police and their controllers knew what they were doing in setting up a search through villages to try and circumvent and demobilize Matigari, their greatest antagonist!

PART III

Short Stories, Plays
& Non-Fiction

The Short Stories

Ngũgĩ reflects in the Preface to *Secret Lives*, the volume published in 1975 which gathers together all his short stories to date, that 'the stories in this collection form my creative autobiography over the last twelve years and touch on ideas and moods affecting me over the same period'. These tales do indeed offer something of a cross-section of Ngũgĩ's preoccupations and stylistic experiments. Certain characters and settings reappear from *The River Between*, *Petals of Blood* and, more fleetingly, from *A Grain of Wheat*, and this underscores the thematic and stylistic relationships between the novels and the stories.

The collection is grouped into three sections, the first two of which date from the author's years in Makerere except for the final piece in Part Two. This and all but the very last story in Part Three were written later after his return from travels overseas.

The first section relates to a more or less self-contained pattern of life still retaining most of its traditional features, and centres on dilemmas within the society resulting from childlessness, from drought, from starvation. Characteristically, the first word of 'And the Rains Came Down!' — which we may regard as representative of the earliest tales — is the name of the central character. In a majority of the stories the protagonist is introduced to us in the opening sentence, and only in one case later than the second paragraph; in the novels, on the other hand, chapters often begin with descriptive passages. This already indicates Ngũgĩ's grasp of the pithiest of all fictional forms. As is also frequently the case, 'And the Rains Came Down!' concerns a woman, and specifically portrays aspects of the woman's lot in life: 'It was good and sweet to rest after a hard day's work, having laboured like a donkey' (9).[1] For Ngũgĩ it is the village mother who is the prototype of womanhood:

> John remained long, looking at her. What made such a woman live on day to day, working hard, yet happy? Had she much faith in life? Or was her faith in the tribe? She and her kind, who had never been touched by ways of the

whiteman, looked as though they had something to cling to. ('A Meeting in the Dark', 59)

This passage serves to highlight the bitter irony of Nyokabi's barrenness in 'And the Rains Came Down!'.

In his earlier stories Ngũgĩ normally adopts the classical mode of plunging at once *in medias res* — starting at the beginning of the final climax and then insetting the events leading up to it. Nyokabi is exhausted at the end of her daily chores, and is about to react violently to the pent-up frustrations which stem from her central problem: 'Her life seemed meaningless and as she sat there looking vacantly into space, she felt really tired, in body and spirit . . . So old. And no child!' (9) Ngũgĩ is often concerned in both the short stories and the novels with characters who reach a moment when they must face, and attempt to resolve, the apparent futility of their existence. Mukami in 'Mugumo' is disillusioned with her marriage, as, for different reasons, is Miriamu in 'Wedding at the Cross'. Wanjiru in 'Minutes of Glory' and Wahinya in 'A Mercedes Funeral' face the unending greyness of life at the bottom of the heap. Existence has no meaning for the old woman in 'Gone with the Drought' after her child's death, nor for Kamau in 'The Return' when he comes back from detention to find that his wife, thinking him dead, has gone off with another man.

Nyokabi feels alienated from the community by her barrenness. Jealousy of her fertile, successful age-mates condemns her to a lonely world, as does Wanjiru's envy of rival prostitutes. Ngũgĩ expresses compassion for individuals who are cut off from their social group and must grapple with problems alone: the childless village woman or the bedraggled town bar-girl — Mangara in 'The Black Bird' and John in 'A Meeting in the Dark', Njoroge in 'The Martyr' or Joshua in 'The Village Priest'. Each is struggling with a problem that is beyond his or her control. Kamau in 'The Return' resolves his situation for himself in the end, as does Nyokabi. Ironically, Njoroge's solution in 'The Martyr' leads to his death. Only Joshua finds help from another human being.

Nyokabi torments herself with girlhood memories of her mother's singing of 'A woman without a child'. The links with oral tradition are both specific and all-pervasive. Though the form and structure that Ngũgĩ adopts for the short stories change over the years, even the earliest show an instinct for the form. His talent relates to the experiences of growing up in a story-telling community, grafted on to natural aptitude. There is no need to look beyond Gikuyu tradition for the original inspiration of these tales, whatever later influences may be traced or conjectured. Such a spur was specially fortunate in the 1960s when short stories were not as yet back in fashion with British publishers.

'And the Rains Came Down!' opens at the moment when something inside Nyokabi is about to snap: 'the pain that had filled up her heart, rose and surged up her soul, up her throat' (10). So she hastens out of the house, avoiding everyone and going she knows not where. The storm within her is to be matched by the storm in nature. As in all Ngũgĩ's fiction, the setting is precisely and intensely realized: Nyokabi's confrontation with the elements is authenticated by everyday, but keenly observed, details. Indeed, our author often evokes tropical rainstorms, in *The River Between*, for instance, as well as in 'Mugumo' and 'The Village Priest'.

Nyokabi's surroundings echo her own strong emotions and seem to take on a certain life of their own to supplement her inner urges:

> She wanted to cry or shout 'Come! Come rain! Wash me, drench me to cold death!'
>
> As if the rain had heard her dumb cry, it poured down with great vigour. Its delicate touch was gone. It was now beating her with a growing fury. (12)

This participation of the environment is a constant feature in the earlier stories. Physical objects seem to restrain Mukami from abandoning her husband's compound: 'The smouldering fire and the small stool by the fireside were calling her back' (2). As Joshua in 'The Village Priest' sets out to propitiate the God of the Gikuyu, 'The dark silhouette of the house and the barn beside it seemed watchful and ominous. He felt afraid' (25). In 'The Black Bird', 'The fluttering shadows on the walls were the incarnation of evil' (35). 'The stars above seemed to be anxiously awaiting Njoroge's decision' (46). 'Yet with every step', Kamau in 'The Return' 'seemed more and more conscious of the hardness and apparent animosity of the road' (49). Instances could readily be multiplied. Yet in the later stories the material world seldom mirrors a character's responses so directly.

Nyokabi must struggle and, as she does so, she finds herself face to face with the challenge of the crying infant at the mercy of the storm, which is the crux of this short narrative. Many of the stories, without overt didacticism, offer their characters a test, but it is here in 'And the Rains Came Down!' that this concept is most clearly spelt out:

> This was a moment of trial; the moment rarely given to us to prove our worth as human beings. The moment is rare. It comes and if not taken goes by, leaving us forever regretful. (12)

Nyokabi accepts the test and triumphs, as does Kamau by implication, and Miriamu in 'Wedding at the Cross'. John in 'A Meeting in the Dark' fails conspicuously. In 'The Mubenzi Tribesman' the protagonist has let himself down before the story begins and is given no second chance since Ruth opts out of her own responsibilities. Different readers will react differently to 'The Martyr', but there is little doubt that Njoroge faces up to his dilemma with courage and determination. The wife in 'Goodbye Africa' is vindicated while her husband is certainly not. In 'Mugumo' supernatural powers relieve Mukami of some of her responsibility, but she has already responded positively to her test. While in the world of sad objective fact Wanjiru achieves nothing, she scores nevertheless a strange and indefinable victory in 'Minutes of Glory'.

Nyokabi's valour is rewarded with the long-unfamiliar glow of human contact, which reminds us in a different vein of the end of 'The Village Priest': 'What did it matter if the child was not hers? Had the child not given her warmth, a warmth that rekindled her cold heart?' (13).

The strength of emotion is ever and again pinpointed in short, sometimes grammatically unconventional, sentences: 'To save another's child! . . . But, oh, the warmth!' (13). The same is true throughout the whole sequence of stories: 'How she loathed him now' ('Mugumo', 3); 'That he hated settlers was quite clear in his mind' ('The Martyr', 45); 'He felt desperate . . . His sense of guilt crushed him' ('A Meeting in the Dark', 64);'Freedom' (Goodbye Africa', 77); 'She wanted love; she wanted life' ('Minutes of Glory', 87); 'Huge sobs of self-pity' ('Minutes of Glory', 92); 'He was numb all over' ('The Mubenzi Tribesman', 144). This device stresses the violent feelings evoked in all the stories. These are tales of high passion and great intensity, though they seldom border on melodrama as do the early plays.

The climax of 'And the Rains Came Down!' is typical in its speed and economy. Nyokabi reaches home and collapses with her load. Her anxious husband brings warm dry clothes and refurbishes the fire. Then he recognizes the child as Njeri's. Nyokabi's latent jealousy of her age-mate is exorcized. Subtly suggested, in the very last sentence we have a characteristic Ngũgĩ 'turn', a miniature apotheosis. Nyokabi the failure has become in her act of human rejuvenation a heroine: 'To think that his wife had done *this!*' (14).

The resolution of 'Mugumo' is also positive. The brief journey that Mukami undertakes gives her time to go over in her mind quite naturally the bitter course of events that has transformed her from the treasured new wife of the husband she idolizes into the beaten, rejected, unfruitful spouse. At length Mukami reaches the haven of the fig-tree, the great sacred symbol of the Gikuyu which features over and over again in Ngũgĩ's writings. There is a constant awareness of tradition. 'Mugumo', 'The Village Priest' and 'The Black Bird' all subscribe to the existence of occult forces, however ambivalent Joshua's own position may be in the second of these. In 'Mugumo', the 'turn' occupies almost a page at the last. Mukami has a vision of Mumbi, the mother of the tribe. Under the influence of the mugumo she has already determined to go back and face her problems in her husband's house before she realizes that her agony will be resolved by the joy of pregnancy.

No relief is available at the end of 'Gone with the Drought'. It is the first of the sombre chronicles of disaster beyond resolution. But fitful contact is achieved in the strange half-relationship between the child through whom we see events and the old woman, broken by her son's death in the past drought. When at length the old woman dies, we are shown in her eyes 'a hovering spot of joy, of exultation, as if she had found something long-lost, long-sought' (19). It is the child's attempt to grasp and minister to the suffering of the aged woman which shapes the familiar happening into a story, while the father's quiet understanding of both completes the design.

Four of the six stories in Part Two of *Secret Lives* are also set in the village, but now Siriana Secondary School and Makerere University College loom in the background. The new influences of Christianity, the colonial regime and the Mau Mau Emergency are at work and play an important part even in determining the curse in 'The Black Bird'. We are in the world of the first two novels. The Christian religion is specifically influential in 'The Village Priest' but also bears down heavily in 'A Meeting in the Dark' through tensions created within John by uncompromising converts to the new religion. 'The Return' is in fact a return to the village, but from a British detention camp to the regimented settlement created artificially in the Emergency: 'The old village of scattered huts spread thinly over the Ridge was no more' (51). This story is thus linked to 'The Martyr' in which Njoroge is torn between conflicting loyalties to Mau Mau and his natural background, and to his hated, paternalistic white liberal memsahib in whose house he has worked for many years. This again provides a bridge to the later story of departing expatriates entitled 'Goodbye Africa'.

A number of the early stories appeared first in *Penpoint,* the journal of creative writing produced by the then English Department of Makerere University College.[2] Of four of these, we have three successive versions since they also figured in the Makerere anthology entitled *Origin East Africa.*[3] This sequence provides valuable evidence of Ngũgĩ's development as a writer. He revised these stories for their appearance in book form, tightening the phrasing and pruning wording that seemed to labour a point or over-simplify emotional subtleties. When he prepared *Secret Lives* ten years later he found few further changes necessary; but in addition to occasional touching up he did take the opportunity of eradicating finally the discredited vocabulary of witch-doctoring on the one hand and of tribalism on the other. Only in one story is the original content itself significantly readjusted: this is 'The Village Priest'.

This story is true to form in opening as the denouement is about to begin. We learn retrospectively that a drought has long been harassing Makuyu, where Joshua has already mustered his band of Christians. Following public confrontation with the rain-maker, Joshua has prayed that rain should not fall at his rival's bidding. But after the rain-maker has sacrificed an unblemished ram beneath the mugumo tree, the 'gathering black clouds' of the first sentence burst. Disgraced and distressed, Joshua sets out secretly to make peace with his traditional deity at the same fig-tree, but he is caught in the very act of this absurd right-about-face by the mugumo priest.

Up to this point the fifty or sixty amendments in the later texts primarily strengthen the style. A sentence that in *Penpoint* read, 'A big raincoat was the only thing that Joshua had put on, on top of his usual clothes and trudged quietly across the courtyard' is tidied up before reaching *Origin East Africa* and split into its two discrete segments: 'Joshua had just put on a big raincoat over his usual clothes. He trudged quietly across the courtyard.' But three sentences earlier, we can discern two levels of change. In October 1962 we had 'Early in the morning he would go all the way to the sacred tree and there make peace with the tribal god.' In 1965 the empty phrase 'all the way' is cut out. Not till 1975 is the term 'his tribal god' replaced by 'his people's god'.

In the second half of the story, in addition to these processes continuing, more radical changes appear. The mellow, humane Livingstone whom we meet in the earlier texts unobtrusively fostering Joshua's more mature Christian awareness, has become a patronizing, dominating white priest with an unequivocally negative influence on the life of Joshua and of Makuyu. The 'rain-maker' (no longer the 'little witch-doctor') first takes up this more strident theme. In previous versions he gets the chance to say very little before Joshua escapes: 'Hmm! So the fox comes to the lion's den. Ha! Ha! So Joshua comes to make peace. Ha! Ha! Ha!' But in *Secret Lives,* 'the fox' becomes 'the whiteman's dog', and the rain-maker is allowed to add: ' "I knew you would come to me Joshua . . . You have brought division into this land in your service to the white strangers. Now you can only be cleansed by the power of your people" ' (25).

At the end of the story it is worth following more closely the author's changes in attitude and approach through all three stages. The present concluding paragraphs replace a somewhat longer ending with a different emphasis. We can illustrate these shifts by setting the texts side by side at points where they diverge significantly. Here is part of the *Penpoint* version towards the end of the story:

> The old sternness and apparent hardness of Livingstone was no longer in his eyes but only a softened, sympathetic understanding of a man who seemed to be looking at a new Joshua . . .
>
> Suddenly the two men met in a hand-shake, hand-shake that made Joshua's heart and love go to [sic] Livingstone for in him, he saw not just a man with a white skin, stern and unpredictable, but a man who could understand another man. For them both it was a great moment, a moment of understanding . . . (6)[4]

The main change in this passage in *Origin East Africa* tends towards understatement and a greater restraint. The last two sentences just quoted are transformed:

> Suddenly the two men met in a hand-shake that made Joshua's heart and love go out to Livingstone. They mutely looked at one another: none broke the silence that settled about them. (64)

In *Secret Lives* the balance of the whole scene shifts:

> The old sternness and apparent hardness of Livingstone was no longer in his eyes but only a softened, condescending sympathy of a man sure of a new and stronger follower . . .
>
> With slow deliberation, Livingstone took Joshua's right hand in his and with the left patted him on the shoulder. He muttered something about a broken heart and contrite spirit. Joshua looked mutely at him. 'Let's pray,' Livingstone said at last. (27)

Originally Joshua played an active role in the final relationship. When his wife asks in surprise if Livingstone is leaving, 'The old village priest looked at his wife and then at Livingstone. "Not yet," he said.' This is eliminated in the 1975 text, and Joshua remains completely silent to the last as he attends to the authoritative eloquence of the white missionary. No longer is there any intimacy or real exchange between them. Ngũgĩ has developed a more radical attitude to the Christian intrusion into Africa.

The concluding words in both earlier versions are: 'When she came back a few minutes later, she found them both busy talking about the problems of Makuyu now that the rain had come and the menacing drought was over.' In the final text the conclusion is: 'When a few minutes later she came back she found Livingstone talking about the problems of Makuyu now that the rain had come and the drought was over. Joshua listened.'

The most striking alteration to any other story that reappeared in *Secret Lives* is at the end of 'The Return'. When Kamau learns that the wife whose image had sustained him throughout the ordeal of detention has been told that he was dead, and has found another husband, he finds that his past suffering, indeed his whole life, loses meaning. He contemplates suicide. But beside the river he discovers a new ability to comprehend his wife's dilemma and to come to terms with a very different future from the one he has contemplated so long: ' "Why should all the changes have waited for my return?" ' (54). Exercising a sterner discipline in his art in 1975, Ngũgĩ terminates the narrative at this point, omitting a somewhat sentimental half page from the previous script in which Kamau turns back to his mother and the author spells out his message too baldly: 'he became aware of the beauty of life in spite of its hardships' (*Origin East Africa*, 59). In now trusting his reader more fully, he evokes a truer and more spontaneous response.

Unlike the protagonists of the stories in Part One or Kamau in 'The Return', Joshua is to a large degree responsible for the situation he has to face, first through his own choice in embracing Christianity and then because of his apostacy — or his continuing perversity as the final version seems to suggest. Elsewhere the initial cause of disaster lies in something the protagonist has done, though we hardly ever feel that the transgression merits the punishment it receives. John has made a girl pregnant without giving thought to the implications of his act. The main character in 'The Mubenzi Tribesman' has stolen money. Both husband and wife in 'Goodbye Africa' are guilty, though she at least is willing to face up to her own actions, without regret (we are glad to observe) but without excuses.

Whereas 'The Village Priest' and 'The Return' both end on a positive note, the final turn in each of the other stories in Part Two, and also of 'The Mubenzi Tribesman', which can conveniently be discussed here, is sad, bitter, tragic. 'A Meeting in the Dark' epitomizes the quandary of cultural rootlessness which plagues a whole generation. John is admired by all the village as an educated young man who, on the verge of going off to Makerere, is without pride and still respects traditional proprieties. But when he makes his well-conducted village girlfriend (whom 'he knew he could have loved') pregnant, he is in torment. Why should he not simply bring the matter into the open and marry the girl? 'Had he been one of the young men he had met, he would not have hesitated in his answer' (63). But with a formidable Calvinist clergyman as father, and another as his past headmaster, John is in an agony of shame and uncertainty: 'His sense of guilt crushed him' (64). What is more, 'Marrying her would probably ruin his chances of ever going to a university' (65). Ironically it is partly because his father cannot forget that he himself slept with his wife before marriage that he intimidates his son with such absolute and severe expectations. John envies the freedom of other young men but cannot bring himself to defy his father in the smallest matter. The Calvinist parent and teacher have induced in their protégé a whirlpool of despair, which leads this gentle young man to the frenzy of throttling the quiet, determined girl, not even aware of the extreme to which he has gone. The darkness of his mental agony has destroyed them both.

'The Martyr' also ends in death as the frightened 'liberal' white colonial mother, filled with terror by her illiberal neighbours after the recent murder of a couple nearby, herself kills the faithful retainer who, despite his hatred of her complacent maternalistic attitude, comes to warn and save her. She has only faint inklings of what she has done. In 'Goodbye Africa' the death of the European couple's one-time house servant as a Mau Mau loyalist is in the past. Now the husband, who had tortured and killed this man in the course of duty while confronting Mau Mau, is haunted by the eyes of his former employee. He seeks to expiate his guilt in a drunken travesty of an African ritual, and then determines instead to relieve his soul by writing the whole thing for his wife to read. Since this is their last night in Africa, she herself plans to wipe the slate clean by admitting her infidelities with this very same 'boy': 'Freedom. And afterward their fevered love-making had finally severed her from the world of her husband and other District Officers' (77). She gets in first with her confession when the moment comes. In a savage pattern of ironies, however, he finds her assertion of life in her adultery far more heinous than the enactment of death in his own past. He suppresses his confession and is left to be pursued by the ghost of this African, whose vitality still calls his own in question.

The final turn in 'The Mubenzi Tribesman' is sadly ironic rather than surprising since we are surely expected to foresee the outcome. We know that the wife who has been spoilt by the pursuit of luxury and status in the city will not welcome from prison the young husband who appropriated money to keep up with her assumed lifestyle. We are sure that she will cling to her sugar-daddy and slam the door in his face. We acknowledge the hollowness of life when it is manipulated by pitiless greed and petty appetite.

The three longer stories in Part Three were written between *A Grain of Wheat* and *Petals of Blood*. They are set in corrupt, get-rich-quick, ruthless independent Kenya, where the unlucky and the unsuccessful are forced to the wall. The fortunes of Wanjiru and Nyaguthii in 'Minutes of Glory', of Wahinya in 'A Mercedes Funeral', and of the happy-go-lucky Wariuki in 'Wedding at the Cross' who becomes mesmerized by position and prosperity, demonstrate Ngũgĩ's concern about the debased conditions in which the poor live. Each of these stories is a protest against the disposition of the new sophisticated society. One tells of the repudiation of stultifying success, another of a flamboyant, if hopeless, gesture in defiance of failure and degradation, and 'A Mercedes Funeral' of how, through a quirk in the political rat-race, one of the wretched of the earth is mocked in death with what he could not attain in life.

'Minutes of Glory' asserts in paradoxical fashion what both human values and human integrity can and should be, in a situation which seems to have finally perverted them. It follows the career of Wanjiru through the bars around Limuru and then in Ilmorog. A school drop-out through no fault of her own, she drifts into being a skivvy in a bar and an unsuccessful part-time prostitute, just as Wahinya with his abortive passion for education stumbles from shop-porter to bus-tout to bar-watchman. Wariuki, full of exuberance and happy, unprofitable skills, is cowed by the establishment, personified in Miriamu's parents: 'They objected to their daughter marrying into sin, misery and poverty' (the first wryly assumed to be automatically associated with the other two); 'He did not want her to marry one of those useless, half-educated upstarts, who disturbed the ordered life, peace and prosperity on European farms' (99).

Wanjiru is an unsuccessful harlot because her romantic soul yearns for a true love relationship and makes her hate this dreary imitation, thus accentuating her lack of seductive graces. Wahinya too has his dreams: 'Beautiful dreams about the future. I imagine that even while sagging under the weight of sacks of sugar, sacks of maize flour, sacks of magadi salt and soda, he would be in a world all his own' (121). Only the wraggle-taggle Wariuki succeeds in actually living out his dreams by dancing his way through poverty and running away with the girl he loves, till he is hypnotized into mediocrity and respectability. At length he embraces the warped standards of a pompous, stereotyped society that wants to hear nothing of dreams, freedom nor happiness.

Wanjiru loses one job when she fights off her employer after he has been turned down by another manhunter. Unlike Wahinya, she retains a fierce pride even at the bottom of the heap. Wariuki does the opposite: he complacently conforms to the antics of soulless social class. Wanjiru's rival, Nyaguthii, is only apparently successful. In fact her bar-room and bedroom victories revolt rather than exhilarate her, and she secretly admires Wanjiru for being detached from the interminable chase: ' "you seemed to be above all this — somehow you had something inside you that I did not have" ' (94).

It is psychologically convincing that Wanjiru's control should finally snap when she finds herself despised and ignored even by someone almost like herself — the lorry-driver who is humbled in his attempts at social climbing and who sleeps with her at intervals because others refuse him. The converse of this ironic situation is played out in Miriamu having to watch and wait while her once heart-free milk-clerk relentlessly mounts the ladder of success, till he proudly emulates the life she has deliberately abandoned. Ngũgĩ is no inverted snob. He is aware of the extent to which many of the underprivileged aspire to bourgeois superiority and assuage their frustrations meanwhile by taking it out on those who are on an even lower rung than themselves.

Angered by the arrogant indifference of her lorry-driver, Wanjiru steals his money and has her fling. She could of course have made a more promising start at the oldest of trades in the big city, with her chic rig-out and consequent new-found confidence. She makes no attempt to do so. It is neither as thief nor as small-time go-getter that she has acted as she has. She thinks only of spitting once, briefly, in the face of fate and calling the bluff of the society whose false values mark her out as a loser. She knows just what she is doing in returning to the scene of her former shame and of her theft. She knows this is a blaze of false glory, a paper conflagration that will burn itself out in a few minutes and leave only ashes. But in these brief moments she has asserted herself. Wanjiru anticipates Wanja of *Petals of Blood*. She proves nothing to anyone else, but she proves to herself (and to the reader) that her lot in life is determined by accidents and external circumstances, not by anything inherent within her. It is Wanjiru's testament and also Ngũgĩ's. In the complex of ironies at the conclusion of the story, the final sentence is as powerful as any ending in the collection, and it is the success of his endings that finally stamps Ngũgĩ as a true short-story writer. Only one person understands what Wanjiru has done and grieves for her, her 'successful' rival: 'But behind the counter Nyaguthii wept' (96).

Miriamu also asserts her inner self in rejecting a life of pious affluence for the second time. Wariuki has destroyed his essential being by sacrificing everything to his trumpery success. So she must deny him at the formal church wedding which is to crown his cardboard ambitions under the new name of Livingstone: ' "No, I cannot . . . I cannot marry Livingstone . . . because . . . because . . . I have been married before. I am married to . . . Wariuki . . . and he is dead" ' (112). We are placed so as to sympathize fully with Miriamu's feelings as she claims her true identity. There is a rare misjudgement by our author in over-explaining the conclusion to us. The last word could have been left just once in Miriamu's keeping. But the ending is so skilfully contrived that it retains its force.

Like 'Gone with the Drought' and 'The Black Bird', 'A Mercedes Funeral' also has a narrator, but here the pattern is more Conradian: the narrator loquaciously interjects remarks to the assembled company. His breezy comic style is superimposed on the author's own sad and serious indictment of society. The multiple levels on which the story operates are neatly handled: though we learn much about the narrator and the four parliamentary candidates, the unfolding tragi-comedy of Wahinya's life and death remains central. The diverse fortunes of the candidates produce also a multiple ending, so the last word must be left to the half-attractive, half-irritating story-teller. But it is the climax of the sombre irony which comes a little earlier that impresses itself on our memories. The winner among the four contestants in the funeral stakes finds that his victory turns sour. The townsfolk cannot accept this making a mockery of the poor man's poverty-stricken existence by tawdry display of wealth. We are left to share a deep compassion for the deprived, and an angry revulsion against those who make a public exhibition of calculated, hollow sympathy so as to promote their own sordid interests:

> But somehow no applause came: not even a murmur of approval. Something had gone wrong, and we all felt it. It was like an elaborate joke that had suddenly misfired. Or as if we had all been witnesses of an indecent act on a public place. The people stood and started moving away as if they did not want to be identified with the indecency. (136)

If we read the earlier stories in *Secret Lives* with a growing awareness of the immense sadness of life and of admiration for those who respond positively to its harsh realities, by the time we reach Part Three we are caught up directly in protest against the new social environment in Africa which is proving in many ways to be as callous and as class-oriented as the old. The basic cause of suffering by the underprivileged is man's inhumanity to man — the black man's inhumanity to the black man. We feel the same passionate righteous anger against those who abuse power — an impulse which underlies *Petals of Blood*. Clearly the removal of the wrongs of colonialism has not produced a just or humanitarian order. If no specific political remedies or policies are spelt out, this is partly because they should be self-evident. One is reminded of George Orwell's assertion in *The Road to Wigan Pier*: 'economic injustice will stop the moment we want it to stop, and no sooner, and if we genuinely want it to stop, the method adopted hardly matters'.[5]

Perhaps Ngũgĩ's real aspiration when he published his collection of stories was to strengthen our will to *want* it to stop', and our refusal to be fobbed off with empty humbug on this issue.

Notes

1. Page references are to the first paperback edition of *Secret Lives* (Heinemann Educational Books, London, 1975).
2. 'The Fig Tree' (retitled 'Mugumo' in *Secret Lives), Penpoint* 9, December 1960, 39; 'The Return', *Penpoint* 11, October 1961, 77–82; 'Gone with the Drought', *Penpoint* 12, March 1962, 2–6; 'The Village Priest', *Penpoint* 13, October 1962, 2–6. 'The Wind', *Penpoint* 10, March 1961, 9–13, has never been reprinted.
3. *Origin East Africa: A Makerere Anthology,* ed. David Cook (Heinemann Educational Books, London, 1965). Ngũgĩ assisted in the selection from *Penpoint* of the material for this volume.
4. An identical sentence has been omitted from this quotation and from the parallel quotation from *Secret Lives.*
5. George Orwell, *The Road to Wigan Pier* (Secker & Warburg, London, 1959).

The Plays

Not only is Ngũgĩ careful and industrious as a novelist, he has also a natural flair, an instinct for the novel form, so that in his best work in prose fiction he combines inspiration and craftsmanship. The same cannot be said of his drama. The plays that he wrote alone show constant signs of strain. The characterization is rudimentary. Key figures tend to become mouthpieces for preconceived attitudes, so that the themes seem forced. The outcome is an often clumsy didacticism.

To date Ngũgĩ has published four plays by himself alone: *The Black Hermit* and the collection of three one-acters named after the short radio drama 'This Time Tomorrow'; and two in collaboration: *The Trial of Dedan Kimathi* in English with Micere Mugo, and *Ngaahika Ndeenda* in Gikuyu together with Ngũgĩ Mirii. Though, as has been suggested, the early plays can readily be faulted for want of both dramatic imagination and technical skill, they nevertheless clearly embody Ngũgĩ's social beliefs and outlook. Like the novels, they reflect the progression in his thinking from his humanist–moralist concern with ethical issues to his later advocacy of a radical transformation of society. *The Black Hermit* belongs at the beginning of this development.

If *The Black Hermit* is not a great play, it nevertheless gained importance because of the shortage for many years of alternative East African material to satisfy the demand for serious indigenous drama in schools, colleges and society at large. The play was written to mark Ugandan independence in September 1962. In fact it was first acted by the Makerere student dramatic society a couple of months after the celebrations in Kampala, partly because the working script was not ready as soon as had been hoped. In the Preface, written at the time of publication in 1968, Ngũgĩ relates the play to his thinking when he wrote it shortly before Kenyan uhuru:

> I thought then that tribalism was the biggest problem besetting the new East African countries. I, along with my fellow undergraduates, had much faith in the post-colonial governments. We thought they genuinely wanted to involve

the masses in the work of reconstruction. After all, weren't the leaders themselves sons and daughters of peasants and workers? All the people had to do was to co-operate. All we had to do was to expose and root out the cantankerous effects of tribalism, racialism and religious factions.[1]

Thus the main target for attack in the play is the blinkered viewpoint of individuals like Remi, the main character. Remi fell in love with Thoni during his village days but was too shy to approach her. Just as he was plucking up courage, he learned that she was to marry his brother. A mere six months after the marriage the brother is killed in a road accident. Traditional pressures impel Remi to take over his dead brother's wife and marry her himself. He does so reluctantly since he now believes she cannot really love him, and so after the ceremony he runs away and buries himself in the city.

The play opens in the village, where various groups are anxious for Remi to return. He is the only university-educated son of a small tribe: the reasons for wishing him back are diverse. His wife is genuinely fond of him and pines for him as her second husband; Remi's mother sympathizes with the abandoned girl and wants her son to come back and build a home and family. Thoni refuses to take another man to her bed to nurture her womanhood, preferring to remain despairingly faithful to Remi, though shamed by his evident rejection of her.

The elders are bewildered. After their compliance with Remi's urgings to vote for the Africanist party in the recent elections, he appears to have deserted them, leaving them without an obvious leader of their own. They assumed that he would become at the very least a DC, and possibly even an important figure in government, to plead their grievances with the authorities. They regard him as a potential source of power for the tribe:

ELDER:	Last month our diviner had a message from God.
	He had a vision,
	And there,
	He saw the tribe expand,
	Becoming powerful,
	Dominating the whole country.
	But here was a problem.
	The tribe had first to tend a plant,
	A green plant in their midst.
	The green life would lead us to power and glory.
NYOBI:	Where will you get the plant?
ELDER:	Remi, Remi. (10–11)

The priest wants Remi to return as his acolyte to help lead the tribe back to Christianity. Nyobi, Remi's mother, torn between these interests, remains motivated by mother-love.

In the second act we find Remi in the midst of an affair with the white girl Jane, though he has by now withdrawn from the night-life of the city. He still shares his belief in a non-tribalistic state with his friend Omange. They are both appalled by the increase of tribal partisanship in public affairs since independence, but it is Remi, Ngũgĩ's leading figure, who argues the government's case against the dissidents. When Omange differs in supporting the right to strike and declares, 'There are other ways of dealing with people who oppose you besides refusing to listen to them and crushing them', Remi demands, 'What, for instance?' Omange snaps back in a voice like the later Ngũgĩ's: 'You could give them what they want, what they fought for. The manpower of the masses ought to be the cornerstone of our economy, not foreign aid' (30). Yet Remi still believes in the first black government and urges the need to throw all available weight behind it:

> You are like any of those politicians who oppose the government. They don't realise that the problems posed by Independence are different from those of colonial days . . . can't we outgrow the opposition mentality and help to build? (30)

When the delegation of elders arrives to plead with Remi to become a leader of the tribe in the administrative or political field, he angrily refuses. However, when the Priest in his turn seeks the younger man's support, Remi withholds the bitter rebuff which he will later deliver in the third act — 'Pastor, you and your religion never did anything for our people. It's only divided them and made them weak before the whiteman' (74). Instead he abruptly sends a message through the Pastor that he will return. Later it turns out that his purpose in doing so is not what any of them expect, but the dramatic opportunities in this temporarily mysterious change of purpose are largely lost. Ngũgĩ does, however, achieve visually a most telling juxtaposition as Remi sees the bundle of charms and the Bible that the two delegations respectively have left behind to influence him:

> These — These — Pieces of superstition
> Meant to lure me home.
> Shall I find my peace and freedom there?
> These are part of me,
> Part of my life,
> My whole life. (45)

Before returning he must break with Jane, who for all her sincerity is romantically unaware that lack of experience disqualifies her from any possibility of settling in the village with Remi:

> I know your father was not a settler, is a teacher, one of the good sort. Still you have not experienced what I have experienced . . . To you tribalism and colonialism, the tyranny of the tribe and the settler are an abstraction . . . To you, African nationalism and what it means to us who suffered under colonial rule for sixty years can only be an intellectual abstraction . . . (47)

These powerful sentiments are somewhat undermined, however, when he has to admit that his real constraint is that he has secretly been married all along and we feel that Jane has good grounds for the contemptuous anger in which she walks out.

All sections of the community are in suspense in the last act awaiting Remi's return, though Thoni feels a deep foreboding which she tries to hide. It is a pity that Ngũgĩ baulks the enactment of the climax of the political theme. Remi's first public speech on his return is only described to us in a report by the 2nd Neighbour: in it he has upbraided his listeners for their chauvinistic tribalism. The play does not set out to exonerate Remi's blustering and self-assertive approach to delicate social problems. Thoni has been crouching unseen when Remi carelessly declares, 'I was wrong to marry her who was another's wife, a woman who did not love me' (65). She runs out and later we learn that she has killed herself.

The play thus sets itself against tribalism, but more particularly against the arrogant, self-obsessed simplifications of the young educated intellectual. When Remi feels trapped by the tribe, he hides himself in the city because 'I wanted to be myself' (32). 'To be a hermit means escaping from what's around you' (46). But in his mission to free his people 'from traditions and bad customs, /Free them from tribal manacles' (45), he can arrogantly claim 'I now know all. My stay in the city has taught me everything' (65). If he is right in principle, he is wrong in spirit when he declares violently, 'I will no longer be led by woman, priest or tribe' (65). Individual sensitivity is sacrificed to abstract principle; long-developed human situations are to be dissolved by ruthless, rigid theory. Remi perceives his mistake too late in the ominous disappearance of his wife just when he realizes that she has always returned his affection. And so the last words of the play are of self-blame:

> I came back to break Tribe and Custom,
> Instead, I've broken you and me. (76)

Whether it is readily clear to an audience that this recantation is not meant to qualify the play's attack on tribalism is open to doubt. In later years this ambiguity might have seemed less important since Ngũgĩ no longer believes that 'tribalism' is 'the biggest problem'. Now he would more likely agree with Omange's declaration in this early play, 'people have a right to destroy a government, any government that continues the practice of the colonial régime' (30).

Several of the key figures in this drama remain somewhat wooden. Jane, Omange and even Remi himself say what is required of them by the pattern of ideas and events but possess no vivid or complex life of their own. If Remi is criticized for his remoteness and egotism, this hardly justifies his external and formal presentation. The elders, on the other hand, are imbued with ritual mystery and dignity. The incantation in Act I Scene II (more powerful as it was when originally performed on stage in Gikuyu) offers an opportunity to the producer to introduce a new dimension into the production. And the swelling sound of what the playwright calls 'Africa's anthem' (63), sung in Kiswahili, looks forward to the group emotion which was to be the greatest strength of *The Trial of Dedan Kimathi*.

But it is the village women who lend some imaginative colour and true feeling to the play — the mother and the rejected wife. Thoni's plight is real. She will not make herself 'cheap before the world' by passing herself 'from hand to hand':

> Yet I can't do without a husband,
> Without a man to warm my bed,
> A man to ask me for a meal in the evening,
> A man to make me wash his clothes;
> And a child of my own,

A child to call me mother
To make me feel a new self. (3)

Her words stir our feelings:

The hut's gloom and loneliness
Has started eating into me. (5)

Her promise to conceal her grief and wander with it alone on the hills is full of sad foreboding. The concern the older woman feels for Thoni amid her own grief about her son deepens their relationship. Ngũgĩ dramatizes movingly his constant awareness of the vital yet often thankless role women play in African society. Thoni, torn between joy and fear at Remi's return, opens the last act. The sense of tragic inevitability in her final appearance is heightened by homely imagery:

I can't stay here in this place.
To be like an unwanted maize plant
That has been pulled out and flung on the bare path.
To be trodden beneath men's feet,
And left to wither and dry up in the sun. (66)

The moment when Thoni moves almost eagerly towards death, handled without sentimentality, is one of the most telling in the play. Here the verse form, which often seems arbitrarily employed among the prose, is vindicated. This vein of imaginative emotional insight constantly enriches the novels, but only seldom the plays. Ngũgĩ's collaborated success on the stage later was to depend more on rhetoric and group response.

The first two pieces in *This Time Tomorrow: Three Plays* are in many respects characteristic student playlets written for immediate production. The Stranger who links the action of 'The Rebels' lends dramatic coherence to the familiar theme of the educated young son of the village returning home with his chosen bride from afar only to be confronted by a traditional bride chosen for him by his father. Atmosphere is created by the forebodings, and a rudimentary attempt is made to consider both sides of the case. That Mary, the outsider, is a Ugandan instead of the usual rather improbable white fiancée creates a more challenging situation. The young man dithers and gracelessly deserts the girl he has brought from a distant land, but too late to save the life of his humiliated prospective wife. He blames himself for the desertion of Mary, and the elders for clinging to a tradition which divides Africa by rejecting a black girl from elsewhere. Ironically, the father had already been cursed in his own time for marrying against his father's wishes and then refusing the summons of his dying parent. The play is the fulfilment of this curse. This is a variation on the pattern of the forces played out in *The Black Hermit*. The son finally declares:

This is your doing. You wanted her to marry against her wishes. It is also my doing. I was not strong enough to stand by the light and truth of my conviction. It is the doing of all of us who forget that Africa is one and it is the home of one black race now bowed down by years of white misery and misshapen education. (15)[2]

The Stranger is there to emphasize these events as part of a cycle, but the action is too abrupt to avoid melodrama.

'The Wound in my Heart' takes up themes from the short story 'The Return' and from *A Grain of Wheat*. The militant, joyful returning Mau Mau detainee, eager to be reunited with his wife, finds her with child by another man — the adulterer here is a white man, again a somewhat melodramatic note. Background circumstances are not filled in and there is barely any complexity of characterization even in the returning Ruhiu. The wife kills herself before she can hear her husband's reaction. Like Gikonyo, his first urge is to take out his frustration on the child. As throughout Ngũgĩ's fiction, the woman in such circumstances is not blamed, directly or by implication: 'It is hard for any woman. Only this time your wife was forced into it' (26). As elsewhere the harsh but heroic lot of village women is emphasized. The sorrowing mother ends the play: 'Come elders, don't grieve for me. I too will bear this wound in my heart' (28).

Though social pressures are the ultimate cause of each of these miniature tragedies, the plays bear the stamp of a chill, bleak fatalism (rather than angry protest or sympathetic concern) which is far from the hallmark of Ngũgĩ's more carefully considered works.

'This Time Tomorrow' was solicited and long awaited for production on the African Theatre programme of the BBC African Service, which had offered a welcome opening for a number of African playwrights. This later play is a fierce protest against an affluent establishment ruthlessly depriving the have-nots even of what little they have. The slight secondary theme of the shanty-town Cinderella being rescued by her taxi-driver lover is rather clumsily related to the main subject of the City Council's Clean-the-City Campaign. This campaign is a cover for demolishing the slum market without offering any substitute, because its shacks are a great shame on our city. 'Tourists from America, Britain, and West Germany are disgusted with the dirt' (41). The idea of the journalist being both a handy commentator and a participant in the action originates in the demands of radio drama. At the same time Ngũgĩ is groping towards the form he was later to find in collaboration with Micere Mugo. The heart of the subject lies in the Shoemaker's response to the Journalist's glib professional probing. This man who has given his life to the cause of liberation is now displaced by those who have always played safe:

> It is not that I don't want to move. But the government should give me a place to go to. After all, I deserve it. I was a member of the Party . . . I took the oath in 1950 . . . We were fighting for freedom . . . I was arrested and sent to Manyani . . . A concentration camp . . . I came home after the Emergency. The white man had not gone. No job for me, no land either. So I came to this city . . . I have not starved. Tell me, tell me good people — why then should I move from here? (43)

Drama is being moulded by the playwright, somewhat crudely, into social protest, a rallying call. The crash of the bulldozer razing to the ground the only human shelters these people possess is an audible indictment of man's inhumanity to man, while the final cry of Njango, till now selling soup from her 'shelter made of cardboard and rotting tin', is an appeal to stand firm next time: 'They are herding us out like cattle. Where shall I go now, tonight? Where shall I be, this time tomorrow? If only we had stood up against them! If only we could stand together!' (50).

171

The Trial of Dedan Kimathi had a long gestation, as the writers explain in their introduction. In addition to the reasons they give for its being eventually completed in 1974, they were spurred on by their, or at least Ngũgĩ's, anger against Kenneth Watene's play *Dedan Kimathi* which was acted in the Nairobi National Theatre and elsewhere earlier in the same year. Neither Ngũgĩ nor Micere Mugo is likely to have underestimated the impressive quality of Watene's writing. They may not even have questioned the data on which he based his play, though in a biography surrounded by myth and controversy they probably had doubts about some of his material. In particular they would have been angered by the presentation of Kimathi as ruthless and selfish. And they may well have deplored the emphasis in the final climax on the killing of Nyati, Kimathi's veteran follower whom he is pictured as sacrificing on suspicion of sympathizing with moves to negotiate with the enemy. Watene clearly places dramatic emphasis on Kimathi's passionate revolutionary idealism, his charismatic leadership, his commitment to unconditional independence. But in placing Kimathi in complex human and historical perspective, Watene also depicts what he saw as inevitable human weaknesses in Kimathi, and withholds any final evaluation of his achievements, of the Mau Mau campaign, or of the validity of claims and criticisms made for and against the movement.

Watene is not neutral: he presents Kimathi as a heroic figure. But to Ngũgĩ and Micere Mugo as they developed their crusading socialist nationalism, the equivocal picture that emerges from Watene's play must have seemed to play down a cause which they sought to blazon. Their ambition was to rally the aspirations of Kenyan workers, stifled by the vested interests of the new black elite almost as effectively as by colonialists, and, it might seem, more irreparably. One starting point in such a campaign was evidently to revive awareness of the freedom fighters' struggles in the forests during the 1950s, aimed at independence with social justice. Kimathi, a key figure, was to be re-created as an inspiration and inciter to fresh positive action. For this, it was not Watene's subtleties and historical balance that were needed. A crusade requires its heroes and its flashpoints. Ngũgĩ and Micere Mugo saw drama as providing these so as to fire a popular audience. To see drama in this way is to give to it a role of immediate social significance. This is not the only important function of drama. But it is easy to see how impatient activists may feel with those who promote its less militant possibilities seemingly at the expense of its revolutionary drive.

The Trial of Dedan Kimathi is thus openly didactic. It aims at teaching Kenyans — and other interested Africans — about the fight for social justice that has already been waged in their country. It celebrates an outstanding leader in this recent struggle, and epitomizes in drama his trial and death at the hands of his colonial enemies, as an active challenge to his successors to continue struggling against cynical exploitation.

Scenes from 'the Black Man's History' (4)[3] are mimed as a background to these events. 'A rich-looking black chief' barters slaves for cloth and trinkets with 'a white hungry-looking slave trader'. A chain of slaves 'drag themselves through the auditorium. 'A cruel, ruthless fellow black overseer' supervises plantation labourers inspected by a white master. This is no desultory pageant but ends in a processional chant of 'anti-imperialist slogans through songs and thunderous shouts' (5). It provides dramatic shape and force when it is repeated later during the torturing of Kimathi under Shaw Henderson's orders. There is a blackout on Kimathi's ordeal, leaving the sound of the whip to accompany the silhouetted cameos of past oppression. The emphasis on black lackeys to colonial domination sets in train the primary theme of the play. The Woman, Kimathi's partisan, who is central to the simple plot-line, is deliberately not named. Like Kimathi, she is first and foremost a symbolic figure. One stage-direction gives the key to producer, actors and readers alike: 'Both Girl and Boy sit at the feet of the woman. It should be symbolic: the woman now represents all the working mothers talking to their children' (59). In the same vein, the Girl and the Boy are given no names.

Early on the Woman inspires the Boy with challenges which later echo through his mind as he grows into a young patriotic insurgent: 'the day you ask yourself: "What can I do so that another shall not be made to die under such grisly circumstances?" that day, my son, you'll become a man (19). The same message returns to him when he and the Girl discover that the loaf of bread contains a gun. After a moment of anger and rejection, he stands by her teaching

> how can I turn
> Against her call
> And
> Live? (43)

The play ends with the desperate gesture by the Boy and Girl with this same gun against unjust 'justice'. The passage in which the Boy and Girl disguise themselves as Masai evidently aims at counteracting the tribal limitations inherent in the subject.

Mythologizing is not falsification. Selected images, events, speeches and individuals embody certain needs of a people. Myths draw upon history. But writers who develop national myths are using history as part of a continuing process which can help determine and shape the future by encouraging certain possibilities in society and perhaps discouraging others. To such writers history is not static, but is material out of which social and economic realities have created the present, providing various openings for the future. The historical Kimathi is important to Ngũgĩ and Micere Mugo as a man whose work must be projected into the future. So their play selects facets of his life-story which can inspire an audience to action in the present. Thus his ideas and what he stood and stands for must be re-interpreted by the writers in terms of the different circumstances of the present time.

We shall consider six different groupings of scenes in the play. The first two are the mimed pageants of slavery, and the scenes with the Woman, Boy and Girl which have already been touched on. There are, thirdly, passages in streets, outside the court, and in prison corridors; there is a flashback scene to wartime in the forest; there are three court scenes in which Kimathi is charged and convicted; and finally there are four 'trials' in Kimathi's cell.

The confrontation between the white 'Johnnie' and the Woman embodies many aspects of the Mau Mau period. The half-interested foreign trooper, prejudiced rather than committed to his cause, is easily beguiled by the determination of the heroic mother figure, whose vitality, however, merely arouses him to casual lasciviousness. Waitana, on the other hand, is the sadistic petty quisling thrown up by every society under duress. The black Warder, while really just doing a job, is callously self-interested enough to wish for his own convenience that the authorities would dispatch Kimathi without the elaborate charade of a trial. The two African soldiers highlight contrasting attitudes on the home front. Second Soldier is alienated from his own people and talks of Mau Mau with arrogant contempt. First Soldier, on the other hand, is sceptical of his role and is aware of the genuine influence exerted by Dedan Kimathi: 'Kimathi is a hero to the people. They love him like anything, say what you will' (13). Later his human concern restrains his fellow from obediently beating Kimathi in transit to the torture chamber, as he whispers, 'Are you a human being? What are you doing this for?' (56). At the end of the play, First Soldier 'shyly joins in' (84) as the People's song and dance builds to a finale, showing that the forces serving the colonial regime included many confused men who put on uniform because they needed a job and in time came to reject the employment they had taken up.

The flashback to the forest occupies a long scene — one fifth of the play — and serves many purposes. It is the only passage which directly re-creates the time of Mau Mau's triumph. It forms part of the Woman's reminiscences as she is re-educating the Boy and Girl. We fade into Nyandarwa Forest on these words:

> He so hated the sight of Africans killing one another that he sometimes became a little soft with our enemies. [*softly*]: He, Great commander that he was, Great organiser that he was, Great fearless fighter that he was, he was human! [*almost savagely, bitterly*]: Too human at times! (62)

All these qualities are displayed in the scene that follows. For their own purposes, our playwrights also present a somewhat complex picture of Kimathi, with his contradictions and weaknesses.

The mini-trial of the two white soldiers brings out several key points. Kimathi says to them:

> It's always the same story. Poor men sent to die so that parasites might live in paradise with ill-gotten. wealth. Know that we are not fighting against the British people. We are fighting against British colonialism and imperialist robbers of our land, our factories, our wealth. Will you denounce British imperialism? (64)

but he is angered by their rote reply: 'We are the Queen's soldiers!' They are summarily executed, as is the soldier from the King's African Rifles. The latter has little to say for himself. One trusts that the First Soldier (who shyly joins the final revolutionary march) would have found more to say if he had been captured, and might have been spared. Kimathi now gives a rallying speech, reminding the forest-fighters that 'We have had great victories' (66): the ground and air forces that the British have had to mobilize are a testimony to Mau Mau's effectiveness. While he advocates seeking aid from all parts, nevertheless 'We must rely on our strength' (67). He praises his forces' self-help, and makes a point directly relevant to the playwrights' purpose:

> We must know our history
> Especially the deeds of those
> Who have always resisted
> The rape of our beautiful Kenya
> Who have always stood firmly
> Against oppression and exploitation. (67)

And he rises to a peroration which is also a direct rhetorical appeal to the audience in the theatre:

> Here we must plant seeds for a
> future society . . .
> We must kill the lie
> That black people never invented anything
> Lay for ever to rest that inferiority
> complex
> Implanted in our minds by centuries
> of oppression.
> Rise, Rise workers and peasants of Kenya
> Our victory is the victory of the working
> people
> The victory of all those in the world
> Who to-day fight and struggle for total
> liberation. (68)

There follows the hearing of the Mau Mau traitors, including Kimathi's brother. We have already heard Henderson taunting Kimathi with his brother's collaboration. And in the first scene the sinister work of betrayal by the 'hooded collaborator' (7) has been re-enacted. Kenyan audiences must include many whose families suffered from the severities of Mau Mau and who eventually in some degree or other condemned the cause — as has become clear during our discussion of *Weep Not, Child*. Now the play asserts that Kimathi was essentially a humane man (who 'hated the sight of Africans killing one another'), but that when he exercised clemency such as this he was in fact wrong to do so (the scene ends in the escape of the reprieved traitors with an outcome already rehearsed). The audience is being subtly persuaded towards a new positive reaction to all that Mau Mau did and stood for.

Each of the three court scenes opens with the reading of the charge against Kimathi. With his refusal to plead, the charge is repeated, emphasizing its relative triviality: 'found in possession of a firearm, namely a revolver, without a licence'. It is as if the prosecution can muster no proper case, or even more significantly as if they think it unwise to have the real issues at stake in the Mau Mau struggle debated in open court. So they resort to a technicality. Meanwhile the silent figure captures the audience's attention in his aloof dignity and integrity.

The court scenes do not simulate actual court proceedings. Rather Kimathi is allowed to take dramatic control of the arena with his restrained but telling rhetoric. He is, convincingly in stage terms, given a platform. Out of his initial silence grows a rejection of the unjust 'justice' of an alien administration. With bitter wit the word 'criminal' is made to revert from its technical to its literal sense: 'To a criminal judge, in a criminal court, set up by criminal law: the law of oppression, I have no words' (25). When the Judge asserts 'There is only one law, one justice,' Kimathi snaps back: 'Two laws. Two justices. One law and one justice protects the man of property, the man of wealth, the foreign exploiter. Another law, another justice, silences the poor, the hungry, our people' (25–6). He elaborates the issue point by point, though the text is consistently directed towards the present audience in their own decade:

> Beaten
> Starved
> Despised
> Spat on
> Whipped
> But refusing to be broken
> Waiting for a new dawn. (26)

The point is bitingly made in a balanced rhetorical 'turn':

JUDGE: There's no liberty without law and order.
KIMATHI: There is no order and law without liberty. (27)

Earlier the scene has provided a stereotyped display of settler arrogance and racism. Now Windhoek finds an outlet for a sincere if totally blinkered statement of the beleaguered settlers' position. Then he draws his gun to pursue the prisoner after he has been taken out. In the scuffle with the white officer and black soldiers, the gun futilely goes off, an incident which forms a pattern with the letting off of the gun at the end by the Boy from exactly opposite motives. The final court scene, in which Kimathi is sentenced, ends the play. Again the reading of the charge leads to a confrontation with the court's version of justice when Kimathi sees the bevy of collaborators drawn up to testify against him. After the flurry of the Woman's appearance, Kimathi is allowed to speak before sentence and once more denounces imperialism and stirs the theatre audience. In the forest he sometimes fears that if he dies, the struggle might subside:

> But now I know that
> for every traitor
> there are a thousand patriots (83),

directly anticipating Karega at the end of *Petals of Blood*. The dock is transformed symbolically into a kind of pulpit as he addresses 'the people':

> So, go!
> Organize in your homes
> Organize in the mountains
> Know that your only
> Kindred blood is he
> who is in the struggle . . .
> Kenyan masses shall be free! (83–4)

The Judge's sentence is engulfed by Dedan's bitter laughter, then by the defiant discharge of the gun, and finally by the surging freedom chorus in Kiswahili.

The real heart of the play is to be found in what the playwrights themselves call Kimathi's four 'trials'. These are not his appearances in the colonial court at all, but four visitations in prison where he is 'craning to catch some light through a tiny barbed wire window' (53). These are four heroic tests which finally qualify him, by implication, as a true leader of the people's struggle. They could be compared to Beckett's four temptations in T. S. Eliot's *Murder in the Cathedral* (without suggesting any such conscious derivation). But while Kimathi's trials are symbolic, they need not be thought of as visionary — though no one could imagine them happening exactly like this in actuality.

The first trial is fairly straightforward. Shaw Henderson attempts to lure Kimathi into betraying the fighters still in the forest in order to save his own life. While Henderson uses some guile, this is not a temptation to which the prisoner is liable: 'Kimathi wa Wachiuri will never betray the people's liberation struggle. Never!' (35). The next two trials are more prophetic, relating the Mau Mau campaign to the continuing struggle against black elitist vested interests that have taken over from colonialism. As Kimathi thinks of his grandmother, and dreams of ethnic unity, a pageant of various Kenyan dances fills the stage until, by ironic juxtaposition, it is replaced by 'a Banker's delegation — or a Trade-cum-businessman's delegation' (38) — a white man, an Indian and an African front-man. Commerce has settled for a black government, but one that can be manipulated by external interests:

> BANKER: We need stability. There never can be progress without stability. Then we can finance big Hotels . . . International Hotels . . . Seaside resorts . . . Night Clubs . . . Casinos . . . Tarmac roads . . . oil refineries and pipelines . . . Then tourists from USA, Germany, France, Switzerland, Japan, will flock in. (40)

What Kenyan could fail to recognize this as his country in the 1970s? Kimathi dismisses this temptation to drop the struggle and to encourage investment:

> And my people? . . . The oppressed of the land . . . all those whose labour power has transformed this land. For it is not true that it was your money that built this country. It was our sweat. It was our hands. Where do our people come in in your partnership for progress? (40)

The third trial is perhaps the most testing and complex, comprising an all-black delegation: a business executive, a politician and a priest. The argument of the business executive operates on two levels. He claims 'we have won the war' (44) and at first Kimathi welcomes this news literally with joy and thanks. But the victory is not what Kimathi had taken it to be: concessions have been made by the new black elite on colonialist terms. The play speaks again directly to its audience who may include many who simplistically believed the current slogans which imply that independence has brought real liberation to the working masses. When it dawns on Kimathi that the victory being spoken of is not the unconditional surrender he had looked for, it should surely also be apparent to his hearers that the independence they have received at Uhuru is not the real emancipation they have the right to expect. And the actual words employed support this double interpretation:

> BUSINESS EXECUTIVE: Is this not what we have been fighting for? Any black man who now works hard and has capital can make it to the top. We can become local directors of foreign companies. We can now buy land in the White Highlands. White Highlands no more. (45)

There was dawning truth in this in 1957, but how infinitely more relevant to the 1960s and 1970s. The politician whines a song which also relates to the time of the trial but speaks much louder of the ex-collaborator new-parliamentarian who has done everything in subsequent decades to keep the surviving freedom-fighters out of political power:

> POLITICIAN: We all fought for Uhuru in our different way. I think it unwise . . . a little hasty . . . divisive politics to single out certain people, certain classes as having fought for Uhuru. There are no classes in Africa. We are all freedom fighters. (47)

Kimathi's contemptuous dismissal of this rationalization must have brought some satisfaction to a section of Kenyan audiences. The black priest, co-operator with the new power group, is in some ways easier prey: 'Can it be wrong even in the eyes of your God for a people to fight against exploitation?' (50). Kimathi seems finally to address his followers in the audience directly before turning back to the delegation:

> This is what I always feared
> How to discern our enemies
> in black clothes, with sweet tongues,
> Chequebook revolutionaries!
> Go. Go. My trial has begun. (50–1)

The last of Dedan Kimathi's four 'trials' is inevitably trial by torture, from which he emerges as the seasoned, authentic hero-figure. As he struggles to his feet after Henderson's fruitless attempts to break him, and tears the letter of surrender he is expected to sign, he thunders a stereotyped cry of defiance across a theatre now tuned to respond to it:

> For four hundred years the oppressor
> has exploited and tortured our people.
> For four hundred years we have risen
> And fought against oppression,
> against humiliation,
> against enslavement of body
> Mind and soul . . . :
> Our people will never surrender! (58)

Clearly *The Trial of Dedan Kimathi* does not aspire to the attributes of the traditional 'well-made play'. In collaborating with Micere Mugo, Ngũgĩ finally found a place in a newer dramatic tradition. The play has more in common with what for a while was called a 'happening' than with a neatly plotted three-act drama. But its purposefulness gives it a clear sense of direction, and the playwrights have done much to impose a pattern on their apparently loose-jointed combination of mime, symbolism, vision and realism. This collaboration achieved what Ngũgĩ for some time wished to set against the drama of playwrights such as Wole Soyinka, which he angrily regarded as uncommitted — though it may seem unlikely that Soyinka would want to compete on these grounds.

Kimathi's rallying speeches express passion and climax. Many passages have rhetorical force. For the rest the style is self-consciously plain. In their anxiety to eliminate barriers of diction, and so to reach a general audience by communicating with anyone who can understand English, the playwrights have deprived themselves of some of the magic powers of language. This sometimes renders the use of slogans belonging to a revolutionary vocabulary somewhat stark, which is a pity in a work seeking to capture the unconverted and the waverers, not just to hearten those already convinced. But these limitations are more likely to catch the attention of a reader than of a spectator in the theatre. Certainly the play did produce the effect intended. It helped to revitalize, at least temporarily, the un-national National Theatre in Nairobi, and vindicated the determination to fire a wider audience in Kenya with revolutionary zeal by creating a militant theatre.

It was a logical development that, as a next dramatic venture, Ngũgĩ should collaborate on a play in Gikuyu, *Ngaahika Ndeenda*, to be acted by, and for, those at the grass-roots of the nation. In consequence, the initial co-authorship with Ngũgĩ Mirii opened out into full-scale cooperation with the whole community group, as they extended, modified and remoulded the draft script into an expression of corporate anger, hope and vitality.[4] The production became a model for a whole community's growth as members of Kamiriithu centre found appropriate channels for their innate energy and creativity. Ngũgĩ expresses his delight in becoming involved in this process in *Detained*:

> I saw how the people had appropriated the text, improving on the language and episodes and metaphors, so that the play which was finally put on to a fee-paying audience on Sunday, 2 October 1977, was a far cry from the tentative awkward efforts originally put together by Ngũgĩ and myself. I felt one with the people. I shared in their rediscovery of their collective strength and abilities, and in their joyous feeling that they could accomplish anything — even transform the whole village and their lives without a single Harambee of charity — and I could see the way the actors were communicating their joyous sense of a new power to their audience who too went home with gladdened hearts. (78)

Ngaahika Ndeenda, later translated as *I Will Marry When I Want*, was specially suited to this sort of communal enlivenment since it incorporates much song, dance and ritual from the people's shared tradition, and from Mau Mau song and celebration, as well as from Christian church ceremony and hymns. The language flowers into proverbs and imagery. More than a quarter of the printed text involves singing and ceremonial forms, which would occupy an even greater proportion of stage time. The play is set in contemporary Kenya, like *Petals of Blood*, and like that novel relates the present to the historic sequence that has led up to it. We look back to the time before the coming of the white man, to colonial times when traditional

society was under siege, and to the patriotic upsurge of the Mau Mau
insurrection. The main action concerns the anti-climax of a betrayed
independence. At length the finale looks forward to the creation of a juster
society in the future.

The collaborators take full advantage of their dramatic form to re-create,
as a novel cannot, the actuality of a traditional communalism. The
wholehearted togetherness of the time-honoured village marriage ceremony
is captured before the audience. The vigorous idealism of Mau Mau
camaraderie is brought live to the stage. And these are then contrasted with
the smug individualism of those who have succeeded in skimming the fat
off the present-day system. The joyful song of the Aagaciku clan:

> Here is the millet gruel, woman of the Mbui clan,
> You who knows how to welcome guests!
> Now hand me my honey
> And my ear-rings and tobacco
> For the beautiful one from the Njiku clan,
> As for you the beautiful one from the Mbui clan,
> I have got your yam,
> And a crop of ripened bananas (66)[5]

harmonizes with the fervour of the revolutionary oath:

> I'll always help this organization,
> With all my strength and property,
> I'll help members of this organization,
> So that if a bean falls to the ground
> We split it amongst ourselves. (69)

But the voice of the modern egotist with its hypocritical Christian emphasis
grates ironically against these voices of fellowship out of the past. Ndugire
describes how the good Lord led him by the hand to the bank to get his
loan:

> Now you see I did not take out
> Even a cent from my pocket.
> And yet I am milking cows,
> And I am harvesting tea.
> That's why I always praise the Lord
> Without any fear. (46)

Thus the plot that forms a framework for the musical and ritual passages
tells how an unjust colonial past has led to an unjust neo-colonial present.
Expropriation of land by white settlers has been reduced to grabbing the
few impoverished acres left to the workers, through chicanery and
confidence tricks, by a ruthless elite subserving the demands of international
corporations. A snobbish class system underpins the exploitation of the
labourer. The complacent, hymn-singing rich extol the virtues of such
minions as have been schooled into willing acceptance of their derisory
wages:

> That tractor driver is very mature.
> He does not argue back.
> He does not demand higher wages.

> He just believes in hard work,
> Praising our Lord all the time.
> He is a true brother-in-Christ. (43–4)

Glib hypocrisy is one of the play's repeated refrains, but against it is pitted the workers' determined protest. Kiguunda, as his employer himself insists, is paid above average wages, and yet can exclaim:

> What do I get a month?
> Two hundred shillings,
> And you call that a lot of money?
> Two hundred shillings a month
> With which to buy clothes, food, water,
> And you know very well
> That prices are daily climbing up!
> A person earning two hundred shillings,
> Can he really cope with the rising prices? (85)

Gicaamba is allowed a long speech detailing the soul-killing life of a factory shift-worker. For instance, on the night shift:

> You meet your wife returning from the fields.
> Bye bye
> You tell her as you run to the machine.
> Sweat.
> Another fortnight.
> Here, take this
> Two hundred shillings.
> The rest to Europe.
> By that time you have sold away
> Your body,
> Your blood,
> Your wife,
> Even your children!
> Why, because you hardly ever see them! (35)

The play also addresses itself boldly to subjects on which there may not up till now have been complete unanimity in the locality. Religion is particularly severely attacked as 'the alcohol of the soul' (61):

> All the missionaries of all the churches
> Held the Bible in the left hand,
> And the gun in the right hand . . .
> And they had the audacity to tell us
> That earthly things were useless! (56–7)

Powerful scorn is poured on the heterogeneous array of foreign-based sects in Africa:

> Are we the rubbish-heap of religions?
> So that wherever the religions are collected,
> They are thrown in our courtyard? (9)

The habitual tension between generations is also frankly aired:

> Do modern girls marry,
> Or do they only go to the bars
> Accompanied by men old enough to be their fathers . . . !
> (17–18)

In *Detained* Ngũgĩ himself comments on the focus of the play. He writes of 'the heroic history of Kenyan people as celebrated in *Ngaahika Ndeenda*' and 'the historical betrayal mourned and condemned in the same drama', adding, 'My involvement with the people of Kamiriithu had given me the sense of a new being and it had made me transcend the alienation to which I had been condemned by years of colonial education' (98). Elsewhere he calls it

> a play that looks at the Kenyan history of struggle against imperialism with pride, delineating the traitorous role of those who sold out and the heroic role of those that held out; a play which correctly reflects the true social conditions in Kenya today, especially in its comparative depiction of the styles of life of the 'privileged' thieving minority and the labouring majority. (188)

The primary strengths of the play remain the vigour of its song and dance patterns, and its forceful, detailed assertion of social injustice as part of an unambiguous, class-based protest. On the first count *Detained* offers further support

> the *Gituro* opera sequence, written word for word at the dictation of an illiterate peasant woman from Kamiriithu village and performed step by step according to her choreography, was one of the finest aesthetic experiences on the Kenyan stage and one of the brightest moments in the show. (190)

On the second count Ngũgĩ gives the creation of the play itself as additional evidence. He attributes his being sent to detention for his part in *Ngaahika Ndeenda* to the reaction of 'powerful propertied elements' against seeing

> peasants and workers whom they have come to regard as only fit for picking tea leaves and coffee beans, prove that out of their own internal resources and the passions born of their unique experience of history, they can outshine the best that can be produced by parroting foreigners, and by following submissively the trodden paths of foreign education, foreign theatres, foreign cultures, foreign initiatives, foreign languages. (190)

The production was heady stuff delivered to an audience composed of those suffering the privations and facing the problems being described.

Kiguunda, though a Mau Mau loyalist, has been able to lay claim to a mere 1½ acres in the post-independence struggle for land in Kenya — a new scramble for Africa! In contrast, Ndugire, Kioi's sanctimonious ex-homeguard lackey, has gathered — as just one of his perquisites — 'a tiny garden of about a hundred acres' (46). The process by which Kioi deprives Kiguunda of his patch of soil, in a society which pivots on land, is the central plot of the play: this epitomizes the impoverishment and dehumanizing of the poor by the rich. Kioi wants Kiguunda's land on behalf of an international consortium as a site for an insecticide factory — a smelly project which must be kept away from the estates of the wealthy. So for dramatic effect, a key visual symbol in Kiguunda's one-roomed house (the main stage setting) is the title-deed for this vital smallholding, which has its place on the wall. The stage directions insist that our attention be focused on this crucial title-deed, and its ultimate disappearance.

Kioi's son, John Muhuuni, is dallying with Kiguunda's daughter, Gathoni. Kioi and his wife, Jezebel, deign to visit Kiguunda's household to persuade him to remarry in church. But Kiguunda angrily repudiates the idea that he and Wangeci have been 'living in sin' (49):

> This is mine own wife,
> Gathoni's mother,
> I have properly married her
> Having paid all the bridewealth
> According to our national ways.
> And you dare call her a whore! (50)

Theatrically he chases Kioi and Jezebel from the house with the sword which has been hanging beside the title-deed.

Now, after a brief struggle with herself, Gathoni dismisses her parents' scruples and motors off with her boyfriend to Mombasa. However, it occurs to Wangeci that the Kiois want her to marry Kiguunda in church as a prerequisite to a wedding between the children of the two houses. In spite of scornful opposition to such imported ways from their close friend, Gicaamba, she prevails upon her husband, and they go off to the grand house to discuss the matter. In an effective stage reversal, whereas the Kiois scorned Wangeci's food when they visited Kiguunda's house, the Kiois now insult their inferiors by excluding them from their own meal and encouraging the house-servant to slight them.

When Kiguunda appeals for help with the expenses of the marriage ceremony which the Kiois are wishing on them, he is offered alternatives: to sell his land or raise a loan with the land as security. He accepts the latter. So Act III opens with Kiguunda's house resplendent in bourgeois trappings, mirroring the Kiois' pharisaical display of a print of hairy Nabucadinezza and a plaque (replacing the title-deed) reading 'Christ is the head of this house . . .' The couple act out their imagined church wedding in anticipation, but are interrupted by a weeping Gathoni who has been abandoned in pregnancy by John Muhuuni. The Kiguundas rush to the Kiois' house to insist on a marriage between Muhuuni and Gathoni but are met with contempt. Kiguunda attacks Kioi with the sword he has carried from home in an attempt to extort a written agreement, but the modern Jezebel frustrates him with a gun.

In the last scene the fine furniture has been reclaimed from Kiguunda's house when he fails in repayments on the loan. Gathoni is a local bar prostitute. Kiguunda is drunk and out of work. Wangeci is in despair amid the ruins of their home.

This outline apparently gives *I Will Marry When I Want* the ring of Victorian melodrama, but these scenes of human disaster are altogether different in tone and import. They express a passionate denunciation of the wrongs suffered by an African working family under a capitalist system, monitored by powerful foreign interests and managed by black Kenyan middlemen. Yet in aping the false values of a hypocritical Christianity and

bourgeois materialism, the Kiguundas lack either vision or commitment
to inherited values. They betray the dignity of man and the spirit of
egalitarianism. They share the moral negligence of Waiyaki, Njoroge, Mugo,
Gikonyo and other protagonists in Ngũgĩ's works. They must suffer the
repercussions of their misguided actions. They are deliberately contrasted
with the Gicaambas who in all things show a proper human pride and
integrity.

The characterization is neither complex nor highly individualized. But
a village cast will readily fill out Kiguunda, Gicaamba and their wives as
recognizable people. The well-to-do figures offer opportunities for some
degree of comic caricature. The snubs provide wry humour, as when
Wangeci wrongly thinks she is being offered tea in Kioi's house, only to
find it whisked away from her grasp. The acting out of the daily wrongs in
this social structure must stir ready response in an experienced village
audience. Disjointed resentment and complaints are marshalled into
coherent protest. And the joys, which are inherent in people's solidarity in
pursuing a life proper to themselves and the country, are reiterated and
celebrated.

The main function of the verse structure is to emphasize the speech
rhythms and patterns and thus make the text more intimate and easier to
read. It also helps to assimilate a new richness in imagery, and above all
considerable dependence on proverbs, with their often uninhibited
pointedness. Kiguunda vindicates his attachment to his tiny plot of land
thus:

> A man brags about his own penis
> However tiny. (4)

The essential pulse of the drama, heightening and complementing the
cry for social justice, is felt in the carefully designed sequences of song,
dance and incantation. As in *The Trial of Dedan Kimathi*, scenes which are
acted out from memories and imaginings are freely augmented by dancers
and singers who appear on stage specially for this purpose. These enact-
ments are relevant to the whole theme and conception: they bring to life
rituals and ceremonies from the past and the present, for instance both
traditional and modern church wedding ceremonies, as well as a wide variety
of communal song and dance patterns, many formalized, some improvised.
A long, pageant-like representation is sparked off by Kiguunda and Wangeci
calling to mind their courting days. Appropriate dances and choruses are
then loosely linked by a few spoken words to a freedom song and a
procession, followed by a chanting women's parade, all as part of 'the
remembrance of things past' (26); then finally a Mau Mau ensemble involves
two more songs before the dialogue slides back fairly casually into the
present and we again take up the plot.

In Act II, a heated discussion of the sacredness and validity of traditional
marriage rites leads into the re-creation of the ceremony itself. This is the
beginning of an even longer sequence fairly arbitrarily maintained by spoken
links:

> It was soon after this
> That the colonial government
> Forbade people to sing or dance . . .

But we went on meeting clandestinely.
We the workers in factories and plantations said in one voice:
We reject slave wages!
Do you remember the 1948 general strike?
A procession of workers with placards bearing political slogans enters ...
(67–8)

There follows a Mau Mau battle with its victory song.

The effect of these musical episodes, combined with the fact that characters are essentially prototypes, achieves a kind of distancing from immediate, personalized emotional involvement, which has something in common with the Brechtian mode. The outcome is less deliberate than Brecht's creation of 'alienation'; the shifts between the particular and the general operate on a relatively *ad hoc* basis. The renewed emphasis on society and away from the individual depends on bringing the audience within the ambit of traditional and revolutionary activities, rather than on inspiring intellectual awareness in us by impinging verbally on a theme while totally shifting the perspective. But *The Trial of Dedan Kimathi* and *I Will Marry When I Want* do similarly focus attention on principles and concepts, not on private dramas.

In recent years Ngũgĩ has insisted on the priority of content over form in his work. As a novelist he is at once such an instinctive artist and a careful, committed craftsman that form and content are fully compatible and the issue hardly arises. This is less true in the drama. In the latest collaboration there are instances of careful structural patterning, such as the appearance of the evangelical fund-raisers in the first and last scenes, or Kiguunda's final pitiful adoption of the Drunk's song and speech at the opening. Moreover the songs and dances are thematically relevant and so take on a certain operatic quality. But for all this, content does appear to take precedence over aesthetic considerations. A comparison between the use of the two genres is encouraged by the close parallels in themes and motifs between *I Will Marry When I Want* and *Devil on the Cross*.

The drama in which Ngũgĩ has lately been involved adopts other criteria than his novel-writing. The form finds a different justification from the complete marriage between medium and intention in the narrative prose works. Ngũgĩ has entered the important field of community drama which gives dynamic expression to a people's experiences, feelings, needs and aspirations. This is *not* to say that art is a superfluous luxury in a village context. Far from it. Anyone connected with varied types of performance in Africa will know that a critical and truly appreciative audience is at least as readily to be found in the village as in any national theatre. Any true artist must deeply respect this audience and give it of his best. But in drama for the people, by the people and between the people, a certain looseness of form may be inevitable. The co-ordinating dramatist will seek to elicit rather than impose assumptions. The corporate form that emerges will have its own felicities, its own kind of force, which Ngũgĩ himself perceived in 'the way the actors were communicating their joyous sense of a new power to their audience who too went home with gladdened hearts'.

The logic of this mode enables the bitter end of the story in *I Will Marry*

When I Want to lead to a new hopeful resolution shared by actors and audience.

> When I left the auction place
> I thought I should revisit the piece of land
> For a last glance,
> A kind of goodbye.
> Who did I find there?
> Kioi wa Kanoru, Ikuua wa Nditika
> Plus a group of Whites.
> I fled.
> But their open laughter followed me. (111)

This is not the end of the stage performance. The horror of such a denial of all true human values leads to a reformulation of the Mau Mau oath of solidarity:

> Our nation took the wrong turn
> When some of us forgot these vows. (113)

Actors and audience are at the last involved in a new self-dedication to the principles of justice and community. The play which has grown out of the two Ngũgĩs' conception ends on a note of triumphant hope:

> *The trumpet of the masses has been blown.*
> *Let's preach to all our friends.*
> *The trumpet of the masses has been blown.*
> *We change to new songs*
> *For the revolution is near.* (115)

It is perhaps little cause for surprise that when this trumpet at length penetrated the ears of the establishment, it resounded somewhat ominously and caused violent reactions. This in itself is an ironic tribute to the power and effectiveness of the kind of drama to which Ngũgĩ committed himself. The value of the published text lies not so much in the possibility of its being performed elsewhere precisely as it stands, as in the way it could inspire other communities to embody their dilemmas and aspirations in creative dramatic enterprises of their own.

Notes

1. Quotations are from the first paperback edition: *The Black Hermit* (Heinemann Educational Books, London, 1968).
2. Quotations are from the original hardback edition: *This Time Tomorrow* (East African Publishing House, Nairobi, 1970). The play 'This Time Tomorrow' also appears in Cosmo Pieterse (ed.) *Short African Plays* (Heinemann Educational Books, London, 1972).
3. Quotations are from the first paperback edition: Ngũgĩ wa Thiong'o and Micere Githae Mugo, *The Trial of Dedan Kimathi* (Heinemann Educational Books, London, 1976).
4. Ngũgĩ explains in detail in *Detained: A Writer's Prison Diary* (Heinemann

Educational Books, London, 1981) how the writing and staging of the play came about. It formed part of a communal effort to revive and invigorate the community centre of his home village, Kamiriithu:

> The script had to be ready by March 1977.
>
> We could not meet the March deadline. But by April 1977, an outline of the script of *Ngaahika Ndeenda* was ready. For the next two months the peasants now added to the script, altering this and that. Reading of the final working script and rehearsals started on 5 June 1977. The actual performances would commence on 2 October, the twenty-fifth anniversary of the declaration of the State of Emergency in Kenya and the beginning of the Mau Mau armed struggle.
>
> The six months between June and November 1977 were the most exciting in my life and the true beginning of my education. I learnt my language anew. I rediscovered the creative nature and power of collective work. (76)

5. Quotations are from the first paperback edition: *I Will Marry When I Want* (Heinemann Educational Books, London and Nairobi, 1982).

The Social
& Literary Criticism

Introduction and Early Period

The practice of examining the beliefs and ideas of a writer is becoming a tradition in the critical evaluation of African literature. This was to be expected in a literature whose successful authors have often voiced clear and coherent bodies of ideas. These beliefs have usually involved commitment to the goals of 'the African revolution'. This concept has influenced the themes of so much significant African writing that criticism has itself had to explore it.

Ngũgĩ, attempting to justify the publication in 1972 of his collection of essays entitled *Homecoming*,[1] asserts that they form 'part of the fictional world' of the first three novels, *Weep Not, Child, The River Between* and *A Grain of Wheat,* and goes on to spell out the different roles which fiction and the essay play in the revelation of a writer's mind:[2]

> In a novel the writer is totally immersed in a world of imagination which is other than his conscious self. At his most intense and creative the writer is transfigured, he is possessed, he becomes a medium. In the essay the writer can be more direct, didactic, polemical, or he merely states his beliefs and faith: his conscious self is here more at work. Nevertheless the boundaries of his imagination are limited by the writer's beliefs, interests, and experience in life, by where in fact he stands in the world of social relations. This must be part of the reasons that readers are curious about a writer's opinion on almost everything under the sun — from politics and religion to conservation of wild life! A writer is thus forced either by the public or the needs of his craft to define his beliefs, attitudes and outlook in the more argumentative form of the essay.

As Ngũgĩ observes, the essay is an important outlet for a writer's ideas, but perhaps equally important are the less neatly organized or articulated commentaries in newspapers and journals, as well as in spoken forms — lectures, addresses, interviews and in casual remarks. Of course the writer's life-style and practical actions serve to demonstrate, perhaps even more than his utterances do, the working of his mind and his 'articles of faith'. Of the more renowned African writers, Ngũgĩ is among the most vocal, and has left little to chance in projecting his thoughts even outside his creative work.

It should be useful to recapitulate some of his real-life activities discussed elsewhere which shed direct light on his ideas. In the years 1962 and 1963 when he was reading for a first degree at Makerere University, he contributed to a column entitled 'As I See It' in the *Daily Nation* newspaper in Nairobi a total of 44 articles in which are already clearly sketched the outlines of a social, moral and political viewpoint. In subsequent years, as he became known as a novelist, he granted several interviews to inquiring scholars and journalists seeking insight into his ideas, and so progressively gave expression to a pattern of thought that steadily grew and deepened in response to the changing contemporary political and social environment. At the University of Leeds from 1964 to 1967, while both working towards his MA thesis on Caribbean Literature and the composition of his most complex novel to date, *A Grain of Wheat*, he met many young radicals, notably in the group led by Alan Hunt as well as at fortnightly literary discussions in the house of Arnold Kettle. After completing an early draft of his Master's thesis he became somewhat disillusioned with postgraduate studies and concentrated on what he saw as the much more important task of wrestling with the novel which was proving to be a most demanding brainchild. Looking back in 1975, he dates his scepticism about higher degrees as elitist symbols from this time.[3] In 1969 he quit his teaching post at the University of Nairobi in protest, not so much against what he saw as the government's encroachment on the university's authority, but against the pussy-footing posture with which the university community countered such government high-handedness. In Makerere, to which he returned in 1969–70, he contributed vigorously to discussions about changing the primary focus of literary studies at the university from European to African literature. In 1972 he issued his book of essays *Homecoming*. Back at his post as Lecturer in Literature and,subsequently, Chairman of the Literature Department in Nairobi, he transformed literary studies so that they gave pride of place to African content. In August of the same year, 1977, as his latest literary assault on the Kenyan social set-up, *Petals of Blood*, appeared, he co-authored and co-presented with an old friend, Ngũgĩ Mirii, a play in Gikuyu, *Ngaahika Ndeenda* which, according to one newspaper review, 'traces the epical development of Kenya from the Mau Mau struggle to date'.[4] This latest demonstration of active commitment earned for him a year's incarceration,and he remains, even to date, not only unreinstated to his post 18 years after his release from prison, but he has also been forced into exile since August 1982.

Ngũgĩ has given abundant expression to the ideas from which his fictional writings have sprung. So in trying to systematize his philosophy of life (for a philosophy has evolved), the difficulty is not in assembling pointers but rather in defining one's own reactions. A newspaper review characterized Ngũgĩ with the detachment of the seasoned journalist:[5]

A Gikuyu — by which birthright he should lay claim to substantial power leverage — he has been known to prefer the self-denial of astute intellectualism and a commitment to reforms along essentially leftist lines.

Micere Mugo, a colleague, and Ime Ikiddeh, once a fellow student in Leeds, write of him as follows:

Ngũgĩ is well-known for his leftist, militant ideas,especially in connection with Kenya, African and Black affairs. In *Homecoming* his militancy and eloquence are simply captivating, and his commitment as a Black writer comes through on every page. Like Wole Soyinka and Chinua Achebe, Ngũgĩ has been courageous enough to challenge political systems for exploiting the masses and denying people genuine freedom. All three have, at some point,challenged the principles of their home governments which is no easy thing to do in their respective countries.[6]

In order to clear up any doubts that may arise, two points of a background nature may be helpful here. The first has to do with Ngũgĩ's Marxist thinking. One cannot go very far in these essays without being assailed by well-known phrases like 'the ruling classes' and 'the exploited peasant masses and urban workers', but if anyone regards these as empty traditional slogans then he cannot have known much of the history of Kenya. The irony is that it was the experience of social and economic relations in Britain, more than in Kenya, that actually settled Ngũgĩ's socialist conviction. Starting from a common sense appraisal of the situation in his country at independence, in particular the need for a redistribution of land in the interests of a deprived peasantry, Ngũgĩ arrived in England in 1964 and settled into the revolutionary atmosphere of Leeds University where he studied for the next few years. Extensive travels around Britain and Europe, acquaintance with some eminent British socialist scholars, including his supervisor, Dr Arnold Kettle, and discussions with the radical student group led by Alan Hunt — these revealed that the root cause of incessant industrial strife in Britain was no more than the old inter-class hostility inherent in the capitalist system. Thus Leeds provided an ideological framework for opinions that he already vaguely held. It was at this time too that we both read two books which became major influences: Frantz Fanon's *The Wretched of the Earth*, that classic analysis of the psychology of colonialism; and Robert Tressell's *The Ragged Trousered Philanthropists*, one of the most moving stories ever told of the plight of the working class in Britain. Echoes of Fanon are to be heard in some of these essays.[7]

Affirmation is to be found in Ngũgĩ's own words:

[1963] We Africans who have been under colonial rule for many years believe that colonialism . . . is basically immoral. For anyone of whatever country to be content with alien rule . . . is to be less than human.[8]

[1969] What has in fact happened since independence is that the African middle-class, irrespective of their ethnic affiliations, have only wanted to put on the shoes of their former colonial rulers. This is a very dangerous thing; we do not want to find a new African ruling class being in exactly the same position as the former colonial rulers.

I think what we want to do is change the whole structure of relationship so that this kind of class is not created, and if it is created it does not economically entrench itself. I think the case of Latin America is important here, where a small clique of people, who have got the benefits of education and of wealth, have unfairly kept themselves in power.[9]

[1973] The ties of geography are easier to see. Africa and Asia, two great continents, shake hands across the Suez Canal. The Indian Ocean anyway has never been a barrier and for centuries East Africa peacefully traded with China, India and Arabia before the arrival of the Portuguese who turned this creative trade into a traffic of destroyed cities and cultures and human beings for a few silver coins to fatten the coffers of Europe.

This is an African story: it is also an Asian story and any cursory glance at the history of China, Vietnam, India, Africa,the West Indies, Afro-America, will see the testimony in tears and blood. We are truly a colonial people whose sweat has been cruelly exploited by Western-monopoly capital to build the monument called Western civilization. We groaned while they ate: our skins were caked dry in the mines and plantations while they drank water in the shade. We built their cities for them and ourselves slept in the gutter. They scattered us all over the globe and then added insult to injury by coming to our homes and using their superior technology, itself built on black cargo across the middle passage, gunned us out and said the home was theirs.

Let me for a few minutes confine myself to Kenya. Here the missionary, the settler and the colonial governor came as three imperial missives of the Western-monopoly capital. The settler grabbed the land and used African labour. The Governor protected him with the political machinery and with the gun. And the missionary stood guarding the door as a colonial spiritual policeman. As black people were taken to work on the tea and coffee plantations for the settler or conscripted to fight in European wars, the missionary had the audacity to tell them to lift up their eyes unto the Lord and sing halleluyah — Aaamen![10]

[1976] We agreed that the most important thing was for us to reconstruct imaginatively our history, envisioning the world of the Mau Mau and Kimathi in terms of the peasants' and workers' struggle before and after constitutional independence.The play is not a reproduction of the farcical 'trial' at Nyeri. It is rather an imaginative recreation and interpretation of the collective will of the Kenyan peasants and workers in their refusal to break under sixty years of colonial torture and ruthless oppression by the British ruling classes and their continued determination to resist exploitation, oppression and new forms of enslavement.[11]

[1982] What is the effect of (Western) domination (of) . . . the developing world? On the international level, the imperialist nations continue robbing the countries they dominate . . . The economic gap between the two grows bigger and bigger. The third world countries . . . have become economic satellites of the imperialist nations. Economic satellites necessarily become political dependencies. The ruling regimes in places like Kenya and South Korea have . . . ceded their territories to the ruling authorities in America for military use . . .

Culturally, these dependencies become ridiculous imitations of the way of life of the ruling class in the exploiting nations. Prostitution, for instance, has become a way of life labelled tourism. The U.S. military personnel must have their amusement parks and beaches and night clubs. Indeed, these satellite states have put their entire womenfolk on the market, for foreigners who hold dollars, sterling, francs, marks, yen.

Internally, that is within the dependent nations, a corrupt regime wields power. This clique grows wealthy out of the handshake it gets for its services as an intermediary between the imperialist bourgeoisie and its people. Massive impoverishment of the peasantry and the working population becomes chronic. Politically, the ruling regimes become even more detached from the people and they can only maintain power by jailing and murdering their democratic opponents, by ruthlessly suppressing any democratic dissent, and terrorising through the military the entire population. Culturally, the ruling regimes in these satellites see their mission as that of carefully preserving feudal background traditions that enhance superstition or else suppressing any progressive popular cultural expressions to the extent of actually destroying people's cultural centres.[12]

[1993] I am concerned with moving the centre in two senses at least. One is the need to move the centre from its assumed location in the West to a multiplicity of spheres in all the cultures of the world. The assumed location of the centre of the universe in the West is what goes by the term Eurocentrism, an assumption which developed with the domination of the world by a handful of Western nations . . .

Although present in all areas, economic, political and so on, the Eurocentric basis of looking at the world is particularly manifest in the field of languages, literature, cultural studies and in the general organization of literature departments in universities in many parts of the globe. The irony is that even that which is genuinely universal in the West is imprisoned by Eurocentrism. Western civilization itself becomes a prisoner, its jailors being its Eurocentric interpreters. But Eurocentrism is the most dangerous to the self-confidence of Third World peoples when it becomes internalized in their conception of the universe.[13]

Linking all these utterances is a consistency of subject matter, but distinguishing them is an increasing intensification. Thus Ngũgĩ's commitment to a leftist line of social-reform thought is amply documented in his assertions and exemplified in his lifestyle and practical actions. Viewed analytically, this body of thought will be seen to have evolved, as indicated in an earlier chapter, in essentially four phases. Central to the present discussion, these phases may be recapitulated as follows:

1. An early period, stretching to about the end of his course in Makerere in 1964, when he evinces an essentially moralist–humanist outlook on human affairs, characterized by a firm hope for a better future and a youthful, almost naive, innocence of trust in the good intentions and goodwill of people in authority in bringing about that future. This period of panoramic interests that were yet to be fully digested and integrated saw the writing of his early novels.

2. A second phase, embracing a period in Leeds and Ngugi's early teaching career — a period of maturing vision in which his interests impinge on large ideas and events such as Mau Mau, capitalism, socialism, and nationalism. This is when most of the essays collected in *Homecoming* were

written and he articulated what has been called his theory of history.

3. The time after resignation of his post in Nairobi University up to the early eighties. A period marked by corrosive disillusionment with the emerging picture of independent Africa, especially Kenya, and bitter revulsion against the growing African middle class.

4. The period of exile from August 1982 into the nineties.

In outlining these phases, it is tempting to try to identify and isolate Ngũgĩ's special concerns in each period. But it is not so much a difference of subjects as his angle and intensity of viewpoint that shifts. The six passages quoted above aptly illustrate this point. They span three decades but they all focus on the inter-related issues of colonialism, capitalism, African elitism, neo-colonialism, and the suppression by the West of Third World cultures. As the earliest period was discussed quite fully in our second chapter, we shall now concentrate on the second and third epochs, and finally the still on-going years of exile.

Second Phase: 1964 to 1971

The logic of Ngũgĩ's thinking in his second period, from the end of his undergraduate days in 1964 to his return from Northwestern University in 1971, is influenced by two key features. First, there is a new selectivity, leading to severe curtailing of his diffuseness in the early period, and to a deepening of insight. Secondly we find a new awareness of the need for practical action in bringing about change. Reflecting on his undergraduate years in 1971, he says: 'I think I was confused at Makerere. I had more questions than answers and by the time I left I was disillusioned about many things. Leeds systematized my thinking.'[14] And interviewed at Leeds by his fellow students, he declared, 'I am not a pacifist. I do not condemn violence indiscriminately, for the oppressed have no option but to use violence.'[15] In 1969 he had observed: 'I too must have changed since I started writing in 1960.'[16]

These are indications of a developing vision which, in the second period and particularly in the third period was to transform Ngũgĩ's personality and direction of thinking. Synoptically one might say that Ngũgĩ's more important ideas from his early days persist into the second period, but in the third period pass through the lens of revolutionary socialism.

A subject of continuing interest is the importance to a nation of a virile culture that can sustain the nation's life. Thus, in his address in Nairobi in March 1970 to the Fifth General Assembly of the Presbyterian Church of East Africa,[17] he essentially re-cast and expanded his earlier article of 1963, 'I Say Kenya's Missions Failed Badly'[18] but in 'Towards a National Culture'[19] the revolutionary socialist undercurrent to his thinking at that time is dominant. He reiterates his condemnation of Europe for subverting Africa's culture, but goes further to point up a direct link between this cultural devaluation and economic exploitation:

> But what was of far-reaching effect was the fact that, again like Prospero, the European took away the material base, and systematically dismantled the political and economic institutions on which the African had built his way of life.

He notes that after independence many African nations commit themselves to a policy of nurturing a national heritage, but point out that little success is achieved in this project because these nations generally fail to establish a proper economic base for the desired national culture:

> There are people, honest people, who confuse culture with irrelevant traditionalism; it is surely not possible to lift traditional structures and cultures intact into modern Africa. A meaningful culture is the one born out of the present hopes and especially the hopes of an impoverished peasantry, and that of the growing body of urban workers. There are still other people who believe that you can somehow maintain colonial, economic, and other social institutions and graft on them an African culture. We have seen that colonial institutions can only produce a colonial mentality.

The frustration of national cultures in independent African nations has, Ngũgĩ believes, been actively abetted by the ambitions and machinations of the African elite:

> The trouble, of course, is that many African middle classes helped to smother the revolutionary demands of the majority of peasants and workers and negotiated a treaty of mutual trust with the white colonial power structure.

This enables them to foist themselves into privileged positions vacated by the colonial masters, and to acquire symbols of social distinction. The racial barrier to their ambitions having been broken after independence, they desire

> to wear the same clothes and shoes, get the same salary, live in the same kind of mansions as their white counterparts . . . Skin-lighteners, straightened hair, irrelevant drawing-room parties, conspicuous consumption in the form of country villas, Mercedes-Benzes and Bentleys, were the order of the day.
>
> Clutching their glasses of whisky and soda, patting their wigs delicately lest they fall, some of these people will, in the course of cocktail parties, sing a few traditional songs: hymns of praise to a mythical past: we must preserve our culture, don't you think?

A total change of economic system is, therefore, essential if a national culture, capable of sustaining the entire spectrum of national aspirations, is to be evolved:

> We must in fact wholly Africanize and socialize our political and economic life. We must break with capitalism, whose imperialistic stage — that of colonialism and neo-colonialism — has done so much harm to Africa and dwarfed our total creative spirit. Capitalism can only produce anti-human culture, or a culture that is only an expression of sectional, warring interests.

Concluding the essay, he declares:

My thesis, when we come to today's Africa, is very simple: a completely socialized economy, collectively owned and controlled by the people, is necessary for a national culture: a complete and total liberation of the people, through the elimination of all exploitative forces, is necessary for a national culture. A stratified society, even in pre-colonial Africa, produces a stratified culture or sub-cultures, sometimes to the total exclusion from the central hub of national life of the *ahois*, the *ndungatas*, the *osus*, the *mbaras*, the slaves and serfs in such pre-colonial societies, and of the peasantry and working people in modern neo-colonial states. An oppressive racist society, like that of South Africa, can only produce an oppressive racist culture that cannot nourish and edify man.

It was to vindicate his deepening commitment to indigenous African culture that, in 1970, Ngũgĩ abandoned his Christian name, James. As Ime Ikiddeh relates in the Foreword to *Homecoming*, Ngũgĩ had been rebuked by a church elder in his audience at his address to the Fifth General Assembly of the Presbyterian Church of East Africa in March 1970, for the impiety and blasphemy of impudently denouncing the Christian church while he bore a Christian name as testimony to his faith. Thereafter, Ngũgĩ has permanently given up the name, perceiving its incompatibility with his increasingly radical turning away from an alien scale of values.

In the preceding year, while he sojourned at Makerere as a Creative Writing Fellow after resigning his lecturing post at Nairobi, the move to restructure the programme in Literature to emphasize the African content had been gathering momentum. Ngũgĩ had thrown his full weight behind this move. It can thus be seen that the radical transformation of the focus of literary studies which Ngũgĩ later championed at Nairobi was the culmination of an ideological design of long standing.

Besides voicing and demonstrating a revolutionary socialist impulse towards cultural emancipation in this second period, Ngũgĩ also continued to develop the distinct line of leftist thought which, as we have seen, had taken root at the earlier period. His radical thinking is demonstrated in his literary criticism, which is predominantly concerned with the situation of the masses (whom he persistently calls peasants and workers) in sovereign African nations. He judges the significance of an African writer by his relevance to the situation of the masses — as Ime Ikiddeh puts it, 'from the point of view of [the writer's] apprehension of the African problem and what serious hope [the writer] can offer for the wellbeing of [his] society'.

In the article 'The Writer and His Past', Ngũgĩ states — as an introduction to his literary critical essays in *Homecoming* — his theory of history, a theory which embodies the idea of inevitability of the success of the proletarian revolt against the bourgeoisie and is thus in line with one important aspect of Marxist social thought. He writes:

> I want to talk about the past as a way of talking about the present . . . I want to argue that what has been — the evolution of human culture throughout the ages, society in motion through time and space — is of grave import to the [writer]. For what has been, especially for the vast majority of submerged, exploited masses in Africa, Asia and Black America, is intimately bound up with what might be our vision of the future, of diverse possibilities of life and human potential, has roots in our experience of the past.

Quoting T.S. Eliot's lines:

> Time present and time past
> Are both perhaps present in time future,
> And time future contained in time past,

he goes on:

> The novelist is haunted by a sense of the past. His work is often an attempt to come to terms with 'the thing that has been', a struggle, as it were, to sensitively register his encounter with history, his people's history.

As pointed out in earlier chapters, this theory of history has had a strong influence on the underlying thematic purposes of his creative writing, and provided him with a philosophical standpoint from which to view the destinies of a wide range of characters, especially those who, either by deliberate action, feebleness of will or indifference to the social cause, seek to frustrate the drive towards the overall good of the society.

Continuing his article, Ngũgĩ surveys the socio-political background to African creative writing, and reaches the verdict that Africa present has been cut off from Africa past by European intellectual deceit. Hence:

> What the African [writer] has attempted to do is to restore the African character to his history. The African [writer] has turned his back on the Christian god and resumed the broken dialogue with the gods of his people. He has given back to the African character the will to act and change the scheme of things.

The African writer then proceeds from this obligation of restoring the dignity of the African past to the tackling of present-day predicaments: 'conflicts between the emergent elitist class and the masses' and (as a condition for 'a successful and objective reclamation' of the African past), 'the dismantling of all colonial institutions, and especially capitalism' ('capitalism, even at its most efficient has failed to create equality and balanced human relationships in Europe and America. Why do we think it can work in Africa?') He praises Achebe's achievement in both phases of the challenge to African writers: to redeem old Africa and point out the direction of growth for new Africa. Repudiating the role which Ogot and Welbourn, in their book *A Place to Feel at Home*, assign to the element of 'luck' in a person's or a people's or a community's ability to continue to rebuild their homes when damaged or destroyed, Ngũgĩ concludes:

> I do not share Ogot's and Welbourn's faith in luck. I believe that the African masses will build a place to feel at home. For they are not alone. In Asia, in Latin America, in Black America, the people are fighting the same battle. I believe the African novelist, the African writer, can help in this struggle. But he must be committed on the side of the majority (as indeed he was during the anti-colonial struggle) whose silent and violent clamour for change is rocking the continent. By diving into himself, deep into the collective unconscious of his people, he can seek the root, the trend, in the revolutionary struggle. He has already done something in restoring the African character to his history, to his past. But in a capitalist society, the past has a romantic glamour: gazing at it, as witness Wordsworth and D.H.Lawrence, or more recently Yukio Mishima of Japan, is often a means of escaping the present. It is only in a socialist context

that a look at yesterday can be meaningful in illuminating today and tomorrow. Whatever his ideological persuasion, this is the African writer's task.

However, looking at Achebe from the standpoint of his overall potential as an agent of change in the direction of a socialist revolution, Ngũgĩ rejects him:

> Achebe-cum-teacher has left too many questions unanswered. Or maybe he has levelled his accusation, has raised questions, and left it to the pupils to find the answers. Can people like Obi Okonkwo, Nanga, Odili, Max — or political parties even like the Common People's Convention — behave in a radically different way while operating within and in fact espousing the same economic and social set-up? Here we are brought back to the image of the house. For what people like Odili, Max and the army have to offer is not the possibility of building a new house on a different kind of foundation, but of extending the old one. The novel seems to suggest the possibility of individual honesty, integrity and maybe greater efficiency in building the extension. However, a given organization of material interests dictates its own morality. Which do you change first in a society — its politico-economic base (new foundations for a new house of a different nature) or the morality of individual men and women?[20]

Similarly, in spite of very genuine admiration for the forthright stand of Soyinka and Aluko on the post-independence problems of Nigeria, Ngũgĩ considers that they do not bear adequate relevance to the challenge of laying a totally new foundation for the social and economic life of Africa:

> Although Soyinka exposes his society in breadth, the picture he draws is static, for he fails to see the present in the historical perspective of conflict and struggle. It is not enough for the African artist, standing aloof, to view society and highlight its weaknesses. He must try to go beyond this, to seek out the sources, the causes and the trends of a revolutionary struggle which has already destroyed the traditional power-map drawn up by the colonialist nations. And Africa is not alone. All over the world the exploited majority, from the Americas across Africa and the Middle East, to the outer edges of Asia, is claiming its own. The artist in his writings is not outside the battle. By diving into its sources, he can give moral direction and vision to a struggle which, though suffering temporary reaction, is continuous and is changing the face of the twentieth century.[21]

In 'Okot p'Bitek and Writing in East Africa', he interprets *Song of Lawino* as 'a satiric assault on the African middle-class elite that has so unabashedly embraced Western bourgeois values and modes of life'. He discerns 'a class basis' in the attack of the heroine on her westernized husband:

> Lawino is the voice of the peasantry and her ridicule and scorn is aimed at the class basis of Ocol's behaviour. The poem is an incisive critique of bourgeois mannerisms and colonial education and values. For it is Ocol's education, with the values it inculcates in him, that drives him away from the community.[22]

It is a matter of debate, of course, whether Okot is as much concerned with the class question as he is with the issue of cultural alienation, but Ngũgĩ's temperament naturally perceives more readily class conflict in the relationship which Okot delineates.

Caribbean literature has been another subject which has excited Ngũgĩ's leftist thoughts to the extent that it formed the subject of his graduate studies at Leeds, and offered him another basis for voicing his beliefs. Clearly, his interest in that literature was set off by the affinity of creative insight and sensitivity — arising from an affinity of cultural history — between Caribbean and African writers. He explores this affinity with learned and stylish perception but, as with regard to Achebe and other West African writers, he concludes his examination of this literature with the inevitable verdict that much of the writing lies essentially outside the significant orbit of revolutionary socialist thought:

> What many West Indian writers ignore is the economic basis of much of this colour distinction. The black man, that is the non-white, has suffered both on the basis of his skin colour, and more fundamentally as one of the class of exploited peasants and workers all over the world. Africa's children (the non-whites) need to realize themselves on these two levels.
>
> To create a religion of skin colour is to despair of a solution for social injustice. But to ignore it is also dangerous. The West Indian black character will discover not only his colour and race, and claim them with pride, but also his class — and seek solidarity with the exploited millions of the islands and throughout the world.[23]

Hence, ultimately, Ngũgĩ's enduring interest in Caribbean literature came to rest on the discovery in some of the writers, notably George Lamming, of an awakening to the essential class and economic foundation of the Caribbean situation. Opening his essay in *Homecoming* on Lamming's *In The Castle of My Skin*, he declares:

> It will be our argument that although it is set in a village in a period well before any of the West Indian islands had achieved independence, *In the Castle of My Skin* is a study of a colonial revolt; that it shows the motive forces behind it and its development through three main stages: a static phase, then a phase of rebellion, ending in a phase of achievement and disillusionment with society poised on the edge of a new struggle; that it sharply delineates the opposition between the aspirations of the peasantry and those of the emergent native elite, an opposition which, masked in the second phase, becomes clear during the stage of apparent achievement.

The world of *In The Castle of My Skin* provides Ngũgĩ with a kind of microcosm of all the social maladies on which he has focused his critical attention throughout his writing and, therefore, an ideal setting for a liberating revolt of the kind he has constantly dreamed of. Here is a feudalistic establishment with a Lord of the Manor (deriving his power from a colonial authority, itself reposed in the imperial majesty of an absent monarch), a middle class, and a servant class of peasants. Inevitably conflict erupts which, true to historical pattern, uplifts the elite class to new heights of privilege, and subjects the peasants to increased deprivation through the loss of their tenant land to the new elite. Ngũgĩ sees in the new dispensation the destruction of an inhibiting relationship of dependence and, therefore, the right climate for setting out on the road to true freedom. Thus one can see how *In the Castle of My Skin* foreshadows *Petals of Blood*.

Perhaps two passages in *Homecoming* represent the culmination of Ngũgĩ's conviction that radical change is needed in the social set-up in African nations. In the first — a continuation of our two earlier quotations from the Author's Note to *Homecoming* — he registers a stinging rebuke to African nations for effecting no significant reforms in economic, political or social institutions inherited at independence:

> Yet the sad truth is that instead of breaking from an economic system whose life-blood is the wholesale exploitation of our continent and the murder of our people, most of our countries have adopted the same system. There has been little attempt at breaking with our inherited colonial past — our inherited economic and other institutions, apart from blackenizing the personnel running them. There has been no basic land reform: the settler owning 600 acres of land is replaced by a single African owning the same 600 acres. There has been no change in the structure and nature of ownership of various companies, banks and industries; the two or three European directors go away to be replaced by two or three indigenous directors — the companies remain foreign-owned. There has been no socialization of the middle commercial sector; the Asian dukawallah goes away, to be replaced by a single African dukawallah. There has not been much structural reform of the educational system; the former white schools remain as special high standard schools, attended only by those who can afford the exorbitant fees.

In the second, which forms part of the essay 'The Writer in a Changing Society', he recalls with touching feeling a childhood witness to the courage and optimism of the peasant women of Kenya in whom was born the fire of the Mau Mau rebellion:

> One day I heard a song. I remember the scene so vividly: the women who sang it are now before me — their sad faces and their plaintive melody. I was then ten or eleven. They were being forcibly ejected from the land they occupied and sent to another part of the country so barren that people called it the land of black rocks. This was the gist of their song:
>
> > And there will be great joy
> > When our land comes back to us
> > For Kenya is the country of black people.
> >
> > And you our children
> > Tighten belts around your waist
> > So you will one day drive away from this land
> > The race of white people
> > For truly, Kenya is a black man's country.
>
> They were in a convoy of lorries, caged, but they had one voice. They sang of a common loss and hope and I felt their voice rock the earth where I stood literally unable to move.
>
> Their words were not the platitudes of our university philosophers who use words as shields from life and truth: these women had lived the words they spoke. There was at once a fatalistic acceptance of the inevitable and also a collective defiance. 'We shall overcome', they seemed to say. The women had taken a correct political stand in the face of an oppressive enemy.

One easily perceives in this view of Kenyan womenfolk the basis of the glowing qualities with which he endows many of his female characters: Muthoni, Nyambura, Mwihaki, Nyokabi, Mumbi, Nyakinyua, Wanja.

In the second period, along with Ngũgĩ's intensified championing of socialized, mass-based institutions in African states, he also displays (as two complementary components of his social thought) a hardening opposition to the elite class and a deepened commitment to the defence of civil liberties. At Leeds, he decided not to complete his Master's degree. This determination had no doubt more than one reason behind it, but it must in part have been related to a growing contempt for esoteric appellations or emblems such as university degrees, particularly higher degrees. Paying a crowning tribute to those who notice the poor and the lowly, he writes in *Homecoming*:

> Leonard Kibera and Samuel Kahiga, in their tough collection of short stories, *Potent Ash*, tell of confused, often conflicting loyalties, of smashed hopes and expectations, and of the enduring though strained relationships of the ordinary men and women during and even after the Mau Mau phase of the struggle. They write about the small man: they show the dignity of the poor and the wretched of the earth, despite the violence of body and feeling around them. Even when they write of the post-independence era, internal and external violence is around the corner.

He discusses at length Kibera's story 'The Spider's Web', in which an old man has been willing to work as a servant in independent Kenya — as a demonstration of his dedication to the new spirit — for a young African girl who, in the time of struggle, had dared to hit back at a haughty European woman. However, the young girl had become high-handed. Realizing that the poor and the privileged have now lost their common focus, the old man has become disenchanted and kills the girl to show that the target of the fight for emancipation has changed.

Regarding his defence of civil liberties, Ngũgĩ's memorable action in this period was his resignation of his post in Nairobi University in March, 1969. To recapitulate, he gave his reasons for resigning as

> . . . the failure of the college administration and a large section of the staff to make a clear and public stand on the issues that led to the crisis at the University College, the mishandling of the crisis by the same administration, and the consequent suspension, itself a form of victimisation, of five students.[24]

Reiterating this later, he said:

> [my resignation] really was in protest against the mishandling of the crisis by the college administration, and also the failure . . . of a large body of members of staff to come out clearly and publicly with their views and attitudes towards issues underlying the crisis.
>
> I was really protesting against the sheer hypocrisy which, I think, exists in the college, when, on the one hand, the members of staff and even the college administration say that they believe in all these ideas — but they won't come out publicly with their statements.[25]

This behaviour gives the 'false impression' to the public

> that the students were engaged in something ugly and sinister and were entirely

to blame for the course the crisis had taken.

And so the public rightly ask, if the teachers don't care about these things, why should the students be so much concerned about [them]? And it is a very dangerous tendency in something which calls itself a university.[26]

In his view, the students had a legitimate cause of protest:

What the students fought for were certain assumptions about a university that they had been led to hold dear. When admitted to the university, they swear, in front of the Principal, the Registrar and the general academic body, to seek the truth . . . A free circulation of ideas is absolutely essential to any quest for truth and knowledge.[27]

He accused the college authorities of betraying this ideal, and condemned the inquiry into, the students' revolt and the entire university administration as undemocratic.

He expressed a preference for the term 'free circulation of ideas' to 'academic freedom', and insisted that the ideal of open discussion is essential for the health of society even at the level of a whole state. Accepting that 'free circulation of ideas' may be curtailed in such exceptional circumstances as during war and social upheavals, he maintained that 'in a free open society, a clash of ideas, or what I am calling the free circulation of ideas, can only help a nation look at itself more truthfully and know itself'.[28] He had quoted Fanon extensively in his letter of resignation and, taken to task over the apparent anomaly that those countries in Africa who approximate most closely to Fanon's models tend towards dictatorships, towards the closed society, he asserted that a government like that run by Nkrumah in Ghana was progressive in so far as it tried to free itself from colonial shackles, but was dictatorial simultaneously in so far as it repressed criticism, and so fell short of Fanon's ideal. He pointed out that Fanon was very critical of African governments which 'instead of welcoming the expression of popular discontent, instead of taking for its fundamental purpose the flow of ideas from the people up to the government, forms a screen and forbids such ideas'.[29]

With growing insight in this second period, Ngũgĩ now has clearer attitudes which presage the practical militancy of later developments. This phase has seen the rejection of half-measures for enshrining justice in society, and insistence on totally new structures of economic, political and social organization as the only basis for social equity and human dignity. The emancipation and welfare of the masses of peasants and workers is held up as an index of growth in society.

Third Phase: 1971 to 1982

We now pass to what we have designated Ngũgĩ's third phase. To appreciate how far Ngũgĩ had travelled in his orientation to his social environment since earlier days, it may be well to remind ourselves of some of his previous positions:

[1964] . . . the problem with the African writer in Kenya is surely one of being able to stand a little bit detached; and see the problem, the human problem, the human relationship in its proper perspective . . .

[While the African writer must be] committed to the situation . . . wholly involved in the problems of Kenya . . . he mustn't allow the involvement in that particular social situation to impinge on his judgment or on his creative activities.[30]

[1969] I'm a writer first and foremost; I don't believe in joining political parties myself, but I believe as a writer, in being a kind of conscience of the nation.[31]

In contrast to the thinking reflected in these assertions, Ngũgĩ of the mid-seventies and beyond made it his business — for instance in *Petals of Blood* — not only to direct public attention unequivocally to the gross social iniquities in his native country, but to do so in language which must be unmistakable to the culprits. Thus Ngũgĩ had gone back into the history of his people to invoke for the current generation the lesson of organized violence against unacceptable regimes. In the search for immediacy and impact he has turned to his native language in his creative exploration of his people's predicaments. As a consequence Ngũgĩ suffered direct persecution for his attack upon official infamy.

He himself reveals awareness of the change which he has undergone over the years when, in answer to a query as to how *Petals of Blood* relates to his earlier works, he said: 'I feel that I have changed, in terms of outlook'.[32] Thus we have an Ngũgĩ who will confront official mendacity and debasement at every opportunity and at any cost to himself, including that of possible permanent loss of employment.

In the third period Ngũgĩ gave expression to his outlook essentially in action rather than polemics: what polemic there was largely accompanied the practical activity. Some particularly important occasions were the launching of his major literary works. For example, in the interviews connected with the publication of *Petals of Blood*, he renewed his attacks upon colonialism, imperialism, cultural infirmity and similar abuses. Asked about the title of the novel, he replied:

Actually this title is taken from a poem by a West Indian writer, Derek Walcott, in which he sees a huge tree preventing a little flower from reaching out into the light.

So I took that as a symbol of the contemporary African situation where imperialism and foreign interests are preventing little flowers (the workers and peasants in Africa) from reaching out into the light.

In the novel, I show imperialism as a monster preventing all our authentic Kenyan and African flowers from reaching out into the light . . . flowering in glory and dignity.[33]

It may be noted here that the earlier title of the book had been 'Wrestlers with God'. Devoted as the book is to the lowly members of society, Ngũgĩ made more potent pronouncements concerning their situation:

Workers and peasants and women form the most important element in this country. They are the true producers of wealth. They produce all the wealth that feeds, clothes, houses everyone in the society. They also produce all the wealth that goes out of the country. Yet they do not get even the barest minimum of that which they produce. The middle-class that feeds on the

workers and peasants is a superfluous, parasitic class . . .
I see no value whatever in the middle-class.[34]

He considers women to be the most exploited of the peasant class — for
the unequal economic situation which determines their status in society
also rules their sexual relationship with men, degrading them to the roles
of prostitutes, barmaids and tourist amusements, as exemplified by his
heroine in the novel. Yet, in Ngũgĩ's words, confirming the tribute noted
earlier which he paid to the peasant women of Kenya for animating the
spirit of the Mau Mau rebellion, '. . . women were the most important
elements in Mau Mau.'[35]

So, in the third period, Ngũgĩ's inclinations are to be discerned not so
much in verbal statements as in practical action. Hence, the change in mode
of utterance in *Petals of Blood* is a deliberate tactical measure to bring home
his message and stress his motives of reform by playing down the literary,
artistic and objective qualities usual in creative writing. The same mood is
expressed in his choice of subjects for his other writings at this time: the
further exploration in depth of the history of armed revolt in Kenya, and
the direct onslaught on what he calls the 'Mubenzi society' in some of his
short stories in the collection *Secret Lives*. His employment of his native
tongue, Gikuyu, in his drama is another gesture of solidarity with the people
at large. *Ngaahika Ndeenda* speaks directly to villagers about the immorality
of those who should be the upholders of fair shares for all. It is little
wonder that Ngũgĩ stirred authority out of its indifference, even though it
reacted only with predictable vindictiveness. His other protests against
insensitive leadership have already been recorded, as also his consequent
hardships. We see Ngũgĩ confident in his convictions, determinedly seeking
by all available means to overcome obstacles to the realization of his vision
of a new Kenya.

Four new works by Ngũgĩ were published: another book of essays, *Writers
in Politics*, his own English translation of *Ngaahika Ndeenda* as *I Will Marry
When I Want*; the prison novel, both in its original Gikuyu with the title
Caithani Mutharaba-ini and in the author's translation as *Devil on the Cross*;
and his record of his experiences and thoughts in detention, *Detained: A
Writer's Prison Diary*. These writings embody Ngũgĩ's mood and attitudes at
this time.

I Will Marry When I Want belongs to the phase of Ngũgĩ's ideological
development expressed by *Petals of Blood*, *The Trial of Dedan Kimathi* and the
latest stories in *Secret Lives*. All pay tribute to the past of a humane and
patriotic culture; denounce the inroads into that culture by colonialist and
neo-colonialist capitalistic institutions; re-create the Mau Mau rebellion and
applaud its spirit of mass action in tackling the problems of modern Kenya;
and assert the inviolable rights of Kenyan workers and peasants to the fruits
of their labour and creativity. *Ngaahika Ndeenda* further marks the beginning
of Ngũgĩ's writing in a Kenyan language — partly as a breakaway from
the European literary tradition which has tended to swamp much of Africa's
heritage, but primarily as a means of communicating with the Kenyan
masses more effectively.

Devil on the Cross takes this process further both in language and content.
The satiric humour of the narrative, in which members of Kenya's capitalist

bourgeoisie compete among themselves to be crowned master of self-confessed exploitation and robbery, derives from an oral story-telling tradition. But further, the open use of the vocabulary of crime, and the mock celebration of a world devoid of human values (which is indicting its own depravity in both its speeches and its deeds) carries further the plainness and directness attempted in *Petals of Blood*. The assertion of the solidarity of the masses is also carried over from the previous novel. But in *Devil on the Cross* the workers' need to be able to press for their rights by armed power is more clearly emphasized in the prominent image of the gun, which plays such an important part in the life of the protagonist.

The essays and the diary express explicitly the direction of Ngũgĩ's thinking at that time. Asserting at the outset that every writer is by definition involved in the 'intense economic, political, cultural and ideological struggles in a society', *Writers in Politics*[36] continues:

> What he can choose is one or the other side in the battle-field: the side of the people, or the side of those social forces and classes that try to keep the people down. What he or she cannot do is remain neutral. Every writer is a writer in politics. The only question is whose and what politics? (*WIP* xii)

It is instructive to compare this quotation with those earlier in this chapter which showed Ngũgĩ excluding the writer from direct action towards social change. In the title essay he prescribes the African writer's specific obligations in the present-day world situation:

> What the African writer is called upon to do is not easy: it demands of him that he recognize the global character of imperialism and the global character or dimension of the forces struggling against it to build a new world. He must reject, repudiate, and negate his roots in the native bourgeoisie and its spokesmen, and find his true creative links with the pan-African masses over the earth in alliance with all the socialist forces of the world. He must of course be very particular, very involved in a grain of sand, but must also see the world past, present and future in that grain. He must write with the vibrations and tremors of the struggles of all the working people in Africa, America, Asia and Europe behind him. Yes, he must actively support and in his writing reflect the struggle of the African working class and its peasant class allies for the total liberation of their labour power. Yes, his work must show commitment, not to the abstract notions of justice and peace, but the actual struggle of the African peoples to seize power and hence be in a position to control all the forces of production and hence lay the only correct basis for peace and justice. (*WIP* 79–80)

The book is dedicated partly to 'all those writers in Kenya and elsewhere who have refused to bow to the neo-colonial culture of silence and fear', and is prefaced by Marx's denunciation of 'bourgeois civilization'. In one of three essays on Josiah Kariuki, Ngũgĩ declares:

> It is time that Kenyan intellectuals and all progressive youth, students, church-leaders, workers, took up Kariuki's call and resolutely denounced and struggled against all the economic, political and cultural forces that condemn our people to starvation wages, to landlessness, to lack of shelter, clothes and schools: forces that have kept us only cultivating, planting, working while others reap and

harvest and eat that which is a product of our collective sweat, forces that are selling us to Euro-American and Japanese imperialism. (*WIP* 92)

In *Detained* Ngũgĩ is past being either intimidated or deflected from championing the advancement of Kenya's post-independence masses. He does not mince his words. All he sees as guilty are openly accused. Comparing political detention in Kenya and South Africa, he writes:

> Maximum security: the idea used to fill me with terror whenever I met it in fiction, Dickens mostly, and I have always associated it with England and Englishmen and with Robben Island in South Africa: it conjured up images of hoards of dangerous killers always ready to escape through thick forests and marshes, to unleash yet more havoc and terror on an otherwise stable, peaceful and godfearing community of property-owners that sees itself as the whole society. A year as an inmate in Kamiti has taught me what should have been obvious: that the prison system is a repressive weapon in the hands of a ruling minority determined to ensure maximum security for its class dictatorship over the rest of the population, and it is not a monopoly exclusive to South Africa and England. (*D* 3–4)[37]

Denying that there has been any improvement after Kenyatta's death, Ngũgĩ reaffirms his concern with the social system rather than with individuals:

> There was an attempt, a subtle attempt, in many of the post-prison interviews, to make me say that things had changed for the better after Kenyatta's death, as if Kenyatta solely and alone was responsible for Kenya's neo-colonial mess ! I have never tried to analyse the Kenya situation in terms of the morality of individuals and 'tribes', as is the fashion in current scholarship. Capitalism cannot be run on any basis other than theft and robbery and corruption. The situation is much worse in a dependent capitalism, as is the case in Kenya and elsewhere. (*D* xiv)

Ngũgĩ's stance at this time involved: bluntness of language, arraignment without sanctity of person or institution, an increased ideological formalism, a sharper focus on evaluating writers, thinkers and literary classics, a reassertion of the role of African languages, and a more militant indignation against both the settler episode in Kenya and the inheritance of its values by the ruling Kenyan elite.

Ngũgĩ exploits the cumulative form of the prison diary to express very strongly all the thoughts and feelings that agitated him in the last years of this period. Its pointed accusations abandon all hope of engineering change by milder indirect criticism and all fear of victimization. He speaks of his determination not to become dehumanized in prison 'despite the Kenya African National Union (KANU) official government programme of animal degradation of political prisoners' (*D* 6). He refers to the power centre as 'Kenyatta's KANU government' (*D* 7), 'the neo-colonial regime of Kenyatta and his comprador KANU cohorts' (*D* 8), 'the KANU-led comprador ruling class' (*D* 10), 'the comprador bourgeois line, led by Kenyatta, Mboya and others' (*D* 54), and 'the KANU comprador regime' (*D* 123). He charges it with denying detainees privacy and herding them together in order that they will turn on one another; with tormenting detainees with illness; and with actively suppressing the development of Kenyan languages as the colonial government had done before them. He concludes his description of the evolution of KANU thus:

> ... by 1966, the comprador bourgeois line, led by Kenyatta, Mboya and others, had triumphed. This faction, using the inherited colonial state machinery, ousted the patriotic elements from the party leadership, silencing those who remained and hounding others to death.
>
> Economically this was reflected in the accelerated purchase of more token shares and directorships in foreign economic enterprises and the abandonment of even lip-service to nationalization ...
>
> Politically, it was reflected in the KANU government becoming a virtual mouthpiece of Anglo-American interests at international forums and in its down-grading relationships with anti-imperialist countries and liberation movements ...
>
> In Africa, the comprador-led KANU government took a less and less pro-Africa position ...
>
> In domestic matters the comprador bourgeoisie abandoned democracy and any lip-service to Kenya's history of struggle, by the 1969 official mass oathing ceremonies meant to psychologically rehabilitate home-guards among the Aagikuyu, Embu and Meru and by extension all those in other nationalities who had played the role of home-guard ...
>
> Ideologically, the ascendancy of the comprador bourgeoisie was reflected in the change of the KANU constitution and manifesto, in effect turning the party into the opposite of what it was in 1961 ...
>
> KANU had changed from a mass nationalist party to a moribund bureaucratic machine ... KANU had thus finally become the organ of the home-guards, and the comprador bourgeoisie. By 1977, only the name remained, a hollow echo of its patriotic origins. (*D* 54–6)

Ngũgĩ also charges the KANU government with quickly reintroducing the provisions of the colonial emergency laws, repealed in 1961 in compliance with the party's manifesto. And he quotes an unsigned manifesto in summarizing an even greater volte-face:

> Before 1965 Kenya's moral enemies were the British colonial settlers and their Kenyan supporters. Their chief supporters were grouped in KADU. KANU fought them hard and defeated them resoundingly. But they regrouped cunningly and joined KANU with Kenyatta's knowledge and approval and slowly turned KANU against its own founders (and) fighters — killed them, jailed them, detained them. In alliance with foreign interests and the Kenyatta clique they murdered the militant KANU spirit. (*D* 52)

He asserts that in Kenya the rich walked in terror of the poor whose property they had stolen, while the 'sole fear [of the poor] was that the police or the General Service Unit (GSU) would molest them' (*D* 70). These accusations culminated in the appraisal of Kenyatta on the occasion of his death:

> ... here was a black Moses who had been called by history to lead his people to the promised land of no exploitation, no oppression, but who failed to rise to the occasion, who ended up surrounding himself with colonial chiefs, home guards and traitors; who ended up being described by the British bourgeoisie

as their best friend in Africa . . . Kenyatta was a twentieth-century tragic figure: he could have been a Lenin, a Mao Tse-tung or a Ho Chi Minh; but he ended being a Chiang Kai-shek, a Park Chung Hee, or a Pinochet . . . warming himself in the reactionary gratitude of Euro-American exploiters and oppressors rather than in the eternal titanic applause of the Kenyan people, sunning himself in the revolutionary gratitude of all the oppressed and exploited. For me, his death, even though he had wrongly jailed me, was not an occasion for rejoicing but one that called for a serious re-evaluation of our history. (*D* 162–3)

Ideologically Ngũgĩ had then moved much closer towards adopting the dialectics and outlook of an avowed Marxist. Already in his earlier writings he was vehement against capitalism and insistent in his demand for a socialist re-ordering of the economy, and he commonly used words and phrases such as 'peasants', 'workers' and 'means of production'. Later he added to this vocabulary, and deployed with determined confidence terms like 'bourgeoisie', 'proletariat', 'the ruling class', 'struggle', 'patriots', 'democrats' and 'militants'. Furthermore Marx and Engels are now frequently quoted. More important still, the tone and movement of prolonged arguments began to adopt a tenor familiar to us from socialist literature. One might cite the one and a half paragraphs on pages 9 and 10 of *Writers in Politics* beginning, 'the economic structure is at the same time a class structure so that at every level of a community's being, that society is characterized by opposing classes with the dominant class, usually a minority, owning and controlling the means of production', or this shorter passage on page 26:

> Under colonialism, this economic and political struggle is often waged under the petty-bourgeois banner of racial nationalism. It is 'we' black people against 'them' whites; Africans versus Europeans. This is only natural since under colonialism, exploitation and privilege masquerade or take the form of an iron race-caste structure. But under neo-colonialism, the political and economic struggle assumes its true class character despite any and every attempt at ethnic mystification. It is now African workers and the peasant masses, together with progressive intellectuals, patriotic elements, students and their class allies from other parts of the world, pitted against the native ruling class and its international imperialist class allies. (*WIP* 26)

The same tone and vocabulary are pervasive in *Detained*, for example in the passage on page 160 in which Ngũgĩ defines the role of a leader in society.

Ngũgĩ's more formal acceptance of the socialist viewpoint focused attention on the concept of class, which is a primary theme both in *Devil on the Cross* and *I Will Marry When I Want* as well as in the explicitly polemical writings. In *Writers in Politics* he ascribes African authors' vacillation on the question of language to their class loyalty:

> But the fact still remains that none of the African writers were able to satisfactorily answer Obi Wali's challenge, because the only way in which they could have meaningfully met the challenge was through a conscious deliberate rejection of their class base, and their total identification with the position of peasants and workers in their struggle against exploitation by an alliance of the

imperialist bourgeoisie and the *comprador* bourgeoisie to end all forms of exploitation, oppression and domination. (*WIP* 58)

He reflects from prison on the goals which the 1962 Kampala conference of African writers set itself:

> Now as I look at Kofi's picture in *Newsweek* at Kamiti Prison, I remember that Chris Okigbo who led the conference with the paper, 'What is African Literature?', is dead, a victim of an intra-bourgeois war which, in the words of Kole Omotoso, was merely for 'redefining the land boundaries rather than redefining the quality of life for those who live within the existing boundaries', a war in which only the Americans, the British and the French emerged as victors; that Wole Soyinka and Kofi Awoonor have served prison terms for saying that things which are not right ARE NOT RIGHT; and that many African writers have witnessed and recorded the terrible anguish of Africans killing innumerable Africans so that Euro-American capital can thrive on grounds made more fertile by African flesh and blood! (*D* 142)

In *Writers in Politics* and *Detained* Ngũgĩ vents his long-festering disgust at the obsequious and treacherous posture adopted by the generality of African intellectuals on all the issues he had been addressing. His passion knows no bounds in the preface to the prison diary which castigates 'petty-bourgeois intellectuals at the university who hide ethnic chauvinism and their mortal terror of progressive class politics behind masks of abstract super-nationalism'(*D* xxi).

Ngũgĩ saw the majority of his fellow writers and critics as 'part of the petty intellectual army of [the] native ruling class' who 'have never really accepted the possibility of their becoming true literary guerillas of the masses in their quest and struggle for total liberation' (*WIP* 24). Instead they write novels in which

> the crowds emerge as gullible, easily fooled, praising now this leader then that leader in return for a drink of beer and five cents . . . The masses are seen as having no minds of their own . . . In African literature, we have very few positive heroes from among the working people, positive heroes who would embody the spirit of struggle and resistance against exploitation and naked robbery by the national bourgeoisie and its global allied classes. (*WIP* 24)

Consequently African intellectuals become the main agents for cultural imperialism: they import personnel to man the Humanities faculties of universities, make foreign literature the centrepiece of their syllabuses, and produce 'the kind of literature that perpetuates the same decadent western bourgeois values and class world outlook' (*WIP* 25). Sadly he found

> our own African critics continuing the same aged approach to literature, the same mouthing of phrases about the anguish of the human condition, universal values that transcend race, class, economics, politics and other social activities or ordinary living. (*WIP* 25)

Ngũgĩ stressed the need to 'understand that cultural imperialism in its era of neo-colonialism is a more dangerous cancer because it takes new subtle forms and can hide even under the cloak of militant African nationalism, the cry for dead authentic cultural symbolism and other native self-assertive banners'. This is possible because:

Suddenly under neo-colonialism it is the African who is building churches in every village under Harambee self-help schemes; who is rushing for the latest literary trash from America or failing that, Africanizing the same thrills and escapism by giving them local colour . . . (*WIP* 25)

Ngũgĩ confessed with chagrin his having himself been blinded in some degree by the myopia that afflicts the intellectual group:

I can remember I myself, in 1965 or 1966 in the deepest ignorance of my colonial education, writing a talk on English as a second language, in which I outlined the advantages of writing in English as opposed to writing in African languages. One of the reasons I gave was that English has a large vocabulary! (*WIP* 57)

Ngũgĩ's militancy about the primacy of African languages in Africa was and is part and parcel of his commitment to communicating with ordinary people. He would therefore not only write in an indigenous language but would collaborate in shaping new uses for these languages in enterprises such as the presentation of *Ngaahika Ndeenda* in a grass-roots community. In both *Writers iŋ Politics* and *Detained* he passionately insists on the incontrovertible importance of African languages in their own context:

Literature as a process of thinking in images utilizes language and draws upon the collective experience — history — embodied in that language. In writing one should hear all the whispering, and the shouting and crying and the loving and the hating of many voices in the past and those voices will never speak to a writer in a foreign language. (*WIP* 60)

As he denounces afresh at this time the obloquy of the settler mentality and settler tactics, we meet a new Ngũgĩ, fortified by research and armed with documents, not dependent on spontaneous reactions alone.Here emerged a knowledgeable and confident spokesman talking back to a band of savage adventurers, devoid of human civilized values, who seized upon a vulnerable phase of African history to lord it over African peoples. In *Detained* he details the cold-blooded brutality of numerous colonial soldiers and officers:

For the white settlers were really parasites in paradise. Kenya, to them, was a huge winter home for aristocrats, which of course meant big game hunting and living it up on the backs of a million field and domestic slaves, the *Watu* as they called them. (*D* 29)

Thus all these eruptions of brutality between the introduction of colonial culture in 1895 and its flowering with blood in the 1950s were not aberrations of an otherwise humane Christian culture. No. They were its very essence, its law, its logic, and the Kenyan settler with his *sjambok*, his dog, his horse, his rickshaw, his sword, his bullet, was the true embodiment of British imperialism. (*D* 40)

Thus the Emergency epitomized the basic logic of settler occupation of Kenya, and the anti-colonialist uprising was a heroic assertion of African dignity and self-discovery. In throwing back the shame of this time in the teeth of those who were responsible, Ngũgĩ was not only setting the record straight and, as it were, washing himself and his fellows clean of abuse, he was also speaking of the present. He was revealing the true foundations of all that had been so eagerly inherited by the new elite. The contemporary Kenyan must recognize the original stock of which the current evils were the latest crop.

In particular Ngũgĩ was concerned to reinterpret the works of those writers, critics and thinkers who exerted most influence in the world at large, as well as more specifically in schools, colleges, and universities. He has always stood out against those he regards as disseminating a settler mentality, such as Elspeth Huxley — 'a scribbler of tourist guides and anaemic settler polemics blown up to the size of books' (*D* 31) — Robert Ruark, Karen Blixen and L.S.B. Leakey, the archaeologist. However, he now subjected a much wider assortment of authors to his new style of questioning, because of either their racist implications or their negative class orientation: Hume, Thomas Jefferson, Hegel, Trevor-Roper, Phyllis Wheatley, Booker T. Washington, Martin Luther King, James Baldwin, Ralph Ellison, Whitney Young, Eldridge Cleaver, Ernest Hemingway, John Updike, Professor Malinowski, Professor Barnard. In the course of reminding us that literature always reflects social reality, he finds that a number of classic authors offer revealing commentaries on their environments. Shakespeare, Marlowe, Ben Jonson, Rabelais reflect

> a feel of sixteenth century English and French societies: the emerging empirical spirit, the bourgeois individualism, the mercantile capitalist spirit struggling against feudalism for the freedom to move and conquer the seas, to colonize and christianize natives, crying in the same breath: my God, my Gold; my Gold, my God. (*WIP* 74)

Even in 'insulating herself from the big upheavals of her day', Jane Austen also 'unwittingly gives a wonderful picture of a leisurely parasitic landed middle class in eighteenth century England', while Emily Brontë provides 'a most incisive examination of the limiting repressive and oppressive ethical values of an industrial bourgeois class' (*WIP* 74). On the other hand he has been critical of the limitations accepted by certain major authors, of whom (perhaps surprisingly) he took George Eliot as a prototype:

> Her world is vast, the issues she is dealing with are wide, but the intellectual and moral conflicts do not arise out of an awareness of a changing world — a world consistently in motion, always in the process of transforming itself from one form to another, and hence giving rise to new class alignments and possibilities of new social orders . . . At their best, these writers can and do produce a literature of sharp social criticism. But such an attitude to society, such an abstraction of human types and moral ideals from their basis in the class structure and class struggle, often gives rise to a literature distinguished for its shallow dive into society and only redeemed from oblivion by those of our critics who have no other critical tools apart from the worn and meaningless phrases like 'human compassion', 'timeless and universal' etc. (*WIP* 75-6)

In profound exasperation Ngũgĩ adds:

> Haven't we heard critics who demand of African writers that they stop writing about colonialism, race, colour, exploitation, and simply write about human beings? Such an attitude to society is often the basis of some European writers' mania for man without history — solitary and free — with unexplainable despair

and anguish and death as the ultimate truth about the human condition. (*WIP* 76)

On such criteria, Ngũgĩ divided the European and American literature with which 'the colonial student was assaulted' (*WIP* 15) into three categories. First is 'the good European literature, the product of the best and most sensitive minds from European culture: Aeschylus, Sophocles, Montaigne, Rabelais, Cervantes, Shakespeare, Goethe, Balzac, Tolstoy, Dostoevsky, Thomas Mann, Ibsen, Yeats, Whitman, Faulkner . . .' But even these writers had a constricted, Europeanized vision, so that 'man' and 'human' were limited in meaning to European stock. Thus African students

> see how Prospero sees Caliban and not how Caliban sees Prospero; how Crusoe discovers and remakes Man Friday, but never how Friday views himself and his heroic struggles against centuries of Crusoe's exploitation and oppression. (*WIP* 36-7)

Second comes the literature 'that tried to define the colonized world for the European colonizer', a literature that 'was downright racist' (*WIP* 16) and made no effort to hide its racism: Rider Haggard, John Buchan, Rudyard Kipling, Robert Ruark, Nicholas Monsarrat, Elspeth Huxley, Karen Blixen. Ngũgĩ sees this approach as being supported by such English expressions as *black market, black sheep, blackmail, blacklist* and so forth. The churches have always compounded such assumptions in associating whiteness with God, Christ, the angels and all goodness, while black is the colour of sin, hell and Satan.

Third, Ngũgĩ isolates the literature which 'set out to sympathetically treat the African world either to appeal to the European liberal conscience or simply to interpret Africa for the Africans' (*WIP* 19), a literature which, none the less, presents the African image negatively. Here Ngũgĩ included Conrad, Joyce Cary, Alan Paton, even William Blake. They were seen as apostles, in different senses and different degrees, of European liberalism. Liberalism too often devolves into a 'sugary ideology of imperialism', which

> fosters the illusion in the exploited of the possibilities of peaceful settlement and painless escape from imperialist violence which anyway is not called violence but law and order. Liberalism blurs all antagonistic class contradictions, all contradictions between imperialist domination and the struggle for national liberation, seeing in the revolutionary violence of the former, the degradation of humanity. (*WIP* 20)

Ngũgĩ relates Christian missions to these liberal groups:

> Why is it that the church is always preaching humility and forgiveness and non-violence to the oppressed? Why do the liberals preach gratitude, humility, kindness, forgiveness and meekness to the oppressed classes? Why is it that the church does not concentrate its preaching and efforts of conversion on the very class and races that have brutalized others, manacled others, robbed others?
>
> The aim is obvious: it is to weaken the resistance of the oppressed classes and here imaginative literature comes in as a useful medium of mental conditioning, making the oppressed believe that the root cause of their problem, and hence the solution, lies deep in their spiritual condition, in their sinful souls. (*WIP* 22)

Ultimately Ngũgĩ fashioned a new definition of literature in defining it as a partisan interest, which must not only reflect social reality — economic, political and cultural — but must reflect it from the point of view of a nation, a race, a class. It must take sides in the vital conflicts which reshape society. One such conflict involves the resistance of peasants and workers to oppression by the controlling, exploitative class:

> A nation's literature which is a sum total of the products of many individuals in that society is then not only a reflection of that people's collective reality, collective experience, but also embodies that community's way of looking at the world and its place in the making of that world. It is partisan on the collective level, because the literature is trying to make us see how that community, class, race, group has defined itself historically and how it defines the world in relationship to itself. (*WIP* 7)

Ngũgĩ cites Achebe's Okonkwo and Ezeulu as 'representatives of the people and [their] spirit of resistance' (*WIP* 30), who make their own history:

> Okonkwo commits suicide rather than submit and live in a world where he is denied the right to make his own history through his control and development of the productive forces. His act of killing an imperialist messenger is as symbolic as it is prophetic. It is the new messenger class, the new errand boys of international monopoly capitalism that make total liberation difficult, for on the surface they do not look like one of Okonkwo's own people. (*WIP* 30)

So Ngũgĩ sought in this third period of his ideological development examined in the foregoing paragraphs 'to bring us all back to school to re-learn our lessons'. He would persuade us to revise certain views which have been regarded as eternal truths. If we sometimes disagree, even in his own terms, with his evaluation of particular authors or texts, or with specific pronouncements, this need not prejudice our response to his thesis as it emerged in the round. In his confirmed revolutionary stance, Ngũgĩ has been determined to ensure that practical results could grow out of his vision of a new Kenya, a vision based on organized thinking and confident knowledge. Clearly he is inextricably involved with the future and fate of his own society.

Fourth Phase: The Period of Exile from 1982

Ngũgĩ's articulation of ideological revolutionary socialist commitment reaches a new peak in the still on-going period of exile from 1982, during which he has perforce lived outside his homeland. Three collections of essays express his frame of mind during these years; (1) *Barrel of a Pen: Resistance to Repression in Neo-colonial Kenya*;[38] (2) *Decolonising the Mind: The Politics of Language in African Literature*;[39] and (3) *Moving the Centre: The Struggle for Cultural Freedom*.[40]

Ngũgĩ himself recognizes this period as a distinct one in his life. Writing in the Preface to *Moving the Centre* (xiii) specifically about the essays in this particular collection, he says that, with the exception of one essay written in 1981, the others were written between 1985 and 1990 and so fall 'within the years of my exile'. Indeed, Ngũgĩ finds a unity of theme among these essays. He identifies one such underlying theme as the inseparable link between (on the one hand) the cultural and (on the other hand) the political and economic dynamics of a society. Another pervading assumption in the essays is that of the inevitability and continuity of change in all phenomena and all societies.

In these essays, Ngũgĩ, applying the seasoned knowledge and insight of mature years and his extensive exposure to world affairs, reconsiders almost all the issues so far analysed in this chapter. However, in view of his extension of the debate to embrace the entire Third World, and his even greater concentration on such subjects as capitalism, colonialism, neo-colonialism, racism, imperialism, education and culture, it is possible to discern a shift from a primarily Kenyan focus on these issues towards their international implications and their philosophical foundations. There is much reiteration from essay to essay; but two cardinal points that can be identified in the arguments are capitalism and imperialism. Indeed, one could propose a schematic representation of Ngũgĩ's preoccupations in this period of exile (as on the following page).

The prototypes of Western nations most severely castigated by Ngũgĩ are predictably the USA, Britain, France and, to some extent, the smaller ex-colonial nations; but Japan and Israel are constantly included among the nations which Ngũgĩ sees as strangulating the Third World by exploitation. Thus, as he tells us in 'Mau Mau Is Coming Back', there were in Kenya in 1982 three military presences — British, Israeli and American, the last maintaining bases in many places in the country, while American and British pilots were flying Kenya's airplanes (*Barrel*, 8). In the same essay Ngũgĩ records how Kenya had, in a false display of neutrality after asserting its 'flag independence' in 1964, opened up the country to wider imperialist interests from Japan, Western Europe and the USA in addition to the traditional link with Britain. The presence of military bases in Kenya traps the country in the tentacles of the war games of Western nations, particularly those of the USA, exposing the people of the country to much danger and making the country part of what Ngũgĩ calls 'the notorious US Rapid Deployment Force and nuclear strategy in the Indian Ocean' (*Barrel* 26).

Ngũgĩ describes the dominance of the West over Third World affairs by the term 'Eurocentrism', which he uses as the title of Part 1 of *Moving the Centre* ('Freeing Culture from Eurocentrism'). Eurocentrism is present in all areas of life and consciousness of Third World peoples — economic, political and so on — but it is most particularly manifest in the fields of languages, literature, cultural studies, and the organization of literature departments in most parts of the globe (Preface to *Moving the Centre* xvii).It is most dangerous when it becomes internalized in the intellectual conception of Third World people — what Ngũgĩ earlier in his career called 'a colonialism of the mind'.

Among the many subjects of Ngũgĩ's thoughts in this current period of exile, as reflected in the three books we are now reviewing, imperialism is dominant. Indeed, imperialism can be said to over-arch everything else that he says. He gives it various definitions: 'the rule of consolidated finance capital' (*Decolonising the Mind*, 2); 'the conquest and subjugation of the entire

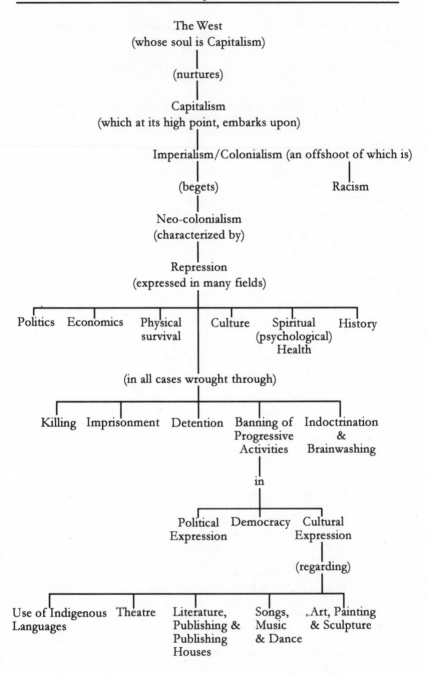

labour force of other countries by concentrated capital'(*Moving the Centre*, 42); and so forth. Imperialism presents itself in two phases: colonial and neo-colonial (*Barrel* 87); its two most obvious manifestations in the contemporary world are its neo-colonial form, and its dominance of the USA (*Moving the Centre* 47). Emerging in the imperialist game in its latter-day neo-colonialist stage, America engineered the overthrow of the Allende government in Chile, achieved ascendancy in the trans-national financial and industrial monopolies in Asia, Africa and Latin America (an ascendancy symbolized by the dominance of the IMF and the World Bank in the determination of the economies and, therefore, the politics and cultures of the subject countries), surrounded all Africa with military bases and other forms of the American presence, and perfected the operation of its Rapid Deployment Forces (*Moving the Centre* 68–69). Ngũgĩ thus forecast that in the 1990s the world would be under the sway of the three main centres of imperialism: a united western Europe, tightening its control over Africa; Japan, consolidating its economic strangle-hold over South-east Asia; and the North American centre, mainly the USA, which would seek to maintain its control over 'the entire imperialist camp' (*Moving the Centre*, 53).

As Ngũgĩ sees it, imperialism puts into disarray the entire fabric of the lives of its victims: in particular their culture, making them ashamed of their names, history, systems of belief, languages, lore, art, dance, song, sculpture, even the colour of their skin; then it thwarts all its victims' forms and means of survival, and furthermore it employs racism. Ngũgĩ analyses four ways in which racism operates as a weapon of assault. First it fosters obscurantism, which conceals the differences between the wealth of the few and the penury of the many — between capital and labour. Second racism manipulates 'divide and rule', the insidious manoeuvres by which capital links up into conglomerates from country to country giving itself the power to subject labour to a destiny of wretchedness. Thirdly by means of discrimination against workers on the basis of skin colour it engineers conflicts and disharmony within the work-force. Fourth, racism is a major basis of exploitation, empowering capital to appropriate to itself the products of labour — which is really the goal of all other modes deployed by racism (*Moving the Centre* 121).

As for capitalism, Ngũgĩ places it in the earliest stage in the growth of exploitative actions which strong nations exercise over the weak ones. Industrial capitalism, which evolved from the Industrial Revolution in Europe, developed into what Ngũgĩ calls 'laissez-faire capitalism'(*Moving the Centre* 47). Laissez-faire capitalism itself developed into monopoly which, to control sources of raw material supply, developed into colonialism, which was sealed at the Berlin conference of 1884. With the 'flag-flying and anthem-singing' independence of African countries in the sixties, capitalism developed into its second stage of neo-colonialism.

Ngũgĩ likens capitalism to the prey-and-victim relationship between the Old Man and Sinbad in *Sinbad the Sailor*, and asserts that, in the contemporary world, the Old Man could be Europe, America or Japan (though primarily the USA), while Sinbad is always the Third World (*Barrel* 71). It is capitalist hunger for more wealth from the exploitation of cheap labour which, according to Ngũgĩ, engenders colonialism and neo-colonialism and caused two world wars. Of all expressions of capitalism, the most destructive has been that of the USA, a country which, between 1899 and 1917, intervened in the internal affairs of at least seven South American states to install comprador regimes (*Moving the Centre* 48), and has been responsible for erecting such reactionary and repressive regimes as those, among others, of Pinochet's Chile, Samoza's Nicaragua, Marco's Philippines, South Korea, Kenya, El Salvador.

Ngũgĩ interprets Vasco da Gama's landing at the Cape of Good Hope as a capitalist-boosting event which placed in Europe's easy reach India's and Africa's riches (*Moving the Centre* 148). He defines imperialism in relation to capitalism as 'the power of dead capital' (*Moving the Centre* 110) by which a few shareholders control the life prospects of millions of people and create deserts, famines, pollution and wars. Ngũgĩ observes that the flaunted success stories of the IMF and the World Bank — the modern citadels of capitalism — are in the main repressing nations (Kenya, Malawi, Cameroon, the Ivory Coast) subservient to the West (*Moving the Centre* 155). He describes in detail how his play, *Ngaahika Ndeenda* (*I Will Marry When I Want*) depicts relentless capitalist persecution of the helpless poor (*Decolonising the Mind* 44), driving them out of any small pieces of land to which they can lay claim.

Colonialism, for its own part, is closely linked in Ngũgĩ's thinking with imperialism, capitalism and racism. He defines it as:

> . . . that situation in which the ruling class of one nation or country imposes its rule and hegemony over another nation or country and subjugates and suppresses all the other classes of the colonial country. ('Education for a National Culture', *Barrel* 93)

He avers that it is established through military conquest and imposition of a political dictatorship. Its aim is the control of the productive forces of the colonized people and, hence, their wealth (*Barrel* 93 and *Decolonising the Mind* 16) their lives, and their culture — their mental universe, which is the medium through which they perceive themselves and their relationship with the world. This control takes the dual forms both of the deliberate destruction of the people's culture (their art, dances, religion, history, geography, education, orature and language) and the superimposition on the colonized people of the colonizer's culture and language. The slave trade, slavery itself, and the settler episode have all, in Ngũgĩ's view, been part of the colonial malady to which the Third World has been subjected.

Ngũgĩ now defines neo-colonialism as 'that process in which a country is nominally independent but its economy is still in the hands of the imperialist bourgeoisie' ('Education for a National Culture', *Barrel* 95). The centrality of the economy in Ngũgĩ's thinking concerning the forces which oppress the Third World is everywhere evident. In a neo-colonialist state nothing has changed from the colonial condition regarding the management of the country's economy. The imperialist bourgeoisie, formerly exploiting the people through feudal or settler organs, simply transfer the mechanisms of exploitation to a native elite, 'nurtured in the womb of colonialism' (*Barrel* 96), but now eternally grateful for having been allowed to raise a flag and sing an anthem and to join the Europeans in plundering and looting.

We have already noted that Ngũgĩ labels neo-colonialism the second stage of imperialism. He x-rays its other features in 'The Writer in a Neo-colonial State' (*Moving the Centre* 71). A neo-colonial state is, by definition, a repressive machine; it progressively isolates itself from the people and compulsively transfers its power base to the police, the army and the imperialist alliance. It suppresses all democratic activities and viewpoints, and becomes a one-party state, which is a one-man rule. It indeed outlaws all democratic procedures and becomes intolerant of democratic creative expression in cultural matters.

Naturally, Kenya is Ngũgĩ's most degraded example of the neo-colonial state. He gives a chilling description in 'Mau Mau is Coming Back' (*Barrel*) of the country's descent from 'a fairly open society'(*Moving the Centre* 71) to a state totally intolerant of all democratic activities.

We have already discussed Ngũgĩ's view of racism as a weapon of imperialism. As an independent element in relations between the West and the Third World, Ngũgĩ defines it as 'the most vicious part of that general ideology that gives rational expression and legitimacy to exploitation, oppression and domination' ('Racism in Literature', *Moving the Centre* 126). It is the principal means by which a ruling junta — applying all sorts of machinations which it disguises as education,history, philosophy, religion, aesthetics and so on — conditions the subject people to develop a negative image of themselves. Literature is one of its most potent weapons, which writers like Karen Blixen (alias Isak Dinesen) have applied in painting obnoxious pictures of Africa.

Another set of subjects thematically linked together in these writings from exile are culture, African languages, African literature,African theatre, education and religion.

Ngũgĩ states that culture 'embodies those moral, ethical and aesthetic values, the set of spiritual eyeglasses through which [people]come to view themselves and their place in the universe ('The Language of African Literature,' *Decolonising the Mind* 14–15). In 'Freeing Culture from Racism' (*Moving the Centre* 128), on the other hand, he defines culture as 'a kind of social body that carries the values [people] have evolved in the course of their economic, political and cultural praxis'. In both these essays and in 'The Universality of Local Knowledge' (*Moving the Centre*), he describes how culture evolves from the process of people's interaction with one another in the course of battling with their common environment for their survival and growth. So culture becomes the means by which people recognize their identity in relation to the entire universe, and construct their self-image. Hence the control of a society's culture is always a matter over which progressive and reactionary forces contend.He devotes 'Post-colonial Politics and Culture' (*Moving the Centre*) to detailing the repressive actions of the colonial authorities and the neo-colonial bourgeoisie of Kenya against the indigenous culture, including the languages of the people.

Ngũgĩ remains passionately committed to the overall development of African languages and their use in African literatures. *Decolonising the Mind* is dedicated to those who use African languages and maintain their dignity. He sees the choice and use of a language as central to a people's definition of themselves since it is central to their identity in relation to their social and their natural environments and thus to the entire universe ('The Language of African Literature', *Decolonising the Mind* 4).Thus he feels strongly that language has played a crucial role in Africa's contention with Europe throughout the twentieth century concerning self-identity. He assigns a dual character to any language: 'a means of communication and a carrier of culture' ('The Language of African Languages', *Decolonising the Mind* 13), and he identifies three attributes of language as a means of communication: namely 'the language of real life'(for establishing relationships among people); 'the speech element' (by which people reveal their inner selves); and 'the written signs' element (by which ideas are imparted on paper).

Ngũgĩ believes that it was because the European colonizers were aware of the powers of language that they waged a virulent war against indigenous tongues. Consequently African languages were denigrated by every possible means, while European languages were held up for esteem: so that the African was led to despise his own language; he was goaded into perceiving his very identity in terms of his colonizers' language.

But Ngũgĩ asserts triumphantly that, in spite of the ruthless imperialist siege against African vernaculars, they have refused to die because they are kept alive by the peasantry and workers. To activate his commitment to resuscitating African languages and to align himself with peasants and workers in keeping them alive, Ngũgĩ himself has now been writing in his own first language for many years. He expressed elation in 1989 when he found that Yale University was already doing a great deal of work on African languages ('Life, Literature and a Longing for Home', *Moving the Centre* 156–7). Of course writing in a local tongue poses such challenges as the reliability of the orthography, the relevance of content, acceptance by readers, and in particular reactions by a neo-colonial government. But Ngũgĩ is convinced that such problems are far from insuperable. For he is sure that ultimately, authentic African literature will simply have to be written in African languages alone.

African literature is the subject of many essays in the three books of non-fiction written in this period. The focus in these essays is on accelerating and deepening the indigenization of literature through writing in native tongues. To achieve this objective, Ngũgĩ prescribes two groups of conditions for African literature. First:

> . . . a willing writer . . . a willing translator . . . a willing publisher . . . a progressive state . . . and, finally and most important, a willing and widening readership. ('The Language of African Fiction', *Decolonising the Mind* 85)

The second set of conditions is that the writer must become part of the African revolution; align himself with the people in their struggle for survival; re-discover and confront the language of the people; learn from their great heritage of orature; imbibe their faith and optimism in the capacity of a people to renew their world and re-make themselves, and join the people's struggle to complete the demolition of neo-colonialism ('Freeing Culture from Colonial Legacies', *Moving the Centre* 74).

He re-animates his familiar venom against European writers ('Freedom of the Artist', *Barrel* 55–69). He lays down three criteria for literary objectivity: a broad perspective on humanity; freedom from state harassment, and an adequate degree of freedom from an inhibiting social structure. On the basis of these conditions, he identifies two kinds of artists:

the state poet laureate and praise-singer who upholds the neo-colonial *status quo* of repression, and the trumpeter of a new world (*Barrel* 61). He recalls the Kenyan government's acts of terrorism against writers, students, teachers, school-children, journalists and others, and declares that, by and large, the real artist of the world is human labour itself which creates the social environment out of which literature emerges.

In 'The Quest for Relevance' (*Decolonising the Mind* 87–108), he re-enacts the old Nairobi debate about placing African literature in the centre of the literature syllabus in Africa's learning institutions. In the few snatches of literary criticism in these essays, Ngũgĩ subjects Achebe's characters to socialist analysis, identifying them with the messenger class and tracing their evolution from actual messengers, clerks, soldiers, policemen, catechists and road foremen in *Things Fall Apart* and *Arrow of God* to their assumption and exercise of power in *A Man of the People* and to their plunging the country into intra-class war in *Girls at War* ('The Language of African Fiction', *Decolonising the Mind* 63).

He considers the writers of the sixties as having had inadequate understanding of the class dynamics of the society which they were attempting to depict so that they tended merely to decry the lack of moral fibre in the new leadership. In 'Imperialism and Revolution' (*Moving the Centre*), he acclaims the Sixth International Radical and Third World Book Fair (London, 1987) for its good work in keeping up the spirit of revolutionary protest in literary writing. His final verdict on African literature is:

> In its search for a genuine homecoming, African literature will truly reflect the universal struggle for a world which truly belongs to us all. ('Freeing Culture from Colonial Legacies', *Moving the Centre* 108).

On African theatre, his most powerful utterance in these essays of the period of exile is 'The Language of African Theatre' (*Decolonising the Mind* 34–62). The thrust of the essay is an account of the running battle which has characterized the relationship between indigenous theatre and colonial and neo-colonial theatre in Kenya from early times to the present.Ngũgĩ sees indigenous theatre as having taken root in community rituals and ceremonies of the peasantry performed to re-enact and celebrate the many events and mysteries which characterize human, animal and plant life and the relationships among these species of creation. They consisted of songs, dance and occasional mime, and formed part of the rhythm of daily and seasonal life of the people.

Colonialism, collaborating with foreign missionary religion, destroyed this indigenous theatrical culture: missionary religion considered the performances idolatrous, while the colonial administration saw the gathering of the inhabitants in the village 'empty space' (38) as a threat to its authority. So the colonial administration began to ban traditional drama, bringing the banning to a climax in the Mau Mau war years of 1952 to 1962 when any gathering of over five people needed a licence. Colonialism tried to replace indigenous drama with plays in the European tradition, most of which presented the African as a clown.

After independence Kenyan Africans began to mount a revolt against European theatre. Beginning in the prominent schools, this revolt broadened during the sixties and early seventies into a country-wide movement with the emergence of notable local playwrights, directors, and actors, and consequently also of theatre companies. Of plays which carried the nationalist, patriotic and anti-colonial spirit of revolt, that by Ngũgĩ himself and Micere Mugo, *The Trial of Dedan Kimathi* (1977), was among the most notable. European monopoly control of the National Theatre in Nairobi was challenged. Alternative theatres were created, and travelling theatres were founded by many institutions.

However, the indigenous theatre was handicapped first by its petty bourgeois base in schools, and secondly by the continuing use of English.But concern about the predominant use of English led to such logical steps as the development of the Kamiriithu Community Educational and Cultural Centre. In the open theatre of Kamiriithu, Ngũgĩ and Ngũgĩ Mirii's *Ngaahika Ndeenda* was produced in 1977, and there Ngũgĩ's musical drama, *Maitu Njugira* (*Mother, Sing for Me*) was developed from November 1981.

Ngũgĩ asserts at the beginning of the essay that although the educated elite (the petty bourgeoisie) were part of Kamiriithu, it was 'the peasants and workers, including the unemployed [who] formed the backbone of the theatre' (*Decolonising the Mind* 35). At the end of the essay, he asks:

> . . . can an idea be killed? Can you destroy a revolutionary shrine . . . itself enshrined in the revolutionary spirit of the people? (61)

Education continues to be another crucial issue for Ngũgĩ during this period of exile. He defines education characteristically in economic terms as 'the process of social production, exchange and distribution of what we eat, wear and shelter under, the whole system of organizing the wealth of a given nation' ('Education for a National Culture', *Barrel* 88). He views education as imparting knowledge about the relationships between man and man and between man and nature, and inculcating a certain attitude about these relationships. So 'education is part of culture and culture is part of education' (88). A valid, positive education, as Ngũgĩ sees it, is a liberating process, which aims at

> producing a fully developed individual who understands the forces at work in society . . . [is] imbued with great hatred of all parasitic relationships of exploitation and oppression . . . with great patriotic pride and courage . . . [and is] desirous of a total control of his natural and social environment. (98)

Such an education is, he believes, what Karl Marx described as 'polytechnic education', which should have the three elements of (1) mental education,endowing scientific knowledge of the world, i.e. one's culture carried in one's history, literature, dances, theatre and so forth for the purpose of changing the world; (2) physical education, embracing training for physical fitness and composed of the simplest gymnastic and military training which prepares people to defend their heritage; and (3) economic and techno-logical training which teaches people the skills which turn everybody into a producer (98).

Ngũgĩ deplores the fact that colonialist and neo-colonialist education thwarted all these positive aims, since it was geared to mystifying, obscuring and denying reality in an attempt to persuade the African that he had no history and could thus have no faith in himself. He returns to the subject in 'The Language of African Theatre', discussed above, where he asserts that bourgeois education weakens the under-privileged, 'making [them] feel that they cannot do this or that — oh, it must take such brains!' overwhelming them with their inadequacies, incapacities and inability to control their environment (*Decolonising the Mind* 57). In his perception, 'Kamiriithu was part of education for demystifying knowledge and reality'.

Though no essay is devoted exclusively to religion, these collections are liberally shot through with his characteristically embittered and disapproving remarks on the subject.

Several other matters come under Ngũgĩ's surveillance in panoramic discharges of his artillery of disapproval, protest, and criticism in this period. His personal life history and experiences might be pieced together from quite detailed information interjected here and there. His familiar idea about the intertwining of influences from the past, present and future resurfaces. Again he insists that there is no neutrality of scholarship: it is either for good or for bad; so he urges the scholar in his utterances, writings and activities to take the side of the masses in their revolutionary struggle for an egalitarian society. He celebrates the heroism of time-honoured Kenyan patriots who fought with the sword, and of contemporaries who battle by campaigning for solidarity with tongue and pen.

Ngũgĩ laments the people's collective fatalistic submission to silence in the face of throttling oppression and blood-sucking tyranny. He traces the genealogy of the present Moi administration in Kenya through a past of only tepid, hypocritical alliances with progressive forces on the one hand, and open villainy on the other. His recurrent exposure of the Kenyan government's repressive tyranny, subservience to imperialism, and consequent widening alienation from the people are perhaps best summarized in Victoria Brittain's preface to *Barrel of a Pen*, a piece which presents a sinister tapestry of the utterly dehumanized society into which Ngũgĩ shows Kenya to have degenerated.

However, Brittain concludes the preface on the optimistic note that opposition to repression is surging in many sectors of the society as evidenced by the spate of resistance writing in various genres. So she affirms that American patronage might ultimately become counterproductive for the USA itself.

The same optimism is resonantly voiced by Ngũgĩ himself in several passages in the three works of non-fiction written in exile. We quoted earlier his query as to whether an idea, an ascendant revolutionary spirit enshrined in people's hearts, can be killed. He declares at the end of 'Women in Cultural Work' that 'Kamiriithi will come back' (*Barrel* 51), and asks:' Can they destroy or abolish the people?' Concluding 'Freeing Culture from Eurocentrism', he asserts defiantly: 'imperialism in its neo-colonial clothes will not be able to destroy the fighting culture of the African peasantry and working class' (*Moving the Centre* 45), and he ends the last essay in *Moving the Centre*, 'Matigari and the Dreams of One East Africa', with the verdict:

> I know, in a sense more deep than words can tell, that Matigari shall one day return to Kenya, to East Africa. (175)

Ngũgĩ strengthens his hope for a better future with doctrines repeated liberally throughout about the positive values of freedom and African socialism. Above everything else, however, his conviction of eventual victory of the now suffering masses is pinned to his recognition (expressed in practically every paragraph of these books) of an undying history and culture among the African masses of unrelenting resistance to oppression and injustice. Tribute to those who have fought for freedom — women being often selected for special acclaim — is a constant refrain in these books of exile.

While still in exile, the second edition of Ngũgĩ's *Writers in Politics* (1997) has just been published. It is evident that this second edition is not dependent on the first for a full exposition of Ngũgĩ's evolving ideas during 15 exiled years. Each edition is a self-contained statement of his ideological position at the time. The general reader acquainted with either edition alone will be well educated on the writer's standpoints concerning the issues then relevant. If the same reader were to know both editions, he would probably be aware only vaguely of any differences between the two.

However, the student and scholar will want to identify what is old and what is new — how Ngũgĩ's thinking has shifted — both in the later edition of *Writers in Politics* and in other recent books of essays discussed in this chapter. We hope that for such enquiring minds the chart on the following page will be helpful:

The three essays in the first edition dropped in the second are:

Kenyan Culture: The National Struggle for Survival
(Part I, Chapter 3);
Handcuffs for a Play (I, 4);
Repression in South Korea (III, 2);
and Postscript to Part I: On Civilization.

New essays in the second edition are four:

Freedom of Expression: The Right to Write is a Human Right (II, 6)
Culture in a Crisis: Problems of Creativity & the New World Order
(III, 12)
Kamau Brathwaite: The Voice of Pan-African Presence (III, 13)
Learning from our Ancestors: the Intellectual Legacy of Pan-Africanism
(III, 14).

The chart shows much of the physical packaging of the new edition. Currency of content has determined retention of some essays; particularity in time the exclusion of others. Essay titles have been changed, altered, prefixed with extra phrases, or suffixed with sub-titles, to reflect more closely the revised concept of each essay, and make the title more specific. Some tidying up has taken place.

Trying to sift out just how the new concept of each essay is arrived at is a daunting task. At first glance, the changes seem to be essentially cosmetic: like trimming a hedge rather than planting a new one. At length one concludes that it is shifts in temper and tone rather than in substance that has determined the alterations. This is illustrated by the new title of Part I, Chapter 3: 'Literature and Double Consciousness: Warring Images in Afro-American Thought' wherein the words 'robber' and 'robbed' have

Second Edition		First Edition		
Part I: War of Images				
Chapter	Title	Title	Part	Chapter
1	Literature & Society: The Politics of the Canon	Literature & Society	I	1
2	Standing on Our Grounds: Literature, Education & Images of Self	Literature in Schools	I	2
3	Literature & Double Consciousness: Warring Images in Afro-American Thought	The Robber & the Robbed: Two Antagonistic Images in Afro-American Thought	III	13
4	Return to the Roots: Language, Culture & Politics in Kenya	Return to the Roots	I	5
Part II: Words & Powers				
5	Writers in Politics: The Power of Words & the Words of Power	Writers in Politics	II	6
7	A Novel in Politics: The Launching of *Petals of Blood*	Petals of Love	II	9
8	J.M. Kariuki: A Writer's Tribute to a Kenyan Hero	J.M.: A Writer's Tribute	II	7
9	The Price of Freedom: The Story of a Mau Mau Detainee	Born Again: Mau Mau Unchained	II	8
Part III: Links of Hope				
10	Afric-Asian Writers: The Links That Bind Us	The Links That Bind Us	III	10
11	Africa & Asia: The History That Refuses to be Silenced	The South Korean People's Struggle is the Struggle of All Oppressed Peoples	III	12

been dropped to tone down the vengeful bluntness of the original vocabulary. In the body of the essay 'rob' and its derivatives appear 12 times in the first three paragraphs of the first edition, not at all in the latest version. Indeed this root is retained only four times mostly in voicing the author's reaction to other writers' ideas, rather than his own original thoughts. The same trend is to be found in other revisions.

In 'Literature and Double Consciousness' the two versions coincide 90 per cent paragraph for paragraph. But the opening two paragraphs of the 1997 edition are re-ordered and heavily reworked. The first paragraph opens with new material introduced to elevate and broaden the argument. Paragraphs 3 to 30 run closely parallel barring minor changes replacing 'rob' and its derivatives with 'dominate' and its derivatives. Certain phrases are made more specific — for instance 'the working majority' becomes 'the body and soul of the dominated who are usually the majority'. In paragraph 8 'by and large' replaces 'thus'; and 'four' in 'four hundred years of repressive socio-political institutions' becomes 'two'; 'in Banneker's reply to Jefferson' is added to 'the consciousness animating the Republican side of the American Civil War'; while 'the struggle of the American people against the occupation of Vietnam' is amplified by references to Malcolm X, Mohamed Ali and Martin Luther King.

In paragraph 11 of the second edition an indented quotation is now integrated into the text; in places two paragraphs are merged into one in the later version; italics are removed; re-wording continues throughout, and significantly Kissinger's name is removed. The second edition's greatest departure from the first in this essay is from paragraph 28 (beginning 'These are as true today . . .') to the end of the essay. Phrases are omitted or shifted around; for instance material in paragraph 30 (1981) is absorbed into the last paragraph in 1997. Two paragraphs are entirely new, while others show little divergence.

This pattern of essentially minor changes prevails in most of the retained essays. Quotations are removed; for instance all the Mau Mau songs on pages 27–8 of the first edition are omitted. Passages are summarized rather than included in full, or are switched between paragraphs.

A uniquely interesting case of changes between editions is 'A Novel in Politics: the Launching of *Petals of Blood*': the second edition is nearly three times the length of the first. One reason for this greater length is that Ngũgĩ elaborates autobiographical material, bringing events in his life up to April 1995. He re-casts into a new mould events (familiar from earlier works of non-fiction) relating both to his career as an author and to his life. He now denounces the imperialists for ravaging Kenya, and the continuing exploitation as evil political figures link up into repressive governments. This recapitulation continues up to the death of Kenyatta in 1978, when, we are reminded, Ngũgĩ himself was in prison. Then, 'My mother died in 1987. I was in exile in London. I am writing this piece in April 1995 in exile, in New York' (*WTP2*, 92).

A further reason for the greater length of the 1997 version of this essay is the chance it gives for Ngũgĩ to discuss more fully the subject of imperialist impoverishment of Kenya, perpetuated by the ganging up of vicious politicians in repressive post-independence neo-colonial regimes. In the new first paragraph this subject is spotlighted by the presence of

Mwai Kibaki, a Kenyan minister, as guest of honour at the launching of *Petals of Blood*. It was Kibaki as a brilliant economist who first introduced Ngũgĩ to the whole subject of economics. Kibaki's presence there refocused Ngũgĩ in 1997, looking back to 1977, on the intensification of colonial and neo-colonial oppression due to the despotic machinery of bodies such as the IMF and the World Bank. The penultimate paragraph of the up-dated essay reads:

> Mwai Kibaki, after years as a faithful Vice-president, is now leader of an opposition party. Daniel Arap Moi is still the President. He has bled the country dry. From personal rule in the decade of the eighties, he has, in the nineties, unleashed the power of state terrorism against opponents or sections of the population. IMF and the World Bank still bankroll his dictatorship. Democracy is not very convenient for finance capital as it roams through the globe looking for conditions that will give it maximum returns. From a free market system, the world is now under the grip of the fundamentalism of finance capital. This era of capital fundamentalism has set in motion all sorts of other absolutist fundamentalisms either in opposition to it or in alliance with it. Any social forces which stand in the way of capitalist fundamentalism are to be crushed. Alas, there is only one God, Finance Capital, and his prophet and temple is the IMF and the World Bank. (*WIP2*, 92–3)

Ngũgĩ then asserts that the 'new faith' (*WIP2* 93) was launched by Thatcher and Reagan in the early eighties. Under this new dispensation, it is the duty of the state, with privatization as its weapon, to ensure the unhindered sway of finance capital, without regard to the many citizens who are driven to exile, jail or untimely death. All democratic forces must be obliterated: state intervention to protect the needs of the poor majority is anathema from now on. Everyone is at the mercy of privatization. The ultimate goal of finance capital is to make African states too weak to oppose its operation but strong enough — with western aid and ammunition — to silence all opposition to its operations. Debts must be serviced and paid. In a nutshell:

> The new faith and its churches must have absolute monopoly in the world. The cold war is over. Socialism is dead. Classes and class struggles were an invention of the evil communist empires! May finance capital unfettered reign long over the globe! (*WIP2*, 93)

The third reason for Ngũgĩ's special interest in the essay about the launching of *Petals of Blood* is that it raises the subject of the role of women, a subject which had always had a doubly strong hold on him because of its connection with his mother. She was now dead, so Ngũgĩ was inspired to write a deeply felt epitaph for her. So while in the first edition he simply introduces his mother to the audience, he now goes further to say that one of the 'three things' making the launching 'memorable' (*WIP2*, 83) was the presence of his mother. For two paragraphs he reminisces about his mother's role in his life and her influence on his writings. Indeed the new thematic focus in this new edition develops from two sentences in the first of these paragraphs where 'the mother' is identified with the Kenyan peasantry — 'the real actor in the novel' (*WIP2*, 85). The peasantry being alienated from the land and turned into proletarians led to 'one of the most crucial social upheavals of the twentieth century . . . fraught with pregnant possibilities for the future' (*WIP2*, 85) The second edition's version of this essay explains how the proletariat and the bourgeoisie relate respectively to rural and urban environments, and describes fully how *Petals of Blood* explores those relationships.

The question then arises after a comparison of the two editions: what is the overall purpose and impact of the revision?

The discussion earlier in this chapter places the original edition of *Writers in Politics* (1981) in the third phase of Ngũgĩ's ideological development. In this phase he employed practical actions, and also in his fiction a mode of utterance oriented to grass-roots, to address the neo-colonialist excesses of the post-independence government in Kenya. We argued on the other hand that in the fourth phase Ngũgĩ brought to a peak his advocacy of revolutionary methods of resistance to repression, extending his philosophy world-wide. So his revision of some third-phase essays is presumably an attempt to take a new look at the issues therein raised through his broader fourth-phase lens.

Our detailed discussion of the rewritten essays has sought to assess their changes of direction. For instance a mellowing in temper reins the earlier undisguised anger and strengthens the theoretical weight of the arguments. Many quotations from other writers and from local Kenyan material have been deleted or shortened, integrated into the text or otherwise amended. Such changes exclude now out-dated topical references, sweeten the tone, fill out philosophical points, or take in newly emerging issues. We can sum up these modifications by suggesting that Ngũgĩ has now moved to a new level of universalization.

As we have observed elsewhere, Ngũgĩ leaves nothing to chance in ensuring his readers' understanding of his writings, both fictional and non-fictional. He takes no delight in mystification or obscurantism. So in the preface, he explains in detail the events in world affairs that have led him to the conclusions elaborated in the 1997 edition of these essays. 'So many things have happened [in the world of academia] since I went into exile in 1982' (*WIP2*, xii). He proceeds in the same paragraph to present almost word for word ideas about capitalist fundamentalism that we partly quoted and partly paraphrased above. He then moves on immediately to urge the establishment of 'a unified African response to the emerging mega-centres . . . of North America, United Europe and Japan' (*WIP2*, xiii). He charges writers and intellectuals with the primary responsibility for formulating the fresh ideas and vision needed to meet the challenges posed by the new frontiers evolving in the developed world.

Ngũgĩ sees links between Africa, Asia and South America as crucial in building mutual strengths to resist threats posed by United Europe, America and Japan. A major target of Africa's efforts must be to further develop indigenous languages to save Africa from becoming 'a linguistic and cultural appendage of Europe' (*WIP2*, xiii) in the next century. In the preface he pays tribute to Ken Saro-Wiwa, a Nigerian writer, and other human rights activists executed by Nigeria's neo-colonialist government; and urges other African writers to ensure that these advocates of justice did not die in vain.

With all these factors in mind, we can now conclude that the revamping of the 1997 version of *Writers in Politics* has been inspired both by the evolutionary course of events, and by Ngũgĩ's specific experiences of exile. Changes in his thinking after the publication in 1993 of *Moving the Centre* are thus expressed in this revised edition. The influence of any new vision he may have had in exile is more difficult to assess; though Ngũgĩ must have been aware of certain achievements by Western-style democracy at least at the level of individual citizens. He states with obvious gratitude in the new preface:

> In 1989 I moved from London to the USA as a visiting professor at Yale . . . To my surprise I discovered how much I had missed the cut and thrust of ideas in a classroom. To be in an atmosphere where I could talk about Lenin and Shakespeare and Sembene Ousmane and speculate about the connections between them without fear of prison was really exhilarating. (*WIP2*, xi)

He recalls his ordeal as a detainee in Kenya and continues,

> I am very grateful for the atmosphere prevailing in the Departments of Comparative Literature and English for it restored to me a kind of inner intellectual peace. There is a kind of solitude at a good campus, Yale in particular, so conducive to contemplation and a life of thought, always reminded me of my days at Makerere. I still look back with gratitude to my four years of association with my wonderful colleagues and students . . . (*WIP2*, xi)

New York University, whither he moved in 1992, presented a down-to-earth environment — a mixture of penury and opulence paralleling conditions in Nairobi and Leeds — to which Ngũgĩ related more readily in terms of his ideological stance.

For the African to engineer his own socio-cultural, economic and political development, he must perceive where his inadequacies lie at the beginning of the 21st century. In Nigeria for example, after 36 years of independence and with its natural endowments of wealth, can we continue in good conscience to blame the colonial legacy for the throttling woes in which people live and die? No minimum standards have been established, let alone maintained, in health services, education, water supply, electricity, roads, telecommunications, or even personal security. Here, the conspicuously wealthy constitute themselves virtually into their own petty governments by resorting to 'senseless accumulation of wealth' (of which Ngũgĩ also accuses Kenyatta) to provide these basic needs for themselves and their selected constituents. Even so they admit with chagrin that the Nigerian executive can hardly provide in toto the level of personal comfort enjoyed by labourers in so-called imperialist countries. But at the same time we cannot reasonably find any excuse in the supposed natural mediocrity of black people claimed by squint-eyed early Western writers whom Ngũgĩ has so piquantly vilified time and again.

We must now recognize new departures in the up-dated *Writers in Politics*. We have so far seen it as an integral part of the fourth phase of Ngũgĩ's ideological progression. But it actually marks a significant change in the general tone in writings within that phase, and seeks to expand their theoretical scope. We have noted that in essays retained from the 1983 edition, passages have been added or deleted, recast or re-phrased, to convey a deeper, more reflective, less temperamental tone, and a more universal focus. The entirely fresh essays in the 1997 edition give greater scope for expression of these new elements. There are no clear-cut departures in subject from the beginning of the fourth phase. Indeed it is possible to match almost one to one topics handled earlier and later in the phase. Any sub-division lies in new approaches to familiar themes.

Freedom of expression is discussed in Chapters 6, 13 and 14. In Chapter 6 ('Freedom of Expression: The Right to Write is a Human Right') we are told that power of expression is both a functional tool and a value in itself with an 'immensity of . . . power to destroy or to create; to wound or heal' (*WIP2*, 78). Conditions hampering freedom of expression are identified, among them economic domination of one group by another; political repression; and inequalities between and within countries. Ngũgĩ's own experience of detention arising from his writing in Gikuyu, and later the banning of his novel *Matigari* illustrate the suppression of freedom of expression by tyrannical political forces. Indeed in Kenya the word 'president' is outlawed for use by anyone but the head of state. For Ngũgĩ the greatest tragedy currently threatening Africans is the likely loss in the next century of their indigenous languages, since many families are now bringing up their children speaking a foreign language as their first language.

In Chapter 13 ('Kamau Brathwaite: The Voice of Pan-African Presence') the theme of freedom of expression resurfaces in Ngũgĩ's enshrining a people's right to *name* themselves (to take names embodying their history, culture and pride). Ngũgĩ recalls that in 1972, in welcoming the Caribbean writer Edward Brathwaite to their village, his mother and other women sang and danced for him, and gave him the name 'Kamau' — a great legendary hero of the Aagikuyu. Ngũgĩ perceives in Brathwaite's works an assertion of

> the right to name ourselves, our landscape; the struggle for the means with which to name ourselves; the search in other words for the true voice of our collective being . . . (*WIP2*, 135–6)

The same belief is seen equally behind Brathwaite's idea of 'the Nation Language, that submerged language of the enslaved, which through evolutionary and at times revolutionary subversion of the dominating, asserts itself, often changing the character of what was supposed to be the mainstream'. (*WIP2*, 136)

In Chapter 14 'Learning from our Ancestors: The Intellectual Legacy of Pan-Africanism', freedom of expression is again spotlighted through the concept of naming. Along with dividing up and scattering groups and families enslaved in the diaspora (to alienate them from their cultural roots and destroy their pride in national belonging), the enslaving Westerners re-enforced the dehumanizing destruction of slaves' 'cultural personality' (*WIP2*, 140) by denying them use of their names and languages and even their self-made naming systems. So slaves were deprived of the power to interact freely and creatively with the world, of 'possessing' the world. So, 'dislocated from their geography, history, culture, spirituality, they were now even to be dislocated from their own body.' (*WIP2*, 140) And while the colour of beauty became white, the Western metropolitan language became the only language for describing that beauty. Hence Ngũgĩ sees members of the African intellectual community as 'cultural aliens' (*WIP2*, 150) because they have to clothe their knowledge in alien languages. They are people who

> search for light and then . . . cover the light under English or French linguistic tents so that only those who are inside the tents can benefit from the light. (*WIP2*, 150)

They have nurtured a culture of taking ideas away from, rather than bringing them to the people.

The topic probably given most sustained attention in the new 1997 essays is that of the past, present and future, a theme at the forefront of Ngũgĩ's concerns from the beginning of his ideological thinking in the regular 'As I See It' *Nation* column. While he invokes the past as an underlying awareness in his excited account of Kamau Brathwaite's writing career in Chapter 13, Chapter 14 ('Learning from our Ancestors . . .') is devoted almost exclusively to this subject in its most profound ramifications.

At the opening of the essay we are reminded that Kenyatta dedicated *Facing Mount Kenya* (1938) to

> the perpetuation of communion with the ancestral spirits through the fight for African Freedom . . . in the firm faith that the dead, the living and the unborn will unite to rebuild the destroyed shrines. (*WIP2*, 138)

This belief evinces the greater underlying truth that life is continuous — the living, begotten by the dead, in turn begetting future generations. Ngũgĩ does not regard continuity as identical repetition, but rather as change and movement which must reproduce the common origins and destiny of any people. So in their true meanings, 'the past becomes the source of inspiration; the present, the arena of perspiration; and the future, our collective aspiration' (*WIP2*, 139).

Ngũgĩ clarifies his position: to revere the ancestors does not mean to worship them or glorify them uncritically as if they had no faults. Rather it means taking the past as a school in which a people can learn from all their communal experiences, good and bad: from all the mountains and valleys they have traversed; from their successes and failures; from victories and defeats: from all the nights and days that make up the past.

Predictably, Ngũgĩ declares the two most traumatic experiences Africa has undergone in the past 400 years (ripples of which will continue to be felt far into the future) to be slavery and colonialism. Each has been an instrument of disunity, alienation and cultural assault, seeking to destroy the African psyche. However, from such depth of subjugation, Africa learnt to fight against oppression, and received, as a gift from their ancestors, political independence. Africa can now 'sing anthems of national pride and fly flags of hope' (*WIP2*, 143), an achievement which must not, under any circumstances, be underestimated. The important issue, however, the key question, is 'what [have we] done with that gift'? (*WIP2*, 143).

Ngũgĩ conceives the answer to that question as most unflattering. For neo-colonialism has totally defiled that gift. Imperfect and slippery as that gift may have been, Africa could have done something positive with it. So, having ruined this gift, Africa must ask itself, 'what gift shall we, the living, bequeath to the unborn?' (*WIP2*, 144) The remainder of the essay is a scathing castigation of tyrannical neo-colonial leaders — of whom Africa has had too many — for their wholesale betrayal of the legacy, the ancestral trust. Ngũgĩ narrows down the issue to African intellectuals continually encoding and decoding their knowledge in alien languages (in particular the use by African writers of foreign tongues in exercising their imagination). He concludes the essay by asking, 'if we are to talk to our ancestors, in what languages shall we talk to them? What will they want to hear and what have we to tell them?' (*WIP2*, 151)

Ngũgĩ also now emphatically re-kindles the flame of his optimism that progressive forces will eventually achieve a positive reversal in African affairs. He sees prospects of instigating progress in every act — however small — of opposition, of resistance, of protest, in challenging and denouncing prevailing irresponsible wickedness. We have already heard his exultant praise of Africa's wrenching of political independence from reluctant colonial powers. He calls 'the defeat of direct colonialism and the emergence of independent states in Africa' . . . 'one of the greatest feats in modern history' (*WIP2*, 143), for

> a continent which for four hundred years had been ravished by slavery, by colonialism; a continent where the inhabitants had been handicapped in every way possible, their very labour and history turned against them, this continent could sing anthems of national pride and fly flags of hope. (*WIP2*, 143)

Earlier in the essay (*WIP2*, 141) Ngũgĩ expresses similar pride in the successes which Africa (in particular Africa of the Diaspora) has demonstrated in 'creating languages that were not a replica of the master's'.

The new thrust in 'Culture in a Crisis . . .' is that the real crisis is and has always been that of facing the colonial culture, followed by the neo-colonial culture. This is because, true to history, the culture of domination exercised by Europe over Africa 'creates its opposite: resistance!' (*WIP2*, 127). So Africans, from the very beginning of slavery and conquest, started to re-group, 'piecing together the fragments of things fallen apart, often making use of the contradictions of the new post-conquest situation to reconstruct themselves anew and . . . planting and nurturing seeds of new societies' (*WIP2*, 127). The instrument of this victory was the vision of unity between continental and diasporan African geniuses from both regions, a vision expressed as a reality in the 1945 Manchester Congress, and attaining its apogee in the Pan-African movement. Thus,

> with unity as the means, they hoped to realize the end: the restoration of the African personality to itself. That vision of wholeness, of unity, the vision that the colour of beauty was after all black, had the greatest effect on the continental struggles against colonialism. (*WIP2*, 141)

Asserting that an unholy alliance even more threatening to Africa's true liberation has been formed — among the IMF, the World Bank, Western nations as a whole, Japan, and repressive African civilian and military governments — Ngũgĩ urges that African resistance struggles (that have so far brought victories in many spheres) must be sustained and intensified. Referring specifically to the neo-colonial onslaught against Africa's indigenous languages, he declares:

> . . . the challenge facing the resistance cultures is very clear. There has to be resolute

opposition to all internal structures of repression. Women's movements, students' movements, workers' movements have to struggle to create a more democratic space for themselves within each country. ('Culture in Crisis . . .' *WIP2*, 131)

A major strategy for the struggle will be to forge a dialogue for solidarity among progressive cultures of Africa, Asia, South America and democratic voices 'within the three centres of world domination' (*WIP2*, 131). Ngũgĩ urges that such an alliance may well offer

a better foundation for a genuinely global common culture that puts human beings and human needs at the centre of any economic, political and cultural arrangements within and between nations . . . (*WIP2*, 131)

and would facilitate the founding of

a new international economic, political and cultural order . . . A united African response to the new world order is the only basis of our survival in the twenty-first century.' (*WIP2*, 131)

One wants to share Ngũgĩ's optimism, however hard it may be to do so, for there is really no other choice. The consequences of despair or resignation are too ghastly to contemplate.

However, when one contemplates the internal excesses which countries like Nigeria are suffering on all fronts, it is even more difficult to sustain hope for a better future. At least Kenya (the immediate arena of Ngũgĩ's experience) has had no official military dictatorship; no sweeping pogrom or *civil* war; its wealth is sufficiently limited to curtail the scope for corruption. It may well have been too unsophisticated in carrying out its political assassinations and forceful detentions, so leaving its flanks poorly covered. In some countries (notably Nigeria, whose despots acclaim it to be the bastion of black power !) holding out against despair is a daunting task. Newspapers and the other media cry out daily with criticisms levelled against government, even naming the most highly placed power-brokers, but their doctrine seems to be: 'Let them say their saying while we do our doing'. So the average Nigerian declines into a fatalistic opportunist; even youths treasure their comfort too much to risk adventures that could imperil it: they seek simply to exploit corruption when they have the chance, and let things be.

Colonialism and neo-colonialism (the two sides of imperialism as Ngũgĩ sees things), their attendant finance capitalism with its rotten harvest of disunity, impoverishment and dictatorship, remain the dominant subjects of the new 1997 edition of *Writers in Politics*. Ngũgĩ also finds space for snatches of his biodata back to his time in Kamiriithu to epitomize the unhappy state of affairs in his home country, and recapitulate his concerns about the status of African literature in African institutions of learning.

Clearly during his exile, Ngũgĩ has graduated (after the fashion of Marx, Lenin, Mao Tse-Tung and Frantz Fanon) into a theoretician: in his case concerning the African and Third World revolution by peasants and workers (the proletariat) seeking socio-political emancipation and a fair share of the profits from their sweat. He has become a pre-eminent teacher, instructing by interpreting and informing on a wide range of subjects. The 'real' Kenyan people should account themselves lucky to have him as their chief spokesman. Countries in even more desperate need of his impassioned vision, courage and sense of sacrifice — one could single out Nigeria, for example — do not have many champions of truth and justice, equally radical, committed, out-spokenly articulate: eager to stand shoulder to shoulder with Ngũgĩ as unflagging exponents of the revolutionary socialist cause to make a tireless literary and polemical onslaught on governmental tyranny. One fears lest in such countries all could be in ruins before humane leadership has the chance to take control and salvage social values so as to build them into an infrastructure of just, egalitarian governments.

This chapter has depicted Ngũgĩ as pre-eminently the committed man of African creative writing. He has traversed a wide spectrum of African experience. He has lived through alien rule and cultural miscegenation to independence of a kind involving political sovereignty: the new/old economic and cultural order (and challenge) of neo-colonialism. On the other hand, after a village childhood and an adolescence in the Gikuyuland of Mau Mau, he passed to university and beyond, renowned as a writer with political commitment after detention and exile have strengthened his resolve.

Ngũgĩ is fighting for a complete change from the old structures, and the establishment of socialist, egalitarian regimes which would redeem the rights of those who are now under-privileged. This change he sees as being made more readily possible by the pervasive influence of books and literature — freshly aligned and interpreted; and as at length being brought about by the organized and unified determination of the majority of the people, if necessary through violent conflict against the oppressors by the oppressed.

Notes

1. Heinemann Educational Books, London, 1972.
2. *Homecoming*, xv.
3. Personal interview with Michael Okenimkpe in Nairobi, 17 February 1975.
4. *Daily Times*, Lagos, 13 February 1978, 2.
5. 'Ngũgĩ in Jail', *Daily Times*, Lagos, 29 January 1979, a report by Andy Akporugo, 2.
6. Micere Githae-Mugo, *Visions of Africa in the Fiction of Achebe, Margaret Lawrence, Elspeth Huxley and Ngũgĩ wa Thiong'o* (Kenya Literature Bureau, Nairobi, 1978), 26.
7. Ime Ikiddeh, Foreword to *Homecoming*, xii–xiii.
8. 'As I See It: Respect Will Come When We Are Self-sufficient', *Daily Nation*, Nairobi, 157 (17 March 1963), 29.
9. 'My protest was against the hypocrisy in the college', interview by Peter Darling with Ngũgĩ wa Thiong'o on his resignation from his post as Lecturer in the University of Nairobi in 1969, *Sunday Nation*, Nairobi (hereafter *SN*)469 (16 March 1969), 15–16.
10. 'The Links that Bind Us', acceptance speech by Ngũgĩ wa Thiong'o of the Lotus Prize in Literature at the First Afro-Asian Writers' Conference, Alma Ata, Khazakhstan, 6 September 1973; *East African Journal of Literature and Society*, vol.2, no.1 (1974), 67–8; in revised edition of Writers in Politics (James Currey, Oxford, 1997).

11. With Micere Githae-Mugo, *The Trial of Dedan Kimathi* (Heinemann Educational Books, London, 1976), viii.
12. *Barrel*, 'Writing for Peace', 72–3.
13. *Moving the Centre*, 'Preface', xvi–xvii.
14. In Ngũgĩ and Githae-Mugo, op.cit., 25.
15. Interview by Allan Marcuson, Mike Gonzalez and Dave Williams, *Leeds University Union News*, 18 November 1966, 6; reprinted in *Cultural Events in Africa*, 31 (June 1967), p. iv of the Supplement.
16. 'The Writer in a Changing Society' in *Homecoming*, 47.
17. 'Church, Culture and Politics', ibid., 31–6.
18. *SN*, 147 (6 January 1963), 5.
19. *Homecoming*, 3–21.
20. 'Chinua Achebe, A Man of the People', ibid., 53–4.
21. 'Wole Soyinka, T.M. Aluko and the Satirical Voice', ibid., 65–6.
22. 'Okot p'Bitek and Writing in East Africa', ibid., 71.
23. 'What is my Colour, What is my Race?', ibid., 108
24. 'Ngugi quits at college: mishandling of crisis', *SN* 467 (2 March 1969), 3.
25. 'My protest was against hypocrisy in the college', interview by Peter Darling with Ngũgĩ wa Thiong'o, op cit., 15.
26. Further extracts from the two foregoing *Sunday Nation* items.
27. Ibid.
28. Ibid.
29. Ibid.
30. Interview by Aminu Abdullahi in Leeds, England, 1964, in *African Writers Talking*, ed. Dennis Duerden and Cosmo Pieterse (Heinemann Educational Books, London, 1972), 128.
31. My protest was against the hypocrisy in the college', interview by Peter Darling with Ngũgĩ wa Thiong'o op. cit., 16.
32. 'Petals of Blood', interview by Anita Shreve with Ngũgĩ wa Thiong'o, *Viva*, Nairobi, vol.3, no.6 (July 1977), 36
33. Interview by John Esibi in *SN*, 17 July 1977, 10.
34. 'Petals of Blood', interview by Anita Shreve op.cit., 36–7.
35. Ibid., 36.
36. Page references to the first edition of *Writers in Politics* (Heinemann Educational Books, London, 1981) are prefixed by the initials *WIP*; and to the second edition (James Currey, Oxford, 1997) by the initials *WIP2*.
37. Page references to *Detained: A Writer's Prison Diary* (Heinemann Educational Books, London, 1981) are prefixed by the initial *D*.
38. Page references to *Barrel of a Pen: Resistance to Oppression in Neo-Colonial Kenya* (New Beacon Books, London and Port of Spain; Africa World Press, Trenton, NJ, 1983) are prefixed by the short form *Barrel*.
39. Page references to *Decolonising the Mind: The Politics of Language in African Literature* (James Currey, London; Heinemann Kenya, Nairobi; Heinemann Educational Books, Portsmouth, NH: 1986) are prefixed by the short title *Decolonising the Mind*.
40. Page references to *Moving the Centre: The Struggle for Cultural Freedoms* (James Currey, London; East African Educational Publishers, Nairobi; Heinemann Educational Books, Portsmouth, NH: 1993) are prefixed by the short title *Moving the Centre*.

PART IV

Conclusion

Style

Ngũgĩ has always aspired to be a popular writer in the most enterprising sense of the phrase. He has aimed at reaching as large a reading public as possible with challenging interpretations of society and serious explorations of human experience. It is not often that a writer can have a measurable effect on his environment as Swift did, in a rare instance, with *The Drapier's Letters*. An Orwell, or even a Fanon may not readily be able to quantify the impact of his books, or point to the precise place and time when any of his writings have produced such and such an outcome. Impatient with the slow and gradual impact of novels, Ngũgĩ at length turned back to drama as a means of stirring people more immediately and more dynamically.

In Africa — though not in Africa alone — there is also the complex question of which language to write in. It was not until a decade and a half after his first public success that Ngũgĩ turned to his own first language, Gikuyu, as a means of penetrating more deeply and widely into a specific African community. Obvious as this expedient may appear, there are acute problems. Publishers may be discouraging concerning the prospects of a work in a language providing a limited market. Young authors themselves may vaguely aspire to speak to an unconfined audience. On the other hand, would-be authors may well find that by the time they have emerged from school or college they have lost all facility and nimbleness in their first language, and may be unable to compete with their own grandparents in their mother tongue. Yet an author who seriously aspires to stir a new consciousness, not just in a largely impervious elite or from an inde-terminate international forum but within a coherent and significant social group, does well to return to grass-roots and attempt a more realistic kind of arithmetic about his potential readership. Where and how does the message of a radical spokesman find a truly meaningful response? It gives food for thought that one of the shrewdest of special police cadres in Africa left Ngũgĩ free to publish *Petals of Blood*, which was even launched by a compatriot minister (though there may have been gathering misgivings in certain quarters); but swooped quickly and selectively when at length he turned to rouse his own people through drama in an indigenous language. They knew their own business and by this time Ngũgĩ knew his.

Yet for all that it is right to start discussing the English novels of an African revolutionary writer by expressing reservations, it is also right to go on to assess his very real achievements as a social prophet in deploying wisely a national lingua franca, a tongue current throughout much of Africa, and one which, perhaps incidentally, has free passage across other continents. Indigenous languages and international languages have vitally different functions in Africa. These functions should ideally be complementary and not competitive. It has been sad to watch a generation of African authors developing English and French at the expense of their own languages instead of side by side with them. It makes better sense for the honourable exceptions like Okot and Ngũgĩ to harness all the languages at their disposal and distinguish, no doubt, different priorities in each. For the moment we shall explore the remarkable success of Ngũgĩ in a second language of widespread validity, which he has used both as 'the chosen tongue' and latterly as a medium for translations from Gikuyu.

For authors in different environments, the English language has offered a supply of open cheques which they can put into circulation bearing their own very distinct signatures, and employ for their own purposes. Every original writer does new things with each language he employs, and in some small degree changes it permanently in adapting it to his own needs and individuality. Ngũgĩ has already made a distinct mark on English.

Since Ngũgĩ was aiming at a wide readership for whom English was a second language, it was essential that he should develop a style neither 'difficult' nor laborious. A fair number of African authors have set out with the same aim in view. Ngũgĩ has made of his quest something very different from any of his contemporaries. It is given to only a few outstanding writers to reach a simplicity which is neither elementary nor a reduction of language to bald outlines, but which is a distilling of all the main possibilities of a tongue so as to arrive at a clarity which has both subtlety and richness. Blake is a supreme example. In a different context Ngũgĩ is a notable instance. As we shall see, he uses the full resources of English. His structures are very varied and highly concentrated. His diction is at once spontaneous and exact. In looking more closely at his short sentences we may at first be surprised to observe how grammatically complex they often are. Yet he achieves sophisticated effects without departing from either a vocabulary or an arrangement which would be comprehensible to average African senior students in their second or third year.

In an important sense *A Grain of Wheat* is the culmination of this style. If *A Grain of Wheat* presents difficulties, this is not because of its language or style but is a consequence of its complex and elaborately patterned content. For good reasons the plot-line does not run straight. But there is scarcely a sentence which is hard to follow in its context or which taxes the ordinary reader unduly. The style is essentially a refinement of that developed earlier, but some of the stiffness of the first novels has fallen away. *Petals of Blood* retains many of the same characteristics, but it is at once more extreme in its variations of style, as well as slower and more involved in much of its narrative manner.

Because of these modulations, *Petals of Blood* illustrates particularly well the general point that we are developing. It is not a book which we would describe as easy to read. But its complexity was not of a kind to prevent it becoming a more popular success than its immediate predecessor. And this is because its style allows the fiery contemporary content to make an immediate impact. Both *Devil on the Cross* and *Matigari* are in certain respects more direct and easily accessible. In reaching English via Gikuyu originals, they retain certain traditional and informal features of style, soon to be discussed, which must help to endear them in particular to a Kenyan audience.

Short, concentrated sentences are the key to the style in which Ngũgĩ launched and developed his career as a writer. It is easy enough to find passages of a page or more in *Weep Not, Child* or *The River Between* wherein at least half of the sentences have ten words apiece or less, among which a surprising number have no more than three, four or five words. Sentences of more than 20 words, on the other hand, are the exception. Considering the matter analytically like this, one would imagine it would be hard to keep such a style flowing easily and harmoniously, and even harder to make its effects echo in the reader's mind. Indeed it is true that there is sometimes a certain rawness and jerkiness in the early writing, but in the main the effect has nothing of the barren utilitarianism of old-fashioned primary school exercises. Nor does it often share the characteristically tense staccato manner of Peter Abrahams' clipped sentences. In the early novels, except in dialogue, even the shortest sentence is a fully expressed grammatical structure according to formal traditional criteria: 'He felt guilty'[1] (*RB* 83/71); 'I found it' ('Gone with the Drought' *SL* 16); 'Njoroge was pleased!' (*WNC* 17/15). More significantly, we often find a sentence of some 15 or so words involving three clauses, or even more: 'So when Kabonyi said that Waiyaki had broken that oath people roared back "No-o-o" ' (*RB* 172/150). 'When the time for circumcision came, it was Kamau who met the cost' (*WNC* 95/84). Glancing forward, we may note that this is still true in *Devil on the Cross* and *Matigari*: ' "Muturi and Wangari, because you know that what is done can never be undone, leave these people alone" ' (*DOC* 159); ' "I slowly crept up to where he lay, just in case he was pretending to be dead" ' (*Mat* 22). It is at once evident that these are natural and easy English formations. Nothing is strained. In using the full resources of the English language, Ngũgĩ tends to make use of each separate element in its most straight-forward form. It is their neat and unforced combination which creates the variety and richness of his language. So it is not surprising that in welding clauses together Ngũgĩ, while employing a wide range of means, shows a marked preference for the neatest of all such linkages: relative and noun clauses. This is especially so in the first two novels, in *Devil on the Cross*, and in *Matigari*.

There is a great variety of sentence openings, sometimes an initial subordinate clause, sometimes a long or short sentence modifier, sometimes a direct plunge into the main structure. Such changes allow a constant alteration of forms without obscurity. Straight-forward English (speech in particular) depends heavily on pronouns as subjects of clauses. Throughout his writings, the subjects of Ngũgĩ's clauses are mainly pronouns (and sometimes names) — seldom in fewer than half, and often in as many as two-thirds of the clauses on a page or even more in the later novels. This gives his prose an easy, unpretentious movement and enables him to keep human beings at the centre of attention. Indeed, though his writing is precise and visually detailed, he does not often build up lengthy nominal groups, as do many good novelists, except as an occasional rhetorical device in *Devil on the Cross* and *Matigari*. Few elements of language are extended so far as to become obtrusive in the first three novels. A specifically literary style might well be characterized by such elaborations, and perhaps in particular by an uninhibited use of non-finite groups dependent on participles and infinitives. Indeed Ngũgĩ uses these valuable adjuncts without hesitation, but sufficiently discreetly for them to have no ponderous or obtrusive effect. At their simplest, such structures are not uncommon even in everyday speech, and so a careful author can always make them blend unobtrusively into their surroundings: 'So he ran blindly, not knowing whither' (*WNC* 66/59); 'In the village, he moved from street to street, meeting new faces' ('The Return', *SL* 52); 'Even before this calamity befell him, life for him had become meaningless, divorced as he had been from what he valued' (*WNC* 134/119); 'To break oath was one of the most serious crimes that a man could commit' (*RB* 172/149–50) — here the infinitive group becomes the subject of the main clause; 'Far beyond, its tip hanging in the grey clouds, was Kerinyaga. Its snow-capped top glimmered slightly, revealing the seat of Murungu' (*RB* 19/16) — we notice also the unassuming inversion in the first sentence; 'The crowd retreated, forming a huge ring as they did so' (*Mat* 166). Another sophisticated structure which Ngũgĩ used simply from the start — and on which he was later to depend more heavily in some passages in *Petals of Blood* — is the appended adjectival phrase: 'He walked across the courtyard, not afraid of the darkness' (WNC 61/53).

As we would expect of a novelist intent on telling a story, Ngũgĩ relies heavily on the most dramatic of the verb tenses — the one-word simple past. This is particularly obvious in *The River Between* and *The Grain of Wheat*. Nevertheless, in using more complex tenses he is exceptionally far-ranging: now one, now another becomes prominent, especially those which bring out self-doubt and hesitations, and those which set side by side two different periods in the past. He never develops a habit of mind which restricts his choice. In *Devil on the Cross* and parts of *Matigari* he finds the use of the present tense especially apt, not only in lengthy speeches, but also in dramatic passages of the historic present which both heighten and generalize the more stylized presentation.

Thus, throughout, Ngũgĩ's apparent simplicity is in a sense deceptive. He *is* simple in that he writes prose which is easy to read, but not in the sense of avoiding the full range and variety of the English language. If ever an author has worked hard and successfully to have the best of both worlds, Ngũgĩ has done so.

As we have observed elsewhere, Ngũgĩ had to struggle determinedly to become a complete master of dialogue. He had deliberately to increase the amount of direct speech written into an earlier draft of *The River Between*. Some lingering signs of this effort remain in the first two novels and conversation is sometimes strained. For instance, this exchange between mother and son may, at least on reflection, have a somewhat stilted ring:

'Mother, you must tell me all those stories again,' he implored as he knelt down to help in spite of her rejection of his offer.

'Hmmmm,' she murmured as she blew some rubbish away from the seeds she had in her hands. She paused for a moment and smiled.

'You cunning young man. Is that why you offered to help, eh?'
(*WNC* 19/16–17)

The qualified success here depends more on the accompanying commentary than on the flow of the speech rhythms. As the children, Njoroge and Mwihaki, become friends, there remains a stiffness in their talk which goes beyond the shyness and earnestness which are sometimes natural at such an age: the text *sounds* like what it is, an over-formal translation:

'My father works here.'

'This place belongs to Mr. Howlands.'

'You know him?'

'No. But my father talks about him. My father visits him and says that he is the best farmer in all the land.'

'Are they friends?'

'I don't know. I don't think so. Europeans cannot be friends with black people. They are so high.'

'Have you been here to his farm?'

'No !'

'I have often come here to see father. There is a boy about my height. His skin is so very white. I think he is the son of Mr Howlands. I did not like the way he clung to his mother's skirt, a frightened thing . . .' (*WNC* 41/36–7)

Yet by the time he comes to write *A Grain of Wheat*, Ngũgĩ is not only master of his characters' speech patterns but he is also sufficiently confident of himself to cast large parts of the novel in the form of spoken narrative, a device which proves to be one of the novel's greatest successes. In the passage that follows, Gikonyo and Mumbi are sparring with each other before becoming lovers. There is no extreme shift towards colloquial diction, but as we read we are in no doubt that the characters are actually talking to each other:

'Why did you stop?' she smiled.

'Oh, I didn't want you to hear my carpenter's voice and see my hands destroying both the song and the strings.'

'Is that why you never speak when you come to our place?' There was a malicious twinkle in her eyes.

'Don't I?'

'*You* should know . . . Anyway, I stood there all the time and heard you sing and play. It was good.'

'My voice or hands?'

'Both !'

'How do you know whether my playing is good or bad? You never come to the dances on Sunday.'

'Aah, true I never do. But do you think all other men are as mean as you? Karanja often plays to me alone at home. I sit, I knit my pullover, he plays. He is a good player.'

'He is a good player,' Gikonyo agreed curtly. (*GOW* 90–1/68–9)

Ngũgĩ's greatly increased facility in dialogue in the later novels and the revival of his interest in drama are obviously interrelated, though it is hardly possible to determine which is the cause and which is the effect. The two developments leapfrog each other.

With so much of the narrative now put in the form of direct speech by various characters — even more so in *Petals of Blood* — we might look for a marked shift in diction, but interestingly enough this is not an aspect of style which yet changes very greatly. From one who now writes so breezily and so profoundly at will, one might expect a movement outward in opposite directions in different passages towards speech forms, on the one hand, and more deliberately literary style, on the other. Both these developments are in fact apparent in *Petals of Blood* but neither is dependent to any significant extent upon shifts in vocabulary or phrasing. We shall now move on to discuss first this relative consistency in diction, and then those changes that are apparent in the fourth novel, before at length discussing *Devil on the Cross* and *Matigari* in more detail.

Let us consider a fairly characteristic narrative passage from *Weep Not, Child* as a starting point: three paragraphs on pages 133–4/119 when Ngotho finds himself in jail — a passage of close on 300 words. This text includes a snatch of colloquial East African English in the quoted proverb: 'We shall not give the hyena twice' (meaning, 'We shall not twice make a gift to the hyena'). At the other extreme we hear one of Ngũgĩ's frequent echoings of biblical language — quite often, as here, employed with conscious irony: 'Now since the white man had reversed the tribal law and cried, "A tooth for a tooth", it was better for Ngotho to offer his old tooth that had failed to bite deep into anything.' For the rest, the language is almost exclusively drawn from what Quirk and Greenbaum refer to in *A Grammar of Contemporary English* as 'the common core of English',[2] that vast unspecialized pool available for all purposes and in all registers. It is doubtful whether the few words that lie on the borderlines of specifically literary vocabulary would cause any great difficulty to readers who have determined to read the book: 'awareness', 'shadowed', 'calamity', 'befell', 'divorced', 'irresolute'. Even if they do, they are too rare to offer a major obstacle. The same is true of the occasional more unusual phrasing, which adds depth without building up any very troublesome barrier: 'a succession of nothingness', 'sitting posture', 'to relieve him', 'conscious of failure'. We must add to these a word or phrase from special areas — 'divine justice', 'tribal law'. Otherwise we have words and groupings from the centre of English usage. We will find the same thing over and over again if we examine other typical passages from the novel, from *The River Between*, or from *A Grain of Wheat*.

Let us now contemplate a key passage from the last of these three novels, which will serve two purposes. It will again illustrate many of the features we have so far observed, and will be apt as a point of departure for discussing differences that do develop here, and more strikingly in *Petals of Blood*:

Nevertheless, when the moment came, and he saw the big crowd, doubts destroyed his calm. He found General R. speaking, and this reminded him of Karanja. Why should I not let Karanja bear the blame? He dismissed the temptation and stood up. How else could he ever look Mumbi in the face? His heart pounded against him, he felt sweat in his hands, as he walked through the huge crowd. His hands shook, his legs were not firm on the ground. In his mind, everything was clear and final. He would stand there and publicly own the crime. He held on to this vision. Nothing, not even the shouting and the songs and the praises would deflect him from this purpose. It was the clarity of this vision which gave him courage as he stood before the microphone and the sudden silence. As soon as the first words were out, Mugo felt light. A load of many years was lifted from his shoulders. He was free, sure, confident. (*GOW* 267/203–4)

As will be easily recognized, much remains constant here. But there are at the same time certain shifts in manner, quite apart from the refinement of a number of techniques, which we have watched develop earlier.

As the narrative is increasingly taken over by the speaking voices of key characters, so the favourite colloquial linkage of clauses by the word 'and' becomes much more frequent, quite often without any repetition of the subject: 'He would stand there and publicly own his crime.' Rhetorical questions are used very often as a way of conveying thought processes. At the same time modulations of the human voice and formulations of thoughts determine a new approach to punctuation. Very often here clauses are amalgamated in the same sentence with only a point of punctuation between them, perhaps dramatically with a full colon, or with the fluid movement of a series of dots, or tentatively with a comma where formal grammar would in the past have prescribed something more: 'His hands shook, his legs were not firm on the ground.' In this instance the device is independent, as not infrequently, of either speech or the stream of consciousness: it provides a tense, more breathless transition. Thus rhythms are sensitive to mood and meaning. A device almost unknown in the first two novels becomes now one of the commonest methods of connecting clauses.

Even in *A Grain of Wheat* sentences are on the average slightly (though only slightly) longer, and the incidence of extremely short sentences drops markedly, though not perhaps enough to make this obvious at a first glance. Moreover deviations from formal traditional grammatical structure are much commoner. The novelist feels freer in his creative urges and in his easy command over English.

These developments mark a difference in degree in *A Grain of Wheat* as well as a new maturity. We may feel that in *Petals of Blood* they amount to a difference in kind. In this fourth novel, as was remarked above, two opposite developments take place in the structures employed which create striking contrasts between adjacent passages of narrative prose such as did not occur in the first novels.

On the other hand, when a specific character becomes the narrator, previous tendencies in style are intensified. As many as half the sentences may now be as short as five words or less, and many of these may comprise fragments of language in traditional terms. (Even in *A Grain of Wheat* the paragraph immediately following the last quotation consists of one four-word sentence without a verb: 'Only for a minute!') In the more developed sentences, clause linkage is commonly by points of punctuation or by 'and';

while one-word tenses take up an even higher proportion of finite verbs. However, there are still non-finite groups and appended adjectival groups here and there.

On the other hand, where in *Petals of Blood* the author takes over the narration or Munira resumes his prison report (subtly, at times, we are unsure which is the case) precisely opposite effects are apparent in the language. The average sentence length doubles compared to the norm in the early novels, and very long sentences make their appearance with 60, 70 or 80 words apiece. Whereas only a tenth of the earlier style was taken up in sentences of above average length for English,[3] now half or more of the prose is in such longer periods. In some passages non-finite groups, various phrases in parallel, and adjectival appendages clearly dominate the structure. Though other features that we discussed earlier remain fairly steady, the total effect in such paragraphs is to produce a much more literary style, still kept sufficiently clear and comprehensible by the diction and the simple subjects. This is not to say that there is any loss of passion or interest. Far from it. As we shall soon see the great climaxes of *Petals of Blood* are in this manner, as well as many outbursts of explicit social protest.

These new features and contrasts will be clear if we look closely at three pages (229–31) of the original edition, and especially the two long paragraphs which occupy the larger part of these pages. These exemplify the contrast between the two extremes of style. The last paragraph of Chapter 8 Section 1 concerns the passionate climax of the love affair between Karega and Wanja. The physical experience is explored with Lawrentian intensity and embodies Ngũgĩ's own deep conviction of the power of genuine human contact to release the positive potentials within man and woman. The outcome is both their own fulfilment and their ability to gain some control over forces which otherwise limit mankind's effectiveness. To compare this consummation with the very different idyll of the first union of Gikonyo and Mumbi on page 106/80 of *A Grain of Wheat* tells much about the difference between the two novels. Let us reproduce a couple of extracts for readers who do not have the full text at hand:

> Karega's heart seethed with a hopeless rage: he bit his lips trying to hold himself together, hold back the impulse toward recognition of their mutual nakedness. But the rage, the impulse, urged him toward her, made him hold her closer to him, gradually laying her on the grass, surely and methodically removing her clothes with her hands making impotent gestures of protest, oh please Karega don't do that, and he hearing that genuine fear of need and desire in the voice, felt hot blood rush up and suffuse his whole system as his body sought out hers in a locked struggle on the ground.

And further on:

> Then they started slowly, almost uncertainly, groping toward one another, gradually working together in rhythmic search for a lost kingdom, for a lost innocence and hope, exploring deeper and deeper, his whole body aflame and tight with painful desire or of belonging.

Immediately afterwards, Section 2 of the chapter opens with Wanja half-remembering, half-dreaming in bed the next morning. It will be seen that, as we have suggested, there is a total contrast in style. Taking the paragraphs as a whole, the average number of words per sentence shifts from over 30 to ten as the great flowing periods, elaborated with parallel structures of many kinds, switch to long series of interjected groups (especially nominal groups) each concentrated in its sentence capsule. Again it is practicable to quote only a small part (the linking dots are Ngũgĩ's):

> Her other affairs were always accompanied by anxiety, bitterness, an overriding need for a palliative, a temporary victory, a tormenting need for blood and vengeance, for gain. This is different. This is peace. This holiness. Her eyelids are heavy, languid. She is sinking into a no man's land but holding on to his face and eyes. Theng'eta . . . the spirit . . . millet power of God . . . millet fingers of God. Harvest. Prickly pains from prickly hairs on maize stalks. Sheaves of maize stalks. Leaves of grass. Micege and maramata on skirts. Clods of clay on feet and hands putting seeds into the earth. The journey. Journeys over the earth, on air, flight. Kărima Ka ihii. Meeting in Limuru in her hut. In her mother's hut. And strange. It is not his face she is looking at. It is that of an awkward youth offering her a gift of a pencil and an indiarubber eaten at the edges.

One of the dominant features of the style of *Devil on the Cross* can be traced back through the earlier novels. The prose has always been gently but firmly patterned, bound together by balances, repetitions, parallels, contrasts: of word, of phrase and clause, of sentence and paragraph. Motifs are taken up and followed through for half a page or more, embedded in the diction. In the earlier novels this patterning is not in the main startling or dramatic and is not easily illustrated in brief quotations, but some instances might be cited, almost at random, as pointers to the more continuous effects in total context. Ideas are clinched by the reiterated word — often with subtle shifts in meaning — and by repeated structures: 'but Mrs. Hill had suddenly crystallized into a woman, a wife, somebody like Njeri or Wambui, and above all, a mother' ('The Martyr', *SL* 45); 'It was no good calling on the name of God for he, Howlands, did not believe in God. There was only one god for him — and that was the farm he had created, the land he had tamed' (*WNC* 87/76); 'Kamau was a neat man with his hair always close-cropped. But there seemed to be something uncanny, something almost inhuman in his neatness' (*RB* 73–4/63). Short sentences may support each other with a faint suggestion of ritual: 'This was a sacred tree. It was the tree of Murungu' (*RB* 19/15). A climax is created as an insistent thought throbs through a character's brain: 'The voice was still urging him: *Go on!* He quickened his steps as if this would hurry the vanishing hours of day. It was night that was now welcome to him. The voice became more insistent: *Go on!*' (*WNC* 152/135) 'What shall I do? What shall I do? Then his way became clear' ('The Village Priest' *SL* 24).

Such fibres binding the texture of the prose are further strengthened in *A Grain of Wheat*. For instance, two contrasting paragraphs immediately following a passage already quoted pivot across a third, which in its brevity embodies a rapid emotional change, so that the words 'light' and 'free' shift significantly in meaning:

> . . . As soon as the first words were out, Mugo felt light. A load of many years

was lifted from his shoulders. He was free, sure, confident.

Only for a minute.

No sooner had he finished speaking than the silence around, the lightness within, and the sudden freedom pressed heavy on him . . . (*GOW* 267/204)

The sentence cited above from *Petals of Blood* illustrates a similar bonding, both by means of variety of reiterated structures in the longer periods, and the incisive drumming of the short ones.

The lengthy rhetorical passages in *Devil on the Cross* develop these techniques to a new complexity and intensity. We are, of course, meant to be aware of the parallels and patternings, but in fact so many correlations are made to interlock that at a first reading we can actually be conscious of only a few of the features that build up into emotional emphases and climaxes. For whole pages of the debate in the taxi, the motifs of hearts and humanity are rallied between Wangari, Mwaura and Muturi, until Muturi develops a weighty peroration to discredit Mwaura's cynicism on pages 51–3. The positive achievements of civilization are presented in a dovetailed series of noun groups. Seven 'and's link the items in the third sentence:

> What marvel could be greater than that? Look at the towns we have built with our hands: Mombasa, Nairobi, Nakuru, Eldoret, Kitale, Kisumu, Ruuwa-ini and Ilmorog. Look at the coffee, and the tea, and the sugar cane, and the cotton, and the rice, and the beans, and the maize we have grown out of a handful of seeds. Look at the fire trapped inside copper wires that stretch from Ruiru, Athi and Sagan Rivers, so that we can have suns and moons and stars in our towns and in our houses after nature's sun, moon and stars have gone to bed! (52)

The reiterated imperatives pile up: 'Look at . . . look at . . . look at'. In the whole sequence rhetorical questions are heaped upon each other. More subtly two sentences (including that preceding our quotation) catch up the same structural sequence of a zero relative followed by 'so that . . .' and 'after . . .' The diction accumulates lists as evidence and repeats refrains such as 'sun . . . moon . . . stars'. Rolling phrases bind parallels with contrasts: 'the fruits of the combined labour of many hands . . . the fruits of that co-operation'; 'the clan of parasites . . . the clan of producers'. And all these techniques are gathered into great sweeping oratorical rhythms as the challenge of hearts and humanity is thrown back in Mwaura's teeth:

> If the fruits of that co-operation had not been grabbed by the clan of parasites, where do you think that we, the clan of producers, would be today? Would we still know the meaning of cold, hunger, thirst and nakedness?
>
> That humanity is the heart of man because the heart of man is linked irrevocably with the growth of his nature as a man. Can you tell us the price of a heart now, you cheap and foolish merchant? (52–3)

At the beginning of our chapter on *Matigari*, we compared the dominant styles deployed in *Devil on the Cross* and *Matigari* itself. However, the general framework of each of the two novels have much in common stylistically on a more detailed scale. This is particularly true of the patterning at every level: vocabulary, phrasing and structures. One respect in which *Matigari* takes earlier tendencies much further is in the detailed repetition of major motifs. The re-iteration of Matigari's life history; of the socio-political principle of the farmer, the tailor, the builder, the factory worker getting their economic rights; of the fundamental question of the ownership of land and everything on it; of truth and justice — these are the foundations and the pillars, the body and soul of the whole fable. The almost word for word repetition binds the work in a traditional frame even stronger than the already powerful consistency of the themes in earlier novels. But in other respects the internal links are familiar in kind. Let us take as an example a passage of about 400 words on pages 166 and 167 beginning 'Suddenly a ball of fire burst out of the windows of the house'.

The already familiar collocation 'the house' recurs 12 times in these paragraphs; the single word 'burning' nine times. Crowd reactions build up the tension step by step: they 'shouted and scrambled' . . . 'surged'; they 'are surging'; and then 'climbed into' the house 'to loot' it and each 'took something'. As the fire burgeons they 'retreated' 'forming a ring'. But the fire chief fears they are 'getting out of control' and 'might attack/ overwhelm' his men. Steadily the conflagration builds up to a climax, fanned as it were by the constant chant 'Bad Boy's house is burning'. The 'ball of fire', 'clouds of smoke', 'tongues of fire' culminate in a 'loud explosion' 'as if blown up by a bomb', 'exploding into flames', raining 'shattered stone' on the onlookers till 'the flames lit up the whole compound, the fields and the surrounding country'. And this is only the beginning. The quick-fire sentences of only one or two clauses keep up the tempo relentlessly. The complex variety of sentence openings in the Minister's speech gives way to sentence after sentence plunging headlong into the action. Nominal groups are brief: everything is action with high content verbs and an exceptionally low incidence of mere 'is' or 'was'.

In the Minister's speech earlier things are linguistically different but there is still intense patterning. In a passage of just over three hundred words beginning on page 102 with 'Yes, this Boy you see here . . .' there are seven rhetorical questions and five exclamation marks. As the Minister boasts, four sentences begin 'I have'; and while he expounds as the demagogue par excellence four other sentences begin 'Look'. Lengthy nominal groups clog the diction: 'those loyalist professors and all holders of Ph.D.s in Parrotology' . . . 'those who are always raising a hue and cry about revolution, revolutionary politics, revolutionary socialism and other *foreign ideologies*'. The Minister unknowingly burlesques himself as in front of an audience of have-nots he itemizes his possessions, some of which are even sub-itemized: 'I have three swimming-pools . . . yes, three . . . one for the children, one for the guests and one for me and my wife.' The Minister exposes his vicious absurdity while Ngũgĩ creates pleasing comic rhythms which carry the reader eagerly along through derision and anger.

This passage of intense satire also illustrates Ngũgĩ's now completely confident mastery of colloquial English. Mocking as our reactions may be, we have no doubt that this is the Minister's speaking voice. Budding grammarians may find themselves tested in trying to parse some of these brilliantly accurate colloquial/rhetorical outbursts:

'Yes, this Boy you see here — his father was killed by terrorists for obeying and abiding by the law. Look how far his son has gone today. Is he scavenging for rubbish in garbage yards? You'll all agree with me that it is clear that he is not.' (102)

The average length of the periods is still not excessive since there are 12 sentences with less than ten words; but there are also three of 30 or more. The Minister pompously wheels out some impressive vocabulary: 'scavenging', 'garbage', 'seven-storey', 'emblem', 'dispassionately', 'distortion'. But colloquial forms far outweigh any essentially literary diction. Subjects of clauses are predominantly pronouns; hardly any subject groups are more than three words. Preferred clause linkages remain tight: relative pronouns, 'and', or simply a punctuation point; nominal clauses are still common. If anything, Ngũgĩ now extends the already wide range of his usage; but his prose in English translation is ever more accessible to the average secondary student. Indeed *Matigari*'s style has proved no barrier to popularity in either of its languages!

It may be with some surprise that we first observe that the author of *The River Between*, a novel brilliantly structured around central symbols, uses unexpectedly little metaphorical language. There are telling images of the countryside, of huts and places, of the sun and the sky', and of people, and these images shift from the narrative present into various layers of past time through memories, dreaming and daydreaming on the part of various characters, and through the author's time-shifts. Such images and the way they are linked produce an imaginative vividness which may seem to reside in similitudes and comparisons. But this is seldom the case. The images are of actual things literally seen in the present or the past of the novel. Not infrequently, however, a specific word or phrase may have metaphorical as well as literal implications: instance the word 'groping' and the phrase 'millet power', with the latter's lingering implications in the last quotation from *Petals of Blood*. 'Bush grew and bowed reverently' around the giant fig-tree in *The River Between* (19/15); 'For a day or two [Ngotho] had walked upright' after hearing of Jacobo's death (*WNC* 134/119); 'Her innermost turmoil had been his lullaby' ('Minutes of Glory', *SL* 92); 'In the shamba, [Mugo] felt hollow' (*GOW* 8/7). When the woman is beaten in the trench, Mugo, before he himself is touched, 'felt the whip eat into his flesh' (*GOW* 196/150).

All this is changed in *Devil on the Cross*. We meet a sudden rich outflow of simile, metaphor and imagery of all kinds. As part of traditional Gikuyu eloquence, proverbs heighten the language at every turn. From first to last the novel is freshly coloured with vivid, evocative language. This is equally true of Wariinga's early narrative manner: 'If he shouts at me, I will remain silent. I will simply look down like the shy leopard or like a lamb cropping grass', (*DOC* 20) or her dramatization of the gross menacing absurdity of the Boss's love-making: 'Didn't I tell you that one doesn't go to a dance wearing old, scentless perfume? Kareendi, my new necklace, my tomato plant growing on the rich soil of an abandoned homestead!' (*DOC* 22) Constantly this new vein of imagery reinforces our closeness to the natural environment and village life. Muturi fears that educated people 'sway from this side to that like water on a leaf' (*DOC* 211).

Things again are different in *Matigari*. It is as if the all-embracing traditional fable pattern takes over from detailed metaphor and simile which are as scarce as in the early novels. The over-arching symbolism is offset by a return to very direct diction. If one scans a cross-section of pages in different parts of the work, our search yields but a few simple analogies — 'like a leaf in the wind' (22) — and familiar idioms — 'the fire of freedom' (23 etc.) — or the Minister's clichés — 'at the bottom of the ladder', 'on a platter' (103). But the intensity of the finale does yield some heightened colouring: 'the pack of dogs looked like a flock of sheep'; of Matigari 'as if on reaching him [the bullets] turned into water'; the rain deluges 'as if all the taps of heaven had been turned on full blast'. The dogs seem to growl, 'Sisi mbwa kali'; and sardonically Matigari likens the last stage of the chase to a fox-hunt.

We have already remarked in a previous chapter how proverbs are spoken in clusters in the traditional manner of debate. This major feature of *Devil on the Cross* is to be found less frequently in *Matigari*. In some degree such wise sayings are replaced by chorus-like refrains forming part of cyclic repetitions: 'the-white-man-who-reaps-where-he-never-sowed', 'the tiller goes to sleep on an empty stomach'. But these litanies themselves catch up proverbial maxims as part and parcel of their insistent messages: 'He who sows must be the one who reaps! We refuse to be the pot that cooks but never eats the food !' (60 etc.) Such choral effects are anticipated in *Devil on the Cross* by certain images that contribute to a larger patterning. They recur time and again as linking threads: the scentless perfume quoted above; the dance of the hunter and the hunted; the single bean that will be shared by hungry workers; the desecration of the mother figure (as an extreme image of callousness); the rich man's fart that does not smell bad in sycophantic nostrils; and so forth.

Behind the force, the sweep, the elegance of Ngũgĩ's style have always lain two special influences which are of particular force in the fifth and sixth novels. It is relatively easy to become aware of these formative elements in Ngũgĩ's artistic control over rhythm and structure. But in the earlier novels it is harder to pinpoint them as shaping specific passages in terms of diction or syntax, except in occasional brief sequences.

First, he is the offspring of an all-pervasive oral tradition, of the genius of the village singer and the family story-teller around the fire. And secondly, we have no doubt that the Bible sang its music to him and excited his emotions less equivocally than its content and message influenced his thinking. Very occasionally we may hear the two traditions blending in the text, as when Chege sets out to inspire Waiyaki with his heritage:

> '. . . it was before Agu; in the beginning of things. Murungu brought the man and woman here and again showed them the whole vastness of the land. He gave the country to them and their children, and the children of the children, *tene na tene*, world without end.' (RB 21/18)

But this is rare. This strain is not even carried over into the pages that immediately follow this quotation.

When Isaka reads the Bible in *Weep Not, Child* there is a distinct contrast with the manner of the adjacent passages:

> A short man went into the pulpit. Njoroge looked at him closely. His face seemed familiar. The man began to speak. And then Njoroge remembered. This

was the worldly teacher they used to call *Uuu*. His moustache was not there. Teacher Isaka had gone to Nyeri the year Njoroge finished the first school . . .

'And Jesus answered and said unto them: Take heed that no man deceive you.' (101–2/89–90)

The balance of phrase, clause and sentence, the dovetailing of grammatical structures within a graceful forward flow — stylistic principles which Ngũgĩ had mastered — find their parallel (though no mirror-image) in the Christian scriptures. And the tuned ear will hear brief echoes at unexpected moments: 'Wanjiku wept' (*GOW* 252/193), side by side with the overt quotations from Kihika's Bible.

Even though in *Devil on the Cross* there are deliberate ironic transpositions from the Bible, these in the main are set in racy modern language, for instance the re-interpretation of the parable of the talents. Indubitable biblical influence on style is still elusive except in specific quotations such as, 'Get thee behind me, Satan' (*DOC* 194). And the same thing is true of *Matigari* though it also contains extensive explicit references to the Bible, notably in Guthera's account of her Christian upbringing, in the version of Jesus's words to his disciples during the Last Supper delivered by the drunken man in the prison, or the passage from chapter 24 of St. Matthew's gospel read out by the priest during the Minister's meeting to squash the rumour that Matigari is the risen Christ.

But the impact of oral tradition is unmistakable and omnipresent. The use of proverbs and cyclic repetitions has been duly noticed. And we have discussed in earlier chapters the way song forms are welded into the prose sequence. Such elements alter the whole balance of language in the later novels. But there is more. In the matatu Muturi and Wangari enter into a time-honoured riddle contest. Kihaahu begins his testimony in the Cave by chanting praises to himself in traditional form. In both *Devil on the Cross* and *Matigari* the prose constantly, and particularly at major climaxes, takes on a ritual manner derived from fable and story-telling:

'He went on, carried away by his words. He did not see Wariinga open her handbag. He did not see Wariinga take out the pistol.' (*DOC* 253)

He put on the cartridge belt across his chest, over his left shoulder, so that it hung on his right side. He passed the strap of the sword over his right shoulder and across his chest so that the sword lay on his left side. Finally he picked up the AK47 and slung it over his shoulder. He stood for a while under the *mugumo* tree. (*Mat* 175)

Evidence from *The Trial of Dedan Kimathi* will restrain us from assuming that these influences from traditional ritual and story-telling would not have appeared in Ngũgĩ's novels if he had continued to write them first in English, but the inspiration of composing works first in Gikuyu undoubtedly gave new impetus to the incorporation of such elements.

In the earlier novels, even as the characters themselves increasingly take over the narrative, there is still little use of specific speech forms, and even in *Devil on the Cross* there is a marked increase only in specific sections and speeches. But for long Ngũgĩ has clearly found it natural and compatible to work unmistakably through the human voice, whether Mumbi's among others in *A Grain of Wheat*, or say Nyakinyua's in *Petals of Blood*:

> Even now, at night, in bed . . . I remember the red flames. There were two huts. One belonged to my mother, the other was mine. *They* told us to remove our bedding and clothes and utensils. They splashed some petrol on the grass-thatch of my mother's hut. I then idly thought this was unnecessary as the grass was dry. Anyway, they poured petrol on the dry thatch. (*GOW* 159/122)

The first-person account is supported by the characteristically colloquial East African 'anyway', the stress on '*they*' and the repetitions among otherwise unobtrusively literary structures. Similarly in the following passage the strings of 'and' clauses and the phonetic spellings counteract the effect of the long complex sentences:

> 'But then came the second big war, and once again our children, our sons, your father among them, were taken away and we heard strange names when they came back: Abithinia, Bama, India, Boboi, Njiovani, Njirimani, and others. And this time our sons were actually holding the guns and helping, unwillingly, in the general slaughter of human lives. My man would whisper all these things to me late at night and the fever would seize him and he would tremble so and I would hold him to still him.' (*POB* 224)

The freedom of the passage quoted earlier in this chapter from Wanja's story is unlike the freedom of a traditional story-teller. Even at its chattiest in 'A Mercedes Funeral', Ngũgĩ's style is in fact a clever simulation of fairly sophisticated modern talk overlaying a carefully articulated written mode:

> You mention Chang'aa. Actually it was Chang'aa, you might say, that saved the campaign. Put it this way. If Wahinya, the other watchman in Ilmorog Bar and Restaurant, had not suddenly died of alcoholic poisoning, our village, our town would never have been mentioned in any daily. Wahinya dead became the most deadly factor in the election. (*SL* 117)

Though we have seen that in *Matigari* Ngũgĩ took another stride towards the literary expression of precise colloquial usage, much of what has just been said is also true of this later novel. Buthera's miniature autobiography well illustrates this. Matigari himself lards much of his plain but fluent talk with rhetorical catch-phrases. By this time Ngũgĩ (even in translation) appears to have true disjointed speech patterns at his disposal but he merges them into smoother talk with authorial discretion. And still the myths and history of Gikuyuland remain one of the staples of Ngũgĩ's fiction.

Our author has a strong and constant sense of place. We are conscious of and familiar with the precise locality in which events are happening, and at the same time there is an awareness in perspective across the undulating ridges. The countryside is a presence in detail and as a total ambience. The Honia is the centrepiece in *The River Between*. Time and again it is described with ever varying subtlety and with many surrounding particularities, apparently casual but in fact exactly matching the immediate mood:

> For a second Nyambura sat as if her thoughts, her feelings, her very being had been paralysed. She could not speak. The announcement was too sudden and too stupefying. How could she believe what she has heard came from Muthoni's mouth? She looked at the river, at the slightly swaying bulrushes lining the banks, and then beyond. Nothing moved on the huge cattle road that wound through the forest towards Kameno. The yellowish streaks of morning light diffused

through the forest, producing long shadows on the cattle path. The insects in the forest kept up an incessant sound which mingled with the noise of falling water farther down the valley. They helped to intensify the silence, created by Muthoni's statement.

'Circumcised?' at last Nyambura found her voice. (*RB* 28/25)

It is characteristic of Ngũgĩ's unified structure that he makes the keenly visualized symbolic house and its vast plantation the scene of Matigari's rebellion, beginning with the attempted assassination of Settler Williams and his rescue by Boy Senior, and of the final confrontation with corrupt authority in the conflagration; just as most key scenes in *The River Between* are enacted beside the Honia.

Chapters constantly open with an awareness of a Gikuyu scene, with or without the specific presence of human beings:

The women and men of Makuyu were already up and about their morning chores by the time the two girls, with their water-barrels weighing heavily on their backs, reached home. (*RB*, Chapter 7)

There was mist everywhere. It covered Kameno, Makuyu and the other ridges in its thin white greyness. It was chilling, chilling the skin. (*RB*, Chapter 10)

Waiyaki emerged from the smoke-clouded hut and walked away slowly, dragging his feet and shambling over things like a drunken man. (*RB*, Chapter 11)

A fairly large 'hill' stood outside Ngotho's household. Years of accumulating rubbish had brought this into being. If you stood there in the daytime, you could more or less see the whole of the land of Jacobo . . . (*WNC*, Chapter 5)

Then, as now, Thabai Ridge sloped gently from the high ground on the west into a small plain on which Rung'ei Trading Centre stood. The centre was a collection of tin-roofed buildings that faced one another in two straight rows. The space enclosed served as a market . . .(*GOW*, Chapter 7)

Although by now the sun had moved a great deal westwards, and the shadows had lengthened, it was still oppressively hot all over the country. The grass wilted, and the leaves wore a tired look about them. The haze in the air was uncomfortable; one saw mirages on tarmac highways. Except for the noise of cars on the road, and that of birds singing in the trees, the whole land was gripped in a deathly stillness. No wind blew. No leaves rustled. No clothes fluttered anywhere. (*Mat*, Part I, Section 11)

The intimacy established between the setting and the reader makes it possible for Ngũgĩ to take the whole social background of Gikuyuland for granted. The mugumo, the circumcision tradition, proverbs, all contribute to a rustic symbolism that establishes the ancient dignity of the tribe. There are no para-sociological explanations thrown in self-consciously. Songs break out spontaneously among the people, expressing the immediate occasion and subjects of immediate concern. The non-Gikuyu reader reacts confidently to the precise depiction of a scene or a situation, having been eased unwittingly into familiarity with the whole character of the society:

The men who came to see Ngotho usually went to his Thingira. But sometimes they went to Nyokabi's or Njeri's hut. This pleased Njoroge for he loved to listen to the mature talk of men. These men were the elders of the village. They talked about affairs of the land. (*WNC* 57/50)

They were coming for her. She ought to have known, to have prepared herself for this. Her wedding day had come. Unceremoniously they swept her off the ground, and for a moment she was really afraid, and was putting up a real struggle to free herself from the firm but gentle hands of the three men who were carrying her shoulder-high. ('Mugomo' *SL* 3).

She commanded them to remove all the money in the pockets, the metal bug that split up homes and drove men to the city. She took all the money and put it away on the floor outside the ritual circle. She sat down.
Millet, power of God.
She poured a few drops on the floor and chanted: for those that went before us and those coming after us, tene wa tene.
Then she put some in a small horn, and continued her admonitions, looking at them, fixing them with her eyes. (*POB* 211)

Matigari dreams of a return to ancient stability:

He wanted to embrace all the children and take them to his house that very moment . . . He saw a vision of himself and his children entering their house together, lighting the fire together and working together for their home, smoke drifting from the roof of their common home. (*Mat* 16)

The novels create their own social terms, so that we are inside the mystery rather than external observers. The publishers have restrained their itch to put unfamiliar words like 'thingira' in italics — that alienating device: so 'thingira' has become part of Ngũgĩ's legitimate English (there being no other English word for it), and we accept it and know it from its associations in context (though it is still a pity that it has a distinguishing capital letter).

In a similar way, people too are realized by the precisely selected, significant detail which makes us feel their presence at close quarters, and their unconscious relationship with others:

Njoroge was lonely and wanted to find companionship. He always admired the big, strong muscles of Kamau as he held the saw, or the hammer, or the smoothing plane. He looked sure, as he hammered in a nail here and sawed a piece of wood there . . . Njoroge often wondered whether he himself could ever have been like this. (*WNC* 96/85)

When Kihika was arrested General R. had remained calm, had shown no surprise or any sign of loss. With years Koinandu, who had wept at the time, forgot Kihika's death and did not feel any urgency for revenge. Now it was the General who trembled with passion. Koinandu looked around at the bare hut, avoiding the pacing figure. A sufuria, two plates, empty bottles and a water-tin lay on the floor, rather disconsolately. He cleared his throat:
'Perhaps it is no use. Perhaps we ought to forget the whole thing.'
General R. abruptly stopped pacing. He looked at Koinandu, weighing him up and down. Koinandu fidgeted on his seat, feeling the antagonism in the other's stare. (*GOW* 32/25)

Then there is the other side of the coin of characterization. We analysed in an earlier chapter how detailed observations humanize the grand archetypal figure of Matigari: his grey hairs, his brow 'creased with fatigue', his immediately recognizable hat and so forth. But his primary symbolic status is not new in Ngũgĩ's canon either, except perhaps in degree. Howlands, Kamau, Jacobo in *Weep Not, Child*; Joshua, Kabonyi, Mumbi in *The River Between*; Kihika, Karanja, General R., Thompson in *A Grain of Wheat*; the Lawyer, Chui, Nderi wa Riera, Wanja in *Petals of Blood* are just a few of the characters to whom we could readily designate symbolic roles.

Such symbolism is even more explicit in *Devil on the Cross* and *Matigari*. Matigari himself stands for more than 'the patriots who survived the liberation war, and their political offspring' (*Mat* 20, footnote) — he embodies the whole Mau Mau campaign and the progressive movement it engendered. Likewise Howard Williams Junior and Senior represent the usurping alien forces that have illegally appropriated the country's wealth; while John Boy Senior and Junior epitomize the quislings who have both aided the multi-corporations in their comprehensive take-over and have grabbed political power in the process of stealing all that remains in the country. The frequent re-telling of the fabled story of these personae, personalized in the first person 'I', reinforces the totality of past victory since the defeat of one individual by another is more conclusive than an on-going struggle between opposing armies: and such a concentrated account implies the hope for a similarly unqualified victory in the future.

This personalization of the themes in the novel's characters is matched by their 'concretization' in inanimate items, notably the house and the plantation. The former 'seemed to stretch out for miles' and the latter apparently 'had no beginning and no end'(42), thus mirroring the vastness of the property and the wealth that the settlers and their lackeys have appropriated. And we must remember that land and house represent spiritual as well as material values.

While we are seldom aware in reading Ngũgĩ of specific passages of description, as we often are with, say, D.H. Lawrence, places and people and ideas are interfused in a manner which is nevertheless reminiscent of Lawrence's fiction. Indeed, the actual localities — Kameno, Kipanga, Rung'ei, Ilmorog — take on for the reader an almost independent existence in a way associated in English literature with Mrs Gaskell or, on a larger scale, George Eliot, whose purposes and methods are otherwise very different.

The effect in Ngũgĩ is of intensification, not of expansiveness. There is economy with no hint of dryness. The memorable scenes are often incredibly short on paper, but they assume a greatly increased significance in being recalled explicitly later by one or other of the characters as part of the author's carefully articulated design. Although earlier there may at times be a certain abruptness in the juxtaposition of the pieces in the jigsaw, the overall effect is surprisingly sophisticated even in the first novels. By the time he comes to write *A Grain of Wheat*, Ngũgĩ is master of his techniques. This is a long novel by African standards. Indeed it is not unreasonable to compare it in complexity with *Nostromo*. Yet it is still only half the length of Conrad's masterpiece.

The acme of this style is the love scene between Gikonyo and Mumbi; the whole sequence is barely more than a page without skimping or undue haste or lack of proportioned development. The very many parts of Ngũgĩ's complex design in this novel never get out of control because none is allowed to over-expand and dislocate the co-ordinating plan.

In certain respects, the techniques are even more complex in *Petals of Blood* wherein different laminations of the plot overlap and interlock continuously: instance the evening when theng'eta is resurrected and many different aspects of the past at different times and in different lives are revealed and interwoven in the present. The climax of the heroic journey, which occupies Part Two and which in the main unfolds chronologically, is the confrontation with Nderi wa Riera. The whole passage, including Riera's return to Nairobi, the preparation for the interview, the actual meeting in his office, the public session in Jevanjee Gardens and the ignominious retreat and arrests, occupies only eight pages. Towards the end of the book, the culmination of the action in the depiction of the fatal evening in Wanja's house, including the fire, requires only about one page (329) in its fullest telling. This concentration is a necessary counterbalance to the involved structure.

Devil on the Cross is an amalgam of modes. Some of the essentially discursive scenes are very long: the journey in the matatu; the great satiric event in the Cave. But these are 'scenes' in a very different sense from that we have just been using. In the realistic narrative, on the other hand, incidents are told with the familiar Ngũgĩ brevity and incisiveness, though the fact that the same event is told twice may give the impression of fuller depiction: for instance the rout of the assemblage by the marchers, told first in a page and a half and later retold even more briefly to Wariinga from Muturi's viewpoint. The para-autobiographical account of the Boss's attempted seduction of his secretary is relatively long — four pages. But the whole day of Wariinga's attempted suicide occupies just one and a half pages. Individual sequences from Wariinga's affair with the Rich Old Man, or from her metamorphosis into an idealistic engineer, are extremely short.

The long, highly discursive central 'scene' in *Matigari* is the Minister's meeting, which takes up about a sixth of the whole work. For the rest we have essentially cinematic sequences which follow the protagonist, mainly in the open air: events in and around the bar/restaurant, spanning 15 pages, include Guthera's fracas with the police and her account of her life; the prison scenario, of equal length, involves a whole series of cameos outlining how the various inmates were arbitrarily arrested. The constant references back to the past telescope a swathe of time within the constantly emphasized three and a half days of action in the present. The relentless impetus of Matigari's search still allows Ngũgĩ to hold back and slow down time for contemplation of the issues owing to his fine control of tempo. The highlit scenes are again briefly concentrated: the police harassment of Guthera, the stoning of Matigari. The breathless chase lasts only three and a half pages, and the revolutionary conflagration just four.

For Ngũgĩ's brief scenes to maintain dramatic appeal, it is necessary for him to achieve the build-up to a peak of intensity in an exceptionally short space. His control over structure makes this possible. A climax in a novel by Ngũgĩ is no sudden disconnected event. It is the outcome, and to some extent the resolution, of forces and events which we have seen gathering with increasing speed and violence towards such a culmination. Any such climax before the conclusion itself is pointedly recalled and referred to, becoming a key point in a cyclic development, and thus achieving significance and resonance out of all proportion to the number of pages it occupies in the primary telling. Parallels intensify this patterning. The love-scene we have just mentioned between Mumbi and Gikonyo in *A Grain of Wheat* clearly determines much of the subsequent action. But more than this, it is re-echoed when the race which leads up to it (the scene between the two lovers is only possible because Karanja outstrips Gikonyo and is lost sight of) is paralleled in another race on uhuru day, which Karanja again wins in fact but loses in effect.

The denouement of each novel is powerfully integrated with all that has gone before. In *The River Between* Waiyaki's crowning defeat is determined as much by his own inadequacy as by Kabonyi's intrigues. It would be impossible, however, without his moral and emotional achievement in allowing the desire for unity to culminate in his commitment to Nyambura. But it also springs from his youthful and modernist obstinacy in refusing to permit affairs of the heart to be discussed publicly. His downfall is swift. Three pages before the novel ends, Waiyaki is at the height of his popularity and influence: 'he was amazed because he did not know that he had such power over the people' (RB 172/149). The almost instantaneous catastrophe is convincing because everything that contributes to it is fully known and prepared for. In the last dramatic reversal, story and themes are interlocked: the challenge to the characters is also in effect the challenge to the reader.

The ending of *Weep Not, Child* is more muted since the protagonist is not involved in any heroic action, unless his final rejection of suicide in readiness to confront the realities of living can be so accounted. But the final reversals are equally abrupt and equally telling. As we read the penultimate page for the first time most of us must have believed that Njoroge's suicide was only minutes away. Yet his physical and moral rescue is fully authentic as we contemplate the complete pattern of the novel.

The whole design of *A Grain of Wheat* is scrupulously planned towards the day of uhuru which is being prepared for at the opening, and which necessitates the cyclic re-enactment of the many-sided struggle that led up to it. And Mugo's speech is planned as the centrepiece of the day in Rung'ei. By the time we reach this moment nothing is concealed from the reader of the paradoxes attendant upon this occasion. Only the actual manner in which Mugo will behave remains to surprise us, but this turns out to be so crucial to our interest and to the final behaviour of the other characters that the anti-climax experienced by the spectators in the novel proves to be a peculiarly sophisticated climax of suspense and drama for the readers. The moment itself is handled with a brevity which we now recognize as a hallmark of Ngũgĩ's style, as also is the eventual rehabilitation of the marriage between Gikonyo and Mumbi which fittingly alters the whole tenor of the novel on the very last page.

Emotional tension and excitement are generated in *Petals of Blood* by the deliberate structuring of the story along the lines of a detective thriller. The plot opens with the apprehension by the police of several individuals for questioning in connection with a sensational crime. Attention shifts to and fro from one suspect to another with increasing pace, until the last breathless round of investigation ends suddenly in a startling conclusion as the detective engineers the unforeseen culprit into a dramatic confession. There are, of course, other ways of considering the patterning of this complex work. But this undeniable ground-plan succeeds in lending immediacy, suspense and climax to a work which aims ultimately at presenting a sad, contemplative analysis of the contemporary social scene, however desperately streaked with hope, and complicated by layer upon layer of irony.

The central act in the finale of *Devil on the Cross* is Wariinga's assassination of the Rich Old Man. In this symbolic moment the two modes of the novel meet. By definition this is not to be seen as an arbitrary, isolated action, but as a preliminary move towards the revolutionary retribution which must eventually be meted out to the oppressors of Kenyan, African, all exploited peoples everywhere. We are meant to recall the two previous attempts by the wealthy and the powerful to seduce Wariinga when she appeared helpless. So at this moment the Rich Old Man echoes the previous image of the perfume that has been lost. With characteristic Ngũgĩ control, the old scene is re-enacted with a difference and the Hunter and the Hunted re-emerge, she again with the gun in her hand which so narrowly missed her ravisher in his perverted game earlier. At that time he 'told her that the game would never end'. But now that he has seen that she could not be trusted with guns, she was not to hunt him again. He would do the hunting all the time (144–5). But at the last her hand is very well to be trusted with a gun; now she knows exactly what she is doing and why; and it is she who will master the hunt, not he. And in this moment of decision the Rich Old Man is at the centre of the cohorts from the thieves' carnival in the Cave. He is finally identified as their prototype by the incriminating presence of Kihaahu and Gitutu. The former revelations in the Cave enable us to understand Wariinga's sentence as she stands 'like a people's judge about to deliver his judgement' (253).

None of the works more clearly spells out from the start its hoped for conclusion than does *Matigari*. Matigari himself, as the representative of the Kenyan people, is to recover from the usurpers his nation's heritage represented by 'the house' and 'the plantation'. Throughout he is on an immemorial journey in search of justice and truth. This will validate and fulfil restitution of their age-old birthright by restoring happiness, prosperity and communal peace to those who labour to create the national wealth. The imagery of decadence, strife, hopelessness, filth, and despair is mellowed by even more powerful images: of the dignity, joy, and hope that grow from spontaneous love, mutual support and togetherness among the people. Throughout there is a sense of actively aspiring and moving towards a universally desired goal in spite of the entrenched wickedness that stands in its path. Hope is affirmed as the children of the old patriots take up arms for a new stage of the combat. The Minister's meeting thus culminates in a furore of devastating satire which anticipates victory. As *Petals of Blood* is spiced with the suspense of a detective thriller, now *Matigari* leads irrevocably to a different popular climax in a hell-for-leather car chase, culminating in a fire-ball which ignites the revolutionary spirit. But for the reader the text concludes with a challenge not an invitation to complacency. The novel dramatizes the need to prepare the ground first for the desired apotheosis. Not enough has yet been done to make it possible for Matigari to re-inhabit his true house and invite all his children to cook and eat there with him. What is now possible is the destruction of the corrupted building to make way for the foundations of a new, more beautiful one. So the work ends with the chase compressed excitingly into three pages, and the conflagration into four. Just three more pages record the final gruesome yet paradoxically triumphant 'hunt' of Matigari and Guthera, and frame the final page as Muriuki seems to invite new-style patriots to reject inertia and join the battle.

Irony is fundamental to Ngũgĩ's style. The complexity of his vision is determined by an ability to see many facets of every action, every situation, every impulse. In reporting an event, he is aware of the conflicting motives that have shaped it, the different ways it may be viewed and reported by different people, and the unintended results that may spring from it. Ngũgĩ's wily smile at human foibles, his sad exploration of the contradictions in society, his angry exposure of specious justifications for individual self-interest are all essentially ironic. Things are not simply as they appear on the surface.

There is one respect in which Ngũgĩ's irony is exceptional in literary terms. We tend to think of the dark, unstated half of the ironic equation as revealing only what is sinister and malign. This is largely borne out by Ngũgĩ's portrayal of experience: in these novels the hidden workings of both Fate and the politician show little pity for a common humanity. But in Ngũgĩ irony is also capable of doubling back on itself and suggesting to us the latent hopes and potentialities inherent in the incredible selflessness that men and women can display In counterbalance to the rapaciousness of their fellows. If the larger ironies in Ngũgĩ deny the possibility of easy optimism, they also firmly close the door on cynicism and despair.

We may do well to exemplify the ironic structure of the novels before investigating the way in which irony influences the fabric of the style.

In *The River Between* Waiyaki's defeat and failure are the outcome of an interlocking set of ironies. In this complex pattern the final irony may be seen as positive if we concede that the reactions of the crowd at the last indicate that this set-back for well-intentioned and right-thinking policies is not final, and that it contains the seeds of incipient success in the long run. Waiyaki fails not because his emphasis on education is misconceived but because he has refused to link his campaign to the political rights, needs and aspirations of the people. But the leader of the movement in Kameno for immediate political action is an out-and-out village demagogue who manipulates this cause for his own ends. Waiyaki is out-manoeuvred by the unscrupulous Kabonyi because he stands by his unannounced commitment to unity in determining to marry Nyambura — a unity which ought to be the end-product of education. Yet in the moment of victory, Kabonyi's followers sense the ironic falseness of their purpose: 'They went away quickly, glad that he was hidden by the darkness. For they did not want to look at the Teacher and they did not want to read their guilt in one another's faces' (*RB* 174–5/152). Waiyaki's vision is thus in effect vindicated; and we end in the reasonable hope that in the longer run the future lies not with the likes of the self-seeking Kabonyi, but with the selfless Waiyaki and his kind, if only, as we now have cause to believe, such a man can learn from his early mistakes and falterings.

The conclusion of *Weep Not, Child* presents Njoroge to our sympathetic but extremely critical judgement when he seeks to escape bewilderment in the final surrender of suicide. He is saved by his mother who is the epitome of the enduring values and fortitude of the people. It is ironic that Njoroge must be redeemed by his renouncing the most decisive act that we have known him to contemplate in the whole course of the novel. As he again embraces life, an inner voice accuses him of cowardice. This voice ironically implies a final positive assertion. Nominally it is the retreat from suicide which the voice is condemning, but to us it is clear that Njoroge's real cowardice, which is being condemned at a deeper level, lay in his determination to kill himself. His new resolve to live and confront his own and his people's troubled future is his first real display of courage.

Mugo's apotheosis in *A Grain of Wheat* is his confession of guilt. The truly guilty can expiate the wrongs they have committed (whatever the extenuating circumstances) only by offering themselves up as a sacrifice. But in the death of Mugo society is made aware that revenge, if not actually irrelevant, is a dead end, and that the real legacy of Kihika to his survivors lies in their building an integrated community to fight against continuing evils, not in harbouring bitterness and self-hatred which would be the fruits of brooding destructively on the past. This realization is crystallized in the rediscovered harmony between Gikonyo and Mumbi.

The assassinations which are central to the plot of *Petals of Blood* turn out to have been committed by a convert to extremist evangelical Christianity. This man first dedicated his life to teaching in an altogether under-privileged primary school, but in doing so he has ranked himself as a failure in the eyes of his family. It is this same man who, after betraying the principles on which this sacrifice was based by having a junior colleague sacked in jealous revenge, determines to balance the wrong of society and 'save' his one-time rival by killing a significant group of the oppressors of the ordinary man. Wanja, who embodies the joy and vigour of life, has herself killed her own offspring. Having been betrayed by society into prostitution, she later will not renounce her profession when she can, but institutionalizes it into a vested interest. The man who has been in the fight for freedom sinks into virtual beggary amid the economic bonanza of those who kowtowed to colonialism. And the man who deliberately gives his life to fighting for social justice ends up behind barbed wire. But as the novel closes, in the eyes of the underdog it is in Karega that the hope for the future is embodied.

At the end of *Devil on the Cross*, likewise, Muturi and Wangari are still in detention. The victory of the marchers which ended the Devil's Feast was no more than a distant foretaste of the new dispensation so desperately needed and eagerly prepared for. Social patterns in Ilmorog and Nairobi remain balanced between the Eaten and the Eater. At the reception which ends the novel, the Eaters, in the persons of Gatuiria's father, Kihaahu and Gitutu, are still in command, ready blandly to engulf and dismiss any puny opposition from Gatuiria and Wariinga. Gatuiria is indeed engulfed. But not so Wariinga. The hunter is now hunted by the People's Judge. The Rich Old Man is executed by the woman whom he had himself driven to the edge of suicide. It is on a note of muted triumph that Wariinga eventually steps proudly out of the novel, illumined through a glass darkly, like Karega, by an imagined future. The fable in the Aristotelian sense is completed. The issues are plain. The possibilities are set out. A forcefully didactic novel has had its say and taught its lesson.

In *Matigari* the Minister is a satiric monster, an alarming exaggeration foreshadowed in miniature by Nderi wa Riera in *Petals of Blood* — but perhaps not *so* much of an exaggeration as the ultra-satiric nightmare figures of *Devil on the Cross* — and all too fearfully recognizable to Kenyans and indeed to many other peoples. We pinpointed earlier some of the powerful, provocative ironies, such as the bland dismissal of rumours of the return of the risen Christ because 'He' has not presented himself on a courtesy visit to His Excellency Ole Excellence. The ironies branch out in all directions: the priest in fear and trembling lest these rumours are well-founded. 'All the roads which were named after the governors or kings or queens during the colonial days are now named after His Excellency' (148). Here too ironies lie within ironies. That the holier-than-thou minister's wife is found copulating adulterously in the deep bush while Guthera pities her lover's wife who will be beaten by the adulterer for asking what her husband was doing out there with another woman. Muriuki announces 'proudly' that the abandoned car wreck that he sleeps in is the shell of a Mercedes-Benz (16), wryly also foreshadowing his dramatic ride later in a resplendent new Mercedes with Matigari. The big destitute orphan boy bullies and steals garnered garbage from the small orphan boy. The irony of a corrupt and sadistic police is perhaps too familiar to the majority of readers to need further emphasis here. The double thinking of those who are in retreat from their own principles — the lecturer and the student who had been so radical as to be imprisoned, and the sycophantic priest — balance the picture.

Ngũgĩ's whole manner leads to great clarity of vision and expression but nothing is over-simplified. At his most bitter and angry he altogether rejects pessimism and draws attention to one or another figure in whom the chances of a just future repose.

If the structure of each novel is thus charged with irony, it is only to be expected that it will be reflected in the texture of the language. In the earlier works the irony is quite often explicitly stated:

Suddenly he realised that he did not want to meet her while he had on that piece of calico which, when blown by the wind, left the lower part of his body without covering. For a time, he was irresolute and hated himself for feeling as he did about the clothes he had on. Before he had started school, in fact even while he made that covenant with his mother, he would never have thought that he would ever be ashamed of the calico, the only dress he had ever known since birth. (*WNC* 22/19)

They had been happy. Then the man became a convert. And everything in the home put on a religious tone. . . She, too, had been converted. But she was never blind to the moral torture he inflicted on the boy. . . She always wondered if it was love for the son. Or could it be a resentment because, well, they two had 'sinned' before marriage? John had been the result of that sin. But that had not been John's fault. It was the boy who ought to complain. ('A Meeting in the Dark', *SL* 56–7)

The rain carried away the soil, not only here but everywhere. That was why land, in some parts, was becoming poor. For a time, he felt like fighting with the rain. The racing drops of water had turned to filth and mud. He subsided. He now felt like laughing heartily. Even here in this natural happening, he could see a contradiction. The rain had to touch the soil. That touch could be a blessing or a curse. (*RB* 76/65–6)

Some themes, like the settlers' possessiveness concerning the land and the people, offer themselves so obviously to irony that no subtlety is demanded or proffered: 'He just warned them that if any man went on strike he would instantly lose his job. How could he allow a damned strike to interfere with any part of his farm?' (*WNC* 59/51-2). The contradictions between Waiyaki's intentions and his actions provide other instances: 'But now he wanted an opportunity to shout what was oppressing his mind. He would tell the people — "Unite". That would be early next year' (*RB* 137/119). He is continuing to procrastinate as part of his very gesture towards activity.

Patterns also develop which make demands upon the reader since the criss-crossing of attitudes is only tangentially revealed, as when Isaka is interrogated by a British patrol:

Where had he left the documents? Satan had made him forget them at home. But the white soldier knew better. Isaka was a Mau Mau. Again Isaka replied that Jesus had saved him and he could not exchange Jesus with Mau Mau. The officer looked at him with reddening eyes. (*WNC* 115/101)

The white officer's own nominal Christian allegiances are weaker than his inherent prejudices against the black man. But the deeper irony is that Isaka speaks the truth: Gikuyu Christians did indeed see their religion standing opposed to the liberation movement. The interplay of irony among the major themes is not always predictable:

Kabonyi and the Kiama were asking him to stand by their beliefs, beliefs that would destroy his mission of healing the rift between Makuyu and Kameno; between Joshua and the others. His mission of enlightenment through education would come to nothing. (*RB* 147/127)

This is true — but Waiyaki has himself failed to set about that part of his mission, and so at the time he is arraigned by the people for making a treacherous alliance, he has done nothing to propagate any alternative view of the matter. '[Ngotho's] awareness that he had failed his children had always shadowed him. Even before this calamity befell him, life for him had become meaningless, divorced as he had been from what he valued' (*WNC* 134/119). Can Ngotho legitimately be blamed — either by his children or by himself — for having failed to halt the colonialists' misappropriation of the land? Even if in part he can be so blamed, is it not himself that he has betrayed (as suggested by the second sentence) before it may be considered whether or not this can also be accounted a 'betrayal' of the children?

In *A Grain of Wheat* significant actions and attitudes of all the characters are constantly re-examined from different viewpoints. There is no resemblance between the actual meeting of Mugo and Kihika and how it has been imagined. We have both Thompson's and Mugo's variant accounts of the moment when the DC spits on the informer's face. There are two versions of the raping of Dr Lynd. We are with the villagers as they dance in celebration around Mugo's hut, and later Ngũgĩ takes us inside the hut to be with Mugo on the same occasion, slumped in terror and remorse. As it is constantly the role of this novel to explore what lies behind assumed 'facts', we can hardly do more than illustrate this from a few of the complex ironies, selected almost at random, with which the text is studded:

> He liked porridge in the morning. But whenever he took it, he remembered the half-cooked porridge he ate in detention. How time drags, everything repeats itself, Mugo thought; the day ahead would be just like yesterday and the day before. (4/3)

> 'Like Kenyatta is telling us,' he went on, 'these are days of Uhuru na Kazi.' He paused and ejected a jet of saliva on to the hedge. (5/4)

> [Of Margery Thompson] Now in the kitchen, washing dishes, she found herself reviving the warmth she had felt earlier in the day. How ridiculous, she told herself, recalling every detail of that brief encounter with Karanja. Perhaps it is because I am leaving Africa. No, maybe I'm growing old. They say the African heat does these things to women. (58/44)

> As soon as Gikonyo had gone, Mugo rushed to the door, flung it open and cried: 'Come back.' (141/107)

> When Gikonyo came home in the evening, Mumbi could tell that he was in a bad mood. First he did not talk to her. This was not unusual. Then, when she gave him food, he only glanced at it once and then continued staring at the wall. Again this was not unusual. But . . . (189/145)

> And then suddenly he heard the village people around his hut singing Uhuru songs. Every word of praise carried for him a piercing irony. What had he done for the village? What had he done for anybody? Yet now he saw this undeserved trust in a new light, as the sweetest thing in the world. Mumbi will tell them, he thought. He saw the scorn and horror, not on Mumbi's face alone, but on every person in the village. (266/203)

Such quotations form part of wider patterns running through *A Grain of Wheat*, but when we turn to *Petals of Blood* the temptation is immediately to quote whole pages at a time rather than a group of sentences since now the bitter ironies (and the strange consolations that sometimes rise from within them) follow through whole passages of its complex structure. One of the most clear-cut examples of specific irony developing throughout a lengthy paragraph is the account of Nderi wa Riera's specious rhetoric in which he rationalizes every disaster that has befallen the original inhabitants of Ilmorog into achievements for which they are to praise him and grounds for them again to vote him into power — as they will do:

> . . . The road had brought trade to the area: small shopping centres were springing on either side of the road. In order to prevent a mushrooming of mere slums and shanties, he had proposed — and indeed the plans were under way — for Chiri County Council to set up a properly planned, sewaged shopping centre at Ilmorog. A few acres of land would of course be taken from the people

for the purpose, but the County Council would pay adequate compensation. Then as a result of his representations and remonstrations with the central government, it had been decided to develop the whole area into ranches and wheat fields. A tourist centre would be set up and a game park . . . (267)

However, Munira's account of the way in which he is drawn into jealousy as he agonizes over the idyllic affair between Wanja (who will allow him to sleep with her only once again, and then as the hardened queen of Ilmorog prostitutes, for one hundred shillings) and Karega (whom he will attempt to 'save' in his obsessive assassination of the corrupt worthies of the new town) is indeed more complexly and subtly ironic (243–5). So also is Abdulla's account of how, himself a social misfit maimed in the Mau Mau struggle, he invents the story of Joseph being his brother as a cover for his virtual adoption of the orphan (285–6). Likewise, Wanja's admission that she snuffed out the life of the child she was later to yearn for, in the course of her bitter testament to Karega and Munira in which she reveals how she has been brought to her unrepentant role of chief avenging prostitute of New Ilmorog: 'You eat or are eaten' (291–4).

There is a somewhat strange, yet representative passage towards the end of *Petals of Blood* which brings together many of the characteristics we have been discussing. It is the moment when Abdulla urges Wanja to marry him. It is strange in that the structural simplicity has now, as it were, come full cycle: anyone unfamiliar with the novel might well get a most distorted view of the book from these few lines snatched out of context. They are indeed full of clichés. One could forgive a newcomer for dismissing the scene as a trite piece of melodramatic sentimentality: the mutilated half-caste seeking to rescue the obdurate whore by marrying her, and being flouted. Yet Ngũgĩ has brought us to a point in the narrative where this is completely convincing and very moving. More than this, it epitomizes much of the sad contradiction at the heart of this debased society in which true feeling seems unable to flourish and flower, although, none the less, it still struggles through the cracks in the concrete to remind us of the ever-present potential for a different dispensation. That Abdulla can find no more than outworn phrases to express such feelings is one more coil in the network of ironies. When Wanja declares: 'But this is my cup,' we are differently taken aback. This travesty of sacrifice is so coloured with healthy defiance that we can hardly hope to disentangle our conflicting reactions either rapidly or neatly. Such is *Petals of Blood*:

> He felt somehow personally humiliated by what seemed her irrevocable and final entry into whoredom. It hurt him, but he understood. He stood at the door, then sat down and went straight into business. He stammered, slightly confused, but he went on. 'Listen. Please. Stop this business. I have a little money. I still have my share of what we got from the recent sale. Marry me. I may not be much to look at: but it was fate.' He finished, almost swallowing the last sentence in his embarrassment. She stood up, turned away and walked into an inner room. Then she came back. She was calm. 'My heart is tearless about what I have committed myself to. You know I have tried. Where was I to throw these girls that were part of the old Theng'eta premises? To others who too would profit from their bodies? No, I am not doing this for their sakes. From now onwards it will always be: Wanja First. I have valued your friendship. And I hope we

can remain friends. But this is my cup. I must drink it.' He had expected this but it did not make it any easier. (311–12)

After this we are sill left to infer at the end — it is never spelt out — that the child Wanja is carrying is Abdulla's. There is thus a muted and somewhat ambivalent echo of the hopeful ending of *A Grain of Wheat* just as *Petals of Blood* might wrongly appear to be on the edge of cynicism. Such a reversal is less equivocally suggested by the last words of the later novel: 'Tomorrow . . . and he knew he was no longer alone.' Out of simplicity has emerged a style which conveys layer under layer of unexpected but complementary meanings.

It may at first seem superfluous to say more about the ironic style of *Devil on the Cross* or *Matigari* since large sections of each are overt satire. But it may still be valuable to emphasize the complex manner in which Ngũgĩ contrives that irony shall interlock with irony. For instance in exploiting the snobbery of status-conscious parents, Kihaahu discovers that they will take the bait only if schools are, at least in appearance, thoroughly westernized. The elite are not attracted by even the most sophisticated indigenous education.

The double irony is even more savage when a proper nationalist patriotism in rejecting foreign exploitation is manipulated into a demand for the exclusive rights of Kenyans to plunder other Kenyans:

I am very sure that we, the Kenyan thieves and robbers, can stand on our own feet and end forever this habit of sharing our loot with foreigners . . . Let us steal from among ourselves, so that the wealth of the country remains in the country, and so that in the flesh of ten million poor we can plant the roots of ten national millionaires.' (*DOC* 166–7)

every robber should go home and rob his own mother. That's true democracy *and equality of nations*! (*DOC* 171)

For his nationalist zeal, Mwireri is later murdered by his own countrymen who are in the pockets of neo-colonialist big-businessmen.

The whole portrait of the opportunist taxi-driver, Robin Mwaura, is a network of paradoxes. '"Don't you believe in anything? Isn't there anything that your heart considers bad or good?"' (49) Muturi asks him, and his reaction is privately to write Muturi off as a religious fanatic!

But the ultimate double ironies, as we have begun to see, are positive. Ngũgĩ has found the answer to the lassitude of Ngotho's generation. He has always looked back in anger to his forebears for having given up the fight in face of apparently overwhelming odds. This Ngũgĩ will not do. Determination can and must be buoyed up by a sense of community. We remember Muturi's words, ' "Despair is the one sin that cannot be forgiven"' (27) Ngũgĩ must consciously have realized that the ending of *Petals of Blood* and *Devil on the Cross* are complementary. Karega and Wariinga are kindred spirits. As she walks out of the novel, head held high but solitary at the last, we may well recall that the final words of *Petals of Blood* have been reduplicated by Muturi. Whether we relate this assurance to Muturi himself and his underground organization, to Ngũgĩ in Kamiti and the network of those who have been steadfastly on his side, or to a whole cross-section of readers of the novel, the ultimate irony is optimistic: ' "Remember, you're not alone." ' (*POB* 345; *DOC* 212)

The reversal between the first and the last pages of *Matigari* is sadly ironic. Its positive implications are subtle and will perhaps be grasped only by a reader who is sympathetically alert to the complete message of the narrative. But the upshot was and is realistic and immediately relevant. The fable opens with the exemplar of all forest fighters burying his weapons in a gesture of final amnesty: 'It was all over now'(3). Later, as it is demonstrated to him that such a renunciation may have been premature, he feels for his fighting gear in vain: 'His hand moved to his waist in a gesture he had often performed in his years of struggle . . . There was nothing there' (30). His conviction steadily grows that 'One had to have the right words; but these words had to be strengthened by the force of arms' (131). Now another major irony compounds the problem. The very people who are everywhere loudly supporting and praising Matigari and his socio-political message, turn away uninterested whenever they are asked to join the search for truth and justice. At the close he has deliberately passed on all his resurrected armoury to his front runner from the younger generation. In this Muriuki himself becomes the successor to Karega and Wariinga. His determined armed defiance spells again hope for the future on, significantly, another last page. But Matigari has already defined the way ahead to his two prototypical lieutenants — Guthera and Muriuki — at this time when it is only possible to take the first preparatory step in clearing the ground and making way for the reconstruction that can follow in due time:

> I will retrace my steps to where I went astray and resume my journey from there . . . It is better to build another house altogether — a new house with a better foundation. (139)

The new earth still lies in the future, but the way ahead has been mapped out; plans have been laid; and within the fabled blue-print the cleansing fire has prepared for that 'better foundation'.

Notes

1. Henceforward when referring to extracts, *The River Between* will be abbreviated to *RB*, *Secret Lives* to *SL*, *Weep Not, Child* to *WNC*, *A Grain of Wheat* to *GOW*, *Petals of Blood* to *POB*, *Devil on the Cross* to *DOC* and *Matigari* to *Mat*. Publication details and the system of page references are given in the Notes to previous chapters.

2. This phrase, which occurs in a tabulation on page 13 of *A Grammar of Contemporary English* compiled by Randolph Quirk, Sidney Greenbaum, Geoffrey Leech and Jan Swartvik (Longman, 1972) reappears verbatim in an identical context on the first page of Quirk and Greenbaum's *A University Grammar of English* (Longman, 1973).

3. In analysing various representative passages from each of the six novels, we have, perhaps somewhat arbitrarily, regarded sentences of 30 words or more as being 'of above average length for English'.

Literature & Society

In this final chapter we propose to raise questions concerning the role of the writer in the ordering of society. How far has Ngũgĩ seen it as his function to identify and advance the good of the community, and to condemn and combat forces that he sees as socially negative? How is his stand to be compared to that of Achebe, who has consciously and clearly articulated goals? In exploring these issues we must evaluate the effect that a clear-cut social viewpoint has on an artist's work, either to its profit or its detriment.

The image that has emerged so far of our author is of a man who identifies himself unequivocally with a progressive, radical line of thought concerning all the pressing social issues of his time, and who eagerly deploys every means at his disposal to further the views and policies that he advocates. His fictional and polemical writings, his activities and his life-style all reinforce this image. The mission of transforming society has dominated the thinking and the writing of both Achebe and Ngũgĩ in their different ways from early in their lives. Achebe has coined watch-words for every student of African literature: 'Here, then, is an adequate revolution for me to espouse — to help my society regain its belief and put away the complexes of the years of denigration and self-denigration.'[1] If Ngũgĩ's declarations have been less personalized — and less often quoted — his art nonetheless has been unceasingly dedicated to heartening the oppressed and exposing the injustices that weigh them down.

So vigorously has Ngũgĩ related his art to social issues that it closely mirrors the changes that have taken place in his reformatory and political thinking. In the process of writing his earlier novels, short stories and plays, Ngũgĩ was still formulating his stand on various issues agitating his society. While the facts of the writer's upbringing and personal experiences form the staple of his subject matter, literary values are not questioned. It is part of the universal heritage of literature that it should seek to highlight the problems which burden, manacle and maim mankind. For the youthful Ngũgĩ these problems included, at one level, family afflictions such as childlessness, marital strife and kindred feuds; and at another level, communal adversities such as droughts or floods, and the vast societal dilemmas of colonialism, confrontation between different religions, creeds and patterns of behaviour, and Mau Mau. Resolution is sought in terms of man's enduring spiritual values. The author's voice is muted; and the manner in general shuns harshness and violence of language or approach. Waiyaki is admired for such personal success as he achieves in the midst of longer-term public failure. Njoroge is saved from suicide and infused with a new courage to face the future.

In the middle period, during which *A Grain of Wheat* is the principle literary work, Ngũgĩ's stand on social issues becomes steadily more radical, but as an artist he is still controlled by his aesthetic awareness. His aim is to embody a major statement on public affairs as the primary theme in an essentially literary artefact. His reinterpretation of past events is conveyed by implication and suggestion rather than by direct statement. The whole history of the Kenyan struggle, particularly Mau Mau's heroic stand during the Emergency, is elevated to the status of a popular mass uprising. So the evil machinations of the MP who out-manoeuvres the land co-operative are seen as thwarting the popular will. This symbolizes the whole conduct of political authority in independent Kenya, rendering the long-awaited, hard-fought-for independence hollow and meaningless. For all this, the socio-political message takes second place to the fate of the individual upon which literature has most often focused.

In the latest period, a rebellious Ngũgĩ seems tired of sifting his message through a genre to which each reader may react differently. So he makes attempts to modify his medium and render it less arbitrary. Logically his new outlook is dynamically expressed in his first language in *Ngaahika Ndeenda, Caitaani Mutharaba-ini* and *Matigari*, which as a later priority he translates or has translated into English to join *The Trial of Dedan Kimathi* and *Petals of Blood*. During this period he twice employs drama as the mode most immediate in its impact.

Had Ngũgĩ turned to Gikuyu earlier in his career, it would have been because of his opposition to the colonial legacy and his desire to re-develop traditional African culture: we recall the cry from his undergraduate journalism for the replacement of English by Kiswahili in East African schools. Now his primary motivation is the need to reach the masses, with whose problems he identifies himself and whose spokesman he has become: developing an indigenous language is an important but secondary aim.

The Trial of Dedan Kimathi seeks to mobilize the popular will against neo-colonialism and the new capitalism which are widening the gap between the Kenyan rich and poor. The play re-defines for the whole population — but in particular for the ordinary man and woman — the role which the Mau Mau insurrection played in gaining Kenya's political sovereignty. It depicts the upheaval as a class reaction against repressive political and economic control in terms of popular Marxist-inspired social conceptions. Ngũgĩ has evidently come to see his earlier works as too reticent on the true nature of the uprising, so that now he rights the imbalance. His choosing to put his message on the stage points to his urgent desire for communication at grass roots.

In pursuit of the same goal of harnessing popular indignation against corrupt, oppressive power-groups, and so instigating revolutionary action by the peasantry and the workers, *Petals of Blood* adopts a new idiom. We are now brought face to face with a world gasping for breath in the grip of neo-colonialist capitalism. We are shown the oppressor and the oppressed, the overfed and the starving, the predators and their victims, the degenerate city and the desolate village. Among the exploited poor are a few architects of change who will lead the populace in redesigning society. Ngũgĩ no longer minces his words or speaks in parables. Corruption and injustice are openly denounced: characters are clearly prototypical across the whole conspectus of this sagging society; the imagery is unambiguous. Ngũgĩ spells out the desperateness of the situation and the urgency of the need for change.

In *Devil on the Cross* Ngũgĩ adds laughter as a new weapon to undermine and expose the profligacy of the elite, expecting that a wide audience will eagerly take part in the satiric unmasking of their over-lords. By contrast the sufferings and triumphs of individuals struggling against their debased environment are seriously, even earnestly, portrayed. The burlesque self-exposure of the demi-gods of neo-colonialism provides, Ngũgĩ realizes, a suitable stylized setting for the directly didactic fictional statement. The sheer daring of the project carries both the denunciation and the revolutionary exhortation to extremes which we might formerly have thought impossible within the framework of a novel, however unconventional.

There is no doubt that Ngũgĩ has been influenced by radical socialist thinking and is familiar with Marxist theory. Among others Frantz Fanon — as already noted — had earlier an important impact on Ngũgĩ's ideas. Latterly, Amilcar Cabral's comprehensive application of Marxist principles to the entirely new situation in Africa and the whole ex-colonial Third World has had even greater force because of its more precise relevance, as we shall observe in greater detail later. Thus right from Ngũgĩ's earliest writing such concepts as a people's government, the power of the proletariat, mass-controlled means of production and distribution and the need for egalitarian social services are the implicit premises of his fiction. In the latest period his entire thinking and writing are cast in the mould of anti-capitalist revolutionary doctrine.

Two important convictions characterize this new phase. First there is the total rejection of the possibility of rebuilding African societies on old colonialist foundations. To build an egalitarian society is not to cleanse outmoded institutions of corruption and make them function more efficiently, but to destroy them altogether, make a fresh beginning, and create new systems. Secondly, Ngũgĩ is disillusioned about reforming those who are at the power bases of society; he virtually despairs of rousing the consciences of the rich. He now concentrates all his efforts on developing among the poor an awareness of the inequalities which are at the root of their sufferings, and of urging them towards a revolution which alone can set the whole situation in the country to rights.

This is the impulse behind *Petals of Blood, Devil on the Cross*, the recent plays, the latest stories in *Secret Lives*, and (most clearly of all) *Matigari*. The social doctrine which has been long maturing is at length comprehensive and coherent: control of the many by the few is blatantly immoral: history is on the side of the oppressed and will ensure their inevitable victory. There is an increasing sharpness and militancy in the call on the poor to engineer their own deliverance. Waiyaki and Njoroge meant well but fumbled, and even Kihika was too ill-informed to prevail over the handicaps that constrained him. But Karega and Muturi know how to marshal the collective will of the work force in labour organizations, ready to dominate the battle looming ahead in this tense environment. Matigari becomes the very spirit of his country, re-mustering the cohorts out of despair and apathy, and symbolically leading them into battle, urging his fictional countrymen — but also more vitally his non-fictional readers — into action. The middle-class is parasitic. Far from being relied on to re-align the class system, it should itself be dissolved in the eventual re-structuring of society.

We observed earlier[2] that in *Petals of Blood* Ngũgĩ felt the need in certain passages to be more explicitly didactic than he had been hitherto, and we left it as an open question whether this might prove productive or counter-productive in getting his message across dynamically to his readers. However, there is no doubt at all that he knew exactly what he was doing in making this shift towards outspokenness. As a novelist Ngũgĩ was taking a calculated risk. He was prepared to jeopardize the 'suspension of disbelief' in order to ensure that his ideas stood out absolutely plainly. He deliberately side-stepped certain conventions of the well-made novel as they had for long been understood in the West, though he had not yet made radical modifications in the mode of his own fiction.

The stylistic leaps that Ngũgĩ ventured upon in composing *Devil on the Cross* and *Matigari* were thus logical developments in his search for an effective pattern for the committed novel. Taken out of its whole context, the story of Wariinga is Ngũgĩ's most uncompromisingly didactic piece of straight fiction to date, while the debates centred on Muturi in the matatu and, after the workers' rally, only thinly veil the author's teaching voice. We have argued elsewhere[3] that the formal control required for the extended parody in the novel creates a fictional world in which the almost equally stylized serious narrative is more readily acceptable than it might otherwise be. Nevertheless, if we consider this part of the work simply as it stands, we find ourselves face to face with a new Ngũgĩ who has chosen a much balder, and consequently more self-conscious manner of story-telling.

If Ngũgĩ was still to move forward thematically in *Matigari*, he had to take another bold leap stylistically. So he moulds the whole oral tradition of his community into the infrastructure for a modern revolutionary fable. The author himself has described some of his aims and methods:

> In *Matigari* even the narrative tone is supposed to be very much like an oral tale . . . I'm interested in how myths grow, how the human imagination captures the essence of things in terms of myths . . . There is one scene where he meets John Boy outside the house and John Boy asks who he is. And, in order to explain who he is, Matigari has to go into history and say he has been there even before the times of the Portuguese in the sixteenth century.[4]

One might say that in many respects Ngũgĩ is now embracing the conventions of the well-made fable, which would certainly have been recognized and appreciated by the majority of his readership for the original

Gikuyu edition. And the fable is expected to be a captivating but essentially didactic story.

We have now reached the point at which we must ask point blank whether it is, in general, legitimate or effective to employ literature as a means of expounding and promoting a social doctrine, and how successful Ngũgĩ has been in doing so. Literature synthesizes and focuses many aspects of human experience and understanding. It is concerned with life as a whole. It is to do with psychology, history, sociology, religion and politics, among many other things. It is inextricably interwoven with an understanding of language as a means of communication, and is deeply involved with form and design. While it constantly employs analysis as a means to an end, literature aims at a controlled and comprehended synthesis of human awareness.

Thus it is vitally true that literature examines human values and reveals to our understanding the constants that run through human experience in all places and at all times. This is one of its most important functions which must never be belittled. But it is also true that it deals with contemporary and particular issues, attitudes and behaviour in contemporary, and particular situations. It presents to us as a unified whole groups of problems and happenings which are anatomized by the sociologist, the political scientist and the psychologist. It does so in a vivid and illuminating manner.[5]

Since literature essentially knows no bounds in its selection of subject matter, the question of legitimacy does not in fact arise, but rather considerations of tact and tactics. We are still bound to ask whether literature is well suited to the task of arousing popular reaction against social abuses, and if so how directly or indirectly it can afford to operate. If ideas are left entirely implicit, unstated, many readers may miss some or even all of the essential points that a writer seeks to convey. If, on the other hand, bare explicitness is in danger of reducing the average reader's interest and receptivity, a novelist must decide where to draw the line. When the activist sees the necessity of sacrifice, he or she will abandon art before principle. But we may conclude that *ideally* this sort of sacrifice is unnecessary and undesirable.

As his socio-political ideas became more cogent and forward-looking, Ngũgĩ's wrestle with his materials has become fiercer and more demanding. The first reaction to *Petals of Blood* by many of us steeped in literary principles (and very fine principles and criteria they are) was to see it as a step backwards from *A Grain of Wheat* since in place of the almost perfectly controlled form and texture of the earlier novel, the intellectual skeleton grins through the vital literary flesh in a number of places in *Petals of Blood*. Readers preoccupied with radical political ideas, on the other hand, readily saw *Petals of Blood* as a big step forward in its uncompromising rejection of capitalist exploitation together with the old class structure, and its definition of the struggle towards a more just society by concerted communal effort. It would be a pity to be carried away entirely to either extreme. A middle position might paradoxically be put like this: *A Grain of Wheat* is the more perfect novel, but *Petals of Blood* is arguably the greater. (Just as, for instance — for different reasons — many critics would see *Romeo and Juliet* as the more formally perfect and *King Lear* as by far the greater Shakespearean tragedy.) *A Grain of Wheat* reconciles the two sets of claims, literary and socio-political, by somewhat muting the latter: not through any dishonesty, but because Ngũgĩ's social view was less fully developed. The new surge of righteous but clear-sighted political anger in *Petals of Blood* tends to pull the literary frame somewhat out of true but not enough to dim its claim to be a major, complexly structured novel. *Petals of Blood* thus stands as a rare literary achievement with all its faults upon it, a skilfully articulated work which in no degree compromises the author's fully-fledged radical political viewpoint.

The same is true of *Devil on the Cross*, though in adopting an entirely new mode it shakes itself free from some of the previous problems and in doing so creates its own. But the solution to these new problems are in part inherent in the genre. Satire is by definition a means of being entertainingly didactic. The comic inversion involved shifting the basic tone away from the ponderously moralistic, towards the scandalously sensational. As we have already seen, Ngũgĩ has avoided the major pitfall of satire, the monotony of a repetitive pattern, and in doing so he has at the same time ensured that his message is not only varied but is maintained at a level which is generally comprehensible. He has surveyed the many and various aspects of economic exploitation without losing any part of his readership in technical detail. What is more remarkable is the way he has combined this ironic extravaganza with the simplified revolutionary idyll of a prototypical victim of the system. Wariinga grows out of a bewildered imitation of bourgeois values into a trained radical self-awareness. Her origins are in the class borderland between the workers and the white-collared pen-pushers. If Gatuiria sadly represents a falling back at the moment of crisis into stereotyped reactions implanted by a conditioned childhood, Wariinga shows how individuals — men or women — can shake themselves free of their past and prepare to participate in what they envisage as a different kind of future. Readers will vary in how far they can accept this formalized parable, much of it written in a newly formalized style which may at times seem rather forced, and even flat after what we have been accustomed to:

> Today Wariinga strides along with energy and purpose, her dark eyes radiating the light of an inner courage, the courage and light of someone with firm aims in life — yes, the firmness and the courage and the faith of someone who has achieved something through self-reliance. What's the use of shuffling along timidly in one's own country? Wariinga, the black beauty! Wariinga of the mind and hands and body and heart, walking in rhythmic harmony on life's journey! Wariinga, the worker!

Ngũgĩ will no doubt judge the success of his moral fables by their impact on the general readership he has aimed at, rather than by any critical consensus. But an unbiased view will hardly deny the boldness and force with which he has handled his later experiments in committed fiction.

In both *A Grain of Wheat* and *Petals of Blood* Ngugi has, in a more established fictional manner, embodied his major themes in his characters, his patterned imagery, his story and setting. Cabral, in modifying and extending Marxist theory through a process of analysing a situation fundamentally different from that in Europe but common throughout the ex-colonial world, makes a clear distinction between the struggle for independence and the later campaign for national liberation. The former takes place in a colonial situation and is the essential subject of *A Grain of Wheat*:

> the colonial situation neither allows nor invites the meaningful existence of vanguard classes (an industrial working class and rural proletariat) which could ensure the vigilance of the mass of the people over the evolution of the liberation movement. On the contrary, the generally embryonic character of the working classes and the economic, social and cultural situation of the major physical force in a national liberation struggle — the peasants — do not allow these two principal forces of that struggle to distinguish on their own genuine national independence from fictitious political independence. Only a revolutionary vanguard, generally an active minority, can have consciousness *ab initio* of this distinction and through the struggle bring it to the awareness of the mass of the people.[6]

In *A Grain of Wheat* Ngũgĩ is chief spokesman of this vanguard in Kenya. The novel shows how untrained men like Kihika made a determined effort through Mau Mau to provide an alternative vanguard class. But we further see how, having made a crucial contribution to the ousting of colonialism, this group is suppressed to allow the MP who double-crosses the land co-operative and his fellows to negotiate a 'fictitious political independence'. These ideas are implicit in their positive and negative aspects in the narrative as it relates to Kihika and Thompson, Gikonyo and Karanja, Mumbi and Mugo. There is almost no overt didacticism. The points are silently emphasized as events comment on each other by juxtaposition. The novelist's control and craftsmanship are of a very high order throughout. We are led to see for ourselves the necessity of moving on to a true independence by the awakening of 'the consciousness of broad popular strata' and the reuniting of 'the population around the ideal of national liberation'.[7]

When Ngũgĩ turns to expose the iniquities and needs of neo-colonialist Africa in *Petals of Blood*, he himself is now unreservedly outspoken:

> These parasites would always demand the sacrifice of blood from the working masses. These few who had prostituted the whole land turning it over to foreigners for thorough exploitation, would drink people's blood and say hypocritical prayers of devotion to skin oneness and to nationalism even as skeletons of bones walked to lonely graves. The system and its gods and its angels had to be fought consciously, consistently and resolutely by all the working people! From Koitalel through Kang'ethe to Kimathi it had been the peasants, aided by the workers, small traders and small landowners, who had mapped out the path. Tomorrow it would be the workers and the peasants leading the struggle and seizing power to overturn the system and all its prying bloodthirsty gods and gnomic angels, bringing to an end the reign of the few over the many and the era of drinking blood and feasting on human flesh. Then, only then, would the kingdom of man and woman really begin, they joying and loving in creative labour. (344)

This rhetorical denunciation and exhortation is stirring stuff. No one can miss the message. Cabral himself was hardly more explicit in expounding the path to national liberation — which is the central subject of *Petals of Blood* — at the 1966 Havana conference:

> On the one hand, the material effects (mainly the nationalization of cadres and the rise in native economic initiative, particularly at the commercial level) and the psychological effects (pride in believing oneself ruled by one's fellow countrymen, exploitation of religious or tribal solidarity between some leaders and a fraction of the mass of the people) serve to demobilize a considerable part of the nationalist forces.
>
> But on the other hand, the necessarily repressive nature of the neo colonial State against the national liberation forces, the aggravation of class contradictions, the objective continuance of agents and signs of foreign domination (settlers who retain their privileges, armed forces, racial discrimination), the growing impoverishment of the peasantry and the more or less flagrant influence of external factors contribute towards keeping the flame of nationalism alight. They serve gradually to awaken the consciousness of broad popular strata and, precisely on the basis of awareness of neo-colonialist frustration, to reunite the majority of the population around the ideal of national liberation.
>
> In addition, while the native ruling class becomes increasingly 'bourgeois' the development of a class of workers composed of urbanized industrial workers and agricultural proletarians — all exploited by the indirect domination of imperialism — opens renewed prospects for the evolution of national liberation. This class of workers, whatever the degree of development of its political consciousness (beyond a certain minimum that is consciousness of its needs), seems to constitute the true popular vanguard of the national liberation struggle in neo colonial cases.[8]

In terms of *Petals of Blood*, here speaks a Karega who has acquired the eloquence of the Lawyer.

Petals of Blood and *Devil on the Cross* both embody such themes but in contrasting styles. In the former these motifs are developed, as in *A Grain of Wheat*, by familiar fictional methods through the narrative, characterization, inter-relationships, imagery and setting. They are related to the emotional needs, problems and intertwinings of the human situation:

> And recalling Abdulla, Karega, Munira, her grandfather and all the other individuals who had been in an out of her life, she decided that maybe everything was simply a matter of love and hate. Love and hate — Siamese twins — back to back in a human heart. Because you loved you also hated: and because you hated you also loved . . . You knew what you loved and what you hated by what you did, what actions, what side you had chosen. You could not, for instance, work with the colonists in suppressing the people and still say you loved the people. You could not stand on the fence in a struggle and still say you were on the side of those fighting the evil. (335)

In exaggerating and concentrating the same ideas, *Devil on the Cross*, on the other hand, alternates deliberately between outlandish satire and a highly formalized narrative. One mode exposes exploitation satirically:

> The other idea I'd like to follow up is how we, the top-grade tycoons, can trap the air in the sky, put it in tins and sell it to peasants and workers, just as water and charcoal are now sold to them. Imagine the profit we would reap if we

were to sell the masses air to breathe in tins or, better, if we could meter it! We could even import some air from abroad, *imported* air, which we could then sell to the people at special prices! (107)

The complementary mode explicitly and solemnly summarizes the ideal of communal living exemplified by the mechanics' co-operative:

> The fruits of each worker's labour went into his own pocket. But at the end of every month each worker would contribute a fixed sum to a common pool, from which they paid the ground rent for the garage to the Nairobi City Council and their other common expenses. And if one of the workers had an unexpected problem, he or she was allowed to borrow from the common pool to meet his or her needs. No one in that community of workers lived on the sweat of another. (222)

The full and many-sided exposition of total commitment to a now rounded and mature set of socio-political convictions in *Petals of Blood* and *Devil on the Cross* left Ngũgĩ's readership perplexed as to what could possibly be Ngũgĩ's next step forward (if any) as a writer of forthright radical fiction. Indeed in terms of beliefs and proto-policies *Matigari* is essentially an unequivocal re-affirmation of the reformatory, activist philosophy embodied in the preceding novels and plays. Thematically nothing could be new. But *Matigari* proved to be a different kind of book, with familiar arguments now in a time-honoured mode. Ngũgĩ has deliberately adopted the fable form to inspire his own and like-minded people. Matigari is a humanized prophet: not just an individual but the representative of an incisive set of ideas who spells out a way forward for a society stagnating in a pseudo-benign dictatorship compounded of international capitalism and indigenous power-hunger. The trio at the centre of the work are interchangeable role-models, as Ngũgĩ himself has said:

> Yes, Matigari is all-consuming. In a sense both the woman and the boy are really different aspects of Matigari, and Matigari is different aspects of the woman and the boy. They are all part of one another. You could say Guthera is Matigari, and Matigari is Guthera, and Guthera is Ngaruro wa Kiriro or Muriuki, any way you like. I just got three figures who could be father and daughter or man and wife and child, or brothers and sisters. They're just different suggestions.[9]

This is the epitome of Ngũgĩ's message: that for his country (or any country) to move forward, the people must shake off apathy imposed by terror and act together under a communal leadership that springs from themselves. No compromise is now possible. Matigari leads the campaign to destroy the symbolic 'house', not now simply to refurbish it. We need to recall once more his words in the compelling, simple, cyclic diction of this fable — a fable that is to be accessible to all his people — words spoken to his other selves:

> I will retrace my steps to where I went astray and resume my journey from there. It is better to build another house altogether — a new house with a better foundation. (139)

While one stylistic extreme of *Devil on the Cross* is echoed in the scene of the Minister's meeting, in the main 'the narrative tone' is indeed 'very much like an oral tale', with the special feature of its lucid, uncomplicated, flowing style being its emphatic repetitions like resonant and easily memorized chants. Ngũgĩ has now put his message to the people in the people's own language in more than one sense.

The socio-political motifs in *Petals of Blood* remain for the most part implicit in the narrative. We have noted exceptional passages in which the author through the Lawyer or by other means becomes more directly didactic. But because these interventions are not intrinsic to the dominant stylistic manner, they are artistically clumsier than the more extreme methods adopted in *Devil on the Cross* as part of its creative essence. The norm in *Petals of Blood* remains the integration of story and ideas. Wanja's testimony is at once a vivid depiction of her life-story and a revelation of all that someone at the mercy of this society suffers; Abdulla's epitomizes both his own heroism and betrayal, and those of the Mau Mau movement as a whole. Such thematic accounts are vividly personalized, full of action, and are central threads in the story which the novel sets out to tell.

The overt didacticism of *Devil on the Cross* is not isolated in occasional passages. It is the soul of the book, both in its satirical exposures and in its more sober demonstrations. The novel stands or falls as a whole by the success or failure (for each individual reader) of its bold experiments, as it directly deploys literature as a means of eliciting specific social reactions.

Though the mode is different, the same is equally true of *Matigari* in which the revolutionary mental stimulus of bitter humour is replaced by the adoption of a genre rooted in immemorial folk experience.

There is a stylistic link between the three novels now under consideration in the means of presenting challenging radical themes through satiric irony. This is a marginal ingredient in *Petals of Blood*, briefly varying its familiar basically novelistic methods. In *Devil on the Cross* bitter burlesque takes centre stage. In *Matigari* satiric exaggeration provides variety during the denunciatory comedy of the Minister's meeting: but its different stylization as a fable is now central. Also each novel has an essentially different satiric style. In *Petals of Blood* Fat Stomach and Insect, while demonstrating dramatically the double-dealing inherent in political rhetoric, remain strictly within the limits of realism: 'One was fat with a shiny bald head which he kept on touching . . . the other was tall and thin and kept his hands in his pockets and never once said one word' (84). The contestants in *Devil on the Cross*, on the other hand, constantly veer towards caricature:

> Gitutu had a belly that protruded so far that it would have touched the ground had it not been supported by the braces that held up his trousers. It seemed as if his belly had absorbed all his limbs and all the other organs of his body. Gitutu had no neck — at least, his neck was not visible. His arms and legs were short stumps. His head had shrunk to the size of a fist. (99)

When the Minister in *Matigari* is described (100) he is a normal human figure satirized by being dressed as a clone of a western business man, by his paraphernalia of Parrotology, the outrageousness of his complacent statements, and so forth. The irony of the appearance of Howard Williams and John Boy Junior lies in the precise similarities between them.

Each of these novels presents a cross-section of society. The journey of the village delegation across the drought-ridden bush in *Petals of Blood* is a heroic exploit by peasants, rallied by upholders of ancient integrity, by refugees from the bourgeoisie and by proletariat leaders. Each of these same groups is also represented in the persons of Wangari, Gatuiria and Muturi respectively, in the long debate on social issues among the taxi passengers in *Devil on the Cross*, wherein they verbally cross swords with representatives of the exploiters — Mwireri wa Murikai, and their henchmen — Robin Mwaura. This is a journey of words — fierce words on burning issues, in contrast to the journey of action following Abdulla's donkey across Ilmorog plain. In *Matigari* we might say there is a symbolic journey: Matigari meets a variety of type figures in prison and in his travels in search of justice and truth; but here the foreground is taken up mainly by prototypes from the urban jungle grouped round the representative of age-old suffering, resistance and communal integrity.

In the later stages of the Ilmorog epic march, as the party reaches the outskirts of Nairobi, the inhumanity of the ruling class (which in *Devil on the Cross* is first satirically self-confessed and then gallantly opposed by the workers) is acted out before our eyes by businessman, administrator and church dignitary — familiar figures from *The Trial of Dedan Kimathi* for instance, and again personalized in Settler Williams, John Boy, the Minister, and the priest in *Matigari*.

The vivid realization of place in *The River Between* and *A Grain of Wheat* is activated again by our awareness of the changing stages in the life of Ilmorog, old and new, so that the community as a whole becomes as essential to the fictional narrative in *Petals of Blood* as is the community in *Middlemarch* to George Eliot's master-work. The central irony of the disastrous 'development' of the township in Part Four is the very life-blood of the novel as a novel. The palaces and slums of this now soulless boom-town are again sketched in as backcloth for *Devil on the Cross*. To the uninitiated, Ilmorog here appropriately takes on the sad, characterless blur of Anytown, but to those familiar with *Petals of Blood*, the setting adds another detailed dimension to disillusionment. In the earlier novel, these now displaced figures that make up our picture of the place were known to us in depth throughout the length of their lives and back through their distant ancestry. But in the symbolic world of *Matigari* sharp focus on place deliberately disappears in the generalized fable environment, so the familiar type-characters stand out sharply as universal personae.

The wedding of theme and story can be traced right down to individual sentences as well as to individual characters in *Petals of Blood*. The grey future looming before the unskilled would-be worker is made specific in Karega: 'Yes, a covenant with fate, he thought, for the future seemed a yawning blank without a break or an opening, like the sky above them' (107). The irony is in detail both bitter and bizarre: 'There was also the foreign press which in their naivety thought this Tea Party was another Mau Mau' (186), when in fact the latter-day oath-taking is meant to bind the rank and file to the capitalist treadmill. Njuguna can capture the keynote of the whole novel when the villagers are contemplating the long trek to Nairobi: 'I think we should go. It is our turn to make things happen' (115). Munira misreads Karega's intentions, but nevertheless individualistic messianic leadership, either political or (ironically) religious, is effectively dismissed: ' "His pride in even contemplating that one man unaided by God through Christ could change himself, could change the world, could improve on it" ' (300). But Karega has no doubt that a concerted effort by suffering humanity can indeed improve their world: ' "Must we have this world? Is there only one world? Then we must create another world, a new earth" ' (294).

This subtle, implicit emergence of theme from the heart of the story itself is foreign to the satiric and explicitly didactic methods of *Devil on the Cross*. Here little is left to the imagination. The artistry lies first in laying bare social evils which normally lie snugly concealed by rationalizations and apologia, so that their monstrous absurdity in human terms is clearly exposed; and secondly in lending revolutionary idealism a new plausibility and human warmth. The familiar inversions of all morality in the conduct of public affairs no longer seems inevitable. A juster alternative appears far from coldly intellectual or impossibly visionary. Single sentences which we might pick out from *Devil on the Cross*, as we have just been doing from *Petals of Blood*, will not therefore reveal and confirm how the narrative crystallizes certain themes. Rather will they be the culmination of ideas which are meant to be plainly evident throughout. They may be satirical: ' "I want to end with the following battle cry: every robber should go home and rob his own mother! That's true democracy *and equality of nations*" ' (171); ' "We could purchase immortality with our money and leave death as the prerogative of the poor" ' (180). They may be exhortations or expressions of principles: ' "Today, here, we refuse to go on being the pot that cooks but never tastes the food" ' (208); ' "That humanity is the heart of man because the heart of man is linked irrevocably with the growth of his nature as man" ' (53). They may remind us that Wariinga's story is patently a parable rather than a diverting tale: 'The other workers welcomed her as one of them, and they allowed her to use their tools until she could buy her own set' (221); 'She began to speak like a people's judge about to deliver his judgement' (253). Wherever we turn in this work, the message is explicit rather than implicit.

If again we select specific sentences from *Matigari*, even though each may be spoken or thought by a named character, they will hardly ever express a unique experience or an idiosyncratic idea. Each encapsulates a general concept or principle, or is a particular expression of an attitude to which many (or so it is hoped) will aspire. Such a sentence does not advance a plot in a step by step progression as in a novel, but rather sets out a communal stage in a cyclic, recurrent fable: ' "Why shouldn't we peasants eat properly? Why should the builder sleep outside? Why should the tailor walk about in rags?" '(63); ' "Too much fear breeds misery in the land" ' (87); 'The farmer does not stop planting seeds just because of the failure of one crop'(84); ' "If the buyer refuses to pay the price being asked for by the seller, has the latter not got the right to refuse to part with the wares until he gets a suitable price for them? . . . Our strike action is just such a refusal" ' (109); ' "I want to do something to change whatever it is that makes people live like animals, especially us women" '(140); 'One had to have the right words; but these words had to be strengthened by the force of arms' (131).

In the critic's lordly presumption, we may sometimes detect here and there in Ngũgĩ's fiction, as in almost any major work, deviations from the ideal blending of theme and mode. But Ngũgĩ has courageously and successfully set out to mould both the novel and — in collaboration — the drama into his own burning socio-political testimony, without over-simplifications, by gearing the most dynamic features of the art of fiction to his passionate purpose.

In *Devil on the Cross*, it is true, he stormed across the usually recognized bounds of fiction into the realms of rhetoric, open satire and didacticism, and in so doing dared to challenge our established assumptions about literary genres. Yet this is no more radical an approach than that adopted by many novelists world-wide in the second half of this century in attempting to re-vitalize 'the novel', whose funeral oration has been prematurely read by numerous critics. And in *Matigari* he has turned back to the symbolic fable which pre-dated the novel in the history of the verbal arts not only in Africa but in Europe and in many other cultural spheres in the world.

No doubt Ngũgĩ would agree with, but re-interpret, Dr Johnson's assertion that there are 'laws of higher authority than those of criticism'. In fact, until he ventured on *Devil on the Cross* he had rarely in the novel sidestepped traditional principles of literature any more than those of socialism. And indeed even in the prison novel he is more concerned to rethink literary criteria than to reject them. So we can justly say that Ngũgĩ seems at all times to have sought the ultimate goal of any committed writer: to harness the 'laws' of art to the dictates of his own conscience.

Notes

1. Chinua Achebe, 'The Novelist as Teacher', *New Statesman* (London), 29 January 1965.
2. Page 101.
3. Pages 117 ff.
4. Jane Wilkinson (ed.), *Talking with African Writers* (James Currey, London; Heinemann Educational Books, Portsmouth, NH, 1992), 133–4.
5. This and the previous paragraph are adapted from David Cook, *Literature: The Great Teaching Power of the World*, Inaugural Lecture, Makerere University (East African Literature Bureau, Nairobi, 1971), 3 and 9.
6. Speech delivered on behalf of the peoples and nationalist organizations of the Portuguese colonies to the First Solidarity Conference of the Peoples of Africa, Asia and Latin America (Havana, 3–12 January 1966), reprinted in Amilcar Cabral, *Unity and Struggle: Speeches and Writings*, translated by Michael Wolfers (Heinemann Educational Books, London, 1980), 132.
7. Ibid., 132–3.
8. Ibid.
9. Jane Wilkinson, op.cit., 133–4.

Index

All named characters in Ngũgĩ's fiction figure in the index. Where a series of pages is listed (e.g. 154–9), this may indicate an extended discussion of the topic concerned or a number of isolated entries on consecutive pages.

Ngũgĩ wa Thiong'o
Writers in Politics
A Re-Engagement with Issues of Literature & Society

Ngũgĩ has put together a new collection under an old title. One of the completely new pieces 'Freedom of Expression' was written for the campaign to try and save Ken Saro-Wiwa and seven other protesters from execution in Nigeria. He has rewritten almost all the other pieces which have been kept.

Ngũgĩ was warned not to return to Kenya in 1992 after his London launch of the first edition of this book and of *Detained: A Writer's Prison Diary*. Many of the people from the University of Nairobi who were imprisoned for crimes of thought in the subsequent period were asked in the torture chambers whether they had read Ngũgĩ's books.

Ngũgĩ says *'It seemed to me then how ironic the title* Writers in Politics *had turned out to be. In re-issuing these essays I didn't want to lose that nexus between culture and power which had been captured by the title.'*

Contents: WAR OF IMAGES Literature & Society: The Politics of the Canon – Standing on our Grounds: Literature, Education & Images of Self – Literature & Double Consciousness: Warring Images in Afro-American Thought – Return to the Roots: Language, Culture & Politics in Kenya – WORDS & POWERS Writers in Politics: The Power of Words & the Words of Power – Freedom of Expression: the Right to Write is a Human Right – A Novel in Politics: The Launching of *Petals of Blood* – J.M. Kariuki: A Writer's Tribute to a Kenyan Hero – The Price of Freedom: The Story of a Mau Mau Detainee – LINKS OF HOPE Afric-Asian Writers: The Links that Bind Us – Africa & Asia: The History that Refuses to be Silenced – Culture in a Crisis: Problems of Creativity & the New World Order – Kamau Brathwaite: The Voice of Pan-African Presence – Learning from our Ancestors: The Intellectual Legacy of Pan-Africanism – Appendix: On Civilization

Ngũgĩ wa Thiong'o
Moving the Centre
The Struggle for Cultural Freedoms

The West came to see itself as the centre of the universe. Cultural power, just as much as political and economic power, was controlled at the centre.

In this collection Ngũgĩ is concerned with moving the centre in two senses – between nations and within nations – in order to contribute to the freeing of world cultures from the restrictive walls of nationalism, class, race and gender.

The compelling emotional force of this book emerges from Ngũgĩ's convincing emphasis on a "truly universal human culture" and his continuing ability to personalize large political issues and to persuasively politicize his own personal experiences.' – Choice

'. . . the poet or storyteller, he argues, cannot perform his function within his own society unless he shares and enriches its tongue. The Kenyan government only moved decisively against him when he began to do precisely that, first imprisoning him, then driving him into exile.' – Gerald Moore in *Le Monde Diplomatique*

'For a long time, Ngũgĩ's was a lone voice howling against the wind. Now people like Edward Said have joined in the war against cultural imperialism.' – Anver Versi in *New African*

Ngũgĩ wa Thiong'o
Decolonising the Mind
The Politics of Language in African Literature

Ngũgĩ describes this book as 'a summary of some of the issues in which I have been passionately involved for the last twenty years of my practice in fiction, theatre, criticism and in the teaching of literature.' *'Ngũgĩ's importance – and that of this book – lies in the courage with which he has confronted this most urgent of issues.'* – Adewale Maja-Pearce in *The New Statesman*

JAMES CURREY
Oxford

EAEP
Nairobi

HEINEMANN
Portsmouth (NH)